Cracking the Praxis

FRITZ STEWART AND RICK SLITER

FIRST EDITION

RANDOM HOUSE, INC.
NEW YORK

www.PrincetonReview.com

The Princeton Review, Inc.
2315 Broadway
New York, NY 10024
E-mail: booksupport@review.com

ISBN 0-375-76458-5

Editor: Kim Eddy
Production Editor: Patricia Dublin
Production Coordinator: Jennifer Arias

Manufactured in the United States of America.

10 9 8 7 6 5 4 3

First Edition

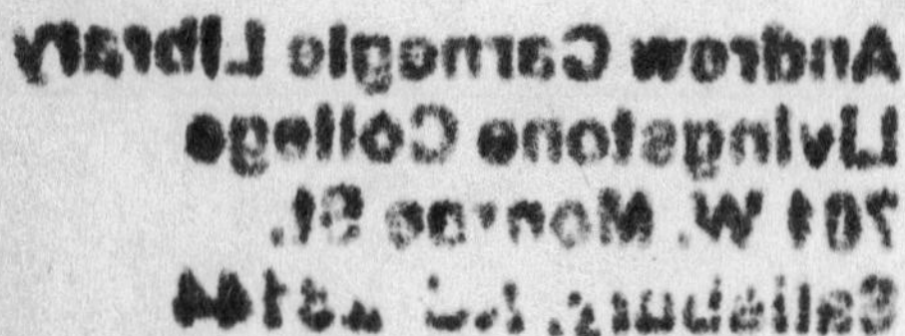

ACKNOWLEDGMENTS

Thanks to Jennifer Auer, Stuart Bammert, Steven and Doris Ott, and Tim Kelley—all of whom answered important questions or provided other assistance in the course writing this book. Thanks also to Ellen Mendlow and Kim Eddy for their constructive criticism and their patience.

DEDICATION

This book is dedicated to the memory of Cathy Schmidel, one of the finest teachers I have ever known.

CONTENTS

Introduction

The Princeton Review started in 1981 by helping 19 students prepare for the SAT and over the past twenty years has grown into one of the largest test-preparation companies in the country. We work with students from all levels to prepare them for college entrance tests, graduate school tests, and professional development tests. Now our goal is to help you pass the Praxis—and we can help you because our methods work.

WHAT CAN I EXPECT FROM THIS BOOK?

This book is designed to help you prepare for the following tests:

Praxis I

Pre-Professional Skills Tests

Reading

Writing

Mathematics

Praxis II

Subject Assessment

Mathematics: Content Knowledge

Social Studies: Content Knowledge

English Language, Literature, and Composition: Content Knowledge

Business Education: Content Knowledge

Earth and Space Sciences: Content Knowledge

Principles of Learning and Teaching

K–6

5–9

7–12

For each of these tests, you will need to know two things:

- what content will be tested
- how that content will be tested

Each of these ideas is important. Merely understanding the content of the material tested is useless if you are unclear as to how the questions seek to test that knowledge. Similarly, understanding the structure of the test is also insufficient if you do not have a basic grasp of the content tested on it.

In addition to a thorough content review and an analysis of the test structure and style, this book includes PPST practice tests in each subject area (Reading, Writing, and Mathematics), PLT practice tests for three separate age ranges (K–6, 5–9, and 7–12), and practice drills for each of the content knowledge tests listed above.

ABOUT THE PRAXIS

What Is It and Who Writes It?

As you probably know, the Praxis series is a collection of tests that many states use to license teachers. The tests are written by the Educational Testing Service (ETS), the same fun-filled folks who brought you the SAT when you were in high school.

There are three sets of Praxis tests, each of which is used for a different purpose:

Praxis I

The Praxis I tests are called the Pre-Professional Skills Tests (we'll call them PPST from here on in), and are used to measure basic competence in three subject areas:

- Mathematics
- Reading
- Writing

The PPSTs are typically used as entry tests for teacher training and certification programs. The content is considered basic knowledge, and in many ways is similar to what is tested on the new SAT.

Praxis II

People typically take the Praxis II tests toward the end of their teacher training programs. The Praxis II tests come in several forms. The two that are discussed in this book are the Principles of Learning and Teaching (PLT) tests and five of the Subject Assessment tests.

The Subject Assessment tests

Each Subject Assessment tests content knowledge related to a specific field. There are Subject Assessment tests for a wide variety of topics, ranging from typical subjects such as Mathematics and English to less common areas such as Agriculture and Driver Education. In this book, we'll cover these five:

- English Language, Literature, and Composition
- Mathematics
- Social Studies
- Earth Science
- Business Education

The Principles of Learning and Teaching (PLT) tests

There are four different PLT tests, for four different age ranges:

- Early Childhood (which is beyond the scope of this book)
- Grades K–6
- Grades 5–9
- Grades 7–12

These tests measure your knowledge of pedagogical topics such as educational psychology and classroom management techniques that are typically covered in teacher training programs.

WHY AM I TAKING THE PRAXIS?

You are taking the Praxis tests because someone in your state decided that the Praxis is an effective way to determine basic teacher competence. Different states require passing scores on different combinations of the Praxis tests in order to become a licensed teacher. For instance, the Praxis score necessary to become a licensed high-school Chemistry teacher in the state of Washington is as follows:

Test	Passing Score
Praxis II Chemistry: Content Knowledge	152

In Nevada, these are the Praxis tests you have to take:

Test	Passing Score
Praxis I	
PPST Reading	174
PPST Writing	172
PPST Mathematics	172
Praxis II	
Principles of Learning and Teaching 7–12	161
Chemistry: Content Knowledge	151
Chemistry: Content Essays	145

If you're currently enrolled in a teacher certification program, your program administrator should be able to tell you what tests you need to take and when. You can also look up which states require which tests by logging on to ETS's website: **www.ets.org/praxis/prxstate.html**.

HOW DO I SIGN UP?

The tests are offered in a paper-and-pencil format six times per school year, usually in September, November, January, March, April, and June.

You can request a Registration Bulletin by calling ETS at (800) 772-9476, or you can register online at **www.ets.org/praxis**. The PPST tests are also offered year-round in a computer-based format. You may register for the computer-based tests only through the website.

WHERE CAN I TAKE THE PRAXIS?

A list of test centers for the paper-and-pencil tests is in the Registration Bulletin, and also online at **www.ets.org/praxis/prxcenters.html**. You can find a list of sites that offer the computer-based tests at **http://etsis4.ets.org/tcenter/cbt_dm.cfm**.

HOW MUCH DO THE TESTS COST?

Way too much, in our opinion. Consider the fees for the Praxis I. The registration fee for any given test day—for either paper- or computer-based tests—is $40. PPST tests cost $30 each. So, to take the three paper-based PPST tests on the same day, you'd be spending $40 (just to walk in the door) plus $30 for each Writing, Reading, and Mathematics test: $40 + $90 = $130, and that's if you take them all on the same day. If you took the tests on different days, you'd need to spend $40 to register for each testing day, so taking the three tests would cost you 3 × ($40 + $30) = $210!

Things aren't much better if you choose to take the computer-based PPST tests. You'll pay the $40 registration fee and per-test fees as follows:

One computer-based test	$ 85
Two computer-based tests	$ 110
Three computer-based tests	$ 135

You can take all three PPSTs in a row, in one sitting, with only one 15-minute break in a 4-½ hour test. They'll charge you $120 for that privilege.

Things get worse if you have to take the Praxis II tests. Any one of the four PLT tests costs $85, so taking the PLT by itself would cost you $40 (yes, you'll pay the registration fee again!) + $85 = $125. The Subject Assessment tests range from $60 to $115 depending on the length and format of the test.

This can add up quickly. A prospective Chemistry teacher in Nevada would have to pay at least $400 in test fees just to be certified.

For a complete list of fees, see ETS's website at **www.ets.org/praxis/fees.html**.

HOW ARE THE TESTS SCORED?

We'll go into the specifics for each individual test type, but one important thing to know right off the bat is that ETS doesn't specify what constitutes a passing score; the individual states do. That explains why a passing score on the Chemistry: Content Knowledge test is 152 in Washington, but only 151 in Nevada.

When we said that ETS hadn't changed at all from your SAT days, we meant it. Standardized tests such as the Praxis (or the SAT) are designed to give standardized results. According to ETS, if you scored a 160 on the Chemistry: Content Knowledge test at one test sitting, you should score about the same at a second sitting. Further, that score should reflect approximately the same percentile rank from test administration to test administration, meaning that the same percentage of people scored above and below 160 on both tests. If ETS couldn't guarantee these standardized, predictable results, then states wouldn't be able to use these tests to certify teachers.

BASIC TEST-TAKING STRATEGIES

ETS guarantees a predictable range of results by designing the multiple-choice sections of the tests in specific ways. First, it's important to know that not all questions are of equal difficulty. Although each question is given equal weight in scoring, some are significantly harder than others. Second, ETS can choose to make some questions more difficult not by testing more complicated material, but by making the correct answer choice harder to recognize. You can combat both of their strategies by applying the strategies you learn in this book.

PACING

You will be under a fair amount of time pressure no matter which test you take. For instance, on the PPST: Mathematics test, you have 60 minutes to answer 40 questions, or 90 seconds per question, and you're not allowed to use a calculator. If you believe that you need to answer each question to the best of your ability, you'll probably end up wasting valuable time working on a very difficult problem that you might get wrong anyway. Instead, we recommend the two-pass system.

The Two-Pass System

On the first pass, answer all the questions that you feel comfortable answering quickly and accurately. If you don't understand a particular question the first time you read it, skip it and go on to the next one. Bubble in your answers on a page-by-page basis, remembering to leave the ones that you've skipped blank.

Then, check the clock and determine how much time you have left. Go back to the beginning of the section and work through the problems you skipped the first time, picking your battles as you go. If you choose to skip a question again on the second pass, bubble in a guess on your answer sheet. Obviously, you should also bubble in answers for the questions that you've worked, too.

> As you begin to bubble in each page, make sure that you begin with the correct question number. It's easy to make a mistake if you aren't careful.

Tip: When there are five minutes left, makes sure that you've bubbled in a guess for every remaining problem. Then, pick one or two problems to work on for those last five minutes, and change your answers if necessary.

PROCESS OF ELIMINATION (POE)

The only advantage that you have on the multiple-choice sections of the Praxis tests is that the right answer is printed on the page in front of you. Unfortunately, the right answer is surrounded by three or four wrong answers. Remember, it's often easier to eliminate a wrong answer than it is to pick the correct answer. Consider the following multiple-choice question:

Which of the following composed *Symphonie Fantastique*?

(A) Wolfgang Amadeus Mozart

(B) Stephen Foster

(C) Hector Berlioz

(D) Camille Saint-Saens

You're not likely to see this question anywhere on any Praxis test (except perhaps the Instrumental Music: Content Knowledge test), and unless you're a classical music fan, you probably don't know the answer. But what if the answer choices looked like this:

Which of the following composed *Symphonie Fantastique*?

(A) George Washington
(B) Stephen Foster
(C) Sigmund Freud
(D) Hector Berlioz

Same question, right? But suddenly the question just got a whole lot easier. Answer choices (A) and (C) aren't even musicians, so we can eliminate them from contention. Now we're down to two:

(B) Stephen Foster
(D) Hector Berlioz

If you're stumped, or pressed for time, you can make a guess at this point, and you'll have a 50% chance of getting the question right. If you have a little more time, you can make a slightly more educated guess. You might remember that Stephen Foster is an American songwriter (*Swanee River, Camptown Races*), or you might just think that his name seems too English-sounding to have written something called *Symphonie Fantastique*. Either way, you'd be right to eliminate him, too. Now, you're down to choice (D), and even if you've never heard of Hector Berlioz, you'd correctly pick him as the composer of *Symphonie Fantastique*.

Never Leave a Question Blank

You have probably taken a standardized test that had a guessing penalty. This penalty would subtract points from your raw score if you missed a question. Thus, the guessing penalty is used to discourage test takers from answering every question.

There is no guessing penalty for a wrong answer on the Praxis tests. Your score on the multiple-choice portions of the Praxis tests you take is determined by the number of questions you answer correctly. You will not lose points for incorrect answers. Therefore, when you take the Praxis tests, there is one thing you must do before you turn in your test:

You must answer every single question on the Praxis!

Ready? Let's get started.

PART I

The PPST: Pre-Professional Skills Tests

THE PRAXIS I: PRE-PROFESSIONAL SKILLS TESTS

These three tests test basic competence in reading, writing, and mathematics. Of the states that use these tests, many require passing scores before a candidate is allowed into a formal teacher education program. However, others require a passing score for final certification. Specific state-by-state information is available on ETS' website: **www.ets.org**.

You can take all three tests on the same day or spread them out over several days. Remember, though: There's a $40 per-test-day registration charge, so it will cost you considerably more to take the tests over several days.

Computer-Based Tests

As of this writing, the PPSTs are the only Praxis tests that are available in a computer-based test (CBT) format. We don't recommend one over the other, because each format has advantages and disadvantages. Listed below are the major differences between the paper-and-pencil tests and the CBTs.

Length

The CBTs are longer than their paper-and-pencil counterparts. For instance, the computer-based PPST: Mathematics lasts 75 minutes and consists of 46 questions. The same pencil-and-paper test lasts 60 minutes and consists of 40 questions.

Pacing

Although the CBTs are longer, you have slightly more time per question to complete them. For instance, you get an average time of about one minute and 38 seconds per question on the Mathematics CBT. On the paper-and-pencil test you get an average of one minute and 30 seconds per question.

Using a Computer

Many people are uncomfortable taking tests on computers. Some dislike the interface, some have a harder time reading information from a computer display than from paper, and some dislike having to take notes or do calculations on scratch paper and then use a mouse to select the answer on the computer.

On the other hand, many people prefer writing essays using a computer, because computers have cut-and-paste functionality and because many people type faster than they write longhand. Unfortunately, there is no spell-check feature on either version of the test.

Flexible Scheduling

The paper-and-pencil tests are offered only six times per school year. The CBTs are offered throughout the school year—you simply reserve a time at the testing center.

Immediate Results

Except for the essay portion of the Writing test, you get your results immediately if you take the CBT. If you take the paper-and-pencil version, you get your scores in the mail after about three weeks.

What Do I Need to Pass?

As mentioned earlier, these tests measure competence in reading, writing, and mathematics. State teacher certification boards don't require mastery, just basic understanding. Further, each state sets its own passing score, so the number of questions you need to answer correctly can vary widely from state to state.

You don't need to ace the PPSTs; you just need to get scores on each that are at or above the cutoff set by your state. To understand how this works, let's look at how ETS grades a PPST test.

Your *raw* score is defined as the number of questions that you answer correctly. For instance, if you answer 26 questions correctly on a 40-question test, your raw score is a 26. If there were 50 questions on the test, your raw score would still be a 26.

Your raw score is then converted to a *scaled* score. The PPST: Mathematics, for example, has scaled scores that range from 150 to 190, although raw scores range from only 0 to 40. If your scaled score is above the cutoff established by a particular state for a particular test, you pass; if not, you fail. ETS doesn't publish exact figures as to how raw scores are translated to scaled scores, but our research indicates that in most states, 75% of the maximum possible raw score is sufficient to pass the three PPSTs. In other words, you could miss (or skip entirely) 10 of the 40 math questions and still pass the test.

What Does that Mean to Me As a Test Taker?

If you're spending too much time on a given problem, narrow down your answer choices, make an educated guess, and move on. Don't get hung up on one particular question to the detriment of those remaining.

The next three chapters are dedicated to an in-depth look at each of the three PPSTs.

1

PPST: Reading

FORMAT OF THE PPST: READING

You'll have one hour to answer 40 multiple-choice questions based on passages of text. Some passages are long, some are of medium length, and some are only a few sentences. There can be anywhere from one to six questions per passage. There is no guessing penalty, so be sure that you answer every question.

ETS says that you can expect a little more than half the questions to test literal comprehension—that is, understanding what the passage says word for word. The rest of the questions test critical and inferential comprehension. To answer these, you'll have to "read between the lines." These questions might ask you to identify an assumption that the author makes, or ask you about the author's attitude toward the topic.

Of course, the passages are on a wide variety of mind-numbingly dull topics, but don't let that bother you. The objective is to get in and out of a given question as quickly as possible.

HOW TO APPROACH PPST: READING QUESTIONS

First, remember these two important truths:

It's an open-book test.

No matter what, the information needed to answer any question will be right in front of you on the page. It doesn't matter whether you've never heard of the passage topic or whether it was the subject of your senior thesis—the information will be right in front of you. It's not like you have to memorize anything: You can always look back at the passage.

The right answer is the one that's better than the other four.

The answer choices on the Praxis are designed to be confusing. Some are even deliberately tricky (are you surprised?). We'll discuss strategies for the different types of questions that you're likely to see, but remember that here, as always, Process of Elimination (as discussed in the Introduction) is your best friend. Often, it'll be easier to identify wrong answers than to pick the right one.

THE PASSAGES

There are two different styles of passages. Some passages are just collections of facts about a topic; these passages look like they might have come straight from a textbook. In the other style of passage, the author makes an argument, and tries to persuade you of his position. Both styles have distinct characteristics.

TEXTBOOK PASSAGES

We're not claiming that textbook passages are as exciting as a John Grisham novel, but they do follow some basic structural rules that your high school English teachers would have approved of. Each passage has a main idea and a topic sentence, and when the author moves from one topic to another she will use transition words such as "although" or "in addition" to let you know how the topics are related.

Argument Passages

If the author tries to make an argument, she will have a conclusion, which will be backed up with evidence. You're not allowed to argue with the evidence (you have to assume it's factual), but you are allowed to argue with the conclusion that she reaches. In fact, if the author makes an argument, it's a safe bet that one or more questions about the passage will ask you about how the argument could be strengthened or weakened with new information.

Despite this variety, you should follow the same step-by-step process for all passages. We'll call this:

The Basic Approach

Here are the four steps:

1. Read the questions first.
2. Ask yourself: What's the Big Idea?
3. Answer the question in your own words.
4. Use POE.

Let's break each one of these down:

1. Read the Questions First.

If you're like most people, you probably approach reading comprehension questions by reading the passage and trying to remember as much information as possible. By the time you read the first question, you've forgotten what the passage said about that particular topic, so you have to go back and read the passage again. If you read the questions first, you'll know what the important parts of the passage are as you read them, and you'll be able to answer the questions far more efficiently.

For instance, if the question asks what the main point of the passage is, and that's the only question asked about the passage, how much time do you think you need to spend reading the nitty-gritty details? That's right, none. On the other hand, if there are two questions that ask about specific details, then you'll probably want to read more of the supporting information.

Further, reading the questions also lets you know whether you're about to read a textbook passage or an argument passage. For example, if you see a question such as, "Which of the following, if true, would most support the author's contention," then you can be sure that you're about to read an argument.

2. What's the Big Idea?

Your first objective as you read the passage should be to figure out, in broad terms, what the author tries to say. What is the passage mostly about? We'll call this the Big Idea. If the questions haven't already tipped you off, you should decide as quickly as possible which type of passage you're reading. The format of the Big Idea will be slightly different depending on which type of passage it is.

While reading a textbook passage, remember that you can rely on its organization. Let's try an example. Quickly read the passage below reading only for the Big Idea. Use the structural clues in the passage to help find it.

Geologists classify rocks on the earth's surface into three categories: igneous, sedimentary, and metamorphic. The names refer not to qualities of the rocks, such as texture or hardness, but rather to the way in which they were formed.

The first category, igneous, describes rocks that were formed by volcanic activity. Flowing red-hot lava burst forth from vents in the earth's surface and cooled quickly into solid rock.

By contrast, sedimentary rock is created over millennia by successive layers of silt from rivers and streams.

Metamorphic rock is created by heat and pressure. The Himalayan mountain range is made up of metamorphic rock created by the collision of two continental plates. The heat and pressure caused by the collision recrystallized the original sedimentary rock and it became metamorphic rock.

Wow, that was exciting. We weren't asked to believe anything, and those sentences could have come from a (really, really, boring) textbook, so this must be a textbook passage. So, what's the Big Idea? You should probably be thinking along these lines:

There are three kinds of rocks.

It really doesn't need to get any more complicated than that. You can look up the specific details later if you need them.

If you're faced with an argument, the Big Idea is what the author wants you to believe, and why he thinks you should believe it. Try this one:

Some scientists and politicians have suggested that automobile engines will soon run on hydrogen fuel cells rather than gasoline. They cite the rising cost of petroleum and a greater awareness of the threat of global warming as two reasons why this change is imminent. However, proponents of hydrogen fuel cell technology fail to consider the enormous cost of retooling auto factories to build these new engines, as well as the cost of upgrading gas stations to accommodate the new power source. Clearly, widespread use of hydrogen power for cars is years away.

What's the Big Idea?

We won't be converting to hydrogen fuel cells anytime soon because it'll cost too much.

3. Answer the Question in Your Own Words.

Many test takers neglect this step, and their scores suffer as a result. If you go into the answer choices saying to yourself, "I'll know the answer when I see it," you'll be more likely to get confused by the language of the wrong answer choices. If you go into the answer choices with a specific idea of what you're looking for, you'll be more likely to avoid the incorrect answers and choose the right one.

4. Use POE.

As we said earlier, a right answer is right only because it's better than all the others. We'll discuss typical patterns that ETS follows in creating wrong answers, and show you how to recognize them.

THE QUESTIONS

Before we apply the four steps to a specific example, let's talk about the types of questions that ETS will ask. As we mentioned earlier, ETS breaks the questions into two main categories: those that test literal comprehension and those that test critical and inferential comprehension.

LITERAL COMPREHENSION

There are four types of literal comprehension questions that comprise about 55 percent of the questions you will see:

- main idea/Main purpose
- supporting idea
- vocabulary-in-context
- organization

Main Idea/Main Purpose

These are both closely related to the Big Idea, but there's an important distinction between the Main Idea and the Main Purpose. A Main Idea question asks, "What did the author say?" A Main Purpose question asks, "Why did the author write the passage?"

Supporting Idea

Supporting Idea questions ask about the evidence used to back up the Big Idea. These questions ask about specific pieces of information in the passage. These questions also ask not only *what* was said, but also *why* it was said.

Vocabulary-in-Context

These questions will ask you what a specific word or phrase means in the context of the passage. A sample question might look like this:

> 1. As used in line 6 of the passage, the word "butaneous" most nearly means which of the following?

Organization

These questions ask about how the pieces of the passage fit together. A sample question might look like this:

> 2. Which of the following best describes the organization of the third paragraph?

Critical and Inferential Comprehension

Critical and inferential comprehension questions comprise about 45 percent of the test and fall into the following categories:

- inference/conclusion
- evaluate evidence
- assumption
- fact vs. opinion
- attitude
- extend/predict
- application

This may seem like a lot, but remember, more than half of the questions will be about literal comprehension. Let's look at each one of these:

Inference/Conclusion

These questions ask you what is provably true based on other information in the passage.

> 3. Which of the following statements can be properly inferred from the information in the passage?

Evaluate Evidence

These questions will ask you to weaken or strengthen the author's position with an additional piece of evidence.

> 4. Which of the following statements, if true, would most weaken the author's reasoning?

Assumption

When the author is stating or defending a point of view, these questions ask what unstated assumptions the author is making in presenting his argument. In other words, the question asks you to identify the gap in the author's reasoning.

> 5. Which of the following is an assumption on which the author's argument depends?

Fact vs. Opinion

These questions ask you to distinguish between the two.

> 6. Which of the following is a fact mentioned by the author?

Attitude

As when we discussed the Big Idea, these questions ask about the author's opinion.

> 7. Which of the following best describes the author's feeling toward logging of old-growth forests?

Extend/Predict

These questions will ask about things that are likely to happen based on the information in the passage.

8. If the trends mentioned in the passage continue, which of the following would be most likely to occur?

Application

These questions ask you to apply the reasoning outlined in the passage in a similar scenario.

9. Which of the following best matches the chain of reasoning used by the author in the third paragraph?

PRIMARY PURPOSE AND ASSUMPTION QUESTIONS

Let's look at an example of a primary purpose question and an assumption question and put the four-step basic approach into action. We'll reuse the second sample passage from page 8:

Some scientists and politicians have suggested that automobile engines will soon run on hydrogen fuel cells rather than gasoline. They cite the rising cost of petroleum and a greater awareness of the threat of global warming as two reasons why this change is imminent. However, proponents of hydrogen fuel cell technology fail to consider the enormous cost of retooling auto factories to build these new engines, as well as the cost of upgrading gas stations to accommodate the new power source. Clearly, widespread use of hydrogen power for cars is years away.

1. The primary purpose of the passage is to

   (A) argue that hydrogen fuel cell technology is not a solution to the growing problem of global warming
   (B) prove that hydrogen fuel cells will never replace gasoline as the main source of automobile fuel
   (C) dispute the contention that cars will soon be powered by hydrogen fuel cells
   (D) show that the cost of retooling auto factories would be greater than the cost of upgrading gas stations
   (E) suggest that gasoline will continue to be less expensive than hydrogen for the foreseeable future

2. Which of the following is an assumption made by the author of the passage?

(A) Widespread use of hydrogen fuel cells in cars would have no impact on global warming.
(B) The cost of petroleum will not rise faster than the cost of hydrogen.
(C) No alternative power source will be found that is cheaper to convert to than hydrogen.
(D) The environmental costs of burning fossil fuels are higher than most people imagine.
(E) The cost of implementing a new technology is related to the time required to implement that technology.

Here's How to Crack It

Step 1: Read the Questions First.

1. The primary purpose of the passage is to

2. Which of the following is an assumption made by the author of the passage?

Based on these two questions, we already know that we're dealing with an argument. If the author's assuming something, then he must be asking us to believe something and supporting that belief with evidence.

We also know that we may need to read for some detail, but both questions seem more concerned with the overall structure of the passage.

Step 2: What's the Big Idea?

We won't be converting to hydrogen fuel cells anytime soon because it'll cost too much.

Step 3: Answer the Question in Your Own Words.

Let's start with question 1:

1. The primary purpose of the passage is to

Remember that a primary purpose question is really asking, "Why did the author write this?" In this case, the author argues against the scientists and politicians who suggested that the conversion to hydrogen is imminent. So we could say, in our own words, something like:

The primary purpose of the passage is to counter the scientists' and politicians' argument.

Step 4: Use POE.

Now, compare what we came up with to each answer choice:

(A) argue that hydrogen fuel cell technology is not a solution to the growing problem of global warming

Does that say, "to counter the scientists' and politicians' argument?" Well, what was their argument? If we go back to the first sentence of the passage, we find the point of their argument is only that the changeover will happen quickly, not that it's necessarily going to fix the problem of global warming. So, no, that's not why our author wrote the argument, and we can cross out answer choice (A).

(B) prove that hydrogen fuel cells will never replace gasoline as the main source of automobile fuel

Here's a hint: The word "never" should jump out at you because it's extreme, and extreme language is usually hard to defend. It's not necessarily wrong, but it should raise a red flag, and you should carefully decide whether it's warranted. In this case, the author does not try to prove that we'll *never* switch to hydrogen cells, only that the switch will take a longer time than the scientists and politicians think. Cross out choice (B).

(C) dispute the contention that cars will soon be powered by hydrogen fuel cells

This one looks pretty good. It matches our statement closely. Let's keep it, but of course we should still check the other two.

(D) show that the cost of retooling auto factories would be greater than the cost of upgrading gas stations

No. We don't have enough information to determine whether the author would even agree with that statement. Cross it out.

(E) suggest that gasoline will continue to be less expensive than hydrogen for the foreseeable future

Be careful here. The author would probably agree with that statement, and for that reason it's a very tempting answer choice. But because we spent the time to answer the question in our own words, we know that that's not *why* the author wrote the passage. The author wrote the passage *to counter the scientists' and politicians' argument.* We can cross out answer choice (E). That leaves us with (C) as the best answer.

Let's Try the Second Problem

Step 3: Answer the Question in Your Own Words.

2. Which of the following is an assumption made by the author of the passage?

Remember that an assumption is a missing piece of evidence between the author's stated reasons and his conclusion. Start by analyzing the structure of the argument. We already know how the author structured the argument since that was the Big Idea:

We won't be converting to hydrogen fuel cells anytime soon because it'll cost too much.

Do you notice anything wrong with that reasoning? The author tells us that just because it costs a lot, that means it won't happen soon. Is that necessarily true? The space program costs a lot, but we put a man on the moon six years ahead of schedule (the target date was 1975). In fact, you could probably make a counter-argument showing that if you threw enough money at the problem, you could get it solved faster. So we could state the author's assumption in our own words like this:

The cost of converting to fuel cell technology will delay the conversion time.

Step 4: Use POE.

Let's compare our answer to the choices provided:

(A) Widespread use of hydrogen fuel cells in cars would have no impact on global warming.

Is that what we're looking for? No. We're looking for a link between cost and time. Cross out answer choice (A).

(B) The cost of petroleum will not rise faster than the cost of hydrogen.

Is that what we're looking for? It's not exactly what we said, but this at least mentions something about cost and speed. We'll keep it for the moment.

(C) No alternative power source will be found that is cheaper to convert to than hydrogen.

No. Other power sources are wholly irrelevant to our argument. Cross it out.

(D) The environmental costs of burning fossil fuels are higher than most people imagine.

This may or may not be true, but it clearly isn't an assumption the author makes. Let's cross it out.

(E) The cost of implementing a new technology is related to the time required to implement that technology.

This seems like a generalized form of what we're looking for. Is it better than answer choice (B)? Well, if we thought that the cost of petroleum did rise faster than the cost of hydrogen, then maybe people would think that the conversion was worth it, and maybe they'd devote the resources to the conversion, and...stop. That's too many "maybes" for one answer choice. If you find yourself building a bridge like that, and there's a better answer choice waiting, go with the better choice. The best answer is (E).

SUPPORTING EVIDENCE AND ORGANIZATION QUESTIONS

Get the idea? Let's try a supporting evidence question and an organization question based on the same passage:

Some scientists and politicians have suggested that automobile engines will soon run on hydrogen fuel cells rather than gasoline. They cite the rising cost of petroleum and a greater awareness of the threat of global warming as two reasons why this change is imminent. However, proponents of hydrogen fuel cell technology fail to consider the enormous cost of retooling auto factories to build these new engines, as well as the cost of upgrading gas stations to accommodate the new power source. Clearly, widespread use of hydrogen power for cars is years away.

3. Which of the following did the passage mention as a reason that some people believe that hydrogen will soon replace gasoline as the main form of fuel for cars?

(A) The cost of fossil fuel-based energy sources is rising.

(B) The burning of gasoline contributes to global warming.

(C) The cost of retooling auto factories is negligible compared to the costs associated with global warming.

(D) Hydrogen is a cleaner-burning fuel than gasoline.

(E) Hydrogen will be cheaper than gasoline in the near future.

4. Which of the following best describes the organization of the passage?

(A) A position is stated, a contrary position is stated, and a synthesis of the two opposing points of view is reached.

(B) Two opposing points of view are described in detail.

(C) The author states a position, and shows that the position is incorrect because the evidence on which it's based is flawed.

(D) The author contradicts a stated position by showing that the position's adherents haven't adequately testined all the evidence.

(E) A position is stated, the reasoning behind the argument is questioned, and additional evidence is offered in support of the position.

Here's How to Crack It

Step 3: Answer the Question in Your Own Words.

3. Which of the following did the passage mention as a reason that some people believe that hydrogen will soon replace gasoline as the main form of fuel for cars?

There were two reasons cited: the rising cost of petroleum, and a greater awareness of the threat of global warming, so the right answer could be either one of those two.

Step 4. Use POE.

(A) The cost of fossil fuel-based energy sources is rising.

Yes. Petroleum is a fossil fuel-based energy source, and that matches one of the things we were looking for. We'll keep it.

(B) The burning of gasoline contributes to global warming.

Be careful here. Although it's true that burning gasoline contributes to global warming, the passage did not mention that as a reason for the scientists' and politicians' beliefs. It's very likely that they would agree with the statement, *but it wasn't mentioned in the passage*, and the question asks for something that *was mentioned in the passage*. Cross it out.

(C) The cost of retooling auto factories is negligible compared to the costs associated with global warming.

No. That wasn't cited as a reason.

(D) Hydrogen is a cleaner-burning fuel than gasoline.

Again, this is true, but it wasn't explicitly mentioned. Cross it out.

(E) Hydrogen will be cheaper than gasoline in the near future.

No. This wasn't mentioned either.

Because we were careful to eliminate otherwise true answer choices that weren't cited as reasons, we're down to the best answer: (A).

And Now Let's Look at Question 4

Step 3: Answer the Question in Your Own Words.

4. Which of the following best describes the organization of the passage?

How was the passage organized? We already know the author argues against a stated opinion. So we're looking for something like

An opinion was stated and supported, and then was argued against.

Step 4: Use POE.

(A) A position is stated, a contrary position is stated, and a synthesis of the two opposing points of view is reached.

This looked great up until the last part. Was there a synthesis? No. Cross it out.

(B) Two opposing points of view are described in detail.

Maybe. There were two opposing points of view, but this answer choice doesn't mention the fact that one was argued against. This probably isn't the right answer, but let's leave it in until something better comes along.

(C) The author states a position, and shows that the position is incorrect because the evidence on which it's based is flawed.

Maybe, and because it matches the structure of the argument more closely than choice (B), we can cross choice (B) out now.

(D) The author contradicts a stated position by showing that the position's adherents haven't adequately testined all the evidence.

This looks pretty good too. Let's keep it.

(E) A position is stated, the reasoning behind the argument is questioned, and additional evidence is offered in support of the position.

No. The additional evidence was against the position. Let's get rid of it.

We're down to choices (C) and (D), which both correctly state that the author argues against a position. Choice (C) says that the author shows that the evidence was flawed. Is that true? No. The author says that there are costs associated with the conversion that the proponents aren't taking into account, but the author doesn't say the proponents' evidence is faulty. How about (D)? Yes. The author does show that the proponents haven't looked at all the evidence.

So although there were two similar answer choices, a closer look revealed how one was better than the other. The best answer is (D).

VOCABULARY-IN-CONTEXT AND INFERENCE/CONCLUSION QUESTIONS

Now let's look at a vocabulary-in-context question and an inference/conclusion question. We'll use the other passage:

Geologists classify rocks on the earth's surface into three categories: igneous, sedimentary, and metamorphic. The names refer not to qualities of the rocks, such as texture or hardness, but rather to the way in which they were formed.

The first category, igneous, describes rocks that were formed by volcanic activity. Flowing red-hot lava burst forth from vents in the earth's surface and cooled quickly into solid rock.

By contrast, sedimentary rock is created over millennia by successive layers of silt from rivers and streams.

Metamorphic rock is created by heat and pressure. The Himalayan mountain range is made up of metamorphic rock created by the collision of two continental plates. The heat and pressure caused by the collision recrystallized the original sedimentary rock and it became metamorphic rock.

5. As used in the passage, the word "qualities" (line 3) most nearly means which one of the following?

(A) Values

(B) Ranks

(C) Characteristics

(D) Worth

(E) Names

6. Which of the following can be inferred from the statements in the passage?

(A) Sedimentary rock is never found near volcanic rock.

(B) Rocks could be classified by categories other than the way in which they were formed.

(C) Lava is composed of melted sedimentary rock.

(D) Most mountain ranges are made up of metamorphic rock.

(E) Metamorphic rock can be created only from heated and pressurized sedimentary rock.

Here's How to Crack It

Step 1: Read the Questions First.

5. As used in the passage, the word "qualities" (line 3) most nearly means which one of the following?

6. Which of the following can be inferred from the statements in the passage?

The first question is a vocabulary-in-context question, so we should pay close attention to line 3 when we get there. The second question is an inference question, so we'll be forced to read the entire passage.

Step 2: What's the Big Idea?

There are three types of rocks.

Step 3: Answer the Question in Your Own Words.

5. As used in the passage, the word "qualities" (line 3) most nearly means which one of the following?

This is how you should approach vocabulary-in-context questions. Go find the word "qualities" in line 3 and cross it out. Then, back up a few sentences and start reading. When you get to the crossed-out word, fill in your own word (sometimes you may have to read a few sentences after the crossed-out word, too). Give it a try.

Did you come up with a word like *attributes* or *properties*?

Step 4: Use POE.

Now, compare your word with the answer choices:

(A) Values

No. Values aren't attributes or properties. Cross it out.

(B) Ranks

No. Ranks aren't attributes or properties. Cross it out.

(C) Characteristics

Yes. Characteristics are attributes or properties. Keep it.

(D) Worth

No. Worth isn't attributes or properties. Cross it out.

(E) Names

No. Names aren't attributes or properties. Cross it out.
The best answer is (C).

Now Let's Try the Other One

Step 3: Answer the Question in Your Own Words.

6. Which of the following can be inferred from the statements in the passage?

In real life when we use the word inference, we typically think of having to make a huge logical leap or deduction. But remember, the Praxis isn't like real life. On the PPST, the right answer to an inference question should be provably true according to the information in the passage. In fact, if it seems too obvious to be right, then it's probably the right answer.

Notice that it's impossible to come up with an answer in your own words for an inference question. That just means that you'll have to be even more careful while working through step 4.

Step 4: Use POE.

(A) Sedimentary rock is never found near volcanic rock.

Can you prove this is true based on facts from the passage? No. Cross it out.

(B) Rocks could be classified by categories other than the way in which they were formed.

Can you prove this is true based on facts from the passage? It seems really obvious. Of course there are other ways you could classify rocks—the passage mentions texture and hardness as examples. Wait! It's really obvious—it might be the right answer. Keep it.

(C) Lava is composed of melted sedimentary rock.

According to the information in the passage, we have no idea what lava is made from. Cross it out.

(D) Most mountain ranges are made up of metamorphic rock.

Most mountain ranges? We only learned about one. Cross it out.

(E) Metamorphic rock can be created only from heated and pressurized sedimentary rock.

We know that's how the Himalayas were formed, but we don't know if that's the only way. Maybe metamorphic rock could be formed by heating and pressurizing igneous rock, too. We don't know. Cross it out.

Choice (B) is the only answer choice that we can prove is true based on facts found in the passage, and is therefore the best answer.

EVIDENCE AND APPLICATION QUESTIONS

Let's look at evidence and application questions in the context of a new passage:

7. At a recent art museum exhibition, more sculptures were shown than photographs or oil paintings. The new curator of the museum invited artists to submit works, and she alone selected the works to be displayed. The curator of the museum is clearly biased in favor of sculptors.

   Which of the following statements, if true, would most weaken the author's argument?

   (A) At last year's exhibition, the old curator also selected more sculptures than photographs or oil paintings.
   (B) A recent survey concluded that most people prefer sculptures to oil paintings.
   (C) The new curator herself is a sculptor.
   (D) More sculptors than photographers or oil painters submitted works to be shown at the exhibition.
   (E) The oil paintings shown at the exhibition were of exceptionally high quality.

8. According to the flawed reasoning the author follows in the passage, in which of the following scenarios would the author be most likely to conclude that bias is present?

   (A) The coach of a little league team assigns his son to play pitcher even though another boy on the team has equally good skills at that position.
   (B) At a local grocery store, there is more shelf space devoted to Brand X than to Brand Y or Brand Z. The manager is solely responsible for allotting shelf space.
   (C) The manager of a local nostalgia movie house surveyed his frequent customers and decided to show more movies starring Cary Grant than either Katharine Hepburn or Henry Fonda, because his patrons had clearly expressed their preference for Cary Grant.
   (D) A moving company hires only people who can lift a 100-pound box over their heads. The new hires at the moving company this week were all men.
   (E) A man interviews for a job, but is told he lacks sufficient relevant experience. As he leaves the building, however, he notices that most of the employees at the firm are at least ten years younger than he is.

Here's How to Crack It

Step 1: Read the Questions First.

7. Which of the following statements, if true, would most weaken the author's argument?

8. According to the flawed reasoning the author follows in the passage, in which of the following scenarios would the author be most likely to conclude that bias is present?

The first is an evidence question and the second is an application question. Because question 7 explicitly mentions an argument, we know that we should look for the point of the argument and the reasons the author gives to back it up.

Step 2: What's the Big Idea?

Based on the passage, the Big Idea is something like this:

The curator's biased because she picked more sculptures.

Step 3: Answer the Question in Your Own Words.

7. Which of the following statements, if true, would most weaken the author's argument?

We're looking for something that suggests that just because she picked more sculptures doesn't necessarily mean she's biased. For instance, maybe most of the submitted oil paintings and photographs were just plain bad.

Notice that we're just getting an idea of what we're looking for rather than an exact answer. Many different statements would weaken the author's argument.

Step 4: Use POE.

(A) At last year's exhibition, the old curator also selected more sculptures than photographs or oil paintings.

Does this show that the new curator isn't necessarily biased? No. What happened last year is not relevant to what happened this year.

(B) A recent survey concluded that most people prefer sculptures to oil paintings.

Does this show that the new curator isn't necessarily biased? No. What most people believe is not relevant to what the curator believes.

(C) The new curator herself is a sculptor.

No. If anything, this would serve to *strengthen* the author's argument by showing that the curator is biased because she is a sculptor and is therefore in favor of sculptors.

(D) More sculptors than photographers or oil painters submitted works to be shown at the exhibition.

Does this show that the new curator isn't necessarily biased? Yes. If there were more sculptures submitted, then the fact that there are more sculptures in the exhibition wouldn't necessarily mean the curator was biased. Keep this one.

(E) The oil paintings shown at the exhibition were of exceptionally high quality.

No. This is irrelevant. The quality of the paintings has nothing to do with whether or not the curator is biased in favor of sculptors.

The best answer is (D).

NOW LET'S TRY THE OTHER ONE

Step 3: Answer the Question in Your Own Words.

8. According to the flawed reasoning the author follows in the passage, in which of the following scenarios would the author be most likely to conclude that bias is present?

This is an example of an application question. The question asks you to find the scenario in which the author would find bias, assuming he applied the flawed reasoning in the passage. To give yourself an idea of what you're looking for, try to state the flawed reasoning in general terms before you look at the answer choices. For instance, in this case you might say:

The fact that someone picked more of one thing than another thing means that the person is biased.

Your own opinion is irrelevant—you're just looking to summarize the author's reasoning. Now we look for an answer choice that follows the same (flawed) logic.

Step 4: Use POE.

(A) The coach of a little league team assigns his son to play pitcher even though another boy on the team has equally good skills at that position.

Does this talk about someone picking more of something? No. Cross it out.

(B) At a local grocery store, there is more shelf space devoted to Brand X than to Brand Y or Brand Z. The manager is solely responsible for allotting shelf space.

Does this talk about someone picking more of something? Kind of. Let's keep it for the moment and see what the other choices are.

(C) The manager of a local nostalgia movie house surveyed his frequent customers and decided to show more movies starring Cary Grant than either Katharine Hepburn or Henry Fonda, because his patrons had clearly expressed their preference for Cary Grant.

This talks about someone picking more of something, but there's a reason explicitly stated that shows the manager isn't biased. Cross it out.

(D) A moving company hires only people who can lift a 100-pound box over their heads. The new hires at the moving company this week were all men.

This, too, talks about someone picking more of something (in this case, all men and no women), but here also there's a reason that suggests there's no bias involved. Cross it out.

(E) A man interviews for a job, but is told he lacks sufficient relevant experience. As he leaves the building, however, he notices that most of the employees at the firm are at least ten years younger than he is.

Does this talk about someone picking more of something? The person doing the hiring isn't explicitly mentioned, and the hiring of the younger people happened earlier than the older man's interview, so this doesn't seem like the best match. But let's look at answer choice B again:

(B) At a local grocery store, there is more shelf space devoted to Brand X than to Brand Y or Brand Z. The manager is solely responsible for allotting shelf space.

Here, as in the original passage, we have one identifiable person in charge of making the decision. We also are asked to compare one item to two others. According to the reasoning in the passage, the author should conclude that the manager is biased in favor of Brand X. Overall, this seems like the best choice. Pick (B).

FACT VS. OPINION, ATTITUDE, AND EXTEND/PREDICT QUESTIONS

Finally, let's take a look at one last passage and the last three question types: fact vs. opinion, attitude, and extend/predict:

Consumers spent far more money on recordings of popular music than on recordings of classical music last year, and they spent a similarly disproportionate amount was spent on live popular music concert tickets than on classical concert tickets. Because popular music lovers outnumber classical music aficionados by a wide margin, these disparities should come as no great shock, and in a free society people have the right to spend money on whatever legal products they choose. But because only classical music has the ability to elevate a listener's soul, the people who bought popular music recordings and concert tickets simply wasted their money.

9. Which of the following statements, taken from the passage, is most clearly an expression of opinion rather than fact?

(A) The people who bought popular music recordings and concert tickets simply wasted their money.

(B) Last year consumers spent far more money on recordings of popular music than on recordings of classical music.

(C) Popular music lovers outnumber classical music aficionados by a wide margin.

(D) In a free society people have the right to spend money on whatever legal products they choose.

(E) A similarly disproportionate amount of money was spent on live popular-music concert tickets than on classical concert tickets.

10. The author's attitude toward people who bought popular music recordings last year can best be described as

(A) contemptuous

(B) strongly disapproving

(C) angry

(D) supportive

(E) tolerant

11. With which of the following statements would the author of the passage be most likely to agree?

(A) Popular music should be banned.

(B) Elevation of one's soul should be one's top priority.

(C) Popular music has no value whatsoever.

(D) People should spend more money on classical music recordings than on popular music recordings.

(E) More people would listen to classical music if it were taught in the schools.

HERE'S HOW TO CRACK IT

Step 1: Read the Questions First.

We've got one fact vs. opinion question, one attitude question, and one extend/predict question. We'll definitely need to get a handle on the author's point and tone.

9. Which of the following statements, taken from the passage, is most clearly an expression of opinion rather than fact?

10. The author's attitude toward people who bought popular music recordings last year can best be described as

11. With which of the following statements would the author of the passage be most likely to agree?

Step 2: What's the Big Idea?

You should have something like:

Money spent on popular music is a waste because classical music is so much more uplifting, even though most people apparently don't agree.

Don't worry if you didn't get all of that—this passage incorporated a lot of information.

Step 3: Answer the Question in Your Own Words.

9. Which of the following statements, taken from the passage, is most clearly an expression of opinion rather than fact?

You probably noticed that most of the passage was fact-based. At the very end, however, the author threw out two big opinions: only classical music can elevate a listener's soul, and people who spent money on popular music threw it away. We don't know which of these ETS will ask for, but the answer's going to be one of those two.

Step 4: Use POE.

(A) The people who bought popular music recordings and concert tickets simply wasted their money.

This is one of the opinions we were looking for, but let's review the others just to make sure.

(B) Last year consumers spent far more money on recordings of popular music than on recordings of classical music.

No. This is a statement of fact.

(C) Popular music lovers outnumber classical music aficionados by a wide margin.

No. This is also an objective fact.

(D) In a free society people have the right to spend money on whatever legal products they choose.

If answer choice (A) weren't there, this would be the best answer only because it's more arguable than the others, but compared to choice (A) it's a fact.

(E) A similarly disproportionate amount of money was spent on live popular-music concert tickets than on classical concert tickets.

No. This is also a fact.

The best answer is (A).

Now Let's Try the Other One

Step 3: Answer the Question in Your Own Words.

10. The author's attitude toward people who bought popular music recordings last year can best be described as

What does the author think about people who bought popular music recordings last year? He thinks they wasted their money! So what's his attitude? How about condescending or scornful? Let's see what we've got:

Step 4: Use POE.

(A) contemptuous

Maybe. Let's keep it.

(B) strongly disapproving

It's not so much that the author disapproves as much as he thinks they made a stupid decision. He even says people are free to do what they want. Cross it out.

(C) angry

No. There's no evidence that the author is angry. Cross it out.

(D) supportive

Supportive? No. He thinks they're idiots. Cross it out.

(E) tolerant

Be careful here. He does tolerate popular music lovers—remember that he believes they can spend money on whatever they want—but that's not his attitude toward them. Cross it out.

The best answer is (A).

Now Let's Try the Last One:

Step 3: Answer the Question in Your Own Words.

11. With which of the following statements would the author of the passage be most likely to agree?

This is an Extend/Predict question. ETS asks you to take what you know about the author and pick the statement with which he'd be most likely to agree. It's impossible to predict what the right answer will be, but you should remind yourself of what you know so far:

The author prefers classical music to popular music.

The author thinks people are foolish to spend money on popular music.

Let's see what the choices are:

Step 4: Use POE.

(A) Popular music should be banned.

That seems awfully extreme. It's hard to defend an extreme answer choice on an extend/predict question. Right answers are usually more middle-of-the-road. Cross it out.

(B) Elevation of one's soul should be one's top priority.

There's no evidence to suggest it should be one's top priority. Cross it out.

(C) Popular music has no value whatsoever.

No value whatsoever? Again, that seems extreme. Get rid of it.

(D) People should spend more money on classical music recordings than on popular music recordings.

That's better. Of course the author would agree with that—he believes that spending money on popular music is wasteful and that classical music is uplifting. It's not too much of stretch to believe that he thinks that everyone should spend more money on classical music than on popular music. Keep it.

(E) More people would listen to classical music if it were taught in the schools.

We have no idea whether the author would agree with this or not. Cross it out.

The best answer is (D).

SUMMARY

You've probably noticed that the two key ideas we discussed at the very beginning are fundamental to being able to answer each question, regardless of the question type.

- **It's an open-book test.**
- **The right answer is the one that's better than the other four.**

Keep both ideas firmly in mind, and remember to follow the four-step process as you work through the following drill. Then check your answers.

DRILL

Directions: Each statement or passage is followed by a question or questions based on its content. After reading a statement or passage, choose the best answer to each question from among the five choices given. Answer all questions following a statement or passage on the basis of what is *stated* or *implied* in that statement or passage; you are not expected to have any previous knowledge of the topics treated in the statements or passages.

Be sure to mark all your answers on your answer sheet and completely fill in the lettered space with a heavy, dark mark so that you cannot see the letter.

Remember, try to answer every question.

Question 1

1. In 1994, approximately two percent of humans who were admitted to hospital emergency rooms after suffering a scorpion bite in Texas died from the attack. Ten years later, this figure has jumped to four percent. Clearly, the venom of the scorpion has become much more toxic to humans.

   Which of the following statements, if true, most seriously weakens the above conclusion?

   (A) The scorpion population in Texas has remained steady since 1994.

   (B) There have been few innovations in the treatment of scorpion bites since 1994.

   (C) Most people who suffer scorpion bites are inexperienced hikers who are unaware of the best methods to avoid contact with a scorpion.

   (D) Since 1994, people have learned that most scorpion bites can be treated in the home as long as they are detected early.

   (E) People who survive one scorpion bite tend to have a better than average chance of surviving a second bite.

Questions 2–4

Mounting evidence suggests that any musical stimulus, from Beethoven to Outkast, can have therapeutic effects. Whether you've had heart surgery or a bad day at the office, soothing sounds may help to lessen stress and promote well-being. Music therapy isn't mainstream health care, but recent studies suggest it can have a wide range of benefits. Most studies have been done with patients recovering from illnesses such as a stroke or cancer.

No one really knows how music helps the body. It is known that listening to music can directly influence pulse, the electrical activity of muscles, and lower blood pressure. Neuroscientists suspect that music can actually help build and strengthen connections among nerve cells. This is probably why listening to Mozart before an IQ test boosts test scores an average of nine points.

2. Which of the following is NOT mentioned as a benefit of listening to music?

   (A) Relieved stress

   (B) Increased neural activity

   (C) Lowered blood pressure

   (D) Increased coordination

   (E) Lower blood pressure

3. Which of the following best summarizes the content of the passage?

   (A) Music therapy has become so widely accepted that many healthcare organizations are adding music therapy coverage to their insurance policies.

   (B) A detailed analysis on how music helps the body.

   (C) Neuroscientists are tracking the neurological effects of music on the body.

   (D) Evidence suggests that music therapy helps the body, even if we aren't sure exactly how.

   (E) Students can perform better on standardized tests if they listen to more classical music.

4. The author's use of the word "mainstream" in the first paragraph means

   (A) conventional
   (B) radical
   (C) musical
   (D) medicinal
   (E) experimental

5. Terry, a high-school senior from State A, expressed an interest in attending Lewis State College, which was located in State B. Terry's parents discovered that Lewis State College offered residents of State B a substantial discount from its normal tuition cost. Therefore, the parents decided to move to State B.

   Which of the following, if true, is the most important reason why the parents might reconsider their decision?

   (A) Scholarships are only given to applicants who establish financial need.
   (B) To qualify for the lower tuition, applicants must prove they have lived in State B for a minimum of three years.
   (C) Several colleges in State A offer tuition discounts.
   (D) State B does not have the same property values as State A.
   (E) Regular tuition at Lewis State College is lower than that of most state colleges.

6. A survey of 1200 residents of a certain state revealed that 34 percent found hunting to be morally wrong and 59 percent had never hunted before. From this information, the surveyors concluded that . . .

   Which of the following best completes the passage above?

   (A) Some respondents expressed their moral convictions more strongly than others.
   (B) The people who expressed an objection to hunting had never hunted before.
   (C) Moral objection is not the only reason why people do not hunt.
   (D) The people who had hunted before but stopped because of a moral objection outnumbered those who had never hunted but didn't find it morally wrong.
   (E) Some people hunt even though they are morally opposed to it.

<u>Questions 7–8</u>

Forced to hunt for new prey, killer whales are upsetting the sea otter population off the Alaskan coast, disrupting the food chain and setting off an ecological cascade. The whales have created damage with such alarming efficiency that a vast ecosystem now seems to be at risk of collapse.

The problem began when fish stocks started to decline in the Bering Sea, probably as a result of commercial fishing, or changes in the ocean currents and temperatures. Because of this lack of food, seals and sea lions are thinning out, losing some of their insulating blubber. Killer whales, therefore, aren't getting the same diet from seals and sea lions as they once did, forcing them to feed on sea otters. The otter populations have collapsed, allowing their prey, sea urchins, to multiply out of control. Sea urchins have now begun to devour the kelp forests on the ocean floor at an alarming rate. The kelp forests are crucial to a number of habitats.

7. Otter populations have declined off the Alaskan coast primarily because

   (A) sea urchins are multiplying at record rates
   (B) the kelp forests are being destroyed
   (C) whales have been forced to search for additional food
   (D) commercial fishing nets trap otters
   (E) global warming and current changes are making the otters sick

8. Which of the following best outlines the structure of the passage?

   (A) A statement is made, and then supported through an example.
   (B) A theory is stated, and the steps leading up to that theory are then explained.
   (C) A question is raised, and then answered.
   (D) An experiment is stated, followed by its conclusion.
   (E) An argument is stated, and then refuted.

ANSWERS AND EXPLANATIONS TO DRILL

1. **D** In order to weaken the conclusion, you need to show that the increase in the death rate to 4% from 2% is due to reasons beyond the toxicity of scorpion venom. Why are a higher percentage of emergency room admits dying if the venom is not more dangerous? (A) is not relevant. (B) indicates that the rates should stay the same, but it does not weaken the argument. (C) and (E) are also irrelevant. (D) indicates that many people are treating their bites at home. This would indicate that only severe cases end up in the emergency room, and these severe cases have a higher death rate. (D) helps to weaken the conclusion.
2. **D** All of the other four answer choices can be found within the passage. On a "NOT" question, eliminate an answer choice once you find that it works.
3. **D** The first paragraph states that music therapy helps a number of different people in different conditions. The second paragraph attempts to give some information on how music may help the body.
4. **A** The author uses the word mainstream to point out how music therapy is beyond the normal practices in medicine.
5. **B** Terry's parents chose to move with the belief that it would help get Terry a lower tuition. In order for that to happen, Terry's parents must be residents of State B. Answer choice (B) indicates that residency alone is not sufficient, which would weaken the decision to move.
6. **C** The number of people who have never hunted exceeds the number of people who find hunting to be morally wrong. Therefore, some people who do not hunt do not find hunting to be morally wrong. If this is the case, there has to be other reasons why people choose not to hunt. No other statement can be logically drawn from the information presented in the brief passage.
7. **C** The third sentence in the second paragraph addresses the whale's need for additional food.
8. **B** The passage starts with the claim that the otter population is in great danger. The theory is supported by explaining how whales are feeding on otters at an alarming rate.

2

PPST: Writing

FORMAT OF THE PPST: WRITING

The test is one hour long, divided into two half-hour sections. The first section contains 45 multiple-choice questions. The second section is an essay. Both sections count equally toward your score.

Let's start with the multiple-choice section:

ERROR ID QUESTIONS

There are only two types of multiple-choice questions on the PPST: Writing. One type asks you to identify an error in a sentence. Here's an example of an Error ID question:

1. Statistically, one (A) is more likely to die in an automobile accident than in a plane crash (B), yet paradoxically people feel safer in their car (C) than (D) in airplanes. No error (E)

All you have to do with these questions is determine which one of the underlined portions of the sentence, if any, contains a grammar or usage error. You don't have to correct the error or explain why it's wrong, you just have to find it. If there's no error, the correct answer is (E).

If you spot an error immediately, that's great. If not, the easiest way to approach these questions is to apply your knowledge of grammar to each of the underlined portions of the sentence. For instance, in the example above you would do this:

(A) *One* is a singular pronoun. Does that match with the verb *is*? Yes. So that's not an error.

(B) Is *plane crash* an acceptable use of words? Yes. So that's not an error.

(C) *Car* is a singular noun. Does that match with the other nouns and pronouns in that clause? No. "People" and "their" are both plural. So *car* is incorrect. (C) is the right answer.

SENTENCE CORRECTION QUESTIONS

The other type of multiple-choice question asks you to correct errors in a sentence. Here's an example of a sentence correction question:

2. To get through an emergency, it demands remaining calm and collected.

(A) it demands remaining calm
(B) it demands calmness
(C) one is demanded to remain calm
(D) one should remain calm
(E) demands one to remain calm

A sentence correction question gives you a sentence, underlines a portion (or all) of it, and asks you to pick the answer choice that best rewrites the underlined portion. If the underlined portion is correct as written, the answer is (A).

If you spot an error immediately on a sentence correction question, that's great. Eliminate choice (A) and all choices that repeat the same error. Then compare the remaining answer choices and eliminate those that contain other errors.

If you don't spot an error immediately, you can use the answer choices to help you. For instance, notice in the example that two answers begin with the word *it*, and two begin with the word *one*. Which is correct? Well, according to the portion of the sentence that's not underlined (which is the part you can't change) someone has to get through an emergency. Therefore, the answer should start with the word *one*. Now we're down to choices (C) and (D). Which is better? Is someone demanding that you remain calm? No. The best answer is (D).

WHAT'S TESTED?

Both of these question formats test the same rules of English, which we'll go over in great detail. You have less than one minute per question on the multiple-choice section, so you'll need to be very familiar with the question types and the grammar rules.

The grammar content tested in the PPST: Writing is actually quite limited. There are literally thousands of English grammar rules that ETS could test, but they stick to a very small subset. Here are the big categories:

Basic Grammar	• Parts of speech
Agreement	• Subject/verb agreement • Pronoun agreement • Verb tense agreement
Building Sentences	• Subjects and predicates • Phrases and clauses • Parallelism • Punctuation • Misplaced modifiers
Style	• Diction • Idiomatic expressions • Clarity

We'll start with an overview of the fundamentals, but don't worry if you start feeling overwhelmed by definitions. Because the questions ask you only to identify errors or correct sentences, ETS can't test you on the definitions of these ideas. You'll be tested only on usage.

BASIC GRAMMAR

Parts of Speech

There are nine altogether, but the PPST: Writing covers only eight:

- noun
- verb
- adjective
- adverb
- preposition
- pronoun
- interjection
- conjunction

(In case you're wondering, the category ETS doesn't test is **articles**—words like *the*, *an*, etc.)

Nouns and Proper Nouns

A **noun** is a person, place, thing, or idea.

The doctor walked into the store.

The nouns are: *doctor* (a person) and *store* (a place).

Beauty is in the eye of the beholder.

The nouns are: *beauty* (an idea), *eye* (a thing), and *beholder* (a person).

Proper nouns are nouns that name a specific person, place, thing, or idea. They should be capitalized.

George Washington was raised on a farm in Virginia.

The nouns are: *George Washington* (a specific person, and therefore a capitalized proper noun), *farm* (an unspecified place and therefore not capitalized), and *Virginia* (a specific place, and therefore a capitalized proper noun).

Verbs

A **verb** is an action word that tells you what's happening.

The policeman apprehended the criminal.
I have eaten worms.
You are a doctor.

The verbs are *apprehended*, *have eaten*, and *are*.

Any form of the verb *to be*, such as *am*, *are*, *were*, *was*, *will be*, and so on, is called a **state of being verb**.

Verb Tense

The **tense** of a verb tells you when the action occurred. The most common tenses are past, present, and future, but there are variations that you should be familiar with. Let's look at the ones that get tested:

Present	Shannon walks to the store every day. Shannon is walking to the store right now.
Past	Shannon walked to the store yesterday.
Future	Shannon will walk to the store tomorrow.

There are two others that show up a lot:

Present perfect	Shannon has walked to the store every day since she got her cast removed.
Past perfect	Shannon had walked to the store every day until she broke her leg.

You use the present perfect tense to show that an action started after a specific point in the past, but continues to occur now. You use the past perfect tense to show that a continued action happened before some specific point in the past.

3. Brian had shown (A) no signs of dissatisfaction (B) with his job (C) before he quit (D). No error (E)

Here's How to Crack It

The correct answer is (E). *He quit* is in the past, and before that time, *he had shown* no signs of dissatisfaction. The sentence correctly uses the past perfect tense, and there are no errors with the words *dissatisfaction* or *job.*

Adjectives

Adjectives are used to describe (or "modify") nouns.

The cat was lazy.
The lazy cat slept on the windowsill.

The adjective in both sentences is *lazy.*

Adverbs

Adverbs are words that modify verbs, adjectives, and other adverbs.

I quickly climbed to the top.

In this case the adverb *quickly* modified the verb *climbed.*

The dog was very stupid.

In this case the adverb *very* modified the adjective *stupid.*

He painted the house very neatly.

There are two adverbs here: *neatly* modifies the verb *painted,* and *very* modifies the adverb *neatly.* Try this one:

3. I was real excited to see my girlfriend.

(A) I was real excited to see my girlfriend.
(B) I was real excitedly to see my girlfriend.
(C) I was really excited to see my girlfriend.
(D) I was really excitedly to see my girlfriend.
(E) I was real, real excited to see my girlfriend.

Here's How to Crack It

In this case, the word *real* is modifying *excited. Excited* is an adjective, so the word that modifies it should be an adverb. *Real* is an adjective, so choice (A) is incorrect, as well as choices (B) and (E). *Really* is an adverb, correctly modifying *excited* in choice (C). In choice (D), there is no adjective at all. (C) is the best answer.

Prepositions

Prepositions are words that show how objects are related with respect to time or space.

I ran to the store.

The preposition is *to*.

By now, you should be able to identify nouns.

The preposition is *by*.

Other common prepositions are *of, at, in*, and *on*.

Let's stop here and introduce one important idea:

Subjects and Objects

The **subject** of the sentence tells you who or what is performing the action.

I ate the sandwich.

The verb is *ate*, so the subject is the noun that is doing the eating. In this case, the subject is *I*.

There are two ways that a noun can be an **object**: it can receive the action that the subject performs (*sandwich*, in the above example), or it can be the noun following a preposition.

John sped past the policeman.

Past is the preposition, so *policeman* is the object of the preposition.

If we're using the full name of each noun, the distinction between subject and object isn't very important. However, the difference between the two becomes very important (especially to ETS) when we use pronouns. Let's return to parts of speech.

Pronouns

Pronouns are short words that take the place of nouns.

I, you, he, she, it, me, they, them, us, him,
and *her* are all pronouns.

Pronouns are convenient because they're typically shorter than the nouns they replace. For instance, you could say:

James bought a dictionary as a birthday present for Elizabeth, and when Elizabeth came over that night, James gave the dictionary to Elizabeth.

But you could say it much more succinctly like this:

James bought a dictionary as a birthday present for Elizabeth, and when she came over that night, he gave it to her.

Not all pronouns are created equal. What if we wanted to use pronouns to shorten this sentence?

Paul went to the store.

What's wrong with this pronoun?

Him went to the store.

That should read:

He went to the store.

The trick is that some pronouns replace subjects, and some pronouns replace objects. Here's the list:

Subject	Object
I	me
you	you
he	him
she	her
we	us
they	them
it	it

Let's see how this works out:

I have a twin brother. Mom loves us, and we love pie, so on our birthday she baked us a banana cream pie. He and I ate most of it that night. The next day, she split the leftovers evenly between him and me.

So, when the twins are the objects of Mom's love, the correct pronoun is *us,* but when they do the loving (of pie, in this case), the correct pronoun is the subject pronoun *we.* Similarly, when they are the subjects eating the cake, the correct pronouns are *he* and *I,* but when the twins are the objects of the preposition *between,* the correct pronouns are *him* and *me.*

One last oddity: state of being verbs (*am, are, was,* etc.) always use subject pronouns. So no matter how strange this may sound,

It is I.

is correct, and

It's me!

is incorrect.

Similarly, if Maria answers the phone and someone asks to speak to her, she should reply

This is she.

not

This is her.

4. Between <u>you</u> and <u>I</u>, this test isn't <u>really</u> that <u>bad</u>.
A B C D
<u>No error</u>
E

Here's How to Crack It

The answer is (B). *I* is a subject pronoun, and the sentence requires an object pronoun there, because of the preposition *between*.

Possessive Pronouns

We're not done with pronouns yet. You also use pronouns to show possession more concisely, and there are two types of these. Sometimes possessive pronouns function as adjectives. Look at this sentence:

Ahmed drove Ahmed's car.

Ahmed's is an adjective modifying *car*. You could use a possessive pronoun to shorten it this way:

Ahmed drove his car.

His replaces *Ahmed's*, but still modifies *car*, and is therefore an adjective. Here's another example:

That pillow is my pillow.

My modifies *pillow*, and again the possessive pronoun functions as an adjective. But you'd probably write it this way:

That pillow is mine.

Aha! Here we have one form of a possessive pronoun replacing another. *Mine* replaces *my pillow* and becomes an object rather than an adjective. Remember that it's not important to know what these things are called, as long as you understand how they're used.

So here's the chart with the possessive pronouns added in:

Subject	Object	Possessive Adjective	Possessive Object
I	me	my	mine
you	you	your	yours
he	him	his	his
she	her	her	hers
we	us	our	ours
they	them	their	theirs
it	it	its	its (not used much)

OK, so think about these sentences:

I ate a sandwich.
The sandwich was eaten by me.
That's my sandwich.
That sandwich is mine.

Try reading these aloud, and then again with each row of the pronouns from the chart. If anything sounds weird to you, think about the rules and persuade yourself that what you're reading is grammatically correct, even if it sounds bad. Most English speakers are notoriously lazy about speaking with correct grammar, so it can be misleading to trust your ear on the PPST.

Who and *whom* are two other pronouns that get tested a lot. You'll never confuse them again if you remember that *who* is used as a subject and *whom* is used as an object. The possessive form (both types) is *whose.* So let's add one last column to our list:

Subject	Object	Possessive Adjective	Possessive Object
I	me	my	mine
you	you	your	yours
he	him	his	his
she	her	her	hers
we	us	our	ours
they	them	their	theirs
it	it	its	its (not used much)
who	whom	whose	whose (also not used much)

Who ate the sandwich?
The sandwich was eaten by whom?
Whose sandwich is that?
That sandwich is whose?

Notice also that none of the possessive pronouns is spelled with an apostrophe. This confuses many people, because we do use apostrophes with regular possessive nouns, like this:

The car is Monique's.

But it would be incorrect to write:

The car is her's.

Instead, you should write:

The car is hers.

Perhaps the most common error in this regard is the misspelling of the possessive pronoun *its.* This is correct:

The dog licked its paws.

This is incorrect:

The dog licked it's paws.

The word *it's* is a contraction of the words *it is,* and is therefore not a pronoun at all, but a subject and verb together. It would be nonsensical to say:

The dog licked it is paws.

Just remember that possessive pronouns never use apostrophes. Okay, back to the other parts of speech.

Interjections

Interjections are words that show excitement or emotion.

They're usually set apart from a sentence by an exclamation point:

Wow! I aced the PPST: Writing!

But you can also you use a comma, if the feeling isn't as strong:

Hey, that's pretty good.

Conjunctions

There are two types of **conjunctions**: coordinate and subordinate.

Coordinate conjunctions are the words *and, but, for, or, nor*, and *yet*.

They link equivalent parts of speech or complete thoughts together. This statement uses the conjunction *and* to link two nouns:

Malika bought a jar and a spoon.

This one links two verbs using the conjunction *or*:

I don't know whether to laugh or to cry.

This one links two complete sentences with the conjunction *but*:

I love you, but I don't want to marry you.

Notice that in each of these examples the items linked by the conjunctions could have come in either order without altering the meaning of the sentence.

Malika bought a spoon and a jar.

means the same thing as

Malika bought a jar and a spoon.

By contrast, a **subordinate conjunction** suggests that one part of the sentence is more important than the other.

Because and *although* are two examples of subordinate conjunctions.

Although he hadn't showered in three days, he didn't smell that bad.
Adam was fired because his job was eliminated.

Notice that in these sentences you can't necessarily switch the order without substantially changing the meaning:

Adam's job was eliminated because he was fired.

Finally, we should mention the conjunctions that come in pairs. The ones that get tested on the PPST are *either...or* and *neither...nor.*

Either that wallpaper goes, or I do.
Neither bats nor rats scare me.

Now that we've got the parts of speech defined, let's look at how they relate to each other, and apply that knowledge to actual questions.

AGREEMENT

All parts of speech in a sentence need to agree with each other. For instance, it wouldn't make sense to say

Harriet Tubman will be remembered for his heroic actions.

because *Harriet Tubman* is a woman, and *his* is a male pronoun. That's considered a pronoun gender disagreement, and that's an error. Let's look at all the parts of speech that must agree in a sentence.

Subject-Verb Agreement

Singular subjects should match with singular verbs, and plural subjects should match with plural verbs. This is called *agreeing in number.* Try this one:

3. The sonnet, a poetic form used by Shakespeare and other writers, <u>has a strict rhyme scheme</u>.

(A) has a strict rhyme scheme

(B) has a rhyme scheme that is considered strict

(C) have a strict rhyme scheme

(D) have strictly a rhyme scheme

(E) have a scheme that rhymes strictly

Here's How to Crack It

If you see the verb of the sentence underlined, make sure that it agrees in number with the subject of the sentence. How will ETS try to trick you? By separating the subject and the verb with a bunch of extra words. To help you locate the subject, cross out prepositional phrases and words that are separated by commas (called subordinate clauses). In this case we'd be left with:

The sonnet has a strict rhyme scheme.

What's the subject? *The sonnet.* Is *the sonnet* singular or plural? Well, it says *the* sonnet, so it must be singular. What's the verb? *has.* Is *has* singular or plural? Singular. So the subject and verb match as written. If you look at the answer choices, you'll notice that choices (A) and (B) start with *has,* while (C), (D), and (E) start with *have.* We've decided that *has* is correct, so we can eliminate answer choice (C), (D), and (E).

Now, if we compare choices (A) and (B), we see that (B) adds an unnecessary new idea (*considered strict*? By whom?) and is longer than (A). Both of these characteristics tend to make answer choices incorrect, so the best answer is (A).

If there's more than one subject of a sentence, things can change. If the multiple subjects are connected by *and*, then the subject is taken to be plural:

Carolyn and Betty walk to school.

If the subjects are connected by *or* or *nor,* the verb should match with the subject closest to it. Both of these sentences are correct:

Neither Akil nor the girls are wrong.
The girls or Akil is wrong.

Pronoun Agreement

Pronouns have to agree with the nouns they replace in both number and gender, and each pronoun must refer unambiguously to exactly one noun in the sentence.

4. When Ben's girlfriend told him that <u>she</u> (A) didn't like <u>his</u> (B) dog Tabitha, <u>he</u> (C) decided to get rid of <u>her</u> (D). <u>No error</u> (E)

Here's How to Crack It

Let's take a look at each of the underlined pronouns. Choice (A), *she,* is correctly used. At this point in the sentence there has only been one female introduced, Ben's girlfriend. Similarly, choices (B) and (C) refer to Ben, because he is the only male in the sentence that those pronouns could refer to. Choice (D), however, could refer to either Tabitha or Ben's girlfriend. The ambiguous pronoun is an error, and the correct answer is (D).

Verb Tense Agreement

The tense of a sentence should be consistent with respect to the action of the sentence.

5. Since 1920, <u>when</u> (A) the 19th Amendment to the U.S. Constitution <u>was ratified</u> (B), women <u>will have the right</u> (C) to vote <u>to elect</u> (D) the President. <u>No error</u> (E)

Here's How to Crack It

The sentence begins with the words "Since 1920," which suggests that an action started in the past and continues to the present time. But later in the sentence, above answer choice (C), the sentence uses the future tense. These tenses are inconsistent, so the correct answer is (C).

Try this one:

6. <u>Although Jorge ate tuna regularly</u>, he stopped after he learned that it might be unhealthy in large amounts due to high levels of mercury.

(A) Although Jorge ate tuna regularly
(B) Although Jorge ate tuna regularly once
(C) Although Jorge was eating tuna regularly
(D) Although Jorge had eaten tuna regularly
(E) Although Jorge was at one time eating tuna regularly

Here's How to Crack It

In this case, we have an action that happened (Jorge's eating) further in the past than another action (his learning that it might be unhealthy). When this situation occurs, ETS believes that you need the past perfect tense to show that time relationship. The correct answer is (D).

Building Sentences

Now that we've got a handle on the parts of speech and some basic grammar rules, let's see how we can string words together to form the sorts of long, convoluted sentences that you're likely to see on the PPST.

Subjects and Predicates

For a sentence to stand alone and make sense, it needs a subject and an action for that subject to perform. That action is called the **predicate**, and in its simplest form it can consist of nothing but a verb. This is a complete sentence:

Kim works.

Kim is the subject, and *works* is the predicate. A more complex sentence looks like this:

Kim works regularly at the grocery store on the corner of Main Street and Elm Avenue every Monday and Wednesday afternoon.

Notice that there's still only one subject and one predicate, but in this case the predicate is much longer.

Phrases and Clauses

At the grocery store, *on the corner of Main Street and Elm Avenue*, and *every Monday and Wednesday afternoon* are all examples of **phrases**. Notice that they contain subjects, but not actions, and therefore they couldn't stand alone as sentences.

A phrase can also contain actions but no subjects:

Standing on the sidewalk, Joan was hit by an out-of-control skateboarder.

The phrase *standing on the sidewalk* has an action, but we don't know who was standing until later in the sentence, after the comma.

A **clause**, then, is anything that has both a subject and an action. However, just because something is a clause doesn't necessarily mean it can stand alone as a sentence.

Although Xian loved her brother.

That doesn't make sense by itself, even though the clause has both a subject (*Xian*) and an action (*loved*). This is an example of a **dependent clause**, because it needs another clause to make it a whole sentence:

Although Xian loved her brother, she didn't want to take him to the movies.

She didn't want to take him to the movies is a clause that could stand alone as a complete sentence. It's called an **independent clause**.

You may have noticed that the word *although* was the only thing that kept the dependent clause from being an independent clause. *Although*, as we mentioned earlier, is an example of a subordinating conjunction. One rule of sentence construction is that in a complete sentence you can't have a dependent clause without an independent clause. Look at this one:

Although Fred was taller than Jim, but Jim was a better basketball player.

What's the problem here? There are two dependent clauses, one using the conjunction *although*, and the other using the conjunction *but*. We could rewrite this two ways:

Although Fred was taller than Jim, Jim was a better basketball player.
Fred was taller than Jim, but Jim was a better basketball player.

In both cases, we changed one of the dependent clauses into an independent clause by removing the conjunction.

You can even have multiple dependent clauses, as long as there's an independent clause in the sentence somewhere.

Although Fred was taller than Jim, Fred couldn't shoot a free throw to save his life, so Jim was a better basketball player.

So far, in every example we've seen, clauses and phrases have been separated by commas. There's one important exception: if you have two closely related independent clauses, you can put them together in the same sentence, but they should be separated by a semicolon, like this:

Jim is an asset to the team; he has a great free throw.

Each of these could stand alone as a complete sentence.

PARALLELISM

One way ETS can make sentences more complex is to introduce lists or comparisons. ETS considers it important that items in lists or items being compared be in the same form as each other. That idea is called **parallelism**, and it's a frequently tested concept on the PPST.

Lists

Two or more elements make up a list. When there are only two elements, you create a list by joining them together with the word *and*:

I went to the store and bought bread and butter.

If there are more than two elements, you still need an *and* at the end, but you'll also need to separate the earlier elements with commas:

I went to the store and bought milk, cereal, bread, and butter.

Notice there is a comma after *bread* but before *and*. This comma, called a serial comma, is not required, but ETS prefers it to be there (as does the editor of this book). ETS won't test you on that one, though. They'll test you on parallelism. Try this one:

7. Ashley's life goals were a successful career and to be a good mother.

(A) a successful career and to be a good mother
(B) a successful career and good motherhood
(C) a successful and good career and motherhood
(D) to have a successful career and a good mother
(E) to have a successful career and to be a good mother

Here's How to Crack It

The two items in the list have something to do with a successful career and being a good mother. Choice (A) isn't the right answer because the two items in the list are *a successful career,* which is a noun, and *to be a good mother,* which is a verb. *Good motherhood* isn't quite the same thing as being *a good mother,* so we can get rid of choices (B) and (C). In choice (D) the items are parallel (*a successful career* and *a good mother* are both nouns), but Ashley doesn't want to have a good mother, she wants to be a good mother. Choice (E) fixes all the problems. *Have a successful career* and *be a good mother* are parallel, and accurately describe her goals.

The questions on the Praxis become harder with really long sentences that try to cause you to get lost in the thicket of words.

8. Last weekend, George washed his car, made his bicycle safer by installing reflectors on the front and back and replacing the brake pads, and mowed the lawn.

(A) Last weekend, George washed his car, made his bicycle safer by installing reflectors on the front and back of the frame and replacing the brake pads, and mowed the lawn.

(B) Last weekend, George, washing his car, made his bicycle safer by installing reflectors on the front and back, and replacing the brake pads, and mowed the lawn.

(C) Last weekend, George washed his car and made his bicycle safer by installing reflectors on the front and back and replacing the brake pads and mowed the lawn.

(D) Last weekend, George, washing his car, making his bicycle safer by installing reflectors in the front and back, and replacing the brake pads, mowed the lawn.

(E) Last weekend, George washed his car, making his bicycle safer by installing reflectors on the front and back, replacing the brake pads, and mowing the lawn.

Wow. What a mess.

Here's How to Crack It

Break this down into smaller lists.

- What are the things that George did? He *washed his car*, *made his bicycle safer*, and *mowed the lawn*. Are those three ideas parallel? Yes.
- What about the reflectors? Well, they're part of making his bicycle safer. How did he do that? By *installing reflectors* and *replacing the brake pads*. Are those ideas parallel? Yes.
- Where did he install the reflectors? On the *front* and *back*. Are those ideas parallel? Yes.

There's no problem with the sentence as it stands. The best answer is (A).

Comparisons

The Praxis also tests parallelism with respect to comparisons. Try this:

Adults eat more vegetables than children.

This sentence is supposed to compare the amount of vegetables that adults eat to the amount of vegetables that children eat. The way it's written, however, this sentence compares the number of vegetables that adults eat to the number of children that adults eat.

You could correct it this way:

Adults eat more vegetables than children eat.

but you're more likely to see it this way:

Adults eat more vegetables than children do.

Try this:

9. The works of John Grisham sell better than Stephen King.

(A) sell better than Stephen King

(B) sell better than Stephen King does

(C) sell better than does Stephen King

(D) sell better than the works of Stephen King

(E) sell better than those of Stephen King

Here's How to Crack It

If you're saying to yourself, "I didn't realize Mr. King was for sale," then you've spotted the error. We're supposed to compare the authors' works, but we're comparing John Grisham's works to Stephen King, the man. Cross out answer choice (A). Because choices (B) and (C) repeat the same error, you can cross those out as well.

Now compare the remaining answer choices. Both compare the works of the authors, but in answer choice (E), the pronoun *those* replaces *the works*. Both sentences are grammatically correct. When faced with two grammatically correct answer choices, pick the shorter of the two. (E) is the correct answer.

PUNCTUATION

We've seen commas show up a lot so far, so let's pause here for a moment, and talk about punctuation. The Praxis tests comma usage the most, but it also tests usage of colons, semicolons, and apostrophes.

Commas

Here are the four places you use a comma. We've already talked about three of them. Use a comma to do the following:

To join independent clauses together with a conjunction.	He didn't like walking to school, but he didn't own a bicycle.
After an introductory phrase or dependent clause.	Although he hated walking to school, he had no choice.
To make lists.	Eat, drink, and be merry.

Here's the new one:

To separate a clause or phrase within the sentence that adds information that is not crucial to the meaning of the sentence.	My grandfather, a World War II veteran, was born in 1902.

Notice that you could omit everything between the commas and still preserve the original meaning of the sentence.

Colons and Semicolons

Colons can be used to begin lists or to show that something is anticipated.

I want only three things out of life: fame, wealth, and happiness.
This is what I think: you smell.

Semicolons, as we mentioned earlier, are used to join two closely related independent clauses. You don't need a conjunction when you use a semicolon.

I knew she was dead; she wasn't moving.

Apostrophes

Apostrophe misuse is rampant, so you can't trust what you see in everyday life.

Use apostrophes:
To replace letters in contractions:

You are not going to do that, are you? Mom said you should not.

becomes

You aren't going to do that are you? Mom said you shouldn't.

To make the possessive form of singular nouns:

The teacher's grade book was stolen.

To make the possessive form of plural nouns that don't end in *s*:

The men's clothes were old-fashioned.

To make the possessive form of plural nouns that do end in *s*:

The students' grades were abysmal.

Notice that the apostrophe goes after the *s* in this case.

Don't use apostrophes:
In personal pronouns:

The book is your's.

should be

The book is yours.

To make nouns plural:

Two dog's fought over a bone.

should be

Two dogs fought over a bone.

To make a singular noun that end in an *s* plural:

We want to keep up with the Jones's.

should be

We want to keep up with the Joneses.

These next four sentences are all correct:

Mr. Jones owned a dog.
Mr. Jones's dog ran away.
The Joneses bought a new dog.
The Joneses' new dog ran away, too.

Misplaced Modifiers

Modifiers are words that more fully explain other words. The examples we've seen so far have been adjectives and adverbs. ETS likes to test the idea that modifiers can change the meaning of a sentence in different ways depending on their location in the sentence. Let's start with a short sentence.

Paula eats fish.

The subject is *Paula*, the verb is *eats*, and the noun that receives the action is *fish*.

Now let's add the modifier *only* in different places. *Only* can function as an adjective or an adverb.

Only Paula eats fish.

Here, we mean that Paula and no one else eats fish.

Paula only eats fish.

This is what we'd probably say in everyday conversation if we meant that Paula didn't eat anything other than fish. A conversation might go like this:

I heard that Paula's on some weird new diet.
Yes, Paula only eats fish.

Again, though, most of us are very bad about the correctness of our spoken English. This sentence means that Paula eats fish, but she doesn't do anything else to them—she doesn't throw them at people, dance with them, or paint them. The conversation should go like this:

I heard that Paula's on some weird new diet.
Yes, Paula eats only fish.

Now, *only* modifies *fish*, which more fully explains what Paula eats.

The general rule is this: a modifier needs to go right next to the thing that it modifies. If the modifier is a single word, it usually goes right before the thing that it modifies.

How will ETS test this? Like so:

10. Standing on the sidewalk, <u>a tomato hit Joan in the face</u>.

(A) a tomato hit Joan in the face
(B) a tomato facially hit Joan
(C) Joan, in the face, was hit by a tomato
(D) Joan was in the face hit by a tomato
(E) Joan was hit in the face by a tomato

Here's How to Crack It

The first thing you should notice is that *Standing on the sidewalk* is a phrase—there's an action but no subject. Given that a modifier should go right next to the thing it modifies, we look for the first noun right after the comma. In this case, we find *a tomato*. Does it make sense that a tomato was standing on the sidewalk? No. In fact, we can tell from context that the first noun after the comma should be *Joan*, and we can therefore cross out answer choices (A) and (B).

Compare choices (C), (D), and (E), and you'll notice that the only difference among them is the placement of the modifying prepositional phrase *in the face*. Ask yourself what that phrase is supposed to describe more fully. You should conclude that it describes where she was hit. Unless they're at the beginning of a sentence, prepositional phrases usually go right after the thing that they're describing. Cross out choice (C) because *in the face* seems to modify *Joan*. Cross out choice (D) because *in the face* seems to modify where she *was*. (E) is the best answer choice because *in the face* correctly describes where she *was hit*.

STYLE

Finally, ETS has some very specific ideas about what constitutes good writing style. We'll start with diction.

DICTION

Good diction means using the right word in the right context. ETS will try to fool you with words that sound similar.

Your invited to a party tomorrow night.

is incorrect; instead, the sentence should read

You're invited to a party tomorrow night.

because *You're* is a contraction of *You are,* which is the subject and verb of the sentence.

In general, if you see a contraction, repeat the sentence in your head using the expanded form of the contraction to see whether it makes sense. Here are some of ETS's favorites:

Their/They're/ There	*They're* saying that *their* car is parked over *there.*
Than/Then	If Doug thinks Led Zeppelin is better *than* Bon Jovi, *then* why does he own so many Bon Jovi t-shirts?
Except/Accept	I *accept* all my limitations *except* my height.
Affect/Effect	Because they cause my nose to run and my eyes to water, my allergies can *affect* the *effect* I have on my girlfriend.

ETS frequently uses other, more complicated words to test diction, so be on your toes if you see a relatively complicated-looking word that just doesn't seem right somehow.

IDIOMATIC EXPRESSIONS

Idiomatic expressions are collections of words that are used together by linguistic convention. In other words, people say something a certain way because everyone says it that way. To ETS, idiomatic expressions are all about prepositions. Look at this one:

She is regarded to be one of the top professionals in her field.

What's wrong with that? The words *regarded to be* may sound wrong to you. Try this instead:

She is regarded as one of the top professional in her field.

The correct idiom is *regarded as.* Why? Just because. This is one place on the PPST: Writing where you can trust your ear a lot of the time, because many idioms are familiar to English speakers. There are some, however, that you're just going to have to memorize. Here's a list of some commonly tested idioms, organized by preposition:

About	
Worry...about	Don't *worry about* me; I'll be fine.
Dispute...about	We had a *dispute about* the amount of money she spent.
Debate...about	The senate *debated about* the bill for three days.

As	
Define...as	A square is *defined as* a polygon with four equal sides and four equal angles.
Regard...as	Tom is *regarded as* New York's finest badminton player.
Not so...as	She is *not so* much beautiful *as* classy.
So...as to be	The movie was *so* bad *as to be* un-watchable.
Think of...as	*Think of* it *as* a vacation rather than a prison sentence.
See...as	Many people *see* the death penalty *as* barbaric.
The same...as	She gave *the same* number of cookies to me *as* to you.
As... as	The boy is *as* dumb *as* a post.
At	
Target…at	The movie was *targeted at* pre-adolescent girls.
For	
Responsible...for	You are *responsible for* your baby.
From	
Prohibit...from	James was *prohibited from* playing baseball in the glass gazebo.
Different...from	After spending more time with her, I discovered that she was not all that *different from* me.
That	
So...that	He was *so* naive *that* he thought politicians told the truth.
Hypothesis...that	The *hypothesis that* dinosaurs were killed off by a meteor crash is increasingly plausible.
To	
Forbid...to	I *forbid* you *to* marry that boy!
Ability...to	He has the *ability to* start fires using his mind.
Attribute...to	The painting, previously *attributed to* Rembrandt, was shown to be a forgery.
Require...to	You are *required to* take the Praxis.

Responsibility...to	You have a *responsibility to* do your job well.
Permit...to	You are *permitted to* leave the hospital grounds only with an escort.
Superior...to	Your math skills are *superior to* mine.
Try...to	*Try to* stay awake during the Praxis.
With	
Credit...with	Marie Curie is *credited with* discovering many radioactive elements.
Associate...with	I don't like you *associating with* those types of people.
No preposition	
Consider...(blank)	Many people *consider* the Taj Mahal the most beautiful building in the world.
More than one preposition	
Distinguish...from	She can't *distinguish* her elbow *from* a hole in the ground.
Distinguish between...and	Many colorblind people can't *distinguish between* red *and* green.
Native (noun)...of	Arnold Schwarzenegger is a *native of* Austria.
Native (adjective)...to	The Nene goose is *native to* Hawaii.
Comparisons and links	
Not only...but also	He is *not only* strong, *but also* fast.
Not...but	The soup was *not* perfect *but* was still edible.
Either...or	*Either* Serena *or* Tara will win the award.
Neither...nor	*Neither* Gabe *nor* Aaron will be chosen for the team.
More...than; less...than	I like ice cream *more than* cabbage, but *less than* beets.
As (to compare actions)	She ate *as* many cookies *as* I did.
Like (to compare nouns)	Her computer is just *like* mine.
Such as (to list examples)	Karen likes bright colors *such as* hot pink and yellow.
More... the -er	The *more* spinach I eat, *the stronger* I get.
From...to	He led the race *from* start *to* finish.
Just as...so too	*Just as* I did well on the Praxis, *so too* will you.

CLARITY

ETS believes that writing is clear if it's not wordy and it's not redundant.

Wordiness

In a sentence correction question, if you're faced with two grammatically correct answer choices, pick the shorter one. Try this:

11. The fingernails of male orangutans tend to be shorter <u>than females</u>.

    (A) than females

    (B) than female orangutans

    (C) than female orangutans are

    (D) than those of female orangutans

    (E) than the fingernails of female orangutans

Here's How to Crack It

The error in the sentence as written is a comparison error. The author intends to compare the length of the orangutans' fingernails, but the sentence compares the length of the males' fingernails to the length of the females' whole bodies. Answer choices (B) and (C) repeat the same error in different forms, so cross both of those out, too.

Now compare choices (D) and (E). Both make the comparison accurately, but choice (D) replaces *the fingernails* with the pronoun *those*. Because shorter grammatically correct answers are preferred, (D) is the best answer.

Redundancy

ETS believes that repeating an idea in a sentence is stylistically incorrect. Try this:

12. If you <u>want</u> (A) to lose weight, <u>you</u> (B) should exercise at least three times <u>per</u> (C) week <u>or more</u> (D). <u>No error</u> (E)

Here's How to Crack It

Because the sentence already says *at least*, it's unnecessary to add *or more*. (D) is the best answer.

DRILL

Ready to practice? Try these questions. Answers and explanations follow.

1. Neither <u>my</u> pet rattlesnake <u>nor</u> my sister's
   A B
   teddy bear <u>is</u> able <u>to talk</u>. <u>No error</u>
   C D E

2. <u>Next year</u>, the Florida legislature is changing
   A
   <u>their procedures</u> used <u>to evaluate</u> teacher qual-
   B C
   ity <u>and</u> tenure eligibility. <u>No error</u>
   D E

3. Like many other blockbuster hits of the last

   five years, <u>the movie</u> <u>had been</u> full of special
   A B
   <u>effects</u>, <u>but shy of</u> character development.
   C D
   <u>No error</u>
   E

4. After the thief <u>left</u> the bank with thousands of
   A
   dollars, <u>he</u> quickly realized <u>he was</u> surrounded
   B C
   by the police <u>on all sides</u>. <u>No error</u>
   D E

5. Having searched for his glasses for hours, <u>they were not found by Paul until morning</u>.

   (A) they were not found by Paul until morning
   (B) they were not found from Paul until morning
   (C) they had not been found until morning
   (D) Paul did not find them until morning
   (E) Paul was not found until morning

6. <u>Neither Andrea or Kathleen could figure out why they got lost.</u>

   (A) Neither Andrea or Kathleen could figure out why they got lost.
   (B) Neither Andrea nor Kathleen could figure out why they got lost.
   (C) Neither Andrea nor Kathleen could figure out why Kathleen got lost.
   (D) Both Andrea and Kathleen could figure out why they got lost.
   (E) Both Andrea and Kathleen could not figure out why she got lost.

7. A human resources study has found that within the past five years, many analysts not considered for promotion <u>had chosen to leave rather than wait until the following year</u>.

   (A) had chosen to leave rather than wait until the following year
   (B) had chosen to leave instead of wait for the following year
   (C) choose to leave rather than waiting until the following year
   (D) choose to leave rather than wait until the following year
   (E) have chosen to leave rather than wait until the following year

8. After the successful IPO, <u>Steve decided to retire over searching for another job</u>.

   (A) Steve decided to retire over searching for another job
   (B) Steve had decided to retire over searching for another job
   (C) Steve decided to retire rather than searching for another job
   (D) Steve decided to retire rather than to search for another job
   (E) Steve decided retirement rather than searching for another job

ANSWERS AND EXPLANATIONS TO DRILL

1. **E** The idiom phrase *neither...nor* is used correctly, and the singular verb aligns with the singular pronoun. The infinitive is structured correctly.
2. **B** The subject of the sentence is *legislature*, which is a singular noun. The pronoun *their* is plural, and therefore incorrect.
3. **B** There is no reason to use the past perfect tense here. The simple past tense, in this case *was*, is sufficient. *Had been* should only be used to describe an event that takes place before another past event.
4. **D** *Surrounded on all sides* is a redundant phrase. There is no reason to add the additional phrase to the end of this sentence. You will find questions where redundancy is the only error.
5. **D** The opening phrase modifies Paul, who is searching for his glasses. Therefore, the subject of the sentence must be Paul, so you can eliminate answer choices (A), (B), and (C). (E) does not convey the proper meaning—Paul was not lost; his glasses were!
6. **C** This is an example of improper pronouns, and an idiomatic phrase. First, the correct phrase is neither....nor. (A) can be eliminated. Next, evaluate the pronoun use that modifies the subject. (B) is incorrect because it uses the plural pronoun *they*; it is unclear to whom *they* refers. (E) is incorrect because it uses the pronoun *she*; it is unclear to whom *she* refers. (D) conveys the opposite meaning of the sentence.
7. **E** The non-underlined portion of the sentence uses the simple past tense in the verb *has found*. There is no need to use the past perfect tense in this example, so (A) and (B) can be eliminated. (C) and (D) use the present tense, while only (E) maintains the correct use of the past tense.
8. **D** This question tests parallel construction. The infinitives *to retire* and *to search* are consistent, which makes (D) correct. All other answer choices do not keep the sentence structure consistent.

THE ESSAY

You'll spend the other 30 minutes of the PPST: Writing test writing an essay. Because you only have 30 minutes, no one (including ETS) expects this essay to be a masterpiece of literature. Instead, it's supposed to demonstrate your ability to organize your thoughts and express them clearly through writing.

SCORING

The essay is scored by two independent graders, both of whom give the essay a score ranging from 1 (lowest) to 6 (highest). If the two scores differ by more than one point, a third scorer is brought in.

It is possible to get a 0, but only if you don't respond to the topic. For instance, a perfectly written diatribe on the evils of standardized testing would get you a score of zero.

It is important to realize that graders will spend about 50–60 seconds grading your essay. That's it. You'll get a high score if you give them what they want. This is what you should do:

- Respond to the prompt.
- Organize.
- Fill 'er up.
- Proofread.

Let's look at each of these:

RESPOND TO THE PROMPT

Here are the official directions:

> Read the opinion stated below. Discuss the extent to which you agree or disagree with this point of view. Support your position with specific reasons and examples from your own experience, observations, or reading.

Then, you are given a statement to write about. It will be a statement of opinion, not fact. Some topics are related to education; some aren't. The statements are purposefully written so that you could easily support either side. Let's try this one:

> "Because professional athletes have such a strong influence on children, they have a responsibility to act as positive role models."

First, pick a side. It doesn't matter which side you pick, but choose one and defend it. If you're not sure which way to go, spend no more than 30 seconds brainstorming reasons for and against the opinion. Then pick the side for which you came up with more support. For the purpose of this example, let's argue against the opinion.

Then, come up with two or three reasons that you'll use to support your position. Let's try these:

- *People known for certain abilities or qualities shouldn't be expected to demonstrate unrelated abilities.*
- *Parents should be primary role models for their children.*
- *Children will learn more about the world if they understand that no one's perfect.*

ORGANIZE

If you only had 50 seconds to read and grade an essay, wouldn't you want it to be well organized? So will your graders. Take about 3–5 minutes and structure your essay before you start writing. Here's the format you should use:

Paragraph 1	Introduce the topic and let the reader know what side you've chosen. If appropriate, give a short preview of the reasons and examples you'll be using. You may restate the prompt directly, or paraphrase it as part of the introduction.
Paragraph 2	Take the first reason and develop it.
Paragraph 3	Take the second reason and develop it.
Paragraph 4	Take the third reason and develop it.
Paragraph 5	Conclude the essay by recapping the major points.

Don't worry if you'd be ashamed to have your favorite English teacher read what you end up creating. This essay isn't supposed to be award winning, it's just supposed to be well organized and literate.

FILL 'ER UP

You'll have about 48 lines on your answer sheet. You should fill between 43 and 48 of them. Length counts. However, you'll find that three reasons, each with a sentence or two of support, plus an introduction and a conclusion, should fill up about that much space.

As you're writing, keep the following things in mind:

- Be neat. Handwriting doesn't count, but your essay does need to be legible. Also, indent at the beginning of each paragraph.
- Use good transition words.
- Words like *although* and *however* show the reader how your next idea relates to the previous idea. Graders like that, because it makes their jobs easier.
- Don't do anything wrong.
- This is not the time to attempt to spell a six-syllable word that you think you know the meaning of. Keep your writing simple and direct.

Let's try it:

The author of the opinion believes that athletes have a responsibility to be positive role models simply because such celebrities face extensive media coverage and therefore influence children. This belief is unfounded. Athletes are just as human as everyone else, and it is unreasonable to hold them to a standard that the rest of society wouldn't be able to meet simply because they are more visible.

Would you expect your auto mechanic to be fluent in French? Would you expect your piano teacher to be able to kick a 35-yard field goal? Of course you wouldn't, even though fluency in French and the ability to kick a 35-yard field goal are both admirable traits. So why would you expect a professional athlete to be a paragon of virtue in his or her everyday life? Granted, I might expect such a high standard of behavior from a priest or a rabbi, because their professions are directly related to morality, but there's no reason to expect such a standard from an athlete.

If the author is concerned about positive role modeling, perhaps he should focus his attention on parental involvement. Parents have a far greater effect on the moral development of their children than any athlete celebrated in the media. Professional athletic leagues filled with positive role models couldn't possibly negate the effects of an abusive home life on a child's development. Conversely, children raised by strong, involved, moral parents are unlikely to be swayed by images of star athletes acting in immoral ways.

In fact, with the right guidance, the visible presence of athletes engaging in questionable activities can be a useful moral lesson. Consider the Kobe Bryant case. Regardless of his guilt or innocence, parents could use his situation to show children that money doesn't buy happiness, that no one is above the law, and that it's important to treat women with respect. In fact, if Mr. Bryant were a perfect moral citizen, parents would be deprived of this lesson because the media certainly wouldn't devote similar time and attention to stories showing him volunteering in a soup kitchen or donating to charity.

So, although the author clearly has the best interests of society in mind, his opinion that athletes have a responsibility to be positive role models is groundless. Let athletes be athletes, let parents be parents, and let us all strive to teach our children well.

Proofread

Leave two or three minutes at the end to proofread your essay. No one's expecting a polished final draft, but you don't want to leave the false impression that you don't understand the rules of written English. If you can quickly correct a few careless errors, you should.

That's it. Ideally, this should be a formulaic exercise, but you should definitely practice this a few times. You're probably not used to writing essays with pencil and paper anymore, and 30 minutes isn't a very long time. Practice writing essays using the following prompts:

"Prospective teachers in any field should be required to study a foreign language."

"Advertisements that promote the use of alcohol or tobacco should be banned."

"Job satisfaction is more important than high wages."

3

PPST: Mathematics

FORMAT OF THE PPST: MATHEMATICS

You'll have one hour to answer 40 multiple-choice math questions. There is no guessing penalty, so be sure that you answer every question.

The level of math tested on the test is surprisingly low: ETS claims that you won't need more than basic elementary school math, but that at least one year of high school mathematics might come in handy.

That doesn't sound so bad, right? Unfortunately, ETS has a few tricks up its sleeve. First, it tests the application of the mathematical knowledge rather than the knowledge itself, so you can expect math questions that ask you to interpret data and make approximations rather than just perform calculations.

Second, despite the fact that we are several years into the twenty-first century, ETS still doesn't allow the use of calculators on the test.

The rest of this chapter consists of a review of the test content combined with strategies for getting to the right answer with as little calculation and time as possible.

CONTENT

Let's start with a vocabulary list:

Integers	. . . , –3, –2, –1, 0, 1, 2, 3, . . .
Positive integers	1, 2, 3, . . .
Negative integers	–1, –2, –3, . . .
Odd numbers	Integers that aren't divisible by 2, such as 3, –5, and 17
Even numbers	Integers that are divisible by 2, such as 4, 8, and –12
Consecutive integers	Integers that are in order from smallest to largest, such as 7, 8, 9, or –2, –1, 0
Prime numbers	A number that is divisible only by itself and 1, such as 2, 3, 5, 7, and 11. 2 is the smallest prime number. 1 is not a prime number.
Real numbers	All numbers, including integers, fractions, decimals, and so on
Zero	0 is an integer. 0 is neither positive nor negative. 0 is even. Anything times 0 is 0. You can't divide by 0.
Factors	Integers that evenly divide into other integers. For example, 5 is a factor of 15, because 3 × 5 = 15.
Multiples	Integers that you get when you take an integer and multiply it by other integers. For instance, 5, 10, 15, 20, . . . are all multiples of 5. So are . . ., –20, –15, –10, –5, and 0.
Fractions	Numbers that looks like this: $\frac{2}{3}$. The top number is called the *numerator*; the bottom is called the *denominator*. Both the numerator and the denominator must be integers, but the denominator can never be 0.

Reciprocals One of a pair of numbers whose product is 1. The reciprocal (or inverse) of 7 is $\frac{1}{7}$; the reciprocal (or inverse) of $\frac{15}{23}$ is $\frac{23}{15}$.

Squares The result of multiplying numbers by themselves. The square of 7 is 49, since $7 \times 7 = 49$.

Exponents Superscripted numbers that tell you how many times to multiply numbers by themselves. 5 is the exponent in the following example: $2^5 = 2 \times 2 \times 2 \times 2 \times 2 = 32$. The exponent is also called a *power*. The number that gets multiplied is called the *base*.

Variables Letters that take the place of numbers in expressions or equations. The variable is x in the following equation: $3x = 15$.

You should also be familiar with these basic concepts:

MEAN, MEDIAN, MODE, AND RANGE

ETS likes to ask questions about sets of numbers. A set can look like this: {1, 7, 3, 9}, or can be described in context (such as in the case of a list of test scores). There are four numbers you need to be able to find with respect to sets:

Mean (or Arithmetic Mean)

You might know the mean better as the *average*. To find the mean, add all of the elements of a set together and divide by the number of elements in the set. The average of the set {1, 7, 3, 9} is 5, because $1 + 7 + 3 + 9 = 20$, there are 4 numbers in the set, and $\frac{20}{4} = 5$.

Median

The *median* is the middle number in the set when the elements of the set are placed in order from smallest to largest. If the set contains an odd number of elements, the median is the number that is in the middle. For example, to find the median of the set $\left\{5, -1, 0, -4, -\frac{1}{2}\right\}$, you'd first arrange the elements in order: $\left\{-4, -1, -\frac{1}{2}, 0, 5\right\}$. Then, pick the middle one: $-\frac{1}{2}$. If there is an even number of elements, the rules change slightly. In that case, the median is the average of the middle two numbers after the set is ordered. So, to find the median of the set {1, 7, 3, 9} you'd order the set: {1, 3, 7, 9}, and then take the average of the middle two numbers. $\frac{3+7}{2} = 5$. So the median of the set {1, 7, 3, 9} is 5.

MODE

The *mode* is the element member that occurs *most* frequently in a list. For instance, the mode of the list {–1, –1, 3, 5, 7, –4, 5, –1} is –1, because –1 appears the *most* (three times in the list).

RANGE

To find the *range* of a set, take the largest element member in the set and subtract the smallest member. That result is the range. For example, the range of the set {1, 7, 3, 9} is 8, because 9 – 1 = 8.

Try this one:

1. What is sum of the average, range, and median of the set {3, 5, 7} ?

(A) 15

(B) 14

(C) 7

(D) 5

(E) 3

Here's How to Crack It

The average of the set is $\frac{3+5+7}{3}=\frac{15}{3}=5$.

The range of the set is 7 – 3 = 4.

The median of the set is 5.

5 + 4 + 5 = 14. The best answer is (B).

UNDERSTANDING DECIMALS

One way of representing numbers that aren't integers is to use a decimal. We use them all the time to represent monetary amounts that aren't whole dollars. For instance, if the price of an item is \$3.92, we know that means three whole dollars, and $\frac{92}{100}$ of another dollar.

Numbers expressed as decimals are especially easy to multiply and divide by powers of ten. To multiply by ten, move the decimal point over one place to the right. To divide by ten, move the decimal point over one place to the left.

For instance, 413.25 × 10 = 4132.5 and 413.25 ÷ 10 = 41.325.

For larger powers of 10, such as 100, 1000, and so on, move the decimal over as many times as there are zeroes. Try this:

23.41735 × 1000 =

There are three zeroes, so we should move the decimal to the right three places:

23.41735 × 1000 = 23,417.35

This works for dividing by powers of 10, too:

41,325.1 ÷ 10,000 =

There are four zeroes, so move the decimal over four places to the left.

41,325.1 ÷ 10,000 = 4.13251

SCIENTIFIC NOTATION

Scientific notation is a special way of writing decimals. In real life it's usually used to represent very large or very small numbers, but you'll see it used for regular-sized numbers on the PPST. Here's an example of a hard-to-read decimal:

452300000

In scientific notation, the number looks like this:

4.523×10^8

In *scientific notation,* the first part of the number must be an integer greater than or equal to 1 and strictly less than 10. The second part of the number tells you how many decimal places to move the number over.

Remember that the exponent tells you how many times to multiply a number by itself. So, $10^2 = 10 \times 10 = 100$, $10^3 = 10 \times 10 \times 10 = 1000$, and so forth. Do you see the pattern? When 10 is the base, the exponent tells you how many zeroes there are. So 4.523×10^8 simply means, "start with 4.523 and move the decimal point over to the right 8 times."

If the decimal point has to move over more spaces than there are decimal places, you have to add zeroes to the end of the number for each extra decimal place required. Try this:

2. Which of the following is equivalent to 923,000 ?

(A) 923×100

(B) $(9.23 \times 10^4) \times 100$

(C $923{,}000{,}000 \div 10$

(D) 92.3×1000

(E) 9.23×10^5

(A) $923 \times 100 = 92{,}300$. Cross out choice (A).

(B) $(9.23 \times 10^4) \times 100 = 92{,}300 \times 100 = 9{,}230{,}000$. Cross out choice (B).

(C) $923{,}000{,}000 \div 10 = 92{,}300{,}000$. Cross out choice (C).

(D) $92.3 \times 1000 = 92{,}300$. Cross out choice (D).

(E) $9.23 \times 10^5 = 923{,}000$. (E) is the correct answer.

MANIPULATING FRACTIONS

You should be able to add, subtract, multiple, divide, compare, and simplify fractions.

ADDING AND SUBTRACTING FRACTIONS

To add or subtract fractions, use the *bowtie.* Let's say we wanted to add these two fractions:

$$\frac{2}{3} + \frac{1}{5} = \frac{}{}$$

The first thing we do is multiply the two denominators together, and write the result on the bottom of the new fraction:

$$\frac{2}{3} + \frac{1}{5} = \frac{}{15}$$

Now, start the bowtie. Multiply the bottom of the second fraction by the top of the first fraction and write the number on the top of the new fraction:

$$\frac{2}{3} + \frac{1}{5} = \frac{10}{15}$$

Since we're adding the fractions, write a plus sign next to the 10:

$$\frac{2}{3} + \frac{1}{5} = \frac{10 +}{15}$$

Now, complete the bowtie by multiplying the bottom of the first fraction by the top of the second fraction:

$$\frac{2}{3} + \frac{1}{5} = \frac{10 + 3}{15}$$

Finally, add the two numbers on top:

$$\frac{2}{3} + \frac{1}{5} = \frac{10 + 3}{15} = \frac{13}{15}$$

Subtracting works the same way, except there's a minus sign instead of a plus sign. Try this one:

$$\frac{3}{4} - \frac{1}{7} =$$

Multiply the bottoms:

$$\frac{3}{4} - \frac{1}{7} = \frac{\quad}{28}$$

Multiply the bottom of the second by the top of the first. Draw that line of the bowtie.

$$\frac{3}{4} - \frac{1}{7} = \frac{21}{28}$$

Copy the minus sign:

$$\frac{3}{4} - \frac{1}{7} = \frac{21 \; -}{28}$$

Complete the bowtie:

$$\frac{3}{4} - \frac{1}{7} = \frac{21 - 4}{28}$$

Subtract the two numbers:

$$\frac{3}{4} - \frac{1}{7} = \frac{21 - 4}{28} = \frac{17}{28}$$

Multiplying Fractions

Multiplying fractions is easy: Multiply the top by the top and the bottom by the bottom. Try this:

$$\frac{3}{5} \times \frac{4}{7}$$

Multiply top by top:

$$\frac{3}{5} \times \frac{4}{7} = \frac{12}{}$$

Multiply bottom by bottom:

$$\frac{3}{5} \times \frac{4}{7} = \frac{12}{35}$$

Dividing Fractions

To divide fractions, invert (flip over) the second one and then multiply:

$$\frac{3}{5} \div \frac{1}{3}$$

Flip the second fraction, and multiply:

$$\frac{3}{5} \times \frac{3}{1}$$

$$\frac{3}{5} \times \frac{3}{1} = \frac{9}{5}$$

But a fraction bar means "divided by" too, so sometimes you'll see division problems written like this:

$$\frac{\frac{7}{9}}{\frac{1}{4}}$$

In cases such as this, you can re-write the fraction to look like this:

$$\frac{7}{9} \div \frac{1}{4}$$

Then invert and multiply:

$$\frac{7}{9} \times \frac{4}{1}$$

$$\frac{7}{9} \times \frac{4}{1} = \frac{28}{9}$$

Comparing Fractions

Sometimes you'll need to be able to tell whether a fraction is bigger or smaller than another. You can use the bowtie for this, too. For example, which is bigger, $\frac{5}{7}$ or $\frac{7}{11}$? First, write the fractions side by side:

$$\frac{5}{7}\ \frac{7}{11}$$

Use the bowtie, always working upward and cross-wise. Write each product at the top of its corresponding arrow:

$$\begin{matrix} 55 & & 49 \\ \frac{5}{7} & \times & \frac{7}{11} \end{matrix}$$

The larger number will appear above the larger fraction. Because 55 is bigger than 49, $\frac{5}{7}$ is bigger than $\frac{7}{11}$.

Simplifying Fractions

Sometimes when you're manipulating fractions, you can end up with large, unwieldy numbers on the top and bottom. Because the fractions on the PPST Math test are often in the simplest form, you should know how to simplify the fraction. In other words, find an equivalent fraction with smaller numbers. To do this, look for factors that are present in both the numerator and denominator, and divide them away. Take a look at this fraction:

$$\frac{21}{49}$$

This fraction can be simplified because both the numerator and denominator are divisible by 7. We could rewrite the fraction like this:

$$\frac{7\times 3}{7\times 7}=\frac{7}{7}\times\frac{3}{7}$$

We can cancel out a 7 from the top and bottom because there's nothing going on here besides multiplication. That leaves us with:

$$\frac{3}{7}$$

Important note: Canceling works only with fractions that have nothing but multiplication in the numerator and denominator. For example, we couldn't get away with canceling if the fraction looked like this:

$$\frac{7+3}{7+7}$$

With larger numbers, you may have to simplify several times to get down to simplest form. Try simplifying this:

$\frac{15}{75}$ Because both numbers end in a 5, we know that 5 must be a factor of both:

$$\frac{15}{75}=\frac{5\times3}{5\times15}=\frac{3}{15}$$

But 3 is a factor of 15, so we can simplify again:

$$\frac{3}{15}=\frac{3\times1}{3\times5}=\frac{1}{5}$$

So, $\frac{15}{75}=\frac{1}{5}$

Try simplifying the following fractions:

$\frac{25}{100}$ $\frac{60}{360}$ $\frac{48}{144}$

Depending on which factors you started with, your work may look different, but you should arrive at the same solutions:

$$\frac{25}{100}=\frac{25\times1}{25\times4}=\frac{1}{4}$$

$$\frac{60}{360}=\frac{10\times6}{10\times36}=\frac{6}{36}=\frac{6\times1}{6\times6}=\frac{1}{6}$$

$$\frac{48}{144}=\frac{12\times4}{12\times12}=\frac{4}{12}=\frac{4\times1}{4\times3}=\frac{1}{3}$$

MANIPULATING ALGEBRAIC EXPRESSIONS AND EQUATIONS

You should be able to create and recognize algebraic representations of mathematical relationships. Try this example:

3. Which of the following expressions best represents "the difference of a certain number and the square of another number"?

(A) $\frac{x}{y^2}$

(B) $x - y^2$

(C) $(x - y)^2$

(D) $x + y^2$

(E) $x^2 - y^2$

The word *difference* means subtraction, so we can eliminate choices (A) and (D). The phrase tells us that only one of the variables is squared, so the best answer is (B).

You should also know how to solve simple algebraic equations. Refresh your skills by working through this example. Solve for x:

$3x + 4 = -2x + 7$

First, you need to make sure that all the x's are on the same side of the equal sign. Whatever operation you perform on one side you must perform on the other. Start by adding $2x$ to both sides:

$$\begin{array}{l} 3x + 4 = -2x + 7 \\ \underline{+2x \qquad\quad +2x} \\ 5x + 4 = 7 \end{array}$$

Next, make sure all of the numbers are on the other side. In this case, we'll need to subtract 4 from both sides of the equation.

$$\begin{array}{l} 5x + 4 = 7 \\ \underline{\qquad -4 \ -4} \\ 5x \qquad = 3 \end{array}$$

Finally, divide both sides by 5 to get x by itself.

$$\frac{5x}{5} = \frac{3}{5}$$

$$x = \frac{3}{5}$$

You should also know how to cross-multiply an equation with fractions.
Try this:

$$\frac{3}{x} = \frac{6}{10}$$

If you see two fractions on either side of an equals sign, cross-multiply. This is similar to the bow-tie process described above. Multiply the bottom right number times the top left number, and write the result on the left side of the equals sign:

$$\frac{3}{x} = \frac{6}{10}$$

$30 =$

Then, multiply the bottom left number by the top right number and write the result on the right side of the equal sign:

$$\frac{3}{x} = \frac{6}{10}$$

$30 = 6x$

Now, solve as usual by dividing both sides by 6:

$$\frac{30}{6} = \frac{6}{6}x$$

So, $x = 5$.

THE DISTRIBUTIVE PROPERTY

If an equation or expression involves parentheses with algebra, you'll need to know how to apply the *distributive property*, which says:

$a(b + c) = ab + bc$

For example, you can see that $4(x + 3)$ can be written as $4x + (4 \times 3)$, or $4x + 12$. You simply take the 4 and multiply it by each number or variable inside the parentheses. Be careful if the number outside the parentheses is a negative. Try this:

$-3(y + 2) =$

You'll need to multiply everything inside the parentheses by a *negative* 3. That'll give you:

$-3y - (3 \times 2)$, or

$-3y - 6$

And look at this one:

$-2(x - 5)$

That turns into

$-2x + 10$, because $(-2) \times (-5) = 10$.

Put it all together by solving this equation for x. Then check your work.

$$\frac{2}{x-2} = \frac{6}{x}$$

Here's the solution, step by step:

$$\frac{2}{x-2} = \frac{6}{x}$$

$$2x = 6(x-2)$$

$$2x = 6x - 12$$

$$-4x = -12$$

$$x = 3$$

RATIOS AND PROPORTIONS

Many questions on the PPST: Mathematics test will ask you to compare relationships between numbers. One way to do this is to use a ratio. For example, in the town of Surf City, immortalized in the Jan and Dean recording, there are "two girls for every boy." This is a *ratio*. It can be expressed as above, or

with the word "to":	2 to 1
or with a colon:	2:1
or even as a fraction:	$\frac{2}{1}$

All of these are equivalent.

The 2 to 1 ratio is not meant to imply that there are only two girls in the entire town. Instead, it means that regardless of the number of people in the town, there will always be twice as many girls as boys.

You can solve ratio problems by setting up a *proportion*, which is just two ratios (usually written as fractions) side by side with an equals sign in between. For instance, let's say you were asked the question on the next page:

4. In Surf City there are two girls for every boy. If there are 30 boys in Surf City, how many girls are there?

(A) 2
(B) 15
(C) 30
(D) 32
(E) 60

Here's How to Crack It

Set up the proportion like this:

$$\frac{2}{1}=\frac{x}{30}$$

On one side of the equals sign you write the ratio you're given. We put the number of girls on top, and the number of boys on the bottom (but we could have written it the other way, too). On the other side, create another ratio, making sure you keep the girls and boys in the same order. We don't know the number of girls (that's what we're being asked to find), so we write an x on the top. We're given that there are 30 boys, so that's what we fill in on the bottom. Now, cross-multiply:

$$30 \times 2 = x \times 1$$
$$60 = x$$

So, there are 60 girls. The answer is (E).

What if the question had looked like this?

5. In the town of Surf City, there are two girls for every boy. If there are 120 people in the town (and there are no adults), how many boys are there?

(A) 1
(B) 20
(C) 40
(D) 60
(E) 80

Here's How to Crack It

This question asks something a little different. Instead of simply focusing on the number of girls and boys, we're asked about the relationship between the total number of girls and boys in the town and the number of boys. To solve a question like this, you need to think about the original ratio, and its implications for the total number of people.

The original ratio is a part-to-part relationship. In other words, we're comparing two parts to each other: the number of girls relative to the number of boys. If you're asked about a part-to-whole relationship, first add the parts together.

Girls		**Boys**		**Whole**
2	+	1	=	3

Now we have a way of expressing the relationship of the parts to the whole, because it's now clear that out of every three people in Surf City, two will be girls and one will be a boy. Armed with this knowledge, we can set up another proportion to answer the question. As we analyzed earlier, the problem asks us the compare the number of boys to the total population. So we can write:

$$\frac{1}{3} = \frac{x}{120}$$

Cross-multiplying and solving, we find that:

$$120 \times 1 = 3 \times x$$
$$120 = 3x$$
$$40 = x$$

The answer is (C).

Sometimes questions will ask you about proportions without mentioning ratios at all. Try this one:

6. On a certain map, two towns that are 100 miles away from each other are represented by dots that are $\frac{7}{8}$ inches apart. How far apart would two dots be if they represented towns that were 200 miles away from each other?

(A) $\frac{3.5}{8}$ inches

(B) $\frac{7}{8}$ inches

(C) $\frac{10.5}{8}$ inches

(D) $\frac{14}{8}$ inches

(E) $\frac{20}{8}$ inches

Here's How to Crack It

Set up the proportion just as we did for the ratio problems, making sure you keep the things you're comparing in the same relative order:

$$\frac{\frac{7}{8}}{100} = \frac{x}{200}$$

$$200 \times \frac{7}{8} = 100 \times x$$

Before you try to multiply out the left-hand side of the equation, save yourself some trouble and divide both sides by 100 first, giving you:

$$\frac{200}{100} \times \frac{7}{8} = x$$

Reducing $\frac{200}{100}$ gives us 2, so now we have:

$$2 \times \frac{7}{8} = x$$

$$\frac{14}{8} = x$$

The best answer is (D).

PERCENTAGES AND PERCENT CHANGE

Percentages are also used to help compare numbers to other numbers. For instance, imagine that a pollster questioned 867 people and found that 292 of them believed that the government should provide free beets to schoolchildren at lunchtime. Rather than have you, the reader of the poll, try to determine whether 292 is a relatively large or small number of people out of the sample of 867, it's more likely that the pollster would express his findings as a *percentage*, meaning that he would tell you the proportional number of people that would have agreed that free beets should be provided had only 100 people been polled. You can calculate the percentage by setting up the following proportion:

$$\frac{292}{867} = \frac{x}{100}$$

If you do the math (which you'd never see on the Praxis because it requires a calculator or some strong long-division skills), you find that $x \approx 33.6$, so you'd know that 33.6%, or about 34 out of every 100 people surveyed believe that the government should provide free beets to schoolchildren at lunchtime.

Percentages always compare other numbers to 100 (the word *percent* literally means "out of 100") because 100 is a nice round number and many of us have developed an intuitive understanding of how other numbers relate to it. For instance, we all know that 50 percent is the same as the fraction $\frac{1}{2}$, and we understand that although a sale sign advertising 10 percent off is a good thing, it's probably not worth making a special trip to the store for.

Because *percent* means "out of one hundred," you can write percentages as fractions by putting 100 in the denominator and simplifying, or as decimals by moving the decimal place over two places to the left. For instance, $25\% = \frac{25}{100} = \frac{1}{4}$, and $25\% = 0.25$.

You should be familiar with these common percentages and their fractional and decimal equivalents:

Percent	Fraction	Decimal
10	$\frac{1}{10}$	0.1
25	$\frac{1}{4}$	0.25
33.3	$\frac{1}{3}$	0.333
50	$\frac{1}{2}$	0.5
66.6	$\frac{2}{3}$	0.666
75	$\frac{3}{4}$	0.75
100	1	1
200	2	2

As we mentioned earlier, the easiest way to divide a number by 10 is to move the decimal place over one position to the left. For instance, 516 divided by 10 equals 51.6. Because dividing by ten is the same as calculating $\frac{1}{10}$ of a number, and because $\frac{1}{10}$ is the same as 10%, you can do the same thing to find 10% of a number. So, $\frac{516}{10} = \frac{1}{10} \times 516 = 10\%$ of 516 = 51.6.

You can carry this same idea one step further to calculate any percentage that is a multiple of ten. For instance, if you're asked to find 40% of a number, that's the same thing as finding 4 × 10% of a number. So, slide the decimal over and multiply that result by four. Try this:

6. 30% of 21 is equal to which of the following?

(A) A little more than 2
(B) A little less than 4
(C) A little less than 6
(D) A little more than 6
(E) Exactly 7

Here's How to Crack It

30% is 3 × 10%. 10% of 21 is 2.1, and 3 times 2.1 is a little more than 6. The best answer is (D).

If you have a solid understanding of how percentages work, you can answer any question you see using these ideas. Try this one:

7. 22 is what percent of 55 ?

(A) 50%
(B) 40%
(C) 22%
(D) 20%
(E) 10%

Here's How to Crack It

First, look at the choices provided. Choice (E) can't be right, because 10% of 55 is only 5.5. Eliminate it. Take a look at choice (A). Could 22 be 50% of 55? 55 is a little more than 50, and half of 50 is 25, so half of 55 must be a little bigger than 25, so choice (A) can't be right either. Eliminate it. Choice (C) can't be right because 22 is 22% of 100, not 22% of 55. Eliminate it. That leaves choice (B) or choice (D). We just said that 10% of 55 is 5.5. 20% of 55 must be twice that, or 11. Choice (D) can't be right. Eliminate it. 40% of 55 must be twice as big as 20% of 55, and in fact 11 × 2 = 22. Choice (B) is the right answer.

Try this one:

8. If 40% of x = 428, then x =

(A) 171. 2
(B) 256
(C) 692
(D) 1070
(E) 2140

The first thing to realize is that x is bigger than 428. If 40% of the number is 428, then the original number must be larger. That eliminates choices (A) and (B). The next question you should ask yourself is, "how much bigger?" We're looking for the whole number, or 100% of it, and we're told that 40% of it is 428. So, 80% of it must be 2×428, or about 850, and that's still less than 100%, so answer choice (C) must be wrong, too. Eliminate it. We're down to choices (D) and (E). Because 80% of the number is 850, we're looking for an answer that's not too much bigger than 850. 2140 is way too big, because it's more than two times 850. Choice (D) is the correct answer.

You should know the following formula for percent increase and decrease problems:

$$\frac{\text{Difference}}{\text{Original}} = \%\ \text{change}$$

Try this one:

9. Not long ago, the cost of a subway ride in New York City went from \$1.50 to \$2.00. By approximately what percent did the cost of a subway ride increase?

   (A) 0.5 %

   (B) 20%

   (C) 33%

   (D) 50%

   (E) 100%

Here's How to Crack It

Use the formula. You should use cents instead of dollars so you can use whole numbers rather than decimals. The difference in price is 200 – 150 = 50. The original is 150. So, the formula says $\frac{50}{150} = \frac{1}{3}$, which we know is 33%. The right answer is (C).

PROBABILITY

You can expect to see a few questions involving probability on the test. The probability of an event occurring is expressed as a fraction or a percentage, always between 0 (meaning that there's no chance of the event occurring) and 1 (meaning that the event will definitely occur). To calculate a probability, fill in the following fraction:

$$\frac{\text{The number of ways the event can occur}}{\text{The total number of possible outcomes}}$$

For instance, let's say you want to calculate the probability of drawing a queen at random from a full deck of cards. Because there are four queens in the deck, there are four ways the event (drawing a queen) could occur. Because there are 52 cards in the deck, there are 52 possible outcomes. Therefore, the probability of drawing a queen is $\frac{4}{52}$, or $\frac{1}{13}$.

There's one other important idea about probability: the probability of an event *not* happening is equal to 1 minus the probability of the event happening. For instance, if there's a 30% chance of rain, there's a 1 – 30% or 70% chance of it *not* raining.

Try this question:

10. What is the probability that on a single roll of a fair die the result will NOT be a multiple of three?

(A) $\frac{1}{6}$

(B) $\frac{1}{3}$

(C) $\frac{1}{2}$

(D) $\frac{2}{3}$

(E) $\frac{5}{6}$

Here's How to Crack It

There are six outcomes possible, the numbers 1 through 6. Of those, the numbers 3 and 6 are the only multiples of three, so there are 2 ways of getting a multiple of three. However, the questions asks to find the probability that the result will NOT be a multiple of three, so we write:

$$1-\frac{2}{6}=\frac{4}{6}=\frac{2}{3}$$

The best answer is (D).

CHARTS AND GRAPHS

You're likely to see many questions on the PPST: Mathematics that ask you to interpret data on charts and graphs. We'll review the most common forms and show you some sample questions so you can see how you'll be expected to apply your knowledge.

Bar Graphs

One common type of graph is a bar graph, in which data are arranged next to each other for ease of comparison. Look at the bar graph on the next page and answer the questions that follow.

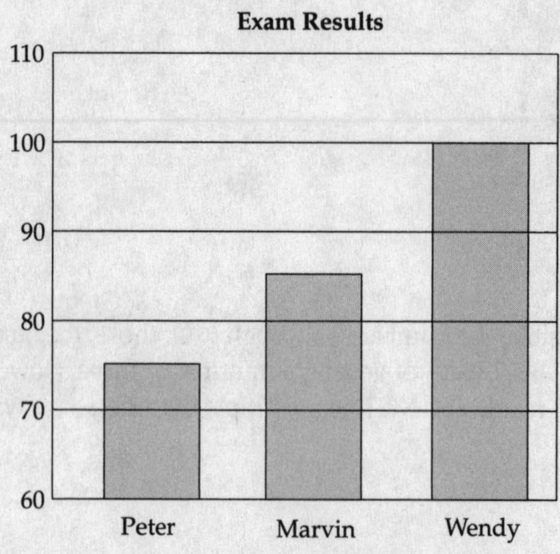

11. Wendy's score is approximately how many points greater than Marvin's score?

(A) 5
(B) 10
(C) 15
(D) 20
(E) 25

Here's How to Crack It

This problem is very straightforward, but it's easy to make a careless mistake either by misreading the student's name or by misreading the score scale on the left. Just read the information on the graph and perform the necessary calculation. In this case, Wendy scored 100 and Marvin scored about 85, because the column corresponding to Marvin's score is about halfway between 80 and 90. Because 100 – 85 = 15, (C) is the correct answer.

Try another.

12. Wendy's score is approximately what percent greater than Peter's?

(A) 10%
(B) 25%
(C) 33%
(D) 50%
(E) 75%

Here's How to Crack It

Use the formula for percent change discussed earlier in the chapter. To find the *percent change* between two numbers, you need to determine the original number and the difference between the two numbers. The difference between the two scores is 100 – 75 = 25. The original score (Peter's) is 75. $\frac{25}{75} = \frac{1}{3}$, which is approximately 33%. The best answer is (C).

PIE CHARTS

Pie charts are useful for comparing different data that, taken together, form a whole. Look at the following chart:

Jeremy's household expenditures as a percentage of monthly income

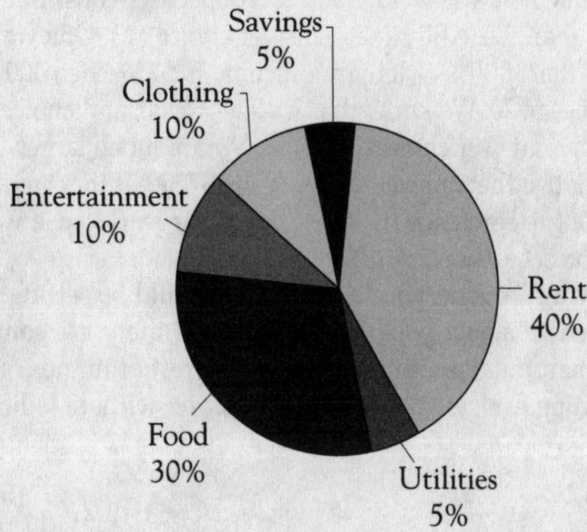

Notice that the sum of the percentages is 100 (40 + 5 + 30 + 10 + 10 + 5 = 100). With a pie chart, the pieces will always add up to a whole. You can expect questions that ask you to compare percentages and read numbers. Try these:

13. If Jeremy spent $100 on utilities in a certain month, how much did he spend on clothing?

    (A) $10
    (B) $50
    (C) $100
    (D) $200
    (E) $500

Here's How to Crack It

According to the chart, Jeremy spent 5% of his income on utilities and 10% of his income of clothing. Because 10% is twice 5%, he spent twice as much money on clothing as he did on utilities. He spent $100 on utilities, so he must have spent $200 on clothing. The best answer is (D).

14. What is Jeremy's monthly income if he spends $720 on food each month?

    (A) $216
    (B) $2400
    (C) $7200
    (D) $14,400
    (E) $21,600

Here's How to Crack It

This one's a little tougher, but here's how to crack it. Food costs constitute 30% of his income, so the answer has to be bigger than $720. Eliminate answer choice (A). One way you can approach the problem from here is to say that if 30% of Jeremy's income is $720, then 100% of his income should be a little bit more than 3 times $720. We know that $3 \times 720 = 2160$, and choice (B) is a little more than that. Furthermore, all the other answer choices (besides (A))are much larger. Another way you could approach the problem is to notice that answer choice (C) is $7200. If that were Jeremy's total monthly income, $720 would be 10% of it, so choice (C) must be too large. Because we've already eliminated choice (A), (B) must be the correct answer.

If this seems like trickery to you, and you feel that you should be setting up an equation to solve a problem like this, you need to adjust your thinking. While there are some problems on the test that may require algebraic manipulation, this is primarily a test of numerical reasoning rather than mathematical skills. If reasoning can get you to the right answer without tedious calculation, then use reasoning.

GEOMETRY

Let's review some terms:

Line

A straight line extends forever in both directions. A *line* is named by any two points on it, in either order. For instance, the line below could be named *AB, BC, AC, BA, CB,* or *CA*. The arrows tell you the line extends past what is drawn.

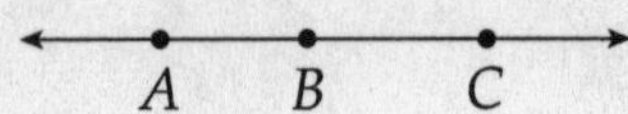

Line Segment

A *line segment* is a finite section of a line with endpoints at either end. Line segments are named by their endpoints. In the line above, *AB* is an example of a line segment.

Parallel Lines

Parallel lines are lines that never intersect. The symbol || means parallel.

Perpendicular Lines

Perpendicular lines meet at a 90-degree angle. The symbol ⊥ means perpendicular. The lines below are perpendicular. In the figure below, the ∟ symbol means that the lines meet at a 90-degree angle, which also means that the lines are perpendicular.

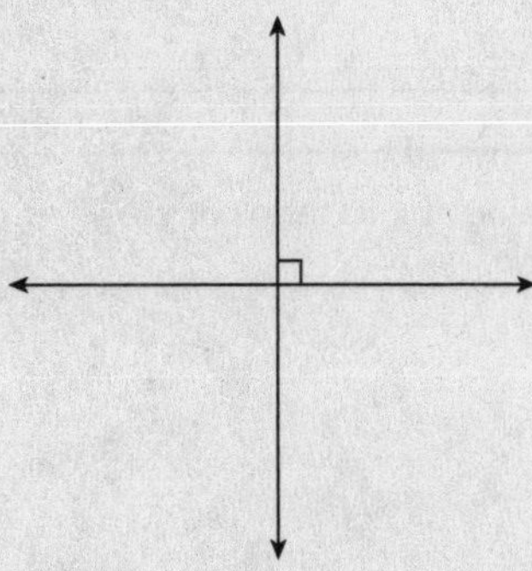

Ray

A *ray* has one endpoint, but extends infinitely in the other direction. A ray is named by its endpoint and any other point on it. The ray below could be named *PQ* or *PR*.

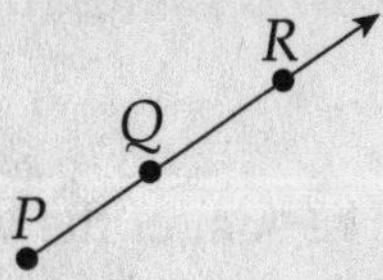

Angle

When two lines, line segments, or rays intersect, *angles* are formed. The point of intersection is called a *vertex*. Angles are named with the vertex point in the middle, and angles across the vertex are equal. In the figure below, the measure of angle *ECD* is equal to the measure of angle *ACB*, and the measure of angle *ACE* is equal to the measure of angle *BCD*.

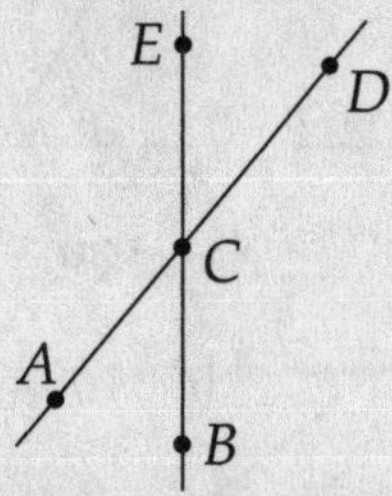

A straight line can also be called a straight angle, and measures 180 degrees. A 90-degree angle is called a right angle.

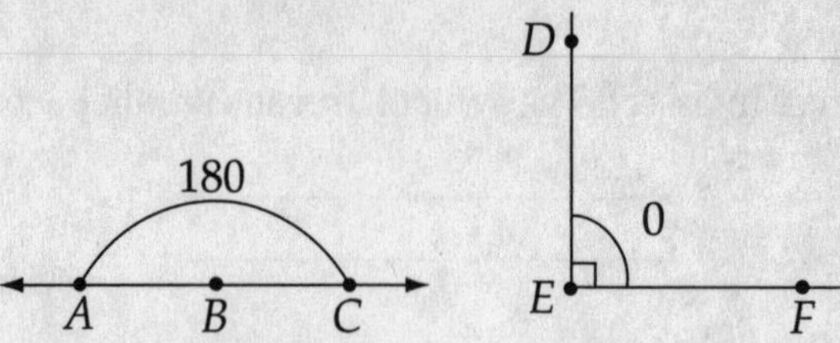

Try applying what you've reviewed so far:

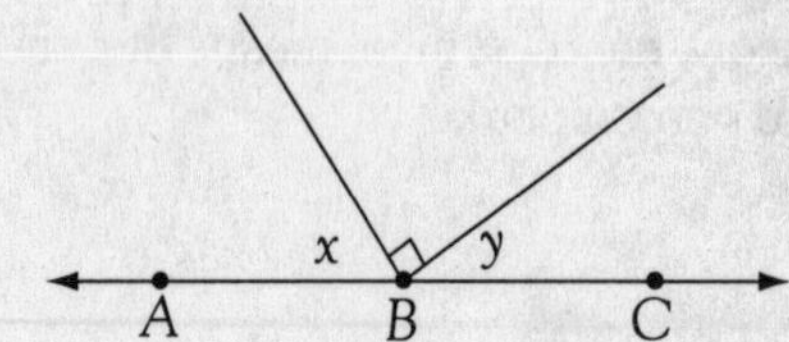

15. What is the value of x in terms of y ?

(A) $90 + y$
(B) $90 - y$
(C) $180 - y$
(D) $180 + y$
(E) $360 - y$

Here's How to Crack It

A straight line has 180 degrees, so $x + y +$ the right angle = 180. Because a right angle has 90 degrees, we know that $x + y + 90 = 180$, or $x + y = 90$. We want the value of x in terms of y, so subtract y from both sides. That leaves $x = 90 - y$, and the best answer is (B).

Triangle

A *triangle* is a three-sided closed figure. The sum of the interior angles of a triangle is 180 degrees. *Equilateral triangles* have equal side lengths, and each angle measure is 60 degrees. *Isosceles triangles* have two equal sides, and the angles opposite those sides are equal in measure. Right triangles contain one right angle. The side opposite the right angle (always the longest side of a right triangle) is called the *hypotenuse*. The other sides of a right triangle are called *legs*.

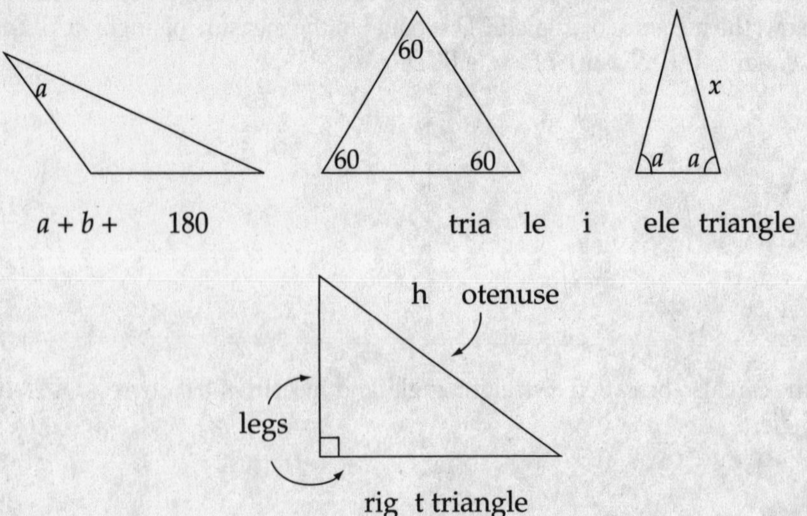

The Pythagorean Theorem

There's one important formula to know about right triangles. The sum of the squares of the legs equals the square of the hypotenuse. In the right triangle below, $3^2 + 4^2 = 5^2$. In the triangle next to it, $5^2 + 12^2 = 13^2$.

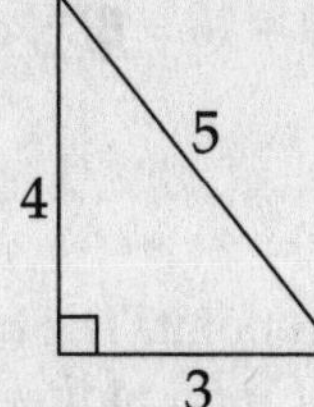

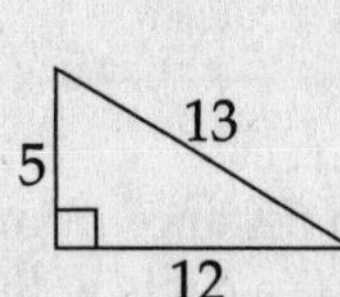

RECTANGLE

A *rectangle* is a four-sided closed figure with four right angles. The opposite sides are parallel and equal in length to each other. If all four sides of a rectangle are of equal length, the rectangle becomes a square.

PERIMETER

The *perimeter* of a figure is the sum of the lengths of all sides of that figure. The perimeter of the triangle below is 12. The perimeter of the rectangle next to it is 20.

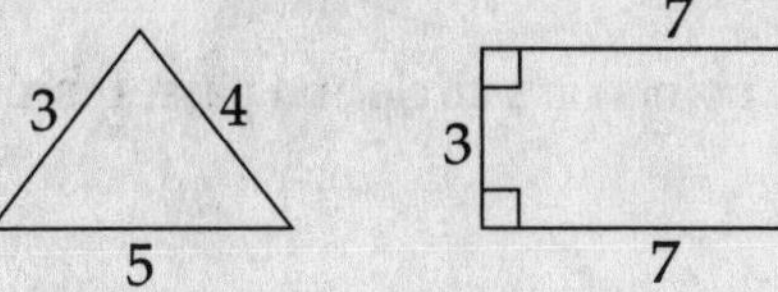

Try this one:

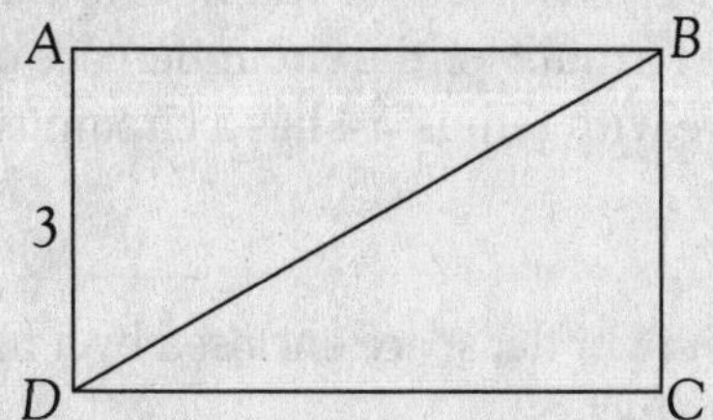

16. If the perimeter of rectangle *ABCD* is 14, what is the length of *BD* ?

    (A) 3
    (B) 4
    (C) 5
    (D) 8
    (E) 14

Here's How to Crack It

The perimeter is the sum of all four sides, so $AB + BC + CD + AD = 14$. Remember that the opposite sides of a rectangle are equal in length. If $AD = 3$, then BC also equals 3. So we have $AB + 3 + CD + 3 = 14$, or $AB + CD = 8$. We know that AB and CD are equal too, so they must both equal 4. Now, use the Pythagorean theorem, which says that $3^2 + 4^2 = BD^2$. So $9 + 16 = BD^2$, or $BD^2 = 25$, so $BD = 5$. The best answer is (C).

Circle

A circle is a set of points a given distance from a given point. The point is called the *center,* and the distance is called a *radius.* Below is a circle with center O and radius 4. All radii are the same length, so $OP = OQ$.

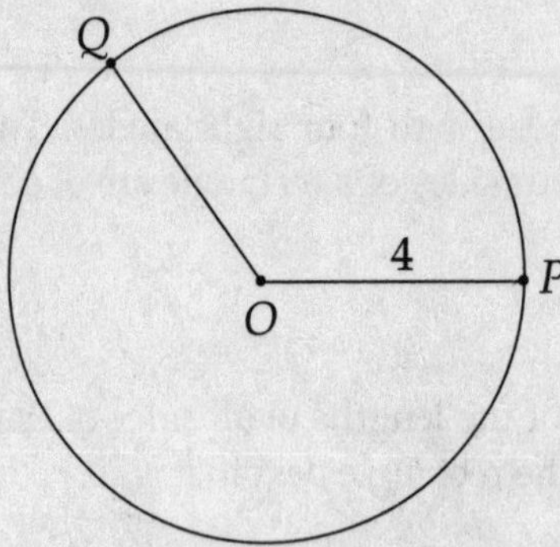

A line segment that connects two points on a circle and passes through the center is called a *diameter.* It is twice as long as a radius.

Circumference

The *circumference* of a circle is distance you'd travel if you were to walk around its edge. You can think of it as the perimeter of a circle. The formula for the circumference of a circle is $C = 2\pi r$, where r is the length of the radius. The circle above with radius = 4 has a circumference of $2 \times \pi \times 4 = 8\pi$.

Area

Area is the measurement of the amount of flat space enclosed by a figure. Area is always expressed in square units (e.g., square feet, square inches).

The formula for the area of a rectangle is $A = lw$, where l is the length of the rectangle and h is the width. The area of the rectangle below is $7 \times 3 = 21$; the area of the square next to it is $5 \times 5 = 25$ (which is also why that amount is called "five squared" or 5^2).

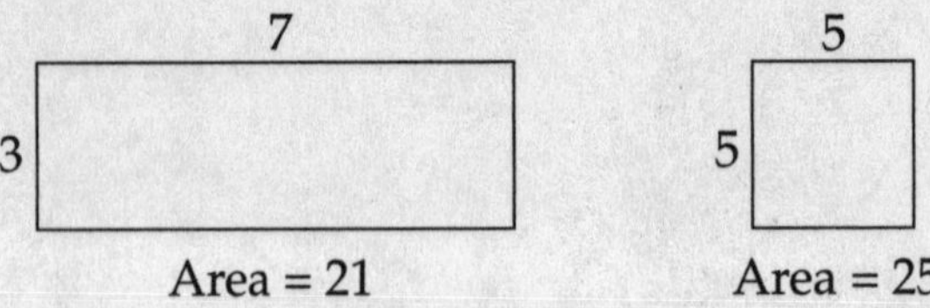

The formula for the area of a circle is $A = \pi r^2$, where r is the length of the radius. The area of the circle below is $\pi \times 3^2$, or 9π.

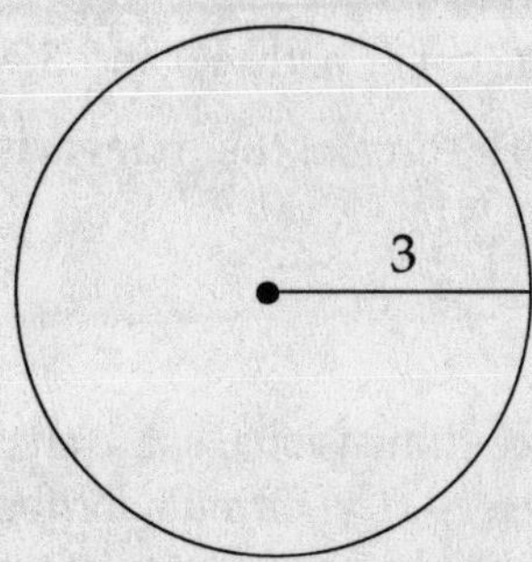

The formula for the area of a triangle is $A = \frac{1}{2}bh$, where b is the base of the triangle and h is the height of the triangle. The height of a triangle is always measured by dropping a perpendicular line from the high point of the triangle to the line containing the base. The area of the triangle below is $\frac{1}{2} \times 6 \times 5 = 15$.

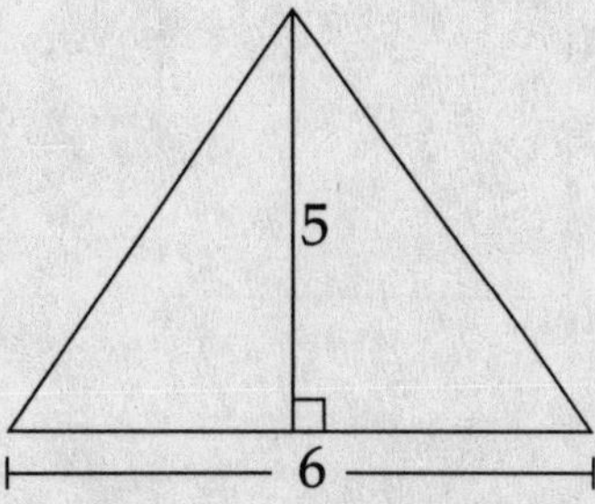

Try this example:

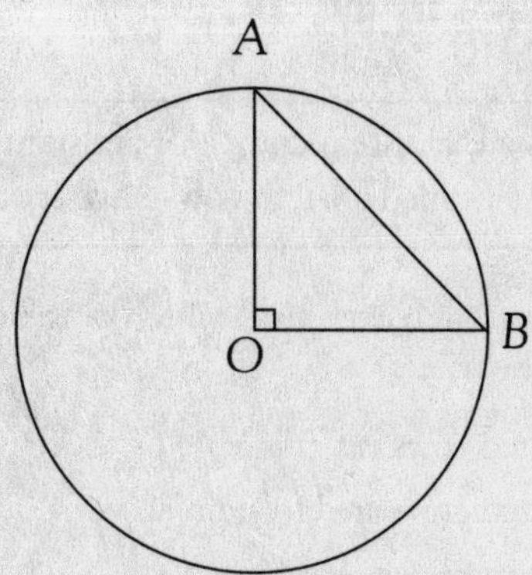

17. If the area of the circle is 16π, what is the area of triangle AOB ?

    (A) 4
    (B) 8
    (C) 4π
    (D) 16
    (E) 8π

Here's How to Crack It

If the area of the circle is 16π, the radius must be 4. Because the radius of the circle is the length of the line from the center to any point on the circle, both *AO* and *BO* must equal 4. *AOB* is a right triangle, so *AO* is the height if *BO* is the base. The area of the triangle is therefore $\frac{1}{2} \times 4 \times 4 = 8$. The best answer is (B).

VOLUME

Volume is the measurement of the three-dimensional space enclosed by a figure. Volume is expressed in cubic units (e.g., cubic feet, cubic meters). The formula for the volume of a box is $V = lwh$, where l is the length, w is the width, and h is the height. The volume of the box below is $3 \times 4 \times 5 = 60$.

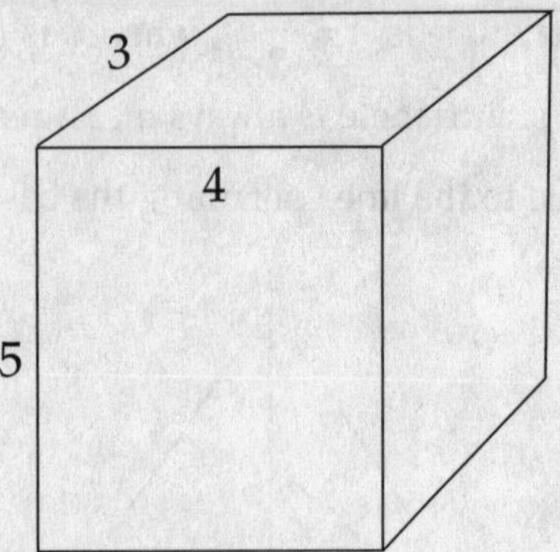

LOGIC

Finally, you can expect some questions that give you logical statements and ask you about the truth or untruth of other statements. For instance, try this:

> Some cows are Holstein cows. All Holstein cows eat grass. Some Holstein cows have spots.

18. If the statements above are true, which of the following must also be true?

(A) All spotted cows eat grass.
(B) All spotted cows are Holstein cows.
(C) Some spotted cows eat grass.
(D) No spotted cows eat grass.
(E) No spotted cows are Holstein cows.

Here's How to Crack It

Take each answer choice and decide whether it *must be true.* One way to go about this is to determine a counterexample for each answer choice. You won't be able to find a counterexample for the correct answer.

(A) No. There could be other spotted cows besides Holstein cows. Those cows wouldn't necessarily eat grass.

(B) No. There could be other spotted cows that are not Holstein cows.

(C) Yes. Some spotted cows are Holsteins, and all Holsteins eat grass. Therefore, some spotted cows eat grass.

(D) No. Some spotted cows are Holsteins, and all Holsteins eat grass. Therefore, some spotted cows must eat grass.

(E) No. Some spotted cows are Holsteins.

DRILL

Practice what you've learned on the following drill.

1. What is the difference between 2.5 and .167 ?

   (A) 0.83
   (B) 2
   (C) 2.333
   (D) 2.667
   (E) 4.17

2. Hugo and Aaron played volleyball for a total of 63 hours in June, and for 89 hours in July. How many more hours did they play in July than the average of hours played in June and July?

   (A) 6 hours
   (B) 13 hours
   (C) 26 hours
   (D) 63 hours
   (E) 89 hours

3. Dale is flipping a coin. On the first five throws, heads has appeared every time. What is the probability that the next flip will appear as tails?

   (A) $\frac{1}{6}$
   (B) $\frac{1}{5}$
   (C) $\frac{1}{3}$
   (D) $\frac{1}{2}$
   (E) $\frac{5}{6}$

4. In his programming class, Chris took three tests. He scored a 78 on his first test, and a 90 on his second test. If Chris had an average of 81 in his class, what did Chris score on his third test?

   (A) 75
   (B) 81
   (C) 83
   (D) 90
   (E) 243

5. $10y - 36 + 4y - 6 + y = 3$. What is the value of y ?

   (A) 3
   (B) 4
   (C) 6
   (D) 10
   (E) 36

6. Judy owns 387 stickers. If she were to purchase three times that amount, approximately how many stickers would she then own?

   (A) 400
   (B) 1,200
   (C) 1,550
   (D) 2,000
   (E) 3,870

7. Which of the payments shown below is greatest?

   (A) 5% of 500
   (B) 25% of 50
   (C) 50% of 5
   (D) 50% of 25
   (E) 25% of 5% of 500

Candidate	Votes Received
Lyn	150
Jolene	10
Brian	80
Adam	?
TOTAL	300

8. Using the chart above, which of the following statements is true?

   (A) Adam received the most votes.
   (B) Brian received 50 more votes than Adam.
   (C) Jolene did not receive the smallest number of votes.
   (D) Adam received 15 more votes than the average number of votes Brian and Jolene received.
   (E) Adam received 10 less than half the number of votes Lyn received.

ANSWERS AND EXPLANATIONS TO DRILL

1. **C** When subtracting decimals, be sure to align the decimals vertically, as shown below:

   2.500

   $-$ .167

   = 2.333

2. **B** The question requires that you know the average number of hours played in June and July. To find an average, take the total (152 hours), and divide by the number of things (2 months). The average is 76 hours per month. To answer question, subtract 76 from the number of hours played in July (89). 89 – 76 = 13.

3. **D** Flipping a coin is an independent event. Prior outcomes do not influence the next event. Dale could have flipped 100 coins that all appear as heads, but that will not change the probability of the next flip (even though this feat is incredibly rare). There are two outcomes—heads or tails, and we want to know one possible event—tails. Therefore, the probably is $\frac{1}{2}$.

4. **A** Start by finding the total score on all three tests. The average is 81, and there are 3 things, so the total is 243 (beware of (E) as a partial answer). Subtracting the first two test scores from 243 yields 75. Note that is a question you can likely estimate. Before his third test, Chris had an average over 81, so his score must be below 81 on the third test. (A) is the only possible answer choice.

5. **A** Simplify the equation to get:

   $$15y - 42 = 3$$
   $$15y = 45$$
   $$y = 3$$

6. **C** The question asks you *approximately* how many stickers Judy would own, so approximate! She has around 400 now. Three times that amount is 1,200. The total amount of stickers is the sum of these two numbers—around 1,600. (C) is the best answer choice. Be careful about answer choice (B), which is a partial answer.

7. **A** Try to estimate these types of questions, so you do not waste time doing needless calculations. (C) should be eliminated immediately—it is visibly less than (D), which is the same percentage, but of a larger number. Further, you should spot that (E) is less than (A). Doing the calculations, you will find that (A) = 25, while (B) and (D) equal 12.5.

8. **D** First, find the total number of votes Adam received. If you subtract 300 from the total of votes listed in the chart, you will find that Adam received 60 votes. From this, you can eliminate (A), (B), and (C) without doing any calculations. The average number of votes Brian and Jolene received is 45 (90 divided by 2). This is 15 less than the number Adam received.

4

PPST: Reading Practice Test 1

The Praxis Series Professional Assessments for Beginning Teachers

Test Name: Pre-Professional Skills Test

Reading

Time – 60 minutes

40 Questions

Directions: Each statement or passage is followed by a question or questions based on its content. After reading a statement or passage, choose the best answer to each question from among the five choices given. Answer all questions following a statement or passage on the basis of what is *stated* or *implied* in that statement or passage; you are not expected to have any previous knowledge of the topics treated in the statements or passages.

Be sure to mark all your answers on your answer sheet and completely fill in the lettered space with a heavy, dark mark so that you cannot see the letter.

Remember, try to answer every question.

Question 1

1. At one time or another, the feeling washes over almost everyone who works in a large corporation: the urge to give it all up, and run his or her own business. But then reality sinks in—bills, the need for a stable job, the low likelihood of success, the long hours—and this great dream simply fades into a passing fancy.

   The passage is primarily concerned with

   (A) critiquing why small businesses fail

   (B) how to choose a career path

   (C) criticizing the career choices for a select group

   (D) analyzing the capital required to start a small business

   (E) an opinion about why there are few entrepreneurs

Questions 2–3

A troubling trend is emerging in the halls of higher learning. After nearly 30 years of rising African-American enrollment at U.S. colleges and universities, blacks are turning their backs on some of the country's elite institutions. At the University of California at Berkeley, 10 percent fewer blacks sought entry for the Fall term this year than last year. This should not be a surprise. The Supreme Court declared the affirmative-action program at the University of Michigan unconstitutional. Admissions officers at Michigan can consider race, but can no longer use this factor to add specific weight to an applicant's score. But the perception in the community is that affirmative action has been killed.

2. With which statement would the author of the passage would most likely agree?

   (A) The perception that affirmative action has been killed has shrunk the pool of black applicants at top colleges and universities.

   (B) The decline in African-American enrollment at top colleges and universities is due solely to affirmative-action program changes.

   (C) Effective outreach to the community would not be helpful in explaining the impacts of changing affirmative-action programs.

   (D) The University of California at Berkeley must change its admissions policies.

   (E) Legislators have made admissions more difficult for minorities.

GO ON TO THE NEXT PAGE

3. The author claims that the new affirmative-action policies by the University of Michigan are

   (A) illegal
   (B) misunderstood
   (C) troubling
   (D) fair
   (E) overdue

4. Scores of aerospace entrepreneurs and astronauts-turned-executives have been waiting for the day when space is no longer dominated by costly, government-funded programs. They believe that alternative, inexpensive access to space is the key to unlocking its commercial potential. Many believe this may be the year. If all goes well, the world's first private space plane, SpaceShipOne, will be shot into space before gliding back to land. And the cost? The cost is $98,000 per ticket per person, on an aircraft that will hold up to 12 passengers.

   The author infers that many aerospace entrepreneurs

   (A) have already been to space, therefore realizing its commercial potential
   (B) were former astronauts
   (C) are willing to pay $98,000 per person for a flight into space
   (D) believe $98,000 is a price many people can afford
   (E) do not believe government-funded space shuttles can be a commercial success

Questions 5–6

Some individuals are beating cancer. Consider the case of Charles Gibson, who was diagnosed with advanced lung cancer three years ago. After chemotherapy, he enrolled in a clinical trial, which provided him with two drugs—the first, a colon cancer drug; the second, an experimental lung cancer treatment. Within a few months, Charles found that his tumors had shrunk by almost 90 percent. Doctors expect Charles to continue to do well, as long as he stays on the two drugs.

But that is the problem. There is an enormous price for taking these two drugs. The colon cancer drug costs almost $4500 per month, while the new experimental drug costs $2000 per month. These prices put tremendous strain on a health-care system that continues to have escalating costs. For Charles, the benefits are obvious. But imagine if every lung cancer patient (175,000 people this year) were treated with these drugs. That would completely exhaust the national health-care budget. It will take more Charles Gibsons for America to realize there is a growing cost problem facing our system.

5. Which of the following best describes the organization of the passage?

   (A) A series of events is arranged chronologically.
   (B) A controversial theory is proposed and then discredited.
   (C) An example is provided, and the problematical issues of the example are discussed.
   (D) An unforeseen problem is presented, followed by examples.
   (E) A criticism is summarized, evaluated, and dismissed.

GO ON TO THE NEXT PAGE

6. The author most likely uses the word "exhaust" in the second paragraph to mean

   (A) bankrupt
   (B) dirty
   (C) tire
   (D) treat
   (E) conserve

7. It is imperative to educate more scientists and engineers in the United States. A recent study shows that American prowess is declining in developing new patents, performing path-breaking research, and creating new technologies. Policies to reverse this trend, starting with less restrictive visa requirements for the best and brightest foreign students, are sorely needed.

   It can be inferred from the passage that the author believes

   (A) the lack of scientists in the United States hurts immigration policies
   (B) more engineers in the United States would improve American prowess
   (C) Americans do not understand new technologies under development
   (D) attracting foreign students to the United States is a necessary step to rebuild American strength in patent creation
   (E) less restrictive visa requirements should apply only to scientists and engineers

Questions 8–9

In his recent novel, James Surowiecki argues that society should take advantage of crowd insights rather than depending on the "expert" advice of select individuals. To prove his point, he cites examples of the capital markets, as well as the disappearance of the 1968 USS *Scorpion*. In order to find the submarine, the Navy asked several individuals to give their best estimate as to where the sub landed. Using a complex formula to aggregate all answers, the Navy made an estimate that ended up only 220 yards from the actual submarine. This final estimate was closer than any one individual's guess. In order to use the advice of a crowd, Surowiecki argues, you need conditions that allows for diverse and independent feedback from individuals, and a method to aggregate the collective judgments.

8. Which of the following statements would Surowiecki most likely agree?

   (A) A crowd can be effective only if it is made up of smart individuals.
   (B) A CEO's insights may not be as effective as the collective insights of the employees of a company.
   (C) Decision markets, such as the Iowa Electronic Market, will not be able to predict outcomes accurately.
   (D) Group feedback is not valuable in business.
   (E) Complex formulas are needed to incorporate feedback from a crowd.

9. Hollywood Stock Exchange is a popular site where people wager and predict box-office returns. It frequently forecasts more accurately than other tools used in Hollywood. This example, if used in the passage, would help to

   (A) support Surowiecki's theories
   (B) contradict opinions held by the author of the passage
   (C) refute prior theories held by Surowiecki
   (D) strengthen the belief in Navy forecasting
   (E) provide insight into how the author views Surowiecki

GO ON TO THE NEXT PAGE

10. Cyberspace appears to be safer than it once was. For the third year in a row, the number of attacks on computer networks has fallen. Clearly, the increase of corporate spending on technology security has helped.

Which of the following is an unstated assumption made by the author of the passage?

(A) Reporting on the number of attacks on computer networks is inaccurate.

(B) Corporate investments in technology security have a direct impact on the number of attacks on computer networks.

(C) New laws against attacks on computer networks have reduced the frequency of attacks.

(D) Attacks on computer networks are no longer a concern.

(E) Corporate spending increased for three consecutive years.

Questions 11–13

Have you ever heard of kiteboarding? If not, don't worry. Twenty years ago, most people said the same thing about snowboarding. If you were to visit the small town of Cabarete, on the northern coast of the Dominican Republic, you would soon realize the tremendous thrill of kiteboarding. This week, in Cabarete, is the Professional Kiteboard Riders Association World Cup Tour (I bet you didn't know there was a professional tour!).

Kiteboarding is a sport in which riders on small boards are propelled by large kites in order to glide over or jump atop bodies of water. It is considered the next popular extreme sport. Trip Forman, an owner of a kiteboarding school, has seen enrollment grow to a projected 6,000 this year from 400 two years ago. Why the growth? Almost everyone that tries it loves it; there is now inexpensive equipment available; and top pro Randy Tennant, who is also an actor, has exposed the sport to a large number of teenagers.

One drawback may be the danger in kiteboarding. According to the Florida Kite Surfing Association, there have been 21 deaths associated with kiteboarding since 2000. The vast majority of these deaths are avoidable if you know what you are doing. I find the sport to be relaxing though. You can ride leisurely or make it as extreme as you want.

11. What role does the author hold in regard to the sport of kiteboarding?

(A) Professional champion

(B) Inventor

(C) Safety advocate

(D) Instructor

(E) Enthusiast

12. What extra information would be helpful in supporting the author's claim that kiteboarding is dangerous?

(A) The number of amateurs and professionals participating in the sport

(B) The types of injuries most commonly suffered

(C) The number of deaths associated with other extreme sports since 2000

(D) The average age of individuals injured while kiteboarding

(E) The number of individuals who were hurt during their first kiteboarding experience

13. The author mentions that the sport is popular due to all of the following reasons EXCEPT

(A) you can ride leisurely or competitively

(B) popular figures are associated with the sport

(C) enjoyment is very high for first time participants

(D) it is very easy to make jumps and do tricks

(E) equipment is affordable

GO ON TO THE NEXT PAGE

14. A helpful way to stave off age-related mental decline is to learn a second language. Researchers compared monolingual to bilingual adults in a test of cognitive function, and bilingualism seemed to offer a protective benefit.

Which of the following, if true, would weaken the author's claim that learning a second language helps reduce the likelihood of mental decline?

(A) The study was performed only in a remote area of the world.

(B) The time and cost of learning a second language is greater than the cost of drugs to treat mental decline.

(C) Only those bilinguals that have used two languages daily since they were children saw benefits.

(D) Women who spoke both Spanish and English saw the greatest benefit.

(E) There were no increased benefits in learning a third language.

Questions 15–16

Scientists at the University of Tokyo have invented a camouflage material that makes the wearer seem transparent by displaying the scene behind the wearer on the front of the material. A camera records the image, and then sends it in real time to a projector that displays the image on the front. Although it works from only one side, the invention could help for many things. For example, pilots could see through the bottom of their planes to help improve landings.

15. The phrase "real time" is used by the author to indicate that transmission of the image is

(A) instantaneous

(B) factual

(C) transparent

(D) camouflage

(E) costly

16. The main goal of the passage is to

(A) discuss a possible use for a new technology

(B) describe the detailed technology requirements for a common item

(C) present a summary of information about a new technology, and a potential use

(D) discuss current dangers in aviation

(E) present the dangers of real time transmission of images

Questions 17–18

Doctors are finding a surprising cause for many of the aches and pains of today's teenagers: playing too hard, too often. While this may seem contradictory for a nation that is concerned about the growing percentage of obese teenagers, there are a number of young athletes that are exercising too much. Year-round play and dreams of going pro are driving these kids, yet many end up with serious injuries.

Overuse injuries are a rising health crisis that derail, or sometimes destroy, promising athletic careers. Just 15 years ago, overuse injuries accounted for 20 percent of patients visiting the Boston Kids' Clinic. Today, however, that number exceeds 70 percent.

Why are kids pushing sports so hard? There are many reasons. Some are driven by dreams of a college scholarship or the lucrative contracts in professional sports. Others are pushed by coaches and parents to participate in year-round leagues, ensuring they remain competitive with their peers. Further, as more kids move towards specialization in one sport at an earlier age, certain segments of the body are more prone to wear and tear. The cross training benefits of diverse sports—for example, soccer in the fall, basketball in the winter, and baseball in the spring—decline as athletes frequently focus on only one sport.

GO ON TO THE NEXT PAGE

17. The passage states that one reason kids are more prone to overuse injuries in sports today is due to

(A) the rising health care crisis

(B) the growing percentage of obese teenagers

(C) the benefits of cross training are outweighed by the challenging travel schedule

(D) the possibility of a college scholarship or professional contract

(E) the increased danger of playing sports in Boston

18. Which of the following would the author most likely support as a way to cut down on the number of teenage sports-related injuries?

(A) A guaranteed salary structure for all major professional sports

(B) Limits to the amount of practice time allowed for athletes in colleges and universities

(C) Mandatory participation by all middle school and high school students in physical education classes

(D) Restriction of parents on the sidelines at competitions, requiring them to remain in the stands

(E) Limits on the number of practices and games a teenager can play in any one sport over a given year

19. Instead of supersizing, a new trend in restaurants is minimizing. Mi Young Kim, owner of three restaurants in Venice, California, is offering two-bite portions of sweets on her lunch menus. The price is right—only $1. Mi Young declares these miniature versions of fancy desserts such as raspberry cheesecake "a spectacular success." These mini-items allow diners to indulge, but without the guilt, which helps keep with today's diet-conscious times. Her next move is to add these treats to dinner menus, and introduce more of them in her restaurants.

The attitude of the author towards the minimizing trend is best described as

(A) neutral

(B) critical

(C) controversial

(D) supportive

(E) ambivalent

20. Instead of sticky, smelly bug repellent, I am going to purchase the new "Buzz Off" clothing, which will repel mosquitoes, ticks, ants, flies, chiggers, and other things that annoy me. These clothes have received an endorsement from the Environmental Protection Agency, so I'm confident that they will work. I look forward to going outside this summer, without the fear of bites or that extremely strong smell.

Which of the following, if true, would most likely weaken the author's intention to purchase the clothing?

(A) The cost of the clothing is equivalent to seven bottles of bug repellent.

(B) The clothing is not recommended for dry cleaning.

(C) There are few chiggers in the region where the author lives.

(D) The clothing produces a smell similar to that of bug repellent.

(E) Before "Buzz Off," the EPA had never given an endorsement for bug repellent clothing.

GO ON TO THE NEXT PAGE

Questions 21–23

One of the most daring deep-space missions NASA has ever planned is about to be launched. Deep Space 1, or DS1, will be unique for two reasons—its ion propulsion engine and its self-navigation system. If DS1 goes well, it will become the model for a new generation of spacecraft.

DS1 is unique in the way in which it will get from place to place. DS1 will be pushed through space by an engine that works by ionizing electrons. Electrons will be fired into xenon gas, stripping the xenon elements of an electron and giving the atoms an electric charge—ionizing them. The ions are then accelerated through an electric field and emitted from thrusters at up to 65,000 m.p.h. This constant push will add 15 to 20 miles per hour daily to the spacecraft's speed, and that impact is significant. Thanks to this process, the spacecraft requires about one-tenth the weight of fuel used in conventional aircraft.

Possibly more innovative is the navigation system. The "brain" of the system will scan stars and asteroids to map the system's location, allowing it to know precisely where it is, and make any necessary adjustments. What would these innovations mean to an automobile? Well, imagine your car finding its own way from San Diego to New York, to a specific shopping mall, while getting 300 miles to the gallon!

21. Which of the following statements would the author most likely agree with regarding NASA's opinion of the DS1 spacecraft?

(A) NASA believes the DS1 technology will eventually lead to cars that can drive themselves.

(B) NASA believes that the DS1 spacecraft, if successful on its mission, will become the model for future space travel technology.

(C) NASA will use DS1 until ion propulsion technology is too costly.

(D) NASA believes that DS1 technology will be the leading pioneer in artificial intelligence.

(E) NASA hopes that DS1 technology can be used for passenger trips to the moon.

22. The author puts the word "brain" in quotations in the third paragraph in order to

(A) imply that NASA has created a new type of intelligent being

(B) show how similar the navigation system is to a human brain

(C) indicate that the navigation system will make decisions similar to decisions a human would make

(D) show that the system is incapable of any decision making without human influence

(E) state a belief that new aliens may be found by the DS1 spacecraft

23. Which of the following techniques does the author use to help the reader better understand the DS1 system?

(A) A technical breakdown of ion propulsion technology

(B) A chart

(C) A hypothetical story that describes the spacecraft

(D) A metaphor that relates DS1 technology to a machine we know how to use

(E) A parable

GO ON TO THE NEXT PAGE

24. Millions of students taking out college loans just received more financial aid. Earlier this year, Congress passed legislation, retroactive to July 1, that lowered the interest rate on new, federally guaranteed student loans to 3.96% from the previous interest rate of 5.13%. Further, the legislation states that those with more than $30,000 in debt may soon have an extra fifteen years to repay outstanding loans.

The passage answer all of the questions below EXCEPT

(A) What is the new interest rate for federal student loans?

(B) Who is eligible to receive additional time to repay college debts?

(C) When does the new loan program begin?

(D) How much will a student who is $30,000 in debt save as a result of the new laws?

(E) What was the old interest rate for federal student loans?

Questions 25–27

I'm not much of a tennis player. Sure, I can go out and hack like any weekend warrior, but I don't need to be worried about new advances in equipment, or having the best technology. Yet, that's exactly what I have. Last week, I went out and purchased a new, oversized-head, titanium-based racquet. I may not be a good player, but boy, do I look good. Apparently, I'm not alone. New racquet technologies have led to a number of advances in the past few years, and sales have exploded. New racquets feature larger heads, longer necks, and lighter body weight. All of this comes at a cost. New racquets range from $175 to $300. Of course, a player of my caliber probably doesn't need to purchase such a racquet, but then again, isn't it cool to tell a fellow competitor you are playing with the PX2 technology (whatever that is!)?

My local tennis pro, someone who could actually use this technology, claims that the new racquets will help all players. The larger racquet size allows greater court coverage, and more power and stability. Lighter weight racquets are easier to move around; however, that comes with the risk of less control of the ball coming off the racquet. In the end, though, I didn't make my decision based on lighter weight versus string control versus a larger racquet head. I made my decision based on the racquet that sounded the most intimidating!

25. The author uses the phrase "weekend warrior" to describe himself as

(A) a top-flight athlete

(B) a recreational player

(C) a temperamental competitor

(D) a tennis professional

(E) a racquet manufacturer

26. The author's main point of the passage is that

(A) advances in technology have harmed the tradition of tennis

(B) oversized racquets provide more reach for players

(C) only professional athletes should be concerned about new advances in racquet technology

(D) looking good is more important than playing well

(E) although some players may not need new tennis racquets, they may enjoy having the best equipment

27. An appropriate title for this passage is

(A) The History of Tennis Racquets

(B) New Tennis Technologies: I Don't Need Them, but I Like Them

(C) Impact of Oversized Racquets on Tennis Scores

(D) Technology in Sports

(E) One Man's Tennis Journey

GO ON TO THE NEXT PAGE

28. It simply isn't fair that big banks continue to charge user fees for customers using "foreign" ATMs. Now, in addition to being charged for using a machine that does not belong to your bank, you must pay an additional fee to the institution that owns the machine. At least small banks understand how much I dislike all these extra charges.

Which of the following is an unstated assumption made by the author of the passage?

(A) Small banks offer checking without ATM fees.

(B) Calling a customer service manager will help to eliminate fees.

(C) Congress has considered making these user transactions illegal.

(D) Banks make the author angry.

(E) Boycotting the banks will force them to change their practices.

Questions 29–32

Tom Purcell, twenty-nine, leaves his job on Wednesday nights at 6 P.M. in order to go back to school. Even with a bachelor's degree in biology, and a master's degree in computer science, Tom still felt he needed to go back to school to further his career. His company agreed, and will be paying the $2,000 per semester tuition.

Tom's story is not unique. More and more, Americans are returning to school for quick, practical courses that allow them to keep up with the competition and rapid changes in technology and business. The rush to these type of "quickie" courses does not mean that graduate degrees are no longer popular. Instead, these courses are used to supplement any employee's education. There is no longer a natural end to when one should complete his or her education. Further, these new courses allow working individuals to learn and work at the same time, eliminating the difficult decision of whether or not to go back to school full time.

The "classroom" is changing as well. More and more, companies are customizing courses for their employees in conjunction with major universities. Classes are held at the workplace, and the curriculum is determined by both leading professors from the university and company administrators. Together, a curriculum is created that provides new information relevant to the workplace. Clearly, adult education has never been better.

29. Which of the following sentences represent an opinion of the author rather than a fact?

(A) 3

(B) 11

(C) 12

(D) 13

(E) 14

30. Which of the following provides the best outline for the passage?

(A) A topic is introduced, followed by supporting examples.

(B) An example is given, followed by counter-arguments against the example.

(C) A specific story is told, followed by general explanations.

(D) A general story is told, followed by specific explanations.

(E) A theory is tested, then refuted, and another theory is created.

31. Which of the following statements would the author most likely support?

(A) Only professional scholars should develop course curricula.

(B) Continuing education in the workplace allows employees more flexibility than traditional post-graduate classes.

(C) Education ends after any post-graduate degrees are completed.

(D) Companies allow employees to take additional courses strictly to keep them at their current jobs longer.

(E) Adult education is on the decline.

GO ON TO THE NEXT PAGE

32. The passage implies that many companies are supporting employees' decisions to go back to school because

(A) companies feel continued education will benefit their employees
(B) companies fear losing employees to other companies that provide additional training
(C) companies need to use federal education grants before they expire
(D) companies feel this is the only way to stay on top of new technological advancements
(E) companies prefer to control the curricula of their employees' classes

Questions 33–34

Stung by broken industry promises, farmers are livid at massive crop failure and damage using "genetically superior" seeds. In the American southeast, growers who used genetically manipulated cottonseeds suffered some of the worst crop failures ever. Farmers' organizations around the world are linking up to stop genetically engineered seeds from being introduced.

33. Which of the following, if true, would weaken the farmers' claim that genetic seeds are to blame for their poor crop production?

(A) The seeds were tried for only one season, which had poor weather conditions.
(B) Growers of the American northwest experienced the same type of problems with genetic seeds.
(C) Cottonseeds are regarded as the best type of genetic seed.
(D) Growers in the southwest were pleased with genetic seeds in tomato and corn production.
(E) Genetically engineered seeds are endorsed by the government.

34. The author's use of the words "linking up" is best defined as

(A) attaching
(B) collaborating
(C) molding
(D) building
(E) connecting

35. Many pregnant women avoid eating fish due to the mercury levels found in many common freshwater and saltwater fish. Doctors recently concluded a study of 720 pregnant women who ate saltwater fish as often as 12 times per week, which found no evidence of harm to the mothers, or their children up to age 5.

Which of the following best describes the results of the study described in the passage above?

(A) Consuming up to 12 servings of fish per week is safe for pregnant mothers.
(B) Freshwater fish contain more mercury than saltwater fish.
(C) Pregnant women who consume saltwater fish have not shown any problems associated with mercury intake during pregnancy, nor have their children.
(D) Children who consume saltwater fish are in danger of mercury poisoning.
(E) Children are in danger of contracting certain diseases later in life if their mothers ate saltwater fish while pregnant.

GO ON TO THE NEXT PAGE

Questions 36–38

Judith Harris wrote a controversial book called *The Nurture Assumption*. Although it has been out for only one year, it has already been provoking passionate debate among scientists and therapists, because it argues that parents make only a single, lasting contribution to their children's future—their genes.

Judith argues that peer groups, not parents, determine the sort of people children will become. Her conclusions are based on her analysis of scientific research, especially with twins. Identical twins raised in the same home are no more alike than those raised apart. And two children adopted by the same parents turn out no more alike than a duo raised separately.

Harris's implications are profound. Does this mean that a parent's love and affection don't matter? Harris, a grandmother and writer of psychology textbooks, without any academic affiliations or a Ph.D., claims, "Good parents sometimes have bad kids." Child development experts tend to disagree. Judith Harris and her work may be the focus of great debate in psychology.

36. In which publication would this passage most likely appear?

(A) A book review publication

(B) A psychology journal

(C) A child development textbook

(D) An editorial page

(E) A parenting book

37. Which one of the following statements would Judith Harris most likely support?

(A) It is okay to ignore your children, because your actions will not affect them.

(B) In order to be an expert in child development theory, one must have a Ph.D. and post-doctorate research.

(C) Peer influence is the primary determinate of how a child will develop.

(D) Parents who spend more time with their children are more likely to raise better kids.

(E) Development during the first two years of a child's life plays a crucial role in determining their future success.

38. Which of the following best describes the main point of the passage?

(A) Parents do not have an influence on their children's behavior.

(B) Judith Harris' book is selling well.

(C) Twins are the best indicators of measuring the influence parents have on children.

(D) Judith Harris is not affiliated with an academic institution.

(E) Judith Harris' book contains new theories about parental influence on children that will likely spark much debate in child psychology.

GO ON TO THE NEXT PAGE

Questions 39–40

Most teachers receive tenure status and lifetime job protection after three years on the job, after which terminating a teacher becomes a very difficult and long process. Teachers faced with termination have a long time before any serious action can be taken—principals seeking to dismiss them must usually file several written reports, wait a year for improvement, file additional poor evaluations, appear at a hearing, and maybe even show up in court to defend the eventual firing. This entire process results in few terminations—just 44 of the 100,000 tenured teachers were dismissed within the last seven years in Illinois. Many states, however, are moving to streamline their firing procedures. Next year, Florida will cut the time a teacher has to show improvement to 90 days from the current time period of one year.

39. Which of the following best summarizes the main point of the passage?

(A) Teachers deserve tenure due to their hard work for low salaries.

(B) Florida's policies are changing regarding teacher dismissal.

(C) There is a debate among teachers about being tenured after only three years.

(D) Most current teacher termination procedures involve many steps, and extend for months, even years.

(E) Teacher unions are concerned about wrongful terminations of teachers who have done nothing wrong.

40. Which of the following sentences, if inserted at the end of the passage, would best complete the meaning of the passage?

(A) Teachers should be given every benefit of the doubt prior to termination.

(B) Firing procedures need to allow more time for appeals.

(C) If teachers aren't fired, there should be a law that protects them from having to go through termination procedures a second time.

(D) Swift procedures will ensure equality for all.

(E) If termination procedures are necessary, it is important that bottlenecks do not slow down the process.

STOP

Diagnostic Test Form

Completely darken bubbles with a No. 2 pencil. If you make a mistake, be sure to erase mark completely. Erase all stray marks.

1. YOUR NAME: (Print) ______________________ Last ______ First ______ M.I.

SIGNATURE: ______________________ **DATE:** ____/____/____

HOME ADDRESS: (Print) ______________________ Number and Street

______ City ______ State ______ Zip **E-MAIL:** ______________________

PHONE NO.: (Print) ____________ **SCHOOL:** ____________ **CLASS OF:** ____________

IMPORTANT: Please fill in these boxes exactly as shown on the back cover of your test book.

OpSCan *i*NSIGHT™ forms by Pearson NCS EM-255325-1:654321
Printed in U.S.A.

2. TEST FORM

3. TEST CODE

0	0	0	0
1	1	1	1
2	2	2	2
3	3	3	3
4	4	4	4
5	5	5	5
6	6	6	6
7	7	7	7
8	8	8	8
9	9	9	9

4. PHONE NUMBER

0	0	0	0	0	0	0
1	1	1	1	1	1	1
2	2	2	2	2	2	2
3	3	3	3	3	3	3
4	4	4	4	4	4	4
5	5	5	5	5	5	5
6	6	6	6	6	6	6
7	7	7	7	7	7	7
8	8	8	8	8	8	8
9	9	9	9	9	9	9

5. YOUR NAME

First 4 letters of last name				FIRST INIT	MID INIT
A	A	A	A	A	A
B	B	B	B	B	B
C	C	C	C	C	C
D	D	D	D	D	D
E	E	E	E	E	E
F	F	F	F	F	F
G	G	G	G	G	G
H	H	H	H	H	H
I	I	I	I	I	I
J	J	J	J	J	J
K	K	K	K	K	K
L	L	L	L	L	L
M	M	M	M	M	M
N	N	N	N	N	N
O	O	O	O	O	O
P	P	P	P	P	P
Q	Q	Q	Q	Q	Q
R	R	R	R	R	R
S	S	S	S	S	S
T	T	T	T	T	T
U	U	U	U	U	U
V	V	V	V	V	V
W	W	W	W	W	W
X	X	X	X	X	X
Y	Y	Y	Y	Y	Y
Z	Z	Z	Z	Z	Z

6. DATE OF BIRTH

MONTH	DAY		YEAR	
JAN				
FEB				
MAR	0	0	0	0
APR	1	1	1	1
MAY	2	2	2	2
JUN	3	3	3	3
JUL		4	4	4
AUG		5	5	5
SEP		6	6	6
OCT		7	7	7
NOV		8	8	8
DEC		9	9	9

7. SEX

- MALE
- FEMALE

8. OTHER

1	A	B	C	D	E
2	A	B	C	D	E
3	A	B	C	D	E

Begin with number 1 for each new section of the test. Leave blank any extra answer spaces.

SECTION 1

1	A	B	C	D	E	26	A	B	C	D	E	51	A	B	C	D	E	76	A	B	C	D	E
2	A	B	C	D	E	27	A	B	C	D	E	52	A	B	C	D	E	77	A	B	C	D	E
3	A	B	C	D	E	28	A	B	C	D	E	53	A	B	C	D	E	78	A	B	C	D	E
4	A	B	C	D	E	29	A	B	C	D	E	54	A	B	C	D	E	79	A	B	C	D	E
5	A	B	C	D	E	30	A	B	C	D	E	55	A	B	C	D	E	80	A	B	C	D	E
6	A	B	C	D	E	31	A	B	C	D	E	56	A	B	C	D	E	81	A	B	C	D	E
7	A	B	C	D	E	32	A	B	C	D	E	57	A	B	C	D	E	82	A	B	C	D	E
8	A	B	C	D	E	33	A	B	C	D	E	58	A	B	C	D	E	83	A	B	C	D	E
9	A	B	C	D	E	34	A	B	C	D	E	59	A	B	C	D	E	84	A	B	C	D	E
10	A	B	C	D	E	35	A	B	C	D	E	60	A	B	C	D	E	85	A	B	C	D	E
11	A	B	C	D	E	36	A	B	C	D	E	61	A	B	C	D	E	86	A	B	C	D	E
12	A	B	C	D	E	37	A	B	C	D	E	62	A	B	C	D	E	87	A	B	C	D	E
13	A	B	C	D	E	38	A	B	C	D	E	63	A	B	C	D	E	88	A	B	C	D	E
14	A	B	C	D	E	39	A	B	C	D	E	64	A	B	C	D	E	89	A	B	C	D	E
15	A	B	C	D	E	40	A	B	C	D	E	65	A	B	C	D	E	90	A	B	C	D	E
16	A	B	C	D	E	41	A	B	C	D	E	66	A	B	C	D	E	91	A	B	C	D	E
17	A	B	C	D	E	42	A	B	C	D	E	67	A	B	C	D	E	92	A	B	C	D	E
18	A	B	C	D	E	43	A	B	C	D	E	68	A	B	C	D	E	93	A	B	C	D	E
19	A	B	C	D	E	44	A	B	C	D	E	69	A	B	C	D	E	94	A	B	C	D	E
20	A	B	C	D	E	45	A	B	C	D	E	70	A	B	C	D	E	95	A	B	C	D	E
21	A	B	C	D	E	46	A	B	C	D	E	71	A	B	C	D	E	96	A	B	C	D	E
22	A	B	C	D	E	47	A	B	C	D	E	72	A	B	C	D	E	97	A	B	C	D	E
23	A	B	C	D	E	48	A	B	C	D	E	73	A	B	C	D	E	98	A	B	C	D	E
24	A	B	C	D	E	49	A	B	C	D	E	74	A	B	C	D	E	99	A	B	C	D	E
25	A	B	C	D	E	50	A	B	C	D	E	75	A	B	C	D	E	100	A	B	C	D	E

5

Answers and Explanations for PPST: Reading Practice Test 1

PPST: READING PRACTICE TEST 1 ANSWER KEY

1. E
2. A
3. B
4. E
5. C
6. A
7. D
8. B
9. A
10. B
11. E
12. C
13. D
14. C
15. A
16. C
17. D
18. E
19. D
20. D
21. B
22. C
23. D
24. D
25. B
26. E
27. B
28. A
29. E
30. C
31. B
32. A
33. A
34. B
35. C
36. A
37. C
38. E
39. D
40. E

ANSWERS AND EXPLANATIONS FOR PPST: READING PRACTICE TEST 1

1. **E** The author makes the following claim—while many individuals consider starting a business, few end up doing so. This is best reflected in answer choice (E).

2. **A** The author attempts to explain the decline in enrollment of African Americans. The author then explains the change in affirmative-action policies. Answer choice (A) helps to link the two statements together. Answer choices (B) and (D) use harsh, definite language—notice the word *solely* and *must* in the two answer choices, which should serve as a warning. (C) contradicts the tone of the passage.

3. **B** This is best supported by the last sentence, which states the perception that affirmative-action policies were killed. The author never claims the change was illegal. Be careful about answer choice (C), which uses a word from the passage. This is a common trick employed by ETS. The word is used to describe the decline in African-American enrollment, not the new policy at Michigan.

4. **E** The author describes SpaceShipOne as the first example of a commercial alternative to government-funded programs. As the first private plane, its scheduled launch serves as what many entrepreneurs believe to be the starting point for commercial success. The author's statements do not support all other answer choices.

5. **C** The passage begins with the example of Charles Gibson. His story is used to describe the high cost of cancer treatments.

6. **A** The author is concerned that the high cost of treatment for cancer patients could financially destroy the health-care budget.

7. **D** This helps create the link between the last sentence (the author's recommendation to solve the problem), and his identification of the problem in the second sentence. Answer choices (A) and (B) take phrases from the passage, but use them in incorrectly. Answer choices (C) and (E) are never stated—beware of harsh language!

8. **B** Surowiecki's argument is that crowds can produce valuable insight, often more valuable than the opinion of one individual. Answer choice (B) conveys this. Notice the use of the words *may not*—it is much easier to assume the author would agree to a qualified statement like (B) as opposed to a harsh statement like (E).

9. **A** Hollywood Stock Exchange would be another example of how group feedback, properly collected, could be used to provide great insight. The example would serve the same purpose as the story of the USS *Scorpion*.

10. **B** The passage talks about how attacks on cyberspace have declined, and states an opinion that increases in corporate spending have worked. Therefore, the author assumes that increased spending yields a safer environment. (E) cannot be verified, and while (C) may be true, the author does not make any assumptions about legal procedures impacting security. (A) and (D) are out of scope.

11. **E** Throughout the passage, the author mentions his enjoyment of the sport. The third paragraph also indicates that he participates in the sport. While professionals, instructors, and safety advocates are mentioned in the passage, the author does not claim to hold any of those roles.

12. **C** The author argues that the sport is more dangerous than other extreme sports. To support the argument, he should provide comparative data. The statistic of 20 deaths in kiteboarding does not show that it is more dangerous than other sports. To compare, the author should show the number of deaths associated with other extreme sports over the same timeframe. Even better, the author could present the number of deaths per participants, in order to give an accurate comparison amongst several sports.

13. **D** Paragraph two lists reasons for the growth and popularity of kiteboarding. (B) is a reference to Randy Tennant, the professional kiteboarder/actor. The level of difficulty, however, is not mentioned in the passage.

14. **C** The author states that bilingual adults tend to perform better in tests of cognitive function, so his advice is to learn a second language. Yet that advice loses strength if (B) is true—learning a second language will not provide incremental benefit. It appears that only those who grow up learning two languages get the benefits.

15. **A** The passage indicates that the image is recorded, transmitted, and then projected. The phrase is used to discuss the amount of time it takes for this process. Only answer choice (A) gives an indication of time.

16. **C** The passage introduces a new material, and briefly discusses how it works. The passage concludes with an example of how the technology could be used. While answer choice (A) occurs during the passage, it is not the primary message of the passage. There are no technical details given in the passage, so you can eliminate (B). Answer choices (D) and (E) are out of scope.

17. **D** In the final paragraph, the author mentions that many kids are pushed by the possibility of college scholarship, or lucrative contract in professional sports.

18. **E** One reason the author gives for the increase in injuries is the movement towards specialization in one sport. Answer choice (E) would reduce the ability of a teenage to specialize in one sport, therefore potentially lowering the risk of injury. (A), (C), and (D) are not related to the topic at hand. Answer choice (B), while helpful, does not address the target group of individuals mentioned in the passage—young teenagers, who are injured long before attending college.

19. **D** The upbeat tone of the passage compliments the restaurant owner and her dessert menu. The phrase "the price is right" indicates acceptance and support to this restaurant trend.

20. **D** The author states two primary reasons for wanting to wear the clothing—the ability to have a repellent for many "annoying" creatures and the opportunity to get rid of the "extremely strong smell" of bug spray. If (D) is true, this could weaken her desire to purchase this clothing. Answer choice (C) seems like a possible answer; however, it does not indicate that there would not be any bugs in the author's region.

21. B The information is contained in the last sentence of the first paragraph in the passage. While aspects of the passage discuss the future possibilities of an automobile, there is no link to NASA believing this will be a direct result of the DS1. Answer choices (C), (D), and (E) are not mentioned in the passage.

22. C Often, an author will use in quotations to imply a meaning similar to the literal meaning of the word. Answer choice (B) is out of scope. Answer choice (D) is wrong, and answer choices (A) and (E) are not stated anywhere in the passage.

23. D The use of the automobile example is designed to show the impressive features of the DS1 system.

24. D Although the number $30,000 is contained in the passage, we cannot tell exactly how much money someone in debt will save. All we know is that person may be eligible for extended payment options.

25. B If you are unfamiliar with the phrase, information in the passage implies that he is not an experienced tennis player. The first sentence of the passage helps to eliminate answer choices (A) and (D).

26. E The author takes a light-hearted tone in this passage, and is the first to acknowledge that he does not need the new racquets. However, he enjoys learning about and using the top-flight racquets.

27. B Answer choices (A) and (D) are out of scope—they are too broad for a small passage. Answer choice (C) is too specific, while (E) is too generic.

28. A The author states that big banks frustrate the author, while small banks understand the author's dislike of bank fees. While the other answer choices could be true, they are not used to help support the statements in the passage.

29. E The statement "adult education has never been better" expresses the feelings of the author, and would be difficult to prove. All other statements represent factual information.

30. C The passage starts with the story of Tom Purcell. From there, we learn about the growing trends in adult education.

31. B In the passage, the author describes the advantages of taking classes while still collecting an income and at the convenient location of the workplace.

32. A We could try to speculate as to why many companies provide educational assistance to their employees, but we cannot prove any of the explanations. Answer choices (B), (D), and (E) all seem like plausible reasons, but we cannot prove them. We can infer, however, that companies believe these programs are beneficial. We know this because companies reimburse employees to take these courses, and because companies develop their own programs. Answer choice (C) is out of scope.

33. A The farmers claim that the reason for their poor crop production is due to the seeds. In order to weaken that claim, another reason needs to be provided to explain the poor crop production. Poor weather does provide a reason.

34. B The goal of the farmers is to gain support from as many other farmers as possible to fight against genetic seeds. The farmers seek to collaborate with as many other groups as possible.

35. C The study found no harm to mothers or their children who consumed saltwater fish during pregnancy. (A) is not specific to saltwater fish.

36. A The passage is very vague and general, therefore we can eliminate answer choices (B), (C), and (E). The passage does not state any strong opinions, making a book review the most likely publication.

37. **C** A statement very similar to this can be found in the first sentence of the second paragraph.

38. **E** If you selected answer choice (A), you selected the main point of Judith Harris' book, NOT the main point of the passage.

39. **D** The passage describes the lengthy procedures used to terminate a teacher who is not in good standing.

40. **E** Answer choices (A) and (B) go against the general point of the passage. Answer choice (D) is out of scope. Answer choice (C) is not supported by the text. Answer choice (E) fits the author's goal—the desire to speed up termination procedures that currently take a very long time.

6

PPST: Reading Practice Test 2

The Praxis Series Professional Assessments for Beginning Teachers

Test Name: Pre-Professional Skills Test

Reading

Time – 60 minutes

40 Questions

Directions: Each statement or passage is followed by a question or questions based on its content. After reading a statement or passage, choose the best answer to each question from among the five choices given. Answer all questions following a statement or passage on the basis of what is *stated* or *implied* in that statement or passage; you are not expected to have any previous knowledge of the topics treated in the statements or passages.

Be sure to mark all your answers on your answer sheet and completely fill in the lettered space with a heavy, dark mark so that you cannot see the letter.

Remember, try to answer every question.

Question 1

1. Summer is a dangerous time for the nation's power lines. Utility companies often turn down the amount of power sent through the high-voltage power lines as temperatures rise. As power lines get hot, they stretch and sag, risking a short-circuit if they touch tree branches or another line. But one company has a fix for this: a ceramic cable that sloughs off heat. This aluminum-oxide material should enable power companies to avert brownouts by distributing two or three times as much juice on peak-demand days.

   Which of the following best describes the organization of the passage?

   (A) A theory is presented, and then refuted.

   (B) An example is discussed, and then explained.

   (C) A problem is described, and a potential solution suggested.

   (D) A criticism is summarized and evaluated.

   (E) An opinion is given, followed by supporting evidence.

Questions 2–3

In a range of diseases, including cancer, stroke, and heart disease, some of the damage is caused by minuscule ions as they travel through the circuitous pathways of a cell. In order to observe the movements of these ions, researchers have developed a new mathematical model that can predict behavior of oddly shaped particles as they flow through porous material. Previous models for this process, called percolation, could track only similarly shaped particles, such as sticks, circles, or squares. The new model won't describe the movement of ions themselves, but it can predict the behavior of nanosize sensor proteins that might be used to track the paths of ions.

2. Which of the following statements is true about the new mathematical model mentioned in the passage above?

   (A) It can track only similarly shaped particles.

   (B) It can describe the movement of ions.

   (C) It can cause some damage in cells.

   (D) It can track particles of oddly shaped sizes.

   (E) It lowers the value of percolation.

3. This passage would most likely be found in a

   (A) commentary section of a magazine

   (B) graduate thesis paper

   (C) science section of a newspaper

   (D) dictionary

   (E) encyclopedia

GO ON TO THE NEXT PAGE

Questions 4–6

In 1956, geologist M. King Hubbert forecasted that U.S. oil production would peak by the early 1970s. His forecast was subject to years of ridicule, until the early 1970s, when he turned out to be correct. Students of Hubbert are now using his same principles to predict the peak in worldwide oil production. Their current conclusion: the world is running out of oil sooner than conventional wisdom would have us believe. In fact, many believe that peak worldwide production may be at hand today.

It is true that at some point the world will run out of petroleum. At debate, therefore, are estimates of supply, consumption, and undiscovered oil. Further, many geologists continue to believe that oil consumption and oil discovery will grow at the same rate forever. Hubbert was the first to prove such a theory to be false. Once the rate of discovery slows, it's possible to extrapolate where production growth ends. Now, Hubbert's followers generally believe that the total amount of oil that was ever on Earth is two trillion barrels and that we have gone through nearly half of that.

One of the scariest points I've seen about those that criticize Hubbert is the belief that there is plenty of oil out there because little exploration has been done in the Middle East during the past 25 years. Even if this were true, why would we want those countries to hold even more power over our future energy needs? As Hubbert pointed out more than 25 years ago, finding an alternative source, and weaning our country off oil, is one of the nation's most important tasks.

4. The use of the word "principles" in the first paragraph means

(A) techniques
(B) morals
(C) leaders
(D) conclusions
(E) first

5. The primary topic of this passage is

(A) how the world will function once oil production peaks
(B) why Hubbert's critics were incorrect
(C) the different measurements of oil production
(D) how Hubbert's techniques indicate a near peak in worldwide production
(E) the danger of the United States' continued reliance on foreign oil production

6. The author would be most likely to agree with which of the following statements about worldwide oil discovery and production?

(A) Skeptics about declining oil do not realize the vast amounts of supply available in the Middle East.
(B) Any prediction of oil production is likely to be inaccurate, because no one knows the amounts of future supply and consumption.
(C) Future stability of the United States requires improvements in solar power technologies.
(D) Technology improvements, which make oil more economically accessible, will definitely delay the peak in worldwide production.
(E) Oil consumption and oil discovery will not continue to grow at the similar rates forever.

GO ON TO THE NEXT PAGE

7. This summer the rock band Phish will perform their last summer tour, 21 years after performing their first concert. While I am a big fan, I think this is the right thing to do. I do not want them to become caricatures of what they are, or even worse, a nostalgia act for years to come. In the end, I'm sure they'll be more respected, even if they aren't as wealthy.

Which of the following is an unstated assumption of the author?

(A) The author is a big fan of the band Phish.

(B) The band would make additional profits if they continued to tour.

(C) A new group will immediately take Phish's place among music fans.

(D) Touring is a tiring and difficult experience for a band.

(E) Phish has continuously performed at a high level.

Questions 8–9

Many popular fish species are endangered. Biotechnology has crafted ways to create fish with more edible flesh. However, few of us are eating biotech-spawned salmon, rainbow trout, and carp. That said, genetically modified crops have already had an impact on animal food, in industrial processes, and in clothing manufacture (for example, most cotton is now bio-engineered). So why the delay in food consumption?

In general, the time between the idea of a new food, and getting a product to market runs around ten years. Government agencies are thorough in validating that newly engineered foods will have no adverse impacts on people or the environment. Further, traditional farmers have lobbied vigorously against these techniques, fearful that their livelihoods will be severely impacted by these new inventions. So while it will be some years before genetically modified foods make it to the dinner table, the success of biotechnology has already had an impact on many aspects of farming.

8. Which of the following questions is the author attempting to answer in the passage above?

(A) How is cotton genetically modified?

(B) Why are farmers resistant to genetically modified foods?

(C) How is biotech food produced?

(D) When will genetically modified foods become mainstream?

(E) What are the long-term impacts of biotech fish on the environment?

9. The author states that traditional farmers view genetically modified foods as

(A) healthy

(B) a solution to today's farming problems

(C) a competing product, and a threat to their livelihood

(D) an undeniable future trend

(E) necessary to sustain a growing population

GO ON TO THE NEXT PAGE

Questions 10–11

Not surprisingly, marriage can have a favorable impact on one's emotional and physical well-being. But that is not guaranteed, and it does not come for free. There is a large body of medical literature showing that married people tend to be healthier and live longer than singles. But newer research adds an important caveat: the quality of the marriage matters. Marital stress can have a negative impact on your health. In a recent study of married men, those with high levels of stress in their marriages were more likely to have an unhealthy thickening of the heart's main pumping chamber. Other studies have shown that happily married women have fewer blockages in their aortas, and that happily married couples are less likely than unhappy couples to suffer from heart disease. Someday, marital stress may be as important an indicator of health as cholesterol, weight, or blood pressure.

10. The author would be LEAST likely to agree with which of the following statements?

(A) A single man should get married quickly in order to ensure the best possible health.

(B) A happy marriage can lead to health benefits for both the man and woman.

(C) Medical literature supports the belief that marriage can lead to better health.

(D) Cholesterol, weight, and blood pressure are all important indicators of health.

(E) Not all marriages are created equal.

11. The author uses the word "body" in the third sentence to mean

(A) volume

(B) torso

(C) theory

(D) discussion

(E) consistency

GO ON TO THE NEXT PAGE

Questions 12–14

Just 50 years after the Salk vaccine was created, Polio in America is a thing of the past. In the fifties, tens of thousands of people fell victim to the disease every year. Polio hit hardest in the summer, when newscasts carried the day's tally of new cases. Parents were afraid to let children swim in public pools or go to the movies. No wonder Dr. Jonas Salk, developer of the first Polio vaccine, became such a revered figure.

While the science that laid the foundation for the vaccine was done by others, it was Salk who moved quickly to develop and test it. In 1949, the breakthrough that paved the way for the vaccine came when John Enders and his team were able to cultivate the Polio virus in test tubes. As Salk perfected the vaccine, he faced critics who argued that his approach, which used an inactivated rather than a weakened form of the virus, was flawed. Dismissing critics, Salk came up with an effective way of inactivating the virus, and personally conducted the early human trials of the vaccine, which demonstrated its effectiveness.

While Salk was praised in the community, he still struggled to gain respect from his colleagues. Critics snipped that his successes were due to the work of others whose brilliant advances made the vaccine possible. This criticism greatly hurt Salk, who avoided work in the labs until he later founded his own Salk Institute in 1963. Until his death in 1995, Salk continued to be motivated by the desire to turn scientific insight into real-world treatments.

12. The main purpose of the passage is

(A) to explain how Salk endured many critics throughout his life

(B) to present alternative theories for vaccine development

(C) to demonstrate that today's parents are much less concerned about their children than the parents of the 1950s

(D) to discuss Jonas Salk's role in the development of the polio vaccine

(E) to criticize the media's treatment of polio's impact on the community

13. Which of the following is an unstated assumption made by the author of the passage?

(A) Using a weakened form of a virus was considered by most scientists the correct way to create a vaccine.

(B) Salk could not handle criticism well.

(C) Other scientists deserved more praise than Salk for their contribution to the polio vaccine.

(D) Alfred Sabin was no longer capable of creating vaccines.

(E) Human trials of the polio vaccine were dangerous, but Salk conducted them anyways.

14. The author most likely believes the criticism directed at Jonas Salk by other scientists was

(A) necessary

(B) illegal

(C) unfortunate

(D) part of a conspiracy

(E) a proper balance to the media's uninformed praise

GO ON TO THE NEXT PAGE

15. An MBA is not as valuable as people believe. After the investment of loads of time and money in getting a master's degree in business administration, the return just isn't there. There is little evidence that mastery of knowledge acquired in business school enhances people's careers, or that attaining an MBA credential itself has much effect on graduates' salaries or career attainment. In the recent strong economy and competitive job market, top consulting firms have begun to hire people who lack MBAs.

The author uses the example of consulting firms in order to demonstrate

(A) the return on investment for an MBA is no longer positive

(B) the amount of time spent obtaining an MBA

(C) that jobs previously held only for MBAs are now open to other professionals

(D) how a strong network in an MBA program can be helpful

(E) why people invest in an MBA

16. A recent book profiled female millionaires. The median millionaire woman is 49 years old, a wife (nearly 40% have been married more than once), and a mother. She wakes up each morning at 5:58 A.M. and crashes at 10:32 P.M. She spends 49 hours per week doing work that she enjoys, and spends an additional four hours per week at the gym. Her average annual income is $414,000, which is 71 percent of her household's income. She has probably been through college, and she owns her own home. She wants to spend time and money working on significant causes.

The author cites numerous statistics in the passage in order to

(A) describe the minimum criteria necessary to become a millionaire

(B) show that female millionaires are younger than their male millionaire counterparts

(C) demonstrate the importance of a college education

(D) present a profile of the average female millionaire

(E) show that even female millionaires contribute only a portion to their household income

GO ON TO THE NEXT PAGE

Questions 17–20

Increasingly, it seems, parents fret over why their children can't behave as much as they fret over anxiety about their educational development. When a lot of parents see how their kids interact with playmates and other adults, they are horrified. These concerns help to account for a surge in enrollment in children's etiquette classes. In the past three years, the number of people signing up for children's etiquette classes in Washington has quadrupled.

The curriculum of these classes stresses social skills and common courtesy. Courses from generations ago tended to focus on the more sophisticated of manners, such as the proper use of cutlery. Today's lessons are more practical to today's society. Coaches teach kids how to greet adults, and how to be considerate to others.

Experts say these courses are essential, especially for a generation raised on pop culture morals that encourage disrespect. Psychologist John Gottman encourages this emotional coaching, because his research shows that children who learn socially appropriate ways to solve problems and handle life's upsets are physically healthier and more attentive. Further, those children have more empathy and more friends, and tend to perform better in school.

17. Which of the following summary statements would the author most likely support?

(A) Parents are no longer concerned about their children's academic performance.

(B) Etiquette schools are needed for all children.

(C) Etiquette schools are necessary for children whose parents do not teach them properly.

(D) Society has influenced children to be too disrespectful.

(E) Etiquette schools are increasingly popular, and can have positive effects on children.

18. The author cites "the proper use of cutlery" in the second paragraph in order to

(A) provide an example of current curricula in today's etiquette classes

(B) criticize the lack of etiquette training from parents

(C) provide an example of how parents are horrified to see the lack of skills their children have

(D) explain what psychologists believe are important lessons for children

(E) demonstrate the differences between today's etiquette curricula and prior generations' curricula

19. Which of the following can be inferred about the author's opinion on the value of etiquette courses?

(A) Etiquette courses can help build important skills for children.

(B) Etiquette courses are an unnecessary cost for most families.

(C) Etiquette courses unfairly prey on the insecurities of parents.

(D) Etiquette courses exist due to the lack of education in the home.

(E) Etiquette courses are too expensive for the value they provide.

20. Which of the following, if true, would help WEAKEN the argument that etiquette courses are more popular than ever in Washington?

(A) The number of children in the Washington area has increased 700% in the last three years.

(B) Few children in Washington watch television, and are therefore not impacted by pop culture influences.

(C) Parents are receiving subsidies from schools to have their children attend etiquette classes.

(D) Much of the information taught in etiquette classes used to be taught in the classroom.

(E) The average household size in Washington has grown from 3.5 to 4.1 over the last 20 years.

GO ON TO THE NEXT PAGE

Questions 21–23

Imagine going to a fast food restaurant a few years from now. You order a burger, and before you receive your order, the burger is placed through gamma-ray treatment. Order some fish, and you'll have to wait for the fish to be placed in a pressure cooker that is three times more pressurized than the pressure in the deepest part of the ocean. Why would restaurants go to such lengths? Simply, to make sure your food is safe.

The threat of bacteria entering into our food is at an all-time high. New bacteria such as *Eschericia coli* and *Vibrio vulnificus* have alarmed many food handlers, and have caused an increasing number of food poisoning deaths for the last five years. As a result, food processors are adopting rigorous standards of cleanliness. Food scientists are helping. Many propose radical alternatives to common food treatment, such as some of the examples described above. While the new techniques are costly, they are not as costly as the potential lawsuits, bad publicity, and human loss that one outbreak could cause.

The real cost to this new technology may not be in dollars, but in overall taste. Scientists admit that tastes may vary in certain foods depending on their processing treatment. As a layman, it seems that placing an oyster under 90,000 pounds of pressure would have some effect on the taste. I just hope that when the gamma rays remove any bacteria, they'll leave me with the wonderful joy of eating a delicious burger.

21. The author's main purpose in writing this passage is to

(A) demonstrate his love for hamburgers

(B) explain why some food processing techniques will change in the future

(C) perform a cost analysis of a food outbreak

(D) demonstrate recent scientific advancements

(E) predict popular foods in the twenty-first century

22. Which of the following best defines the word "layman" as it is used in the passage?

(A) Non-scientist

(B) Expert

(C) Private citizen

(D) Clergyman

(E) Carpenter

23. Which of the following best describes the author's attitude towards the new food processing techniques?

(A) Amazed

(B) Concerned

(C) Angry

(D) Frustrated

(E) Optimistic

24. Whenever a major train accident occurs, there is a dramatic increase in the number of train mishaps reported in the media, a phenomenon that may last for as long as a few months after the accident. Railroad officials assert that the publicity given to the horror of major train accidents focuses media attention on the train industry, and that the increase in the number of reported accidents is caused by an in increase in the number of news sources covering train accidents, not by an increase in the number of accidents.

Which of the following, if true, would seriously weaken the assertion of the train officials?

(A) The publicity surrounding train accidents is largely limited to the country in which the crash occurred.

(B) Train accidents tend to occur far more often during certain peak travel months.

(C) News organizations have no guidelines to help them determine how severe an accident must be for it to receive coverage.

(D) Accidents receive coverage by news sources only when the news sources find it advantageous to do so.

(E) Studies by regulators show that the number of train accidents remains relatively constant from month to month.

GO ON TO THE NEXT PAGE

Questions 25–26

High definition television, or HDTV, is finally available to consumers, approximately ten years after most companies promised the systems. Consumers love HDTV. More than 10,000 people inquired about HDTV at a local store on the first day that it became available. The appeal of HDTV is the clearer picture that the signal produces, which holds approximately three times as many horizontal and vertical lines as a standard television, resulting in a picture that rivals movie screens.

Despite these benefits, consumers who purchase these sets now may be disappointed with the results. There are very few digitally produced programs on television, and the number of these programs is unlikely to increase in the near future. The major networks plan to offer only five hours of digital programming per week next year, and only in the top ten major markets. It will not be until 2006 that more than 75 percent of network television will broadcast in digital form. Further, cable companies are not under any regulation to switch to carrying digital programming. Because two-thirds of Americans receive their television through cable, the delay may be even longer.

25. Which statement best describes the main point of the passage?

(A) Current HDTV sets are much larger than most standard televisions.

(B) The arrival of HDTV is much later than expected.

(C) The cable television industry is thriving.

(D) HDTV provides a clearer resolution picture.

(E) HDTV is available, although there is not much programming currently available.

26. Which of the following best describes the word "major" in the seventh sentence of the passage?

(A) Officer

(B) Large

(C) Subject

(D) Legal

(E) Important

Questions 27–29

In recent years, Americans have gotten the message—eat more vegetables! However, we're still not eating enough of the leafy green vegetables, such as spinach, broccoli, and kale, which do the most to promote good health. Currently, half of all the vegetable servings we consume are potatoes, and half of those are French fries.

Research reported from the Nurses' Health Study confirms the benefits of leafy greens. Researchers determined that women who consumed at least 400 micrograms of folic acid daily in either leafy green vegetables or multivitamin pills reduced their risk of colon cancer as much as 75 percent over 15 years. Remember not to simply substitute vitamins for vegetables, because there are thousands of healthy compounds present in vegetables that cannot be duplicated in a pill.

27. What is the main point of the passage?

(A) Multivitamin pills contain folic acid, as do leafy green vegetables.

(B) Recent studies confirm that leafy green vegetables help to promote good health.

(C) Eating more vegetables can reduce the risk of colon cancer.

(D) Important research was presented at the Nurses' Health Study.

(E) Almost half of the vegetables consumed by Americans are potatoes.

GO ON TO THE NEXT PAGE

28. The author argues that vitamins may not be an ideal replacement for leafy vegetables because

(A) increasing dependence on multivitamins can lead to poor nutritional habits

(B) multivitamins are not proven to fight against colon cancer

(C) folic acid is not contained in multivitamins

(D) a vitamin supplement may not replace the thousands of compounds found in leafy green vegetables

(E) caloric intake may decrease sharply

29. Which of the following changes would the author most likely wish to see in the way Americans consume vegetables?

(A) A lower overall consumption in vegetables

(B) An increase in the number of potatoes consumed

(C) An overall increase in the number of leafy green vegetables consumed

(D) A switch from leafy green vegetables to carrots

(E) More spinach and less kale

Questions 30–31

Recent findings from paleontologists have sparked great debate over whether birds evolved from dinosaurs. Two new artifacts of small dinosaurs have been found, each of which was clearly covered with feathers. This has led many in the scientific community to believe the increasingly popular theory that birds are descended directly from dinosaurs. Some have suggested that even the mighty velociraptor may have been covered with its own feathers. If the dinosaur-bird connection was persuasive before, it is now almost certain.

With any new discovery come skeptics and this recent finding is no exception. Even these startling discoveries do not impress some scientists. These scientists contend that both birds and dinosaurs evolved from the same older common ancestor. They assert that any similarities between birds and dinosaurs are due to the common parentage, not due to a direct evolutionary relationship.

30. What is the author's attitude toward the belief that birds are descended directly from dinosaurs?

(A) Skeptical support

(B) Unwavering conviction

(C) Indifference

(D) Confident support

(E) Utter disbelief

31. Which of the following best summarizes the passage?

(A) Whenever a new anthropological study is done, it will be subject to controversy and debate.

(B) The velociraptor was covered with feathers.

(C) New evidence lends greater weight to the theory that birds are descended from dinosaurs.

(D) Critics of recent studies contend common parentage links birds and dinosaurs.

(E) Evolutionary relationships are difficult to define with certainty.

GO ON TO THE NEXT PAGE

Questions 32–33

Despite years of publicity about the problem, the percentage of college students who binge-drink, that is, consume five or more drinks in one sitting, has declined only to 43 percent from 44 percent. Further, half of all students who binge-drink do so regularly—at least three times within a two-week period. Finally, 33 percent more students admit that they drink simply to be intoxicated. Dangerous drinking is at its worst in fraternities and sororities, where four out of five members acknowledge that they binge.

Public pressure had shown some previous influence regarding students' drinking habits. A University of Michigan researcher says the percentage of drinkers who binged dropped through the late 1980s and early 1990s, largely because of the widespread publicity about the dangers of drinking and driving.

32. Which of the following sentences, if inserted as the final sentence of the passage, would complete the passage?

(A) Currently, there seems to be no way of stopping binge-drinking.

(B) Schools should consider using the same messages used in the 1980s in order to curb binge-drinking.

(C) Those messages are unfortunately not being given to college students today.

(D) University officials should evaluate how to use public pressure more effectively to help curb the current binge-drinking problem.

(E) If schools first reduce the number of fraternity students who binge-drink, the rest of the campus will follow.

33. Which of the following statements, if true, would weaken the claim that publicity efforts helped to curb binge drinking in the late 1980s?

(A) Drunk driving convictions decreased 12 percent over that same time period.

(B) Students did not watch as much television as other groups, decreasing the number of times they heard those ads.

(C) New state laws for drunk driving became much more severe—one conviction went from a suspended license to three years in jail.

(D) Binge-drinking was listed as a "favorite activity" by many college students.

(E) Membership in a designated driver program increased 500 percent during the late 1980s at the University of Michigan.

Questions 34–37

The United States is currently home to an unprecedented 4,000 non-native plant species and 2,300 alien animal species. These plants and animals arrive by air and by sea from other continents, often in the bilge water of tankers and as stowaways on aircraft. Previously, very little was done to stop this transport of alien plants and animals. But now, aliens are so out of control that they are threatening the very existence of America's native species. Of the 1,900 imperiled American species, 49 percent are endangered by aliens. These alien species are the leading threat to native populations, with habitat destruction a distant second. In Hawaii, more than 95 percent of the 282 imperiled species of plants and birds are threatened by aliens.

In general, a plant or animal is kept in check by species that compete with it, eat it, or sicken it. On new grounds, though, aliens often have no such constraints. Many foreign creatures have flourished in delicate ecosystems. Our environment cannot quickly adapt to the presence of a new plant species.

GO ON TO THE NEXT PAGE

A crucial preventative measure is to outlaw the release of ballast water in ports. Some ports, like the port in San Francisco Bay, are populated by almost 99 percent alien species. Yet, limiting the inclusion of alien species will not be easy. Many new species enter undetected. Further, some alien species provide great help to our environment. America's economy thrives on many immigrants—soybeans, wheat, cotton, rye, and fruiting trees, all originated on other continents. Without any data or observations, it is difficult to predict if an alien species will be beneficial or harmful to our environment.

34. Which of the following is the best summary of the passage?

(A) The United States is home to more than 6,000 alien plant and animal species.

(B) It is difficult to predict the effects of an alien species in our environment.

(C) Alien animals and plants can help our environment.

(D) Certain parts of the United States are upset at the number of alien plants and animals in our environment.

(E) Alien species provide a number of problems to our ecosystems, which do not have easy solutions.

35. The author specifically mentions the state of Hawaii in the passage because it has

(A) benefited the most from alien species

(B) been greatly hurt by alien species

(C) been largely unharmed by alien plants or animals

(D) new laws outlining the entry of alien species

(E) a port that contains 99 percent alien species

36. Why does the author suggest outlawing the release of ballast water in ports?

(A) Ballast water pollutes the ocean.

(B) Ballast filters are costly to port operators.

(C) Alien species do more harm in the water than on land.

(D) The San Francisco port does not want any more alien species.

(E) Alien species often enter our environment through ballast water.

37. Why do scientists fear aliens entering our ecosystems?

(A) Alien species will always harm our ecosystem.

(B) Alien species have the potential to disrupt our ecosystems, endangering species unique to our country.

(C) The cost of damage done by aliens is in the billions of dollars per year.

(D) Our ecosystems would always work better without alien species.

(E) Alien species multiply much faster in new environments.

GO ON TO THE NEXT PAGE

Questions 38–40

Insulin is a critical hormone that allows individuals to absorb simple sugars (like glucose and fructose) from their food as it is digested. Most individuals produce the right amount of insulin. In fact, most individuals are not aware of the presence of insulin in the bloodstream.

Recently, nutritionists have discovered that foods known as complex carbohydrates—potatoes, carrots, and pasta among them—break down into simple sugars. Sometimes, this breakdown into sugars occurs so rapidly that the sugars may trigger a strong insulin response. This can be a problem, because a high level of insulin will inhibit the breakdown of fatty deposits. Therefore, eating too many carbohydrates leads to too much insulin, which in turn promotes the accumulation of fat. If you want to watch your weight, be sure to watch the number of complex carbohydrates you consume.

38. Which of the following statements, if true, would weaken the argument in the author's last sentence?

(A) Certain foods, like whole grains and cereals, can counteract the tendency of other complex carbohydrates to raise insulin levels.

(B) Weight gain can be countered by more exercise.

(C) Stress is also a factor in the body's ability to break down fatty deposits.

(D) Complex carbohydrates such as carrots do not contain many calories.

(E) A combination of proper diet and sleep can decrease insulin levels in the body.

39. What is the best definition for the author's use of the word "trigger" in the second paragraph?

(A) Encourage

(B) Decrease

(C) Inspire

(D) Influence

(E) Stimulate

40. According to the passage, high levels of insulin may promote weight gain by

(A) decreasing the heart rate

(B) inhibiting the ability to break down fatty deposits

(C) diminishing the health benefit of foods like carrots and pasta

(D) combining with complex carbohydrates, which then become difficult to break down

(E) slowing the transport of nutrients in the bloodstream

STOP

The Princeton Review

Diagnostic Test Form

Completely darken bubbles with a No. 2 pencil. If you make a mistake, be sure to erase mark completely. Erase all stray marks.

1. YOUR NAME: ______________________________ (Print) Last First M.I.

SIGNATURE: ______________________________ DATE: ___/___/___

HOME ADDRESS: ______________________________ (Print) Number and Street

______________________________ City State Zip E-MAIL: ______________________________

PHONE NO.: ______________ (Print) SCHOOL: ______________ CLASS OF: ______________

IMPORTANT: Please fill in these boxes exactly as shown on the back cover of your test book.

OpScan *i*NSIGHT™ forms by Pearson NCS EM-255325-1:654321
Printed in U.S.A.

2. TEST FORM

3. TEST CODE

0	0	0	0
1	1	1	1
2	2	2	2
3	3	3	3
4	4	4	4
5	5	5	5
6	6	6	6
7	7	7	7
8	8	8	8
9	9	9	9

4. PHONE NUMBER

0	0	0	0	0	0	0
1	1	1	1	1	1	1
2	2	2	2	2	2	2
3	3	3	3	3	3	3
4	4	4	4	4	4	4
5	5	5	5	5	5	5
6	6	6	6	6	6	6
7	7	7	7	7	7	7
8	8	8	8	8	8	8
9	9	9	9	9	9	9

5. YOUR NAME

First 4 letters of last name				FIRST INIT	MID INIT
A	A	A	A	A	A
B	B	B	B	B	B
C	C	C	C	C	C
D	D	D	D	D	D
E	E	E	E	E	E
F	F	F	F	F	F
G	G	G	G	G	G
H	H	H	H	H	H
I	I	I	I	I	I
J	J	J	J	J	J
K	K	K	K	K	K
L	L	L	L	L	L
M	M	M	M	M	M
N	N	N	N	N	N
O	O	O	O	O	O
P	P	P	P	P	P
Q	Q	Q	Q	Q	Q
R	R	R	R	R	R
S	S	S	S	S	S
T	T	T	T	T	T
U	U	U	U	U	U
V	V	V	V	V	V
W	W	W	W	W	W
X	X	X	X	X	X
Y	Y	Y	Y	Y	Y
Z	Z	Z	Z	Z	Z

6. DATE OF BIRTH

MONTH	DAY		YEAR	
JAN				
FEB				
MAR	0	0	0	0
APR	1	1	1	1
MAY	2	2	2	2
JUN	3	3	3	3
JUL		4	4	4
AUG		5	5	5
SEP		6	6	6
OCT		7	7	7
NOV		8	8	8
DEC		9	9	9

7. SEX

- MALE
- FEMALE

8. OTHER

1 A B C D E
2 A B C D E
3 A B C D E

Begin with number 1 for each new section of the test. Leave blank any extra answer spaces.

SECTION 1

1	A B C D E		26	A B C D E		51	A B C D E		76	A B C D E
2	A B C D E		27	A B C D E		52	A B C D E		77	A B C D E
3	A B C D E		28	A B C D E		53	A B C D E		78	A B C D E
4	A B C D E		29	A B C D E		54	A B C D E		79	A B C D E
5	A B C D E		30	A B C D E		55	A B C D E		80	A B C D E
6	A B C D E		31	A B C D E		56	A B C D E		81	A B C D E
7	A B C D E		32	A B C D E		57	A B C D E		82	A B C D E
8	A B C D E		33	A B C D E		58	A B C D E		83	A B C D E
9	A B C D E		34	A B C D E		59	A B C D E		84	A B C D E
10	A B C D E		35	A B C D E		60	A B C D E		85	A B C D E
11	A B C D E		36	A B C D E		61	A B C D E		86	A B C D E
12	A B C D E		37	A B C D E		62	A B C D E		87	A B C D E
13	A B C D E		38	A B C D E		63	A B C D E		88	A B C D E
14	A B C D E		39	A B C D E		64	A B C D E		89	A B C D E
15	A B C D E		40	A B C D E		65	A B C D E		90	A B C D E
16	A B C D E		41	A B C D E		66	A B C D E		91	A B C D E
17	A B C D E		42	A B C D E		67	A B C D E		92	A B C D E
18	A B C D E		43	A B C D E		68	A B C D E		93	A B C D E
19	A B C D E		44	A B C D E		69	A B C D E		94	A B C D E
20	A B C D E		45	A B C D E		70	A B C D E		95	A B C D E
21	A B C D E		46	A B C D E		71	A B C D E		96	A B C D E
22	A B C D E		47	A B C D E		72	A B C D E		97	A B C D E
23	A B C D E		48	A B C D E		73	A B C D E		98	A B C D E
24	A B C D E		49	A B C D E		74	A B C D E		99	A B C D E
25	A B C D E		50	A B C D E		75	A B C D E		100	A B C D E

7

Answers and Explanations for PPST: Reading Practice Test 2

PPST: READING PRACTICE TEST 2 ANSWER KEY

1. C
2. D
3. C
4. A
5. D
6. E
7. B
8. D
9. C
10. A
11. A
12. D
13. A
14. C
15. C
16. D
17. E
18. E
19. A
20. A
21. B
22. A
23. E
24. B
25. E
26. B
27. B
28. D
29. C
30. D
31. C
32. D
33. C
34. E
35. B
36. E
37. B
38. A
39. E
40. B

ANSWERS AND EXPLANATIONS FOR PPST: READING PRACTICE TEST 2

1. **C** The passage starts with a description of a problem involving power lines in the summertime. Later, the creation of a ceramic cable is presented as a possible solution.

2. **D** The second sentence mentions that the model can *predict behavior of oddly shaped particles as they flow through porous material.*

3. **C** The section is too brief for a thesis paper. There are not many opinions stated in the passage, which should allow you to eliminate answer choice (A). (D) and (E) are not appropriate forums for this passage.

4. **A** Students are using the same principles that Hubbert once employed to predict worldwide production. The passage references that Hubbert had innovative calculations and methodologies to predict oil production. Therefore, the passage refers to these techniques used by Hubbert.

5. **D** While the author may agree with answer choice (E), the primary point of the passage was to explain Hubbert's prior success, and the belief that world production may be nearing its peak.

6. **E** The second paragraph mentions that the theory of similar growth between consumption and discovery was not true, according to Hubbert. The author supports Hubbert and his theories, which therefore would lead the author to support answer choice (E). Note that the answer choice (D) may be true, but the harsh language makes it a difficult answer choice to select. *Will definitely delay* is an absolute statement that the passage does not support.

7. **B** Answer choice (A) is true, but it is stated directly in the passage. There is nothing in the passage that references answer choices (C), (D), and (E). The last sentence in the passage states that the band will not be as wealthy as if they were to continue to tour. Therefore, the assumption is that touring is profitable for the band.

8. **D** The passage addresses biotech-spawned fish, and the delays in allowing for this food to reach the marketplace.

9. **C** The second paragraph mentions that one reason genetically modified foods have not reached the dinner table is due to vigorous lobbying against the foods by traditional farmers, fearful for their livelihoods.

10. **A** The author states that marriage alone is not a guarantee of better health. Therefore, the author would not agree with the suggestion that all single men should rush to get married.

11. **A** While there are many meanings for the word *body,* in the passage the author uses it to convey the amount of medical research on the topic.

12. **D** While (A) is mentioned in the passage, the primary message is the creation of the polio vaccine. (B) is also mentioned, but is a secondary message of the passage. (C) and (E) are difficult to defend, as both misinterpret the author's words.

13. **A** Scientists were critical of Salk's decision to use an inactivated form of the virus, which was a departure from the traditional method of development—using a weakened form of a virus. Therefore, scientists believed that method was effective in creating a vaccine.

14. **C** The author profiles the achievements of Salk, and the tone seems to discredit the criticism from other scientists. Answer choices (B) and (D) are too harsh—the author never assumes their criticism was illegal, or part of a conspiracy to discredit Salk.

15. **C** The author argues that an MBA does not help individuals with career attainment. One example is in consulting firms, where the companies began to hire non-MBAs.

16. **D** The statistics profile the average female millionaire.

17. **E** The passage discusses both the rise in enrollment, and the benefits of etiquette courses.

18. **E** The example is used in the second paragraph to discuss how today's lessons differ from the curricula of prior generations' courses.

19. **A** The author, while not directly stating an opinion on etiquette courses, seems to support the idea of having children attend. She cites a psychologist who provides favorable comments about the value of such courses. The other answer choices all state negative opinions of these courses, which are not present in the style of the author's writing.

20. **A** In the first paragraph, we are told that enrollment has quadrupled over the last few years. Therefore, with the total number of children increasing in these courses, if we are to show that the popularity is not increasing, you have to demonstrate that there are more children in the area. Answer choice (A) does this. Essentially, the growth of children in the area has outpaced the growth of these enrollments.

21. **B** The passage tells us that new steps are being taken to ensure food safety because of the increasing threat of new diseases. Answer choice (A) is partial—this is trivial to the overall message. Answer choices (D) and (E) are too broad, and out of scope.

22. **A** The author uses sarcasm in this sentence, and uses the term to convey that he does not have a technical understanding of placing an oyster under 90,000 pounds of pressure, but he assumes that something must be happening.

23. **E** The author presents a playful tone within the passage. The author jokes about the taste of food, but never states that he is against the new techniques. Answer choices (B), (C), and (D) are all negative.

24. **B** This is one of the more challenging questions you will see on this section. First, we need to understand the argument of the railroad officials. They argue that there is in fact no increase in actual mishaps, just an increase in the number of news reports. Answer choices (C), (D), and (E) strengthen this claim. Answer choice (B) weakens the claim by implying that certain months are more likely to have accidents due to high volume of train rides.

25. **E** In the passage, the author praises the features of HDTV, but goes on to announce the programming challenges of HDTV. Answer choices (A), (B), and (D) are all true, but do not address the central theme. Answer choice (C) may be true, but is secondary to the main point of the passage.

26. **B** The author uses the word "major" to describe how the large networks will not increase their HDTV programming, thereby limiting the effectiveness of an HDTV set. The words "top ten" also given an indication that the use of the word "major" indicates a large amount.

27. **B** The passage discusses the importance of leafy green vegetables, and then describes a study that supports the author's claim.

28. **D** Multivitamins do contain folic acid that is contained in leafy green vegetables. However, leafy green vegetables contain many more beneficial compounds.

29. **C** In the first paragraph, the author is satisfied with the increase in the overall consumption of vegetables, but encourages us to eat more leafy green vegetables.

30. **D** The last line of the first paragraph states the author's opinion on the topic. The phrase *almost certain* makes answer choice (B) too extreme, while answer choice (A) is too wishy-washy. (D) finds a nice balance.

31. **C** The topic sentence of the first paragraph states similar information. Answer choices (B) and (D) are too specific, while answer choices (A) and (E) are too broad.

32. **D** The second paragraph states that public pressure has worked in the past. The sentence concludes the paragraph by tying it back to the original point—current efforts to curb binge drinking are not successful.

33. **C** The researcher claims that public pressure against drunk driving led to a decrease in binge-drinking incidents. In order to weaken this claim, you need to show that another factor helped to decrease binge-drinking incidents. Answer choice (C) does this—stiff law penalties could be a reason for the decline in binge drinking.

34. **E** The passage describes the negative effects of alien species in our environment, and explains the difficulty of finding solutions.

35. **B** Read a few lines above the word *Hawaii.* The author mentions the state to show an example of an ecosystem ravaged by alien species.

36. **E** The author proposes this solution as one way to curb the increasing number of alien species being introduced into our environment. Answer choice (C) is not stated in the passage.

37. **B** Again, not all alien species do harm to our ecosystem, so answer choices (A) and (D) are not always true. (C) is a true statement, but scientists are more likely concerned with the environmental impact than a financial impact. Answer choice (E) is not supported by the passage.

38. **A** The passage supports the claim that complex carbohydrates lead to increased weight gain. To weaken the argument, we need to show that it is possible to counteract rising insulin levels caused by complex carbohydrates. Answer choice (A) does this. Other answer choices may be true, but do not impact the author's warning about complex carbohydrates.

39. **E** The additional sugars in the body will stimulate a rush of insulin into the body. While answer choices (A), (C), and (D) are all possible definitions for the word *trigger*, this passage uses the word to covey a stimulation of sugars creating an insulin release.

40. **B** This statement is found directly in the passage, in the second paragraph.

8

PPST: Writing Practice Test 1

The Praxis Series Professional Assessments for Beginning Teachers

Test Name: Pre-Professional Skills Test

Writing

Time – 60 minutes

38 Multiple-Choice Questions

1 Essay

Section 1

Multiple-Choice Questions

Time – 30 minutes

Part A: Usage

23 Questions

(Suggested time – 10 minutes)

Directions: In each of the sentences below, four portions are underlined and lettered. Read each sentence and decide whether any of the underlined parts contains a grammatical construction, a word use, or an instance of incorrect or omitted punctuation or capitalization that would be inappropriate in carefully written English. If so, note the letter printed beneath the underlined portion and completely fill in the corresponding lettered space on the answer sheet with a heavy, dark mark so that you cannot see the letter.

If there are no errors in any of the underlined portions, fill in space E. *No sentence has more than one error.*

Remember, try to answer every question.

1. Today's athlete may feel such great pressure
   A (Today's) B (great)
   to succeed that they begin taking steroids at an
   C (to succeed) D (they begin)
   early age. No error
   E

2. The college newspaper will print those who win
   A (those who win)
   prizes for haiku, commentary, and humor;
   B (;)
   poetry, however, will not be accepted for
   C (will not) D (be accepted for)
   publication. No error
   E

3. Small galaxies have such scanty supplies of
   A (have)
   stars that they are extremely hard to spot.
   B (that) C (they are) D (to spot)
   No error
   E

4. Scientists in Iceland said they would kill 25
   A (they) B (would kill)
   Minke whales this year as part of a scientific
   study, less than originally planned. No error
   C (less) D (than) E

5. Most space experts consider viewing a total
   eclipse with the naked eye safe but stress that
   A (but stress that)
   partial eclipses, including partial eclipse phases
   before and after a total eclipse, observed with
   B (and after) C (observed with)
   certain safety precautions to prevent possibly
   D (to prevent)
   serious eye damage. No error
   E

6. The noise of him chewing his food so disturbed
   A (him) B (disturbed)
   the other students that he was asked to leave.
   C (students) D (was asked)
   No error
   E

7. Police can search a parked car for drugs, guns,
   A (can search) B (drugs, guns,
   or other evidence of a crime while arresting a
   or other evidence) C (while arresting)
   nearby driver or passengers. No error
   D (nearby) E

GO ON TO THE NEXT PAGE

8. To evaluate Internet stocks using
A
antiquated valuation models is like competing
B C
in the Tour de France with a mountain bike.
D
No error
E

9. The audio presentation include music, nar-
A
ration, expert descriptions and re-created
B C
eye-witness accounts of the circumstances and
C
events of World War I. No error
D E

10. Gran Roque is not only an island
with a village on it and it has a selection of
A B
small, brightly colored posadas on its sandy
streets, many of which offer both lodging and
C D
dining. No error
E

11. Because air bags had been proved to reduce
A B
the number of fatal accidents, they were made
C D
mandatory. No error
E

12. Assigned to handle both the academic and
A
emotional challenges from children,
B
counselors find themselves stretched by case-
C D
loads that average 477 students. No error
E

13. Tim scored 15 points and Susie scored 18
A
points, but they're team still lost by fewer than
B C D
8 points. No error
E

14. The government building, built more than 100
A
years ago, is located between the train station
B C
and the freeway. No error
D E

15. The woman who's purse I found on the trolley
A B
came to the lost-and-found window to claim it.
C D
No error
E

16. To impress a supervisor, one should dress ap-
A B
propriately, be prompt, and showing interest in
C D
the work. No error
E

17. The influence of baseball on American life
A
during the Great Depression years were
B C
profound. No error
D E

18. In the four years since the company stock
was listed on NASDAQ, no more than ten
A B
executives has sold insider shares in any one
C D
quarter. No error
E

19. The list of those that can attend next week's
A B
session includes Phil, Mark, and I. No error
C D E

20. Frank is fortunate in that he has seen his
A B
income rise annually each year for the last five
C D
years. No error
E

GO ON TO THE NEXT PAGE

21. Running and leaping while fetching his ball, Jolene was pleased to see her dog so excited on this sunny Sunday afternoon. No error

(A) while (B) Jolene (C) was pleased to see (D) on this (E) No error

22. Because of a rash of elbow injuries among high school baseball players, anxious parents often seek out experimental procedures. No error

(A) Because of (B) among (C) often (D) seek out (E) No error

23. The Colorado River, the largest river in the United States west of the mississippi, contains almost one million cubic miles of water. No error

(A) The Colorado River (B) west (C) mississippi (D) almost (E) No error

GO ON TO THE NEXT PAGE

Part B: Sentence Correction

15 Questions

(Suggested time – 20 minutes)

Directions: In each of the following sentences, some part of the sentence is underlined. Beneath each sentence you will find five ways of writing the underlined part. The first of these repeats the original, but the other four are all different. If you think the original sentence is better than any of the suggested changes, you should choose answer (A); otherwise you should mark one of the other choices. Select the best answer and completely fill in the corresponding lettered space on the answer sheet with a heavy, dark mark so that you cannot see the letter.

This is a test of correctness and effectiveness of expression. In choosing answers, follow the requirements of standard written English; that is, pay attention to acceptable usage in grammar, diction (choice of words), sentence construction, and punctuation. Choose the answer that expresses most effectively what is presented in the original sentence; this answer should be clear and exact, without awkwardness, ambiguity, or redundancy.

Remember, try to answer every question.

24. Carbon-14 dating reveals that the fossils discovered in Africa are nearly 2,000 years as old as any of their supposed predecessors.

(A) as old as any of their supposed
(B) older than any of their supposed
(C) as old as their supposed
(D) older than any of their supposedly
(E) as old as their supposedly

25. The Center for Gun Policy revealed that half of all American men keep a gun in the house, and that on any given day, one out of every thirty adults carry a handgun away from home.

(A) one out of every thirty adults carry
(B) every one out of thirty adults carry
(C) out of every thirty adults, one carries
(D) one adult in thirty carries
(E) each adult among the thirty carries

26. The price of a flat of strawberries has fallen so drastically that some farmers have found it to be more cost-effective to destroy their crops as to make the effort to get them to market.

(A) have found it to be more cost-effective to destroy their crops as to make
(B) found that the destruction of their crops is more cost-effective than making
(C) find the destruction of their crops as more cost-effective than making
(D) find it more cost-effective to destroy their crops than to make
(E) are finding that the destruction of their crops is more cost-effective than the making of

27. Scientists have trained their telescopes on Arp 229, a pair of merging galaxies, and saw stars exploding in numbers far greater than expected.

(A) and saw stars exploding in numbers far greater than expected
(B) and saw stars exploding in numbers far greater than they were expecting
(C) and saw stars exploding in far greater numbers than expected
(D) and seen stars exploding in far greater numbers than being expected
(E) and have seen stars exploding in far greater numbers than expected

28. Just three years ago, the lute, a stringed instrument invented centuries ago, has experienced a rapid rise in popularity due to renewed interest in acoustic music.

(A) has experienced a rapid rise in popularity
(B) experienced a rapid rise in popularity
(C) has experienced what was a rapid rise in popularity
(D) the popularity of which experienced a rapid rise
(E) had experienced a rapid rise in popularity

GO ON TO THE NEXT PAGE

29. Any political figure <u>who is intending on running</u> for president will not succeed without a large quantity of campaign money contributed by wealthy benefactors.

(A) who is intending on running
(B) who has the intention of running
(C) who is intent to run
(D) intending on running
(E) intent on running

30. Threatened by encroaching civilization and hunted by poachers, <u>the bamboo-devouring giant panda has been long studied by naturalists, concentrating</u> on the panda's limited ability to breed in captivity.

(A) the bamboo-devouring giant panda has been long studied by naturalists, concentrating
(B) the bamboo-devouring giant panda has been long studied by naturalists who concentrate
(C) naturalists have long studied the bamboo-devouring giant panda and concentrated
(D) naturalists have long studied the bamboo-devouring giant panda, concentrating
(E) naturalists have long studied the bamboo-devouring giant panda; they concentrated

31. Universities have begun to focus more and more on recommendations from teachers and personal statements from students, <u>in part that their student body should acquire diversity</u> and partly because recommendations provide more appraisals of students' abilities.

(A) in part that their student body should acquire diversity
(B) in part for the acquisition of diversity in their student body
(C) partly because of their student body acquiring diversity
(D) partly because diversity should be acquired by their student body
(E) partly to acquire diversity in their student body

32. Invented by Dr. James Naismith in the late 1800s, <u>the importance of basketball is felt worldwide</u>.

(A) the importance of basketball is felt worldwide
(B) the importance of basketball had been felt around the world
(C) basketball is as important as the world
(D) basketball's importance has been felt worldwide
(E) basketball is important worldwide

33. Any real estate professional will tell you that the value of a parcel of land is most directly affected by <u>the extent of its development</u> and how close it is to a major business center.

(A) the extent of its development
(B) whether it has been developed extensively
(C) how extensively it has developed
(D) how extensively it has been developed
(E) the extent to which it has been developed

34. <u>As</u> many other newer American cities, Dallas doubled in size in only its first ten years of existence.

(A) As
(B) As have
(C) Like
(D) Just like
(E) As with

GO ON TO THE NEXT PAGE

35. Both Penn and Teller achieved success in his career before they collaborated at The Magic Castle in 1979.

(A) success in his career before they collaborated at The Magic Castle in 1979

(B) success in his career before he collaborated at The Magic Castle in 1979

(C) success in their careers before they collaborated at The Magic Castle in 1979

(D) succeeded in careers before he collaborated at The Magic Castle in 1979

(E) success in his career before collaborating at The Magic Castle in 1979

36. The government's attempts to store chemical weapons in a rural community in Oregon, a state with a decidedly environmentalist history, have encountered massive political resistance from Oregon's state legislature.

(A) have encountered massive political resistance

(B) has encountered massive resistance politically

(C) have politically encountered massive resistance

(D) has encountered massive political resistance

(E) had encountered politically massive resistance

37. The size of Texas is somewhat like California.

(A) like California

(B) similar to California

(C) as California

(D) like California's

(E) so as to be like California's

38. Her artwork is not only colorful, but is innovative.

(A) but is innovative

(B) but also innovative

(C) and is innovative

(D) but is said to be innovative

(E) but innovative

STOP

Section 2

Essay

Time – 30 minutes

Directions: You will have 30 minutes to plan and write an essay on the topic presented on page 141.

Read the topic carefully. You will probably find it best to spend a little time considering the topic and organizing your thoughts before you begin writing. DO NOT WRITE ON A TOPIC OTHER THAN THE ONE SPECIFIED. An essay on a topic of your own choice will not be accepted. In order for your test to be scored, your response must be in English.

The essay question is included in this test to give you an opportunity to demonstrate how well you can write. You should, therefore, take care to write clearly and effectively, using specific examples where appropriate. Remember that how well you write is much more important than how much you write, but to cover the topic adequately, you will probably need to write more than a paragraph.

Your essay will be scored on the basis of its total quality—i.e., holistically. Each essay score is the sum of points (0–6) given by two readers. When your total writing score is computed, your essay score will be combined with your score for the multiple-choice section of the test.

You are to write your essay on the answer sheet; you will receive no other paper on which to write. Please write neatly and legibly. To be certain you have enough space on the answer sheet for your entire essay, please do NOT skip lines, do NOT write in excessively large letters, and do NOT leave wide margins. You may use the bottom of page 141 for any notes you may wish to make before you begin writing.

GO ON TO THE NEXT PAGE

Section 2

Essay

Time – 30 minutes

Read the opinion stated below:

"To address the problem of chronic truancy, schools should fine the parents of students who are frequently absent from school. "

Discuss the extent to which you agree or disagree with this opinion. Support your position with specific reasons and examples from your own experience, observations, or reading.

The space below is for your NOTES. Write your essay in the space provided on the answer sheet.

DO NOT TURN BACK TO SECTIONS 1 AND 2 OF THIS TEST.

Diagnostic Test Form

Completely darken bubbles with a No. 2 pencil. If you make a mistake, be sure to erase mark completely. Erase all stray marks.

1. YOUR NAME: (Print) ______ Last ______ First ______ M.I.

SIGNATURE: ______ **DATE:** ___/___/___

HOME ADDRESS: (Print) ______ Number and Street

______ City ______ State ______ Zip **E-MAIL:** ______

PHONE NO.: (Print) ______ **SCHOOL:** ______ **CLASS OF:** ______

IMPORTANT: Please fill in these boxes exactly as shown on the back cover of your test book.

OpScan *i*NSIGHT™ forms by Pearson NCS EM-255325-1:654321
Printed in U.S.A.

2. TEST FORM

3. TEST CODE (4 columns: 0 1 2 3 4 5 6 7 8 9)

4. PHONE NUMBER (7 columns: 0 1 2 3 4 5 6 7 8 9)

5. YOUR NAME

First 4 letters of last name | FIRST INIT | MID INIT

(6 columns: A B C D E F G H I J K L M N O P Q R S T U V W X Y Z)

6. DATE OF BIRTH

MONTH	DAY		YEAR	
JAN				
FEB				
MAR	0	0	0	0
APR	1	1	1	1
MAY	2	2	2	2
JUN	3	3	3	3
JUL		4	4	4
AUG		5	5	5
SEP		6	6	6
OCT		7	7	7
NOV		8	8	8
DEC		9	9	9

7. SEX

- MALE
- FEMALE

8. OTHER

1 A B C D E
2 A B C D E
3 A B C D E

Begin with number 1 for each new section of the test. Leave blank any extra answer spaces.

SECTION 1

1–100: A B C D E (each numbered item, 1 through 100)

9

Answers and Explanations for PPST: Writing Practice Test 1

PPST: WRITING PRACTICE TEST 1 ANSWER KEY

1. D
2. A
3. C
4. C
5. C
6. A
7. E
8. A
9. A
10. B
11. D
12. B
13. B
14. E
15. A
16. D
17. C
18. C
19. D
20. C
21. B
22. E
23. C
24. B
25. D
26. D
27. E
28. B
29. E
30. B
31. E
32. E
33. D
34. C
35. C
36. A
37. D
38. B

ANSWERS AND EXPLANATIONS FOR PPST: WRITING PRACTICE TEST 1

1. **D** The subject of the sentence is athlete, which is singular. The pronoun *they* is not in agreement with the subject.
2. **A** The pronoun *those* likely refers to the individuals that submit winning publications. The newspaper will print their work, and will not print the individuals.
3. **C** Galaxies is a plural subject and the verb tense is in agreement. All verbs are in the present tense, and the use of the infinitive in (D) is fine. However, the pronoun *they* is ambiguous; it is not clear what the pronoun refers to: galaxies or stars.
4. **C** The noun is countable (in this case, 25 Minke whales), so the word *fewer* should be used instead of *less*.
5. **C** The subject of the subordinate clause, *partial eclipses*, needs to be completed by a verb. *Partial eclipses* does not agree with *observed*. (A) uses the correct verb tense, and (D) properly uses a present infinitive. There are no problems with answer choice (B). You need to explain why observed isn't enough for the verb.
6. **A** The noise is a result of *his* chewing, not of him. The use of *him* to refer to the chewing noise is not correct.
7. **E** All verb tenses align to the present tense, the sentence follows parallel construction in (B), and the adverb is used properly.
8. **A** *Competing* is part of the non-underlined portion of the sentence. In order to keep parallel construction, the first verb should be written as *Evaluating*.
9. **A** *Audio presentation* is a singular noun, so the verb should be *includes*.
10. **B** There is an idiomatic phase present in this question, *not only...but also..* (B) should include the phrase *but also* instead of *and*.
11. **D** Subject and verb are in agreement. In answer choice (C), *number* is correctly used, because there can be a specific count; in this case, the number of fatal accidents. The pronoun *they* is ambiguous; it is unclear whether the pronouns refers to the air bags or the number of accidents.
12. **B** The children face both academic and emotional challenges. *From* is not the correct preposition, as it implies that children place these pressures on to the counselors.
13. **B** The incorrect word is used here. It should be *their*, which indicates possession, instead of *they're*, which is a contraction for *they are*.
14. **E** There is subject-verb agreement (both are singular), and the idiomatic phrase *between...and* is formed properly.
15. **A** *Whose* is the correct pronoun to describe the woman. The contraction *who's* is used to indicate "who is."
16. **D** This is a question of parallel construction. The non-underlined portion of the sequence is in the present verb tense (*dress*). *And showing* does not meet the same construction; instead, the correct phrase should be written as *and show*.
17. **C** The subject of the sentence is singular (*influence*), which should take the singular verb tense (*was*).

18. **C** The subject of this clause is plural—*ten executives*. This requires a plural verb, and *has sold* is in the singular voice. The correct verb is *have sold.*

19. **D** The correct pronoun should be *me*, and not *I*. *I* is used as a subject, but in this example, it is used as the object of the sentence.

20. **C** This is a redundant phrase question, and the phrase *annually each year* is redundant. *Annually* would have been sufficient to complete the sentence.

21. **B** This is a typical misplaced modifier sentence. The dog was running and leaping while fetching his ball, not Jolene!

22. **E** The verbs are in the present tense. *Because of* is a correct idiomatic phrase.

23. **C** *Mississippi* refers to the river, which as a proper noun should be capitalized.

24. **B** First, segment the answer choices using *supposed* and *supposedly*. The word serves as an adjective to predecessors, and is best written as *supposed*. Thus, eliminate answer choices (D) and (E). The statement conveys that the new fossils are older than the prior fossils. The phrase *as old as* is used to compare terms. Therefore, (A) and (C) can be eliminated.

25. **D** The subject of this sentence is *one*, which indicates that the verb tense must be *carries*. Eliminate answer choices (A) and (B). (D) does not convey the correct meaning—it states that all 30 adults carry a handgun. (C) is too specific, whereas the correct answer gives a more general ratio of 1:30.

26. **D** First, the word *more* should be paired with *than*, so you can eliminate answer choice (A). (B) does not contain verb tense agreement. (C) is a violation of parallelism (*destruction* and *making*), while (E) is verbose.

27. **E** This is an example of verb tense and parallelism. The scientists *have trained...* and *have seen...*, therefore all other answer choices can be eliminated.

28. **B** The time reference is three years ago, so the verb tense must be in the past tense. (A), (C), and (E) can be eliminated. (D) is in error, as the subject *lute* needs a verb to complete the sentence.

29. **E** This is an example of the idiomatic phrase *intent...on*. The use of *who* in (A), (B), and (C) is allowed, but (E) is better because the word is not necessary to convey the meaning of the sentence.

30. **B** The subject of the sentence is the panda, so (C), (D), and (E), can be eliminated. Who is doing the concentrating? Not the pandas (except maybe on their food)! Therefore, eliminate answer choice (A).

31. **E** For the sake of parallelism, eliminate answer choices (A) and (B). The verb tense of the second phrase is present (*provide*). Of the remaining answer choices, only (E) uses the present tense.

32. **E** Dr. Naismith invented basketball, and this is the subject of sentence. Thus, answer choices (A), (B), and (D) can be eliminated. (C) distorts the meaning of the sentence, leaving (E) as the only remaining answer choice.

33. **D** This is a parallelism example. Notice the use of *how* in the non-underlined potion of the sentence. This leaves only (C) and (D) as possible answer choices. The remaining issue is verb tense. The parcel of land has not developed; instead it has been developed by others. Eliminate answer choice (C).

34. **C** Dallas is like other cities, which means that (C) is sufficient. *As* is used to indicate that processes are the same, which is not correct in this context.

35. **C** The use of *and* in the subject makes the subject plural. Therefore, the pronoun must refer to both Penn and Teller (*their*). Eliminate answer choices (A), (B), and (E). (D) changes success to a verb, succeeded, which is incorrect.

36. **A** The subject of the sentence is *attempts*, which indicates that the verb must be plural tense. Therefore, eliminate answer choices (B) and (D). (E) uses the past tense incorrectly, while (C) uses a misplaced adjective.

37. **D** This is a parallel construction question. Texas's size is somewhat like California's (size). Answer choices (A), (B), and (C) incorrectly compare the area of Texas to the state of California instead of the size of California. Answer choice (E) is verbose.

38. **B** This sentence contains a common idiomatic phrase: *not only...but also*.

Essay

"To address the problem of chronic truancy, schools should fine the parents of students who are frequently absent from school."

Sample Essay #1: Overall Score = 6 (High Degree of Competence)

There is no doubt that chronic truancy and tardiness have an impact on the success of students in school. It is very difficult for students to stay on top of school curricula if they miss any significant time. I fully support initiatives designed to reduce the amount of chronic truancy within schools. However, I strongly disagree that the proper way to address this problem is through financial measures. Fining parents when their children are absent from school can have unintended negative consequences, and will create an adversarial relationship between parents and schools; two parties that increasingly need to work in collaboration to further the development of children.

The proposal to charge parents for their child's truancy assumes that financial penalties will correct the problem. However, I believe that the problem of truancy stems from underlying reasons that cannot easily be fixed through the addition of financial pressure. For example, if a child is frequently sick, and therefore misses significant time in school recovering at home, how will a fine help the child or family? If anything, the additional fine could keep the child out of school longer, if such a fine were to cause low-income families not to spend money on healthcare treatment. On the other hand, some families are so wealthy that a financial charge would not likely drive any behavioral changes. What's an extra $50 to someone that has millions?

In addition to sickness, another reason for chronic truancy is the belief from certain parents that a child's schedule should revolve around the parent's schedule, and not the school schedule. My neighbors frequently remove their children from school for two weeks per year to take a family vacation. This vacation takes place right in the middle of the school year, as the father cannot take any time off during the summer. I don't think that a fine would change their behavior. Instead, the parents would need to understand how such actions are putting their children at an educational disadvantage.

In summary, truancy is a serious problem that deserves attention from schools and parents. There are many possible reasons for chronic truancy, and in order to truly serve the child, teachers, and parents must work together to identify the unique challenges and potential solutions for each specific child. Additional financial pressure could further complicate matters, causing more harm than good.

Sample Essay #2: Overall Score = 3 (Some Competence)

Finally, someone has a great idea. If parents are ever going to learn the importance of sending their kids to school, they'll understand when they have to pay for it. Money talks, and this is no exception.

The average student misses 12 days per year. Let's say that whenever a child misses more than 10 days per year, the parents are fined $100. The money generated will go to schools that are already lacking in budgets. This way, parents will always think twice about having their kids absent for a day when they really don't need to. If a child has missed like seven days, and their parents want to travel with them, they'll think about it twice because if they take that time off then there is no room for sick days that may occur during the remainder of the year. So there you go, a policy that has a definite impact.

My only recommendation to make a strong impact would be to charge parents different amounts based on how much money they make each year. You want each parent to feel the impact on their truant child, but you don't want to penalize the poor, or give breaks to those that are rich.

Sample Essay #3: Overall Score = 1 (Fundamental Deficiencies)

I remember when I was in school, and it really bothered me when other kids were not there and I was told by my mom that I had to be. That type of double-standard really bothers me, how some people get to do something different from others for no epparant reason. That's why when I have kids I'm not sure how I'm gonna answer them when they ask me for the day off of school cause there friends are taking the day off as well. You want to be a good parent, but it is hard to say things like your parents did to you, when you vowed that you would always be different than they were.

10

PPST: Writing Practice Test 2

The Praxis Series Professional Assessments for Beginning Teachers

Test Name: Pre-Professional Skills Test

Writing

Time–60 minutes

38 Multiple-Choice Questions

1 Essay

Section 1

Multiple-Choice Questions

Time – 30 minutes

Part A: Usage

23 Questions

(Suggested time – 10 minutes)

Directions: In each of the sentences below, four portions are underlined and lettered. Read each sentence and decide whether any of the underlined parts contains a grammatical construction, a word use, or an instance of incorrect or omitted punctuation or capitalization that would be inappropriate in carefully written English. If so, note the letter printed beneath the underlined portion and completely fill in the corresponding lettered space on the answer sheet with a heavy, dark mark so that you cannot see the letter.

If there are no errors in any of the underlined portions, fill in space E. *No sentence has more than one error.*

Remember, try to answer every question.

1. Of the five players on the court, Steven has
   A B
   the lower free throw percentage. No error
   C D E

2. Whom do you think should be promoted to
   A B
   run the new expansion team in Texas?
   C D
   No error
   E

3. Though no one believed it, Paula and Tim are
   A B
   as old as we. No error
   C D E

4. Neither Cindy nor Sue believe that Grady
   A B
   would be the last to arrive. No error
   C D E

5. Several people thought the book's author is
   A B
   him, but it is I. No error
   C D E

6. Tax cuts and a new unemployment program
   A
   helps to improve the state of the economy.
   B C D
   No error
   E

7. Lyndon, together with his five team members,
   A B
   is excited to have won the competition.
   C D
   No error
   E

8. After studying the atlas, Mary discovered that
   A
   Asia is larger than any continent on Earth.
   B C D
   No error
   E

9. He spent his college years talking
   A
   on the phone, sleeping, and occasionally
   B C
   on his studies. No error
   D E

GO ON TO THE NEXT PAGE

10. Everyone needs to listen [A] to the professor so that they [B] will understand [C] what to study [D] for the final. No error [E]

11. Terri is gifted [A] in that she can speak [B] in front of 2,000 people as easy as [C] in front of her family. [D] No error [E]

12. I cannot hardly [A] believe that the team was able [B] to win [C] the championship, after it [D] lost its first seven games. No error [E]

13. This week we traveled [A] to the Grand Canyon, and [B] next week we're [C] going south [D] towards the border of Mexico. No error [E]

14. "Please do not call me after 10:00 P.M.," [A] Steven [B] reminded me, [C] "because [D] I will be going to bed." No error [E]

15. From what I've been told, [A] neither [B] Paul nor Amy believe [C] in Santa Claus. [D] No error [E]

16. After [A] he changed his tire, he drives [B] home quickly [C] to watch [D] the game. No error [E]

17. Each of the students believe [A] they can pass [B] any pop quiz that [C] the teacher may give. [D] No error [E]

18. When it became apparent to Shirley that not one of the companies were [A] going to [B] endorse her client's product, she began to reconsider [C] the offer of [D] a leveraged buyout. No error [E]

19. Though [A] some critics deride Bonds' playmaking ability, others hail [B] him as the most [C] impressive [D] baseball player of the past century. No error [E]

20. Of [A] the four members [B] of the executive committee, none were [C] more experienced or wiser than he. [D] No error [E]

21. Political analysts were surprised that neither [A] the crisis facing health care nor [B] the impact of capital gains tax cuts were [C] included in the politician's [D] speech. No error [E]

22. If one wishes to succeed [A] in life, you should [B] acquire strong communication skills, and a strong work ethic, which [C] leaders agree are of the utmost [D] importance. No error [E]

23. Among [A] the many factors contributing to the revival of the American economy was [B] the expansion of [C] trade agreements and the development of [D] new technologies. No error [E]

GO ON TO THE NEXT PAGE

Part B: Sentence Correction

15 Questions

(Suggested Time – 20 minutes)

Directions: In each of the following sentences some part of the sentence is underlined. Beneath each sentence you will find five ways of writing the underlined part. The first of these repeats the original, but the other four are all different. If you think the original sentence is better than any of the suggested changes, you should choose answer (A); otherwise you should mark one of the other choices. Select the best answer and completely fill in the corresponding lettered space on the answer sheet with a heavy, dark mark so that you cannot see the letter.

This is a test of correctness and effectiveness of expression. In choosing answers, follow the requirements of standard written English; that is, pay attention to acceptable usage in grammar, diction (choice of words), sentence construction, and punctuation. Choose the answer that expresses most effectively what is presented in the original sentence; this answer should be clear and exact, without awkwardness, ambiguity, or redundancy.

Remember, try to answer every question.

24. It's all in a days work.

(A) It's all in a days work.
(B) Its all in a days' work.
(C) Its all in a days work.
(D) Its all in a day's work.
(E) It's all in a day's work.

25. "If it is sunny on Monday," he said, "We will go to the ocean."

(A) Monday," he said, "We will go to the ocean."
(B) monday," he said, "we will go to the ocean."
(C) Monday," he said, We will go to the ocean.
(D) Monday," he said, "we will go to the ocean."
(E) Monday, he said, We will go to the ocean."

26. The woman whom he loved moved to Chicago.

(A) The woman whom he loved moved to Chicago.
(B) The woman, who he loved, moved to Chicago.
(C) The woman who he loved moved to Chicago.
(D) The Woman, whom he loved, moved to Chicago.
(E) The woman who he loved had been moved to Chicago.

27. When asked what he wanted to be when he grew up, Tim said, "I wish I was a movie star."

(A) Tim said, "I wish I was a movie star."
(B) Tim said, "I wish I were a movie star."
(C) Tim said "I wish I was a movie star."
(D) Tim said I wish I were a movie star.
(E) tim said, "I wish I was a movie star."

28. Susan's favorite subject is Algebra, but Science is also enjoyed by her.

(A) Algebra, but Science is also enjoyed by her
(B) Algebra, but Science is also her favorite subject
(C) Algebra, but she also enjoyed Science
(D) Algebra, but she also enjoys Science
(E) algebra, but she also enjoys science

29. Stacy climbed up the hill and soon the valley came in sight.

(A) Stacy climbed up the hill and soon the valley came in sight.
(B) Stacy climbed up the hill and soon came in sight of the valley.
(C) Stacy climbed up the hill, and soon the valley came in sight.
(D) Stacy climbed up the hill and soon she had come to the valley.
(E) Stacy climbed up the hill with the valley coming into sight.

GO ON TO THE NEXT PAGE

30. Her face a constant smile, Stephanie told us over and over again how much she appreciated us coming to her fiftieth birthday party.

(A) she appreciated us coming to her
(B) she appreciated that we come to her
(C) she appreciated us having come to her
(D) she appreciated our coming to her
(E) she appreciated that we had been coming to her

31. The stereotype of snobby, wealthy, lazy kids bears no resemblance to the real students at Mater Dei High School, the majority of them work after school jobs.

(A) the majority of them work
(B) the majority of which work
(C) the majority which works
(D) the majority of them working
(E) the majority of whom

32. Drinking alcoholic beverages and eating food that contain preservatives can be unhealthy when indulged in large quantities.

(A) and eating food that contain preservatives can be
(B) and eating foods that contains preservatives can be
(C) and eating foods which contains preservatives can be
(D) and eating food that contains preservatives can be
(E) and eating food that contain preservatives might be

33. Most students would probably perform better in school if they studied Latin.

(A) if they studied Latin
(B) if Latin were to be studied by them
(C) if Latin was studied by them
(D) if they would have studied Latin
(E) if Latin would have been studied by them

34. In Mexico, an increasing number of commuters that believe their families to be immune from the dangers of life in the city.

(A) that believe their families to be
(B) that believe their families are
(C) believes their families to be
(D) who believe their families to be
(E) believe their families to be

35. The journalist lived and conversed with the rebellion army and he was finally accepted as an informed conveyer of its cause.

(A) The journalist lived and conversed with the rebellion army and he
(B) The journalist lived and conversing with the rebellion army, and he
(C) The journalist's living and conversing with the rebellion army,
(D) The journalist, who lived and conversed with the rebellion army,
(E) While living and conversing with the rebellion army, the journalist

GO ON TO THE NEXT PAGE

36. Kareem Abdul-Jabaar, who was born with the name Lew Alcindor, holds the NBA record for most points scored in a career.

(A) Kareem Abdul-Jabaar, who was born with the name Lew Alcindor, holds the NBA record for most points scored in a career.

(B) Kareem Abdul-Jabaar held the NBA record for most points scored in a career, who was born with the name Lew Alcindor.

(C) Being the person who holds the NBA record for most points scored in a career, Kareem Abdul-Jabaar was born as Lew Alcindor.

(D) Kareem Abdul-Jabaar holds the NBA record for most points scored in a career and was born with the name Lew Alcindor.

(E) Kareem Abdul-Jabaar holds the NBA record for most points scored in a career and he was born with the name Lew Alcindor.

37. Each of the books were excellent, and the choice for the best one among the three was very difficult.

(A) Each of the books were excellent, and the choice for the best one among the three was very difficult.

(B) Each of the books was excellent, and the choice for the best one among the three was very difficult.

(C) Each of the books were excellent, and the choice for the best between all three was very difficult.

(D) Each of the books was excellent, and the choice for the best between all three was very difficult.

(E) Each of the books were excellent, and the choices between all three was very difficult.

38. I always manage to get frustrated when playing golf: nonetheless, I promise to continue my involving in the game.

(A) when playing golf: nonetheless, I promise to continue my involving in the game

(B) when playing golf but I always still manage to find a way to promise continuing my involving in the game

(C) when playing golf: nonetheless, I promise to continue my involvement in the game

(D) when playing golf; nonetheless, I promise to continue my involving in the game

(E) when playing golf; nonetheless, I promise to continue my involvement in the game

STOP

Section 2

Essay

Time – 30 minutes

Directions: You will have 30 minutes to plan and write an essay on the topic presented on page 160. Read the topic carefully. You will probably find it best to spend a little time considering the topic and organizing your thoughts before you begin writing. DO NOT WRITE ON A TOPIC OTHER THAN THE ONE SPECIFIED. An essay on a topic of your own choice will not be acceptable. In order for your test to be scored, your response must be in English.

The essay question is included in this test to give you an opportunity to demonstrate how well you can write. You should, therefore, take care to write clearly and effectively, using specific examples where appropriate. Remember that how well you write is much more important than how much you write, but to cover the topic adequately, you will probably need to write more than a paragraph.

Your essay will be scored on the basis of its total quality—i.e., holistically. Each essay score is the sum of points (0-6) given by two readers. When your total writing score is computed, your essay score will be combined with your score for the multiple-choice section of the test.

You are to write your essay on the answer sheet; you will receive no other paper on which to write. Please write neatly and legibly. To be certain you have enough space on the answer sheet for your entire essay, please do NOT skip lines, do NOT write in excessively large letters, and do NOT leave wide margins. You may use the bottom of page 160 for any notes you may wish to make before you begin writing.

GO ON TO THE NEXT PAGE

Section 2

Essay

Time – 30 minutes

Read the opinion stated below:

"All schools should have school uniforms."

Discuss the extent to which you agree or disagree with this opinion. Support your position with specific reasons and examples from your own experience, observations, or reading.

The space below is for your NOTES. Write your essay in the space provided on the answer sheet.

DO NOT TURN BACK TO SECTIONS 1 AND 2 OF THIS TEST.

Diagnostic Test Form

Completely darken bubbles with a No. 2 pencil. If you make a mistake, be sure to erase mark completely. Erase all stray marks.

1. YOUR NAME: ______________________________
(Print) Last First M.I.

SIGNATURE: ______________________________ **DATE:** ____/____/____

HOME ADDRESS: ______________________________
(Print) Number and Street

______________________________ **E-MAIL:** ______________________________
City State Zip

PHONE NO.: ______________ **SCHOOL:** ______________ **CLASS OF:** ______________
(Print)

IMPORTANT: Please fill in these boxes exactly as shown on the back cover of your test book.

OpScan *i*NSIGHT™ forms by Pearson NCS EM-255325-1:654321
Printed in U.S.A.

2. TEST FORM

____

3. TEST CODE / **4. PHONE NUMBER**

3	3	3	3	4	4	4	4	4	4	4
0	0	0	0	0	0	0	0	0	0	0
1	1	1	1	1	1	1	1	1	1	1
2	2	2	2	2	2	2	2	2	2	2
3	3	3	3	3	3	3	3	3	3	3
4	4	4	4	4	4	4	4	4	4	4
5	5	5	5	5	5	5	5	5	5	5
6	6	6	6	6	6	6	6	6	6	6
7	7	7	7	7	7	7	7	7	7	7
8	8	8	8	8	8	8	8	8	8	8
9	9	9	9	9	9	9	9	9	9	9

5. YOUR NAME

First 4 letters of last name				FIRST INIT	MID INIT
A	A	A	A	A	A
B	B	B	B	B	B
C	C	C	C	C	C
D	D	D	D	D	D
E	E	E	E	E	E
F	F	F	F	F	F
G	G	G	G	G	G
H	H	H	H	H	H
I	I	I	I	I	I
J	J	J	J	J	J
K	K	K	K	K	K
L	L	L	L	L	L
M	M	M	M	M	M
N	N	N	N	N	N
O	O	O	O	O	O
P	P	P	P	P	P
Q	Q	Q	Q	Q	Q
R	R	R	R	R	R
S	S	S	S	S	S
T	T	T	T	T	T
U	U	U	U	U	U
V	V	V	V	V	V
W	W	W	W	W	W
X	X	X	X	X	X
Y	Y	Y	Y	Y	Y
Z	Z	Z	Z	Z	Z

6. DATE OF BIRTH

MONTH	DAY		YEAR	
JAN				
FEB				
MAR	0	0	0	0
APR	1	1	1	1
MAY	2	2	2	2
JUN	3	3	3	3
JUL		4	4	4
AUG		5	5	5
SEP		6	6	6
OCT		7	7	7
NOV		8	8	8
DEC		9	9	9

7. SEX

- MALE
- FEMALE

8. OTHER

1	A	B	C	D	E
2	A	B	C	D	E
3	A	B	C	D	E

Begin with number 1 for each new section of the test. Leave blank any extra answer spaces.

SECTION 1

#						#						#						#					
1	A	B	C	D	E	26	A	B	C	D	E	51	A	B	C	D	E	76	A	B	C	D	E
2	A	B	C	D	E	27	A	B	C	D	E	52	A	B	C	D	E	77	A	B	C	D	E
3	A	B	C	D	E	28	A	B	C	D	E	53	A	B	C	D	E	78	A	B	C	D	E
4	A	B	C	D	E	29	A	B	C	D	E	54	A	B	C	D	E	79	A	B	C	D	E
5	A	B	C	D	E	30	A	B	C	D	E	55	A	B	C	D	E	80	A	B	C	D	E
6	A	B	C	D	E	31	A	B	C	D	E	56	A	B	C	D	E	81	A	B	C	D	E
7	A	B	C	D	E	32	A	B	C	D	E	57	A	B	C	D	E	82	A	B	C	D	E
8	A	B	C	D	E	33	A	B	C	D	E	58	A	B	C	D	E	83	A	B	C	D	E
9	A	B	C	D	E	34	A	B	C	D	E	59	A	B	C	D	E	84	A	B	C	D	E
10	A	B	C	D	E	35	A	B	C	D	E	60	A	B	C	D	E	85	A	B	C	D	E
11	A	B	C	D	E	36	A	B	C	D	E	61	A	B	C	D	E	86	A	B	C	D	E
12	A	B	C	D	E	37	A	B	C	D	E	62	A	B	C	D	E	87	A	B	C	D	E
13	A	B	C	D	E	38	A	B	C	D	E	63	A	B	C	D	E	88	A	B	C	D	E
14	A	B	C	D	E	39	A	B	C	D	E	64	A	B	C	D	E	89	A	B	C	D	E
15	A	B	C	D	E	40	A	B	C	D	E	65	A	B	C	D	E	90	A	B	C	D	E
16	A	B	C	D	E	41	A	B	C	D	E	66	A	B	C	D	E	91	A	B	C	D	E
17	A	B	C	D	E	42	A	B	C	D	E	67	A	B	C	D	E	92	A	B	C	D	E
18	A	B	C	D	E	43	A	B	C	D	E	68	A	B	C	D	E	93	A	B	C	D	E
19	A	B	C	D	E	44	A	B	C	D	E	69	A	B	C	D	E	94	A	B	C	D	E
20	A	B	C	D	E	45	A	B	C	D	E	70	A	B	C	D	E	95	A	B	C	D	E
21	A	B	C	D	E	46	A	B	C	D	E	71	A	B	C	D	E	96	A	B	C	D	E
22	A	B	C	D	E	47	A	B	C	D	E	72	A	B	C	D	E	97	A	B	C	D	E
23	A	B	C	D	E	48	A	B	C	D	E	73	A	B	C	D	E	98	A	B	C	D	E
24	A	B	C	D	E	49	A	B	C	D	E	74	A	B	C	D	E	99	A	B	C	D	E
25	A	B	C	D	E	50	A	B	C	D	E	75	A	B	C	D	E	100	A	B	C	D	E

11

Answers and Explanations for PPST: Writing Practice Test 2

PPST: WRITING PRACTICE TEST 2 ANSWER KEY

1. C
2. A
3. E
4. A
5. C
6. B
7. E
8. C
9. D
10. B
11. C
12. A
13. E
14. E
15. C
16. B
17. A
18. A
19. E
20. C
21. C
22. B
23. B
24. E
25. D
26. A
27. B
28. D
29. B
30. D
31. E
32. D
33. A
34. E
35. D
36. A
37. B
38. E

ANSWERS AND EXPLANATIONS FOR PPST: WRITING PRACTICE TEST 2

1. **C** The word should be *lowest*, as there are five players being compared. *Lower* would be appropriate when comparing two things. Three or more requires the *-est* ending.
2. **A** The correct word is *who.* Review the use of *who versus whom* in the PPST review chapters. *Who* is in the nominative case and is being used as a subject.
3. **E** There are no grammatical problems with this sentence. The most confusing aspect of this sentence is the use of *we.* The verb *are* is understood and not expressed in the sentence (ask yourself if the phrase *as old as we are* makes sense—clearly, this works, and *as old as us are*, does not. *No one* is a common trap—it is not written as one word.
4. **A** *Neither...nor* is a correct idiomatic phrase that uses single pronouns. The verb tense in (A) is plural, not singular, and therefore incorrect.
5. **C** Whenever a form of the verb *to be* is used, the pronoun must take the nominative case. The correct word is *he.* While few people would say *but it is I* in conversation, this is a grammatically correct phrase.
6. **B** The verb needs to be in the plural form, as two subjects are combined with the conjunction *and.* Whenever *and* is used, regardless of the tense of the connecting words, the subject is plural.
7. **E** Many believe that answer choice (C) is incorrect. However, the verb is singular, which modifies the singular subject *Lyndon.*
8. **C** This is a comparison error. The correct phrase should be *larger than any other continent.* The comparison is between Asia and the other continents.
9. **D** This is an error in parallelism. The words *talking, sleeping*, and *studying* should be in agreement.
10. **B** *Everyone* is a singular pronoun, which is not underlined. Thus, the pronoun in (B) must be singular. The correct term is *so that he or she.*
11. **C** This is a modifier error, as the adverb should be in the form *easily.* This modifies the verb *speak.*
12. **A** *Hardly* is a negative word, so it cannot be used with another negative word (in this case, the word *cannot*). The pronoun *it* is used to describe the noun *team.*
13. **E** There is no error in this sentence.
14. **E** There is no error in this sentence. You may have been tempted to choose (D), *because.* However, this word is not capitalized, because it is the second half of a sentence that has been broken.
15. **C** The rule is that the verb agrees with the nearest subject. Because *Amy* is a singular subject, the verb must be singular. The verb should be believes.
16. **B** The verb tense needs to remain in the past tense, similar to the verb *changed.* The correct phrase is *he drove.*
17. **A** The subject is *each. Each* is singular and therefore needs the singular verb believes.
18. **A** *One* is the subject, so the verb must be in the singular tense.
19. **E** There is no error in this sentence.
20. **C** The subject *none* is singular, which should take the verb *was.*
21. **C** *Neither* and *nor* are singular pronouns. Therefore, a singular verb tense should be used. In this case, the verb should be *was.*
22. **B** The subject of the sentence is *one.* You cannot change the subject to *you* immediately thereafter. The correct phrase would be to write *one should...*

23. **B** The subject of the sentence actually follows the verb here. The subject is plural, joined by the conjunction *and.*

24. **E** Use the apostrophe to mark omissions in contractions. (*It* is becomes *it's.*) Use the apostrophe to show possession for nouns. For singular nouns, add the apostrophe and *-s* (day's).

25. **D** Use quotation marks to enclose all directly related material. Further, the word *we* does not need to be capitalized, as it is still a part of the original quotation. If a second sentence were quoted, then a capital letter would be correct.

26. **A** The main challenge in this sentence is distinguishing between *who* and *whom.* In this case, *whom* is the correct word, as it is the object of the verb *loved.*

27. **B** This is a tricky question. However, you should be able to eliminate answer choices (C), (D), and (E) as a result of obvious errors. The best use of the verb here is to use the case *were.* When a condition is expressed contrary to fact, the subjunctive form of the verb should be used. That sounds technical, but remember the phrase *I wish I were a movie star* to give you clues on similar questions.

28. **D** The initial sentence shifts the point of view unnecessarily. The sentence is also in the present tense, which eliminates answer choice (C). (B) takes away from the original meaning of the sentence. (E) is incorrect because Algebra and Science should be capitalized as titles of courses.

29. **B** The subject of the sentence is *Stacy;* in answer choice (C), the subject needlessly changes to *valley.* The sentence is describing the actions of Stacy, and rules of parallelism require us to keep the sentence about Stacy. Therefore, (B) is the best answer.

30. **D** What does Stephanie appreciate? Not us (well, maybe she does), but the event of us coming to her party. The object of her appreciation is the event, which makes (D) correct.

31. **E** *Whom* is used properly to refer to the students at the high school. Students are the subject, and the pronoun follows a preposition, so the word should be *whom.*

32. **D** (D) is the only answer choice that contains the correct subject/verb agreement.

33. **A** The original sentence is correct as written.

34. **E** The original sentence does not have a verb in the main clause. This changes in answer choices (C) and (E). However, (C) is singular, while the subject *commuters* is plural.

35. **D** This original sentence does the best job describing the person and the event with the use of the modifying clause. No other answer choice improves on the sentence structure.

36. **A** This original sentence does the best job describing the person and the event with the use of the modifying clause. No other answer choice improves on the sentence structure.

37. **B** First, identify the correct verb tense for the singular pronoun *each.* The pronoun takes the verb *was,* so you can eliminate answer choices (A), (C), and (E). The word *among* should be used when the number of items is greater than two, therefore answer choice (B) is preferable to answer choice (D).

38. **E** There are two errors in this sentence. The author uses a semicolon instead of a colon, so you can eliminate answer choices (A) and (C). Instead of *involving* the author needs the noun form *involvement* to complete the infinitive phrase *to continue.* (D) can be eliminated, leaving a wordy choice (B), and the best answer (E).

ESSAY

"All schools should have school uniforms."

Sample Essay #1: Overall Score = 6 (High Degree of Competence)

I strongly agree with the belief that all schools, even public schools, should have school uniforms. A common dress code, with limited apparel selection, will help to minimize the often apparent socio-economic differences present among children. The amount of time and energy spent by children on their dress can be redirected towards learning. Further, a common dress code will allow students to develop socially based on factors outside of the clothing they wear.

I came from a relatively poor family, and attended a school where the median household income was well more than $250,000. Many of the girls at school would brag about the new clothes they purchased, often at outrageous prices. I immediately felt left out because I could not wear the same things they could. I became bitter towards my parents at their inability to provide for me the same things other girls would receive whenever they wanted. In addition to impacting my relationship with my parents, I was very tentative at school. I never raised my hand or volunteered; in part, perhaps, because I did not want to call attention to myself, often clothed in hand-me-downs from my older sister.

Many critics of a universal uniform policy criticize the financial costs of such a program. I do not think this is a valid argument. Parents should be asked to pay for the basic set of clothing required for school. In theory, parents can use the money allocated for school clothes for the school year, and focus those dollars towards the uniforms. For some parents, however, I understand that there is not always a sufficient "school clothes" budget to cover the cost of uniforms. In that case, these families should receive a subsidy for uniforms. Schools have already shown the ability to execute these programs—the free lunch program is widely praised for its fair approach and ease of execution.

In the final analysis, I think the benefits of a school uniform policy far outweigh any deficits. Children need not worry about the pressures of "looking cool" or fitting in with those of different financial backgrounds. Instead, students can focus on expressing their individuality through their education, a positive effect for all involved.

Sample Essay #2: Overall Score = 3 (Some Competence)

It sounds very easy—give children the same clothes to wear at school, and things will be great. Well I'm not so sure. The belief is that school uniforms will allow children to focus more and not worry about what they wear. In fact, they'll just find other ways to differentiate themselves, which may be worse or more extreme than if they could wear what they wanted in the first place.

My niece goes to a private school, which has uniforms. Because the kids can't express themselves through their clothes, they do it through other ways. One girl has her ear pierced seven times. Another one has dyed her hair purple. Would these extreme measures be necessary if they didn't have a uniform policy? I don't think so. I'm worried about these kids going too far trying to be recognized or different from their peer groups.

In conclusion, uniforms are not a very good idea. They just lead to more extreme behaviors, as I have shown above.

Sample Essay #3: Overall Score = 1 (Fundamental Deficiencies)

I went to school were there was a uniform policy, and man was it no fun. There were only five shirts you could wear—a blue button down, a yellow button down, a button down that was white, one of those white golf shirts, and the fifth one was a blue golf shirt. As for pants, we could wear any type of khaki that we wanted. Shoes were not fun to wear either—no tennis shoes, only on free dress days. Unless students want to be as miserable as me back then, I don't think there should be a uniform policy anywhere.

12

PPST: Mathematics Practice Test 1

The Praxis Series Professional Assessments for Beginning Teachers

Test Name: Pre-Professional Skills Test

Mathematics

Time – 60 minutes

40 Questions

Directions: Each of the questions or incomplete statements below is followed by five suggested answers or completions. Select the one that is best in each and then fill in the corresponding lettered space on the answer sheet with a heavy, dark mark so that you cannot see the letter.

Remember, try to answer every question.

Special Note: Figures that accompany problems in the test are intended to provide information useful in solving the problem. The figures are drawn as accurately as possible except when it is stated in a specific problem that its figure is not drawn to scale Figures can be assumed to lie in a plane unless otherwise indicated. Position of points can be assumed to be in the order shown, and lines shown as straight can be assumed to be straight. The symbol ∟ denotes a right angle.

1. Which of the following contains the three numbers in order from smallest to largest?

(A) 3.092, 3.5, 3.52
(B) 3.092, 3.52, 3.5
(C) 3.5, 3.52, 3.092
(D) 3.52, 3.5, 3.092
(E) 3.5, 3.092, 3.52

Questions 2–3 refer to the following information.

A vending machine contains 42 items. There are 13 candy bars, 14 bags of pretzels, and 15 packs of gum. After recess, there are 11 items remaining in the vending machine.

2. Which of the following facts can be determined from the information give above?

(A) The number of candy bars sold
(B) The cost of a bag of pretzels
(C) The total capacity of the vending machine
(D) The amount of money collected by the vending machine during recess
(E) The number of items that were sold during recess

3. In order to calculate the total value of the items not sold during recess, what additional information would be needed?

(A) The cost of a bag of pretzels, the cost of a candy bar, and the cost of a pack of gum
(B) The number of candy bars left in the vending machine after recess
(C) The number of bags of pretzels left in the vending machine after recess
(D) (A), (B), and (C)
(E) None of the above provides sufficient information.

4. Kathleen has completed five tests in her real estate course. She has scored 83, 86, 94, 73, and 89 on her five tests. What is her mean score on these five tests?

(A) 83 (B) 84 (C) 85 (D) 89 (E) 94

GO ON TO THE NEXT PAGE

Questions 5–6 refer to the chart below.

Population Distribution in Town C

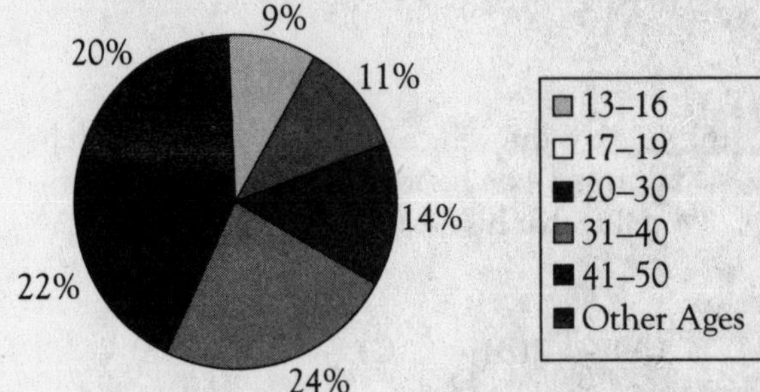

5. What percent of the total population is made up of teenagers?

(A) 12% (B) 14% (C) 17% (D) 19% (E) 20%

6. There are 125,000 people in Town C. Given this additional piece of information, which of the following statements CANNOT be solved from the chart above?

(A) The percent of the total population of adults over 50
(B) The number of people between the ages of 20 and 50, inclusive
(C) How many more 31-40 year olds there are than 41-50 year olds
(D) The percent of the total population that are teenagers
(E) The number of 20-30 year olds

7. In the number 345.678, what is the sum of the digit in the hundreds place and the digit in the tenths place?

(A) 7 (B) 8 (C) 9 (D) 10 (E) 11

x	y
0	–6
2	0
4	6
5	9

8. Which of the following formulas expresses the relationship between x and y in the table above?

(A) $y = 3x - 6$
(B) $y = x + 6$
(C) $y = -6$
(D) $y = 4x + 6$
(E) $y = 2x - 1$

$$(10)(25) + (35)(10) + (27.5)(10)$$

9. Which of the following calculations will lead to the same result as the statement above?

(A) (10)(25 + 35 + 27.5)
(B) (30)(25 + 35 + 27.5)
(C) (35)(45)(37.5)
(D) (10)(10)(10) + (25)(35)(27.5)
(E) (1000)(87.5)

10. If $3 - 6x < 12y$, what is the value of x ?

(A) $x < 3$
(B) $x < 2y + 0.5$
(C) $x > 2y + 0.5$
(D) $x > -2y + .5$
(E) $x > -2y - .5$

GO ON TO THE NEXT PAGE

Student	Questions Answered Correctly	Percentile Score
Justin	27	85%
Julie	23	
Mark		40%
Karen	15	44%

11. Using the information above, which of the following denotes the students' scores in order, from lowest to highest?

(A) Justin, Julie, Mark, Karen
(B) Julie, Justin, Karen, Mark
(C) Karen, Mark, Julie, Justin
(D) Mark, Julie, Justin, Karen
(E) Mark, Karen, Julie, Justin

2, 3, 5, 9, 17, 33, x

12. The numbers above follow a specific pattern. What is the value of x ?

(A) 42 (B) 50 (C) 51 (D) 55 (E) 65

13. If $3A \div 7 = B$, then $6A \div 14 =$

(A) B
(B) 2B
(C) $B \div 2$
(D) $3B \div 7$
(E) 2

14. Brett works 35 hours per week and earns $12.50 per hour. His employer gave him a raise that increases his weekly gross pay to $480.00. What is the increase in Brett's weekly gross pay?

(A) $37.50
(B) $42.50
(C) $47.50
(D) $48.00
(E) $50.00

15. Of the following fractions, which is smallest?

(A) $\frac{3}{5}$ (B) $\frac{4}{9}$ (C) $\frac{7}{13}$ (D) $\frac{1}{3}$ (E) $\frac{2}{9}$

16. Steve is throwing a standard six-sided die. If he throws a 4 on his first throw, what is the probability that his next throw will NOT be a 4 ?

(A) $\frac{1}{6}$ (B) $\frac{1}{3}$ (C) $\frac{1}{2}$ (D) $\frac{2}{3}$ (E) $\frac{5}{6}$

> Some dolls have brown hair.
> All dolls with black hair have a red bow.

17. Considering the two statements above, which of the following statements must be true?

(A) Not all dolls have black hair.
(B) No dolls with brown hair have a red bow.
(C) Some dolls with red bows have brown hair.
(D) There are no dolls with red hair.
(E) Not all dolls have red bows.

18. Zachary needs to order ribbon to decorate gifts for his parents. Each gift requires 31 inches of ribbon. If he has 22 gifts, what is the total length of ribbon that Zachary needs to order?

(A) 10 feet, 6 inches
(B) 31 feet
(C) 56 feet, 10 inches
(D) 62 feet, 4 inches
(E) 682 feet

19. Triangle ABC is a right triangle at angle B. If side AB is 6, and side BC is 8, what is the length of $\overline{AC}$?

(A) 7 (B) 8.5 (C) 10 (D) 14 (E) 28

GO ON TO THE NEXT PAGE

20. Julie can grade 20 spelling tests per hour. If she starts grading tests at 9:00 A.M., which of the following is the best estimate as to when she will be finished grading 134 tests?

(A) 12:30 P.M.
(B) 1:30 P.M.
(C) 2:00 P.M.
(D) 3:30 P.M.
(E) 5:00 P.M.

21. If 3 less than 8 times a number is 37, what is the number?

(A) 34 (B) 29 (C) 21 (D) 5 (E) 4

22. How many times greater than $\frac{1}{4}$ is $\frac{1}{2}$?

(A) $\frac{1}{2}$ (B) 2 (C) 4 (D) 6 (E) 8

23. On a recent test, Valerie answered 2 questions correctly for every 3 questions she missed. If the test had a total of 80 questions, how many questions did Valerie answer correctly on the test?

(A) 5 (B) 32 (C) 48 (D) 80 (E) 160

24. Helen, Anna, and Emily want to go to the baseball game together. They agree to combine their money. Helen has $11.00; Anna has $15.00; and Emily has $16.00. Admission to the game is $21.00 per person. How much more money will they each need to obtain, on average, in order for everyone to be able to go to the game together?

(A) $5.00
(B) $6.00
(C) $7.00
(D) $14.00
(E) $21.00

25. Which of the following expressions finds 20 percent of 130 ?

(A) $\frac{20}{100} \times 130$
(B) $\frac{130}{20}$
(C) $\frac{130}{.2}$
(D) 130×5
(E) $\frac{130}{2}$

26. Connie owns a laundry service. She charges $3.50 for a small load of laundry, and $4.25 for a large load. One day, Octavio brings her 7 small loads and 4 large loads. Assuming no tax is charged, how much will Connie charge Octavio for this laundry order?

(A) $35.00
(B) $38.75
(C) $41.50
(D) $47.25
(E) $54.25

GO ON TO THE NEXT PAGE

Questions 27–28 refer to the following table.

Sales for Company X		
Product	**2005 Sales**	**2006 Sales**
Product A	200,000	250,000
Product B	150,000	150,000
Product C	30,000	60,000
Product D	145,000	160,000
Product E	75,000	65,000

27. Which product saw the greatest percent increase in sales from 2005 to 2006 ?

    (A) Product A
    (B) Product B
    (C) Product C
    (D) Product D
    (E) Product E

28. By approximately what percent did Company X increase in product sales from 2005 to 2006?

    (A) 14% (B) 25% (C) 33% (D) 45% (E) 85%

29. Howard wants to raise his weekly gross pay to $114.00 per week, and currently makes $6.00 per hour. How many additional hours must he work per week?

    (A) 4 hours
    (B) 5 hours
    (C) 6 hours
    (D) 7 hours
    (E) It cannot be determined from the information given.

> If Kyle finishes his homework, he will get ice cream for dessert.

30. Given the statement above, which of the following must be true?

    (A) Kyle did not get ice cream for dessert, so he did not do his homework.
    (B) Kyle did not finish his homework, so he did not get ice cream.
    (C) If Kyle ever gets ice cream, it is because he finished his homework.
    (D) Sometimes Kyle does not finish his homework.
    (E) Kyle can only have ice cream for dessert.

31. Ben's garden has a collection of roses, tulips, and carnations, in a ratio of 3:2:1. If Ben has a total of 72 flowers in his garden, how many roses are in his garden?

    (A) 6 roses
    (B) 12 roses
    (C) 24 roses
    (D) 36 roses
    (E) It cannot be determined from the information given.

32. If the value of y is between .00268 and .0339, which of the following could be y ?

    (A) 0.00175
    (B) 0.0134
    (C) 0.0389
    (D) 0.268
    (E) 2.6

33. $3x + 12 = 7x - 16$. What is x ?

    (A) 3 (B) 7 (C) 12 (D) 16 (E) 28

34. Laura is scheduled to perform 24 surgeries this week. If she performs 4 surgeries on Monday, how many surgeries must she perform each day, on average, to finish by Friday?

    (A) 2 (B) 3 (C) 4 (D) 5 (E) 6

GO ON TO THE NEXT PAGE

35. It is 260 miles between Santa Escuela and Santa Novia. Mr. Lewis drives 40 miles per hour. Assuming he takes a direct route between the two cities, how many hours will it take Mr. Lewis to drive from Santa Escuela to Santa Novia?

(A) 5 hours
(B) 5.5 hours
(C) 6 hours
(D) 6.5 hours
(E) 7 hours

36. Two different whole numbers are multiplied. Which of the following could NOT result?

(A) 0 (B) 1 (C) 7 (D) 24 (E) 423

37. Kathleen bought a new suit at 25 percent off the regular price of $400.00. She had an additional coupon, which saved her an additional 15 percent off the sale price. What price did she pay for the suit?

(A) $85.00
(B) $112.50
(C) $240.00
(D) $255.00
(E) $285.00

38. If the value of z is between –0.1 and 0.8, then which of the following could be z ?

(A) –1.8 (B) –0.8 (C) 0 (D) 1.8 (E) 8.1

Questions 39–40 refer to the following table.

List of Television Shows		
Television Show	**Start Time**	**End Time**
Show A	9:30	
Show B	10:15	10:45
Show C	11:00	11:20
Show D	12:00	12:45
Show E		2:30

39. If Show A is 20 minutes longer than Show C, what time does Show A end?

(A) 9:50
(B) 10:10
(C) 10:20
(D) 10:30
(E) 11:40

40. If Show E is the longest of all five shows, what is one possible start time for Show E ?

(A) 2:20
(B) 2:10
(C) 2:00
(D) 1:45
(E) 1:40

STOP

Diagnostic Test Form

Completely darken bubbles with a No. 2 pencil. If you make a mistake, be sure to erase mark completely. Erase all stray marks.

1. YOUR NAME: (Print) ____________________ Last ____________________ First ______ M.I.

SIGNATURE: ______________________________ **DATE:** ____/____/____

HOME ADDRESS: (Print) ______________________________ Number and Street

______________ City ______________ State ______________ Zip **E-MAIL:** ______________________

PHONE NO.: (Print) ______________ **SCHOOL:** ______________ **CLASS OF:** ______________

IMPORTANT: Please fill in these boxes exactly as shown on the back cover of your test book.

OpScan *i*NSIGHT™ forms by Pearson NCS EM-255325-1:654321
Printed in U.S.A.

2. TEST FORM

____

3. TEST CODE / **4. PHONE NUMBER**

3. TEST CODE				4. PHONE NUMBER						
0	0	0	0	0	0	0	0	0	0	0
1	1	1	1	1	1	1	1	1	1	1
2	2	2	2	2	2	2	2	2	2	2
3	3	3	3	3	3	3	3	3	3	3
4	4	4	4	4	4	4	4	4	4	4
5	5	5	5	5	5	5	5	5	5	5
6	6	6	6	6	6	6	6	6	6	6
7	7	7	7	7	7	7	7	7	7	7
8	8	8	8	8	8	8	8	8	8	8
9	9	9	9	9	9	9	9	9	9	9

5. YOUR NAME

First 4 letters of last name				FIRST INIT	MID INIT
A	A	A	A	A	A
B	B	B	B	B	B
C	C	C	C	C	C
D	D	D	D	D	D
E	E	E	E	E	E
F	F	F	F	F	F
G	G	G	G	G	G
H	H	H	H	H	H
I	I	I	I	I	I
J	J	J	J	J	J
K	K	K	K	K	K
L	L	L	L	L	L
M	M	M	M	M	M
N	N	N	N	N	N
O	O	O	O	O	O
P	P	P	P	P	P
Q	Q	Q	Q	Q	Q
R	R	R	R	R	R
S	S	S	S	S	S
T	T	T	T	T	T
U	U	U	U	U	U
V	V	V	V	V	V
W	W	W	W	W	W
X	X	X	X	X	X
Y	Y	Y	Y	Y	Y
Z	Z	Z	Z	Z	Z

6. DATE OF BIRTH

MONTH	DAY		YEAR	
JAN				
FEB				
MAR	0	0	0	0
APR	1	1	1	1
MAY	2	2	2	2
JUN	3	3	3	3
JUL		4	4	4
AUG		5	5	5
SEP		6	6	6
OCT		7	7	7
NOV		8	8	8
DEC		9	9	9

7. SEX

- MALE
- FEMALE

8. OTHER

1 A B C D E
2 A B C D E
3 A B C D E

Begin with number 1 for each new section of the test. Leave blank any extra answer spaces.

SECTION 1

1 A B C D E	26 A B C D E	51 A B C D E	76 A B C D E
2 A B C D E	27 A B C D E	52 A B C D E	77 A B C D E
3 A B C D E	28 A B C D E	53 A B C D E	78 A B C D E
4 A B C D E	29 A B C D E	54 A B C D E	79 A B C D E
5 A B C D E	30 A B C D E	55 A B C D E	80 A B C D E
6 A B C D E	31 A B C D E	56 A B C D E	81 A B C D E
7 A B C D E	32 A B C D E	57 A B C D E	82 A B C D E
8 A B C D E	33 A B C D E	58 A B C D E	83 A B C D E
9 A B C D E	34 A B C D E	59 A B C D E	84 A B C D E
10 A B C D E	35 A B C D E	60 A B C D E	85 A B C D E
11 A B C D E	36 A B C D E	61 A B C D E	86 A B C D E
12 A B C D E	37 A B C D E	62 A B C D E	87 A B C D E
13 A B C D E	38 A B C D E	63 A B C D E	88 A B C D E
14 A B C D E	39 A B C D E	64 A B C D E	89 A B C D E
15 A B C D E	40 A B C D E	65 A B C D E	90 A B C D E
16 A B C D E	41 A B C D E	66 A B C D E	91 A B C D E
17 A B C D E	42 A B C D E	67 A B C D E	92 A B C D E
18 A B C D E	43 A B C D E	68 A B C D E	93 A B C D E
19 A B C D E	44 A B C D E	69 A B C D E	94 A B C D E
20 A B C D E	45 A B C D E	70 A B C D E	95 A B C D E
21 A B C D E	46 A B C D E	71 A B C D E	96 A B C D E
22 A B C D E	47 A B C D E	72 A B C D E	97 A B C D E
23 A B C D E	48 A B C D E	73 A B C D E	98 A B C D E
24 A B C D E	49 A B C D E	74 A B C D E	99 A B C D E
25 A B C D E	50 A B C D E	75 A B C D E	100 A B C D E

13

Answers and Explanations for PPST: Mathematics Practice Test 1

PPST: MATHEMATICS PRACTICE TEST 1 ANSWER KEY

1. A
2. E
3. D
4. C
5. E
6. A
7. C
8. A
9. A
10. D
11. E
12. E
13. B
14. B
15. E
16. E
17. A
18. C
19. C
20. D
21. D
22. B
23. B
24. C
25. A
26. C
27. C
28. A
29. E
30. A
31. D
32. B
33. B
34. D
35. D
36. B
37. D
38. C
39. B
40. E

ANSWERS AND EXPLANATIONS FOR PPST: MATHEMATICS PRACTICE TEST 1

1. **A** Each number starts with 3. Compare each number in the tenths place, and you'll find two numbers with a 5. Therefore, you know that 3.092 is the smallest number, and you can eliminate answer choices (C), (D), and (E). 3.52 is larger than 3.5, as it has a 2 in the hundredths column, compared to a 0 in the number 3.5.

2. **E** We know that the vending machine contained 42 items, and was left with 11 items. We can subtract to find that 31 items were sold during recess. Note that it is not necessary to do this calculation, just that you recognize it can be solved.

3. **D** In order to calculate the value of the items not sold during recess, we need to know the cost of each item, plus the number of items sold.

4. **C** A *mean*, or average, is calculated by taking a total and dividing by the number of things you added up. On this question, the total is 425, and the number of things is 5. The average is 85.

5. **E** We are told that 9% of the population is made up of 13–16 year olds. The percentage of 17–19 year olds is 11%, making the percent of teenagers equal to 20%.

6. **A** We are not given any specific information about the population over 50 year olds. All we know is that 20% of the population is made up of children under 13 and adults over 50.

7. **C** The hundreds place is 3, and the tenths place is 6. The sum of these two numbers is 9.

x	y
0	−6
2	0
4	6
5	9

8. **A** The best way to solve these problems is to plug-in the answer choices. A quick glance at the table should help you eliminate answer choice (C), as only one pair of numbers has $y = -6$. Neither (B) nor (D) work with any of the pairs, and (E) works only when $x = 5$, and $y = 9$.

9. **A** This is an example of the associative property (though you don't need to know that!). If possible, try to recognize the pattern when answering this question; otherwise, you will spend a lot of valuable time performing unnecessary calculations. Each term in the statement above contains a 10, so they can be combined. For example, $25x + 35x + 27.5x = (25 + 35 + 27.5)x$. All of the remaining answer choices violate one or more rules in combining terms.

10. **D** When solving for x, start by isolating the variable. Subtracting 3 on both sides yields $-6x < 12y - 3$. Next, divide both sides by −6. Remember, when dividing an inequality by a negative number, the sign flips! Therefore, $x > -2y + .5$. Note that the sign flipped when we divided by −6.

11. **E** From the second column, we can rank three students based upon the information given: Karen, Julie, and Justin. Only answer choices (C) and (E) contain those three in that order. Because Mark scored in the 40th percentile, he scored lower than Karen. Thus, his name will appear before Karen's, making (E) the correct answer.

12. **E** Each succeeding number is twice the previous number, minus one. In questions involving patterns, look for something in common from one number to the next. At first glance, this problem looks like an addition sequence—$2 + 3 = 5$; however, that quickly ends, as the next number is 9 ($3 + 5$ does not equal 9). This will help you eliminate (B). 9 is one less than twice 5; 17 is one less than twice 9; and 65 is one less than twice 33.

13. **B** To get from the first equation to the second, the left side of the equation was multiplied by 2. $3A \div 7$ becomes $6A \div 14$. Therefore, the right side of the equation must be multiplied by 2. B becomes $2B$.

14. **B** First, we need to find Brett's weekly gross pay. If you multiply 35 by $12.50, you'll get $437.50 in weekly gross pay. Subtracting that from the new total of $480.00, there is an increase of $42.50.

15. **E** Start by approximating the values. Answer choice (A) is greater than .5, and answer choices (B) and (C) are close to that value. You can compare (D) and (E) by using the same denominator. (D) can be rewritten as $\frac{3}{9}$, which is greater than answer choice (E).

16. **E** Throws of a die are independent events—one outcome will not have an effect on the next outcome. We can ignore the second sentence when determining the outcome. There are 5 desired outcomes that are "Not a 4"—1, 2, 3, 5, and 6, out a total of 6 possible outcomes. The probability is $\frac{5}{6}$.

17. **A** From the statements above, we are told that some dolls have brown hair. Therefore, not all dolls have black hair.

18. **C** First, Zachary is a great son, because he gives so many gifts to his parents! This is a measurement question that requires you know there are 12 inches to 1 foot. First multiply to find the total number of inches of ribbon required. Multiply 31 by 22 to get 682 total inches. Then, convert this to feet by dividing by 12. The result is 56, with a remainder of 10. Be careful about answer choice (E), which is labeled with feet, not inches.

19. **C** This is an example of a right triangle, which requires the Pythagorean theorem. This is a common 6-8-10 triangle (3-4-5 is the most common right triangle lengths). If you square each side and sum them, you get 100 ($36 + 64$). The square root of 100 is 10.

20. **D** Julie must grade 134 tests—a good estimate of this is 130 tests. It takes 6.5 hours to grade 130 tests at 20 tests per hour, so Julie will finish a short time after 3:30 P.M. Be sure to approximate during the problem. The phrase "best estimate" is your key.

21. **D** Try plugging in the answer choices. If you start with answer choice (C), 8 times 21 is 168, and three less yields 165. Because this value is too high, move to a smaller number, such as 5. 8 times 5 is 40, and three less is 37. If you do find the need to write an equation, it can be written as $8x - 3 = 37$.

22. **B** You can try using the answer choices here, too. Starting with answer choice (C), multiply $\frac{1}{4}$ by 4. The result is 1, which is too high. Eliminate (C) and try a smaller number. (B) works. If you set up an equation to solve, it should look like this: $x \times \frac{1}{4} = \frac{1}{2}$. Solving that gives you $x = 2$.

23. **B** We're asked to compare the number correct to the total number of questions, so we should write the following proportion: $\frac{2}{2+3} = \frac{x}{80}$, or $\frac{2}{5} = \frac{x}{80}$. Solving that, you get $x = 32$.

24. **C** Together, the three have $42.00, and need a total of $63.00. Together, they need an additional $21.00, which works out to an average of $7.00 per person.

25. **A** Translate 20 percent to $\frac{20}{100}$. "Of" means multiply.

26. **C** The total cost can be found by multiplying $3.50 by 7, and $4.25 by 4. These totals are $24.50 and $17.00, respectively. Sum the two for a total of $41.50.

27. **C** First, eliminate any answer choice that does not increase from 2005 to 2006. This will eliminate answer choices (B) and (E). Next, approximate the increase of the three other answer choices. Product A increases by 50,000 and C increases by 30,000. Yet to find the percent increase, use the percent change formula (difference divided by original). Product C has the largest increase (an improvement of 100%).

28. **A** To find the percent increase, first find the total in product sales for 2005 and 2006. The totals are 600,000 and 685,000, respectively. The change is 85,000, with an original amount of 600,000. Only one answer choice is close to this fraction. 10% of 600,000 is 60,000, which is the only close answer choice.

29. **E** We know that Howard makes $6.00 per hour, but we do not know the number of hours he currently works. In order to determine the additional hours, he'll need to work to increase his weekly pay, we need a starting point.

30. **A** This is a logic question that follows the "If A, then B" construction. The only true statement that always applies is "If not B, then not A." Answer choice (A) retains that structure.

31. **D** We're asked to compare the number of roses to the total number of flowers, so we should set up this proportion: $\frac{3}{3+2+1} = \frac{x}{72}$, or $\frac{3}{6} = \frac{x}{72}$. Solving that gives you $x = 36$.

32. **B** The tenths place of the answer must be a zero, so you can eliminate (D) and (E). Answer choice (A) is too small, while (C) is larger than .0339.

33. **B** Rearrange the equation to get: $28 = 4x$. Dividing both sides by 4, $x = 7$.

34. **D** With 24 surgeries to complete, and 4 completed on Monday, there are 20 surgeries remaining, with 4 days left. Divide 20 by 4 to get the average of 5 surgeries per day.

35. **D** Divide the total number of miles (260) by the miles driven per hour (40). This total is 6.5 hours.

36. **B** Two different whole numbers cannot be multiplied for a total of 1.

37. **D** Be careful if you chose (C), you likely combined percents incorrectly. The sale price was \$300, or 25% off of \$400.00. Next, the coupon gives an additional 15% off the sale price (NOT the original price). 15% of \$300 is \$45, making the total \$255.00.

38. **C** Answer choices (A) and (B) are both too small. (D) and (E) are both too large.

39. **B** Show C runs for 20 minutes, so Show A runs for a total of 40 minutes. 40 minutes after 9:30 is 10:10.

40. **E** The longest show we currently know about is Show D, which runs for 45 minutes. If Show E ends at 2:30, it must start at least 45 minutes earlier, or before 1:45.

14

PPST: Mathematics Practice Test 2

The Praxis Series Professional Assessments for Beginning Teachers

Test Name: Pre-Professional Skills Test

Mathematics

Time – 60 minutes

40 Questions

Directions: Each of the questions or incomplete statements below is followed by five suggested answers or completions. Select the one that is best in each, and then fill in the corresponding lettered space on the answer sheet with a heavy, dark mark so that you cannot see the letter.

Remember, try to answer every question.

Special Note: Figures that accompany problems in the test are intended to provide information useful in solving the problem. The figures are drawn as accurately as possible except when it is stated in a specific problem that its figure is not drawn to scale. Figures can be assumed to lie in a plane unless otherwise indicated. Position of points can be assumed to be in the order shown, and lines shown as straight can be assumed to be straight. The symbol ∟ denotes a right angle.

Percent of Colored Balloons at Party

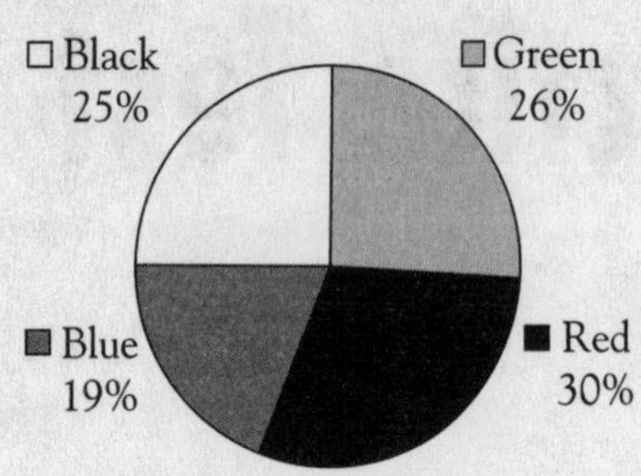

1. According to the above chart, there are a total of 300 balloons at the party. How many more red balloons are there than blue balloons?

   (A) 33 (B) 57 (C) 75 (D) 78 (E) 90

2. Sarah earns \$1300 per month. If she pays \$520 per month for her student loans, which of the following shows the percent of Sarah's earnings that is used to pay student loans?

   (A) $\frac{\$1300}{(\$1300-\$520)}$

   (B) $\frac{\$520}{(\$1300-\$520)}$

   (C) $\frac{\$520}{(\$1300\times\$100)}$

   (D) $\frac{\$520}{(\$1300-\$520)}\times 100$

   (E) $\frac{\$520}{\$1300}\times 100$

3. The scores of the 9 students on the test were as follows: 27, 83, 45, 81, 22, 19, 34, 9, and 22. What is the average score on the test?

   (A) 22
   (B) 38
   (C) 38.25
   (D) 45
   (E) 342

4. The drawing contained only rectangles, but no squares. Which of the following statements must be true?

   (A) Some of the rectangles contained four sides of equal length.
   (B) Triangles were present in the drawing.
   (C) There were no right angles in the drawing.
   (D) None of the rectangles have four sides of equal length.
   (E) Some squares must have been present in the drawing.

GO ON TO THE NEXT PAGE

5. Lisa loves pets. Currently, she has 3 dogs and 5 turtles. What fraction of her animals are dogs?

(A) $\frac{3}{2}$ (B) $\frac{2}{5}$ (C) $\frac{3}{5}$ (D) $\frac{3}{8}$ (E) $\frac{5}{8}$

6. Adam arrived at school at 9:45 A.M. and left school 11 hours and 15 minutes later. What time did Adam leave school?

(A) 6:15 P.M.
(B) 7:45 P.M.
(C) 8:00 P.M.
(D) 8:30 P.M.
(E) 9:00 P.M.

The prices for four townhouses in Texas are:	
Townhouse 1:	$235,015
Townhouse 2:	$139,475
Townhouse 3:	$185,675
Townhouse 4:	$198,130

7. Using the information above, which of the following is the best estimate of the total price for the four townhouses listed above?

(A) $76,000
(B) $700,000
(C) $750,000
(D) $850,000
(E) $7,500,000

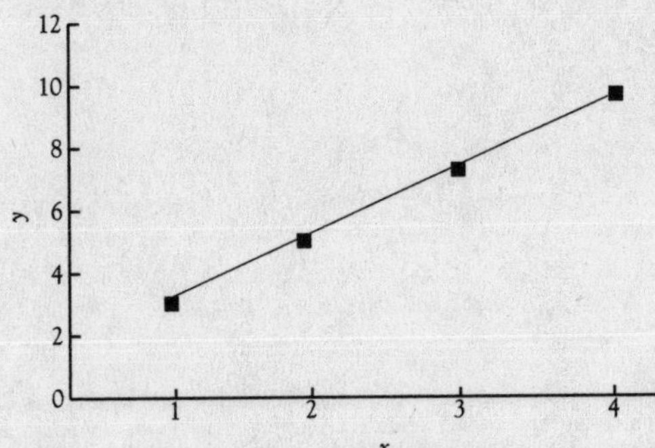

8. Which of the following is true about the graph above?

(A) As x increases, y increases.
(B) As x increases, y decreases.
(C) As x decreases, y increases.
(D) As x increases, y remains the same.
(E) As x decreases, y remains the same.

9. If z is 60% of 500, then what is the value of z ?

(A) 30 (B) 125 (C) 200 (D) 260 (E) 300

10. If a standard six-sided die is thrown, what is the probability of an even number appearing?

(A) $\frac{1}{36}$ (B) $\frac{2}{6}$ (C) $\frac{1}{2}$ (D) $\frac{4}{6}$ (E) $\frac{32}{36}$

11. If $8x + 2z = 10$, which of the following choices are possible values for x and z ?

(A) $x = 1, z = 5$
(B) $x = 1, z = 1$
(C) $x = 0, z = 10$
(D) $x = 3, z = 7$
(E) $x = 4, z = -10$

12. A crate of strawberries costs $4 each, or three crates for $10. What is the minimum cost for 20 crates?

(A) $68 (B) $70 (C) $74 (D) $80 (E) $84

13. If $4x + 6 = 2(y - 3)$, then $y =$

(A) $2x$
(B) $2x - 6$
(C) $3x + 12$
(D) $x + 12$
(E) $2x + 6$

14. Which of the following is not equal to the others?

(A) 45 meters
(B) 0.45 kilometers
(C) 4500 centimeters
(D) 45,000 millimeters
(E) 4.5 hectometers

15. Which of the following answer choices is a multiple of 5 when 4 is added to it?

(A) 45 (B) 46 (C) 55 (D) 63 (E) 67

GO ON TO THE NEXT PAGE

16. Brian has rode 31 miles of his daily 50-mile bike ride. How many more miles has he left to ride?

(A) Less than half the ride remaining
(B) More than 30 miles remaining
(C) Just over 20 miles remaining
(D) Just under 20 miles remaining
(E) Just under 14 miles remaining

17. For every two apple pies that Kathleen bakes, she gets paid $26. How much money will she earn if she works for 6 hours?

(A) $13
(B) $32
(C) $52
(D) $78
(E) It cannot be determined from the information given.

18. Multiplying a number by $\frac{3}{4}$ is the same as dividing that number by

(A) $\frac{9}{16}$ (B) $\frac{3}{4}$ (C) 1 (D) $\frac{4}{3}$ (E) 4

19. At a school supplies store, the price of a blackboard is reduced from $70.00 to $56.00. By what percent is the price of the blackboard decreased?

(A) 10% (B) 14% (C) 20% (D) 56% (E) 86%

20. At his office, Aaron did a survey on what his employees wanted for lunch—sandwiches or pizza. Adam received 34 more votes for pizza than sandwiches. If Adam received a total of 76 votes, how many votes did he receive for sandwiches?

(A) 21 (B) 40 (C) 42 (D) 84 (E) 110

21. What is 2.589 rounded to the nearest hundredth?

(A) 2.5
(B) 2.6
(C) 3.0
(D) 2.58
(E) 2.59

22. The price of a new pair of tennis shoes is $120.00. If during a sale the price is marked down 15%, what is the new price of the shoes?

(A) $18.00
(B) $90.00
(C) $102.00
(D) $105.00
(E) $135.00

23. Justin and Julie collect pictures. They want to place all of their pictures into photo albums. If Justin and Julie own 412 pictures, and each album holds a maximum of 34 pictures, what is the minimum number of photo albums they must purchase so that every picture is contained in a photo album?

(A) 11 (B) 12 (C) 13 (D) 20 (E) 34

24. If two sides of a rectangle are 11 and 6, what is the perimeter of the rectangle?

(A) 10 (B) 17 (C) 22 (D) 23 (E) 34

GO ON TO THE NEXT PAGE

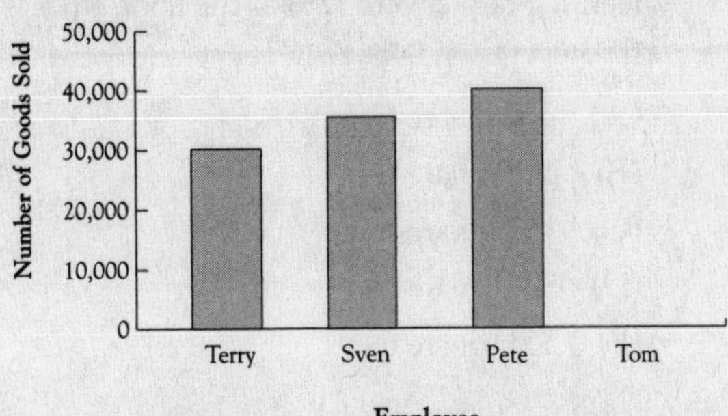

25. According to the above chart, in order for the total amount of goods to equal 150,000, how many goods were sold by Tom?

(A) 30,000
(B) 35,000
(C) 40,000
(D) 45,000
(E) 55,000

26. $14p - 16 + 3p - 4 + p = 16$. What is the value of p ?

(A) 2 (B) 3 (C) 16 (D) 18 (E) 36

27. Seventy-one percent is between

(A) $\frac{1}{2}$ and $\frac{3}{5}$

(B) $\frac{3}{5}$ and $\frac{3}{4}$

(C) $\frac{3}{5}$ and $\frac{7}{10}$

(D) $\frac{3}{4}$ and $\frac{7}{8}$

(E) $\frac{1}{7}$ and $\frac{7}{10}$

28. David walked 485 yards from class to the cafeteria. How many feet did David walk?

(A) 40 feet
(B) 161 feet
(C) 1455 feet
(D) 2100 feet
(E) 5820 feet

29. At a high school, 2 out of every 5 students plan to go to Butterick College. If there are 240 students, how many are expected to go to Butterick College?

(A) 24 students
(B) 96 students
(C) 120 students
(D) 144 students
(E) 180 students

If Jed scores a goal, then his team will win.

30. If the sentence above is true, which of the following statements must also be true?

(A) Jed's team can win only if he scores a goal.
(B) If Jed does not score, his team will lose.
(C) Jed is the best player on the team.
(D) Only Jed can score on his team.
(E) If Jed's team lost, he did not score a goal.

31. In 2004, the total number of CDs sold at Dan's record store was 250,000. In 2005, that number rose to 300,000. What was the percent increase in the number of CDs sold at Dan's store?

(A) 17% (B) 20% (C) 50% (D) 75% (E)105%

32. The school board is proposing a 5% increase in the number of students per classroom. Currently, there are 20 students per class. How many students would there be per class with the proposed increase?

(A) 21 (B) 22 (C) 23 (D) 24 (E) 25

GO ON TO THE NEXT PAGE

Questions 33–34 refer to the following table.

Shareholders in Company W	
Shareholder	**Shares of Stock Owned**
Lyn	150
Jolene	10
Adam	80
Brian	60

33. What percent of stock does Lyn own of Company W ?

(A) 15% (B) 33% (C) 50% (D) 60% (E) 75%

34. What is the average number of shares owned by each shareholder?

(A) 60 (B) 65 (C) 70 (D) 75 (E) 80

35. Dale is playing with a complete deck of 52 cards. If he draws one card at random, what is the probability he will select an Ace, King, or Queen?

(A) $\frac{3}{13}$ (B) $\frac{1}{4}$ (C) $\frac{1}{2}$ (D) $\frac{7}{8}$ (E) $\frac{41}{52}$

36. Which of the following numbers is less than −12?

(A) −14
(B) −10
(C) 0
(D) 11
(E) 13

37. The area of a gymnasium floor is 425 square feet. If a tarp covers 72% of the floor, what is the area of the tarp?

(A) 30 square feet
(B) 119 square feet
(C) 187 square feet
(D) 306 square feet
(E) 353 square feet

38. If the area of a triangle is 24, and the height of the triangle is 6, then the base of the triangle is

(A) 3 (B) 4 (C) 6 (D) 8 (E) 12

39. What is the next term in the following sequence: 3, 4, 6, 9, 13, 18 ?

(A) 23 (B) 24 (C) 31 (D) 36 (E) 37

40. A student correctly answered 80% of 90 science questions. How many science questions did she answer incorrectly?

(A) 8 (B) 9 (C) 18 (D) 71 (E) 72

STOP

Diagnostic Test Form

Completely darken bubbles with a No. 2 pencil. If you make a mistake, be sure to erase mark completely. Erase all stray marks.

1. YOUR NAME: ______________________________ (Print) Last First M.I.

SIGNATURE: ______________________________ DATE: ___/___/___

HOME ADDRESS: ______________________________ (Print) Number and Street

______________________________ E-MAIL: ______________________________
City State Zip

PHONE NO.: ______________ (Print) SCHOOL: ______________ CLASS OF: ______________

IMPORTANT: Please fill in these boxes exactly as shown on the back cover of your test book.

OpScan *i*NSIGHT™ forms by Pearson NCS EM-255325-1:654321
Printed in U.S.A.

2. TEST FORM

3. TEST CODE

0	0	0	0
1	1	1	1
2	2	2	2
3	3	3	3
4	4	4	4
5	5	5	5
6	6	6	6
7	7	7	7
8	8	8	8
9	9	9	9

4. PHONE NUMBER

0	0	0	0	0	0	0
1	1	1	1	1	1	1
2	2	2	2	2	2	2
3	3	3	3	3	3	3
4	4	4	4	4	4	4
5	5	5	5	5	5	5
6	6	6	6	6	6	6
7	7	7	7	7	7	7
8	8	8	8	8	8	8
9	9	9	9	9	9	9

5. YOUR NAME

First 4 letters of last name				FIRST INIT	MID INIT
A	A	A	A	A	A
B	B	B	B	B	B
C	C	C	C	C	C
D	D	D	D	D	D
E	E	E	E	E	E
F	F	F	F	F	F
G	G	G	G	G	G
H	H	H	H	H	H
I	I	I	I	I	I
J	J	J	J	J	J
K	K	K	K	K	K
L	L	L	L	L	L
M	M	M	M	M	M
N	N	N	N	N	N
O	O	O	O	O	O
P	P	P	P	P	P
Q	Q	Q	Q	Q	Q
R	R	R	R	R	R
S	S	S	S	S	S
T	T	T	T	T	T
U	U	U	U	U	U
V	V	V	V	V	V
W	W	W	W	W	W
X	X	X	X	X	X
Y	Y	Y	Y	Y	Y
Z	Z	Z	Z	Z	Z

6. DATE OF BIRTH

MONTH	DAY		YEAR	
JAN				
FEB				
MAR	0	0	0	0
APR	1	1	1	1
MAY	2	2	2	2
JUN	3	3	3	3
JUL		4	4	4
AUG		5	5	5
SEP		6	6	6
OCT		7	7	7
NOV		8	8	8
DEC		9	9	9

7. SEX

- MALE
- FEMALE

8. OTHER

1 A B C D E
2 A B C D E
3 A B C D E

Begin with number 1 for each new section of the test. Leave blank any extra answer spaces.

SECTION 1

1 A B C D E	26 A B C D E	51 A B C D E	76 A B C D E
2 A B C D E	27 A B C D E	52 A B C D E	77 A B C D E
3 A B C D E	28 A B C D E	53 A B C D E	78 A B C D E
4 A B C D E	29 A B C D E	54 A B C D E	79 A B C D E
5 A B C D E	30 A B C D E	55 A B C D E	80 A B C D E
6 A B C D E	31 A B C D E	56 A B C D E	81 A B C D E
7 A B C D E	32 A B C D E	57 A B C D E	82 A B C D E
8 A B C D E	33 A B C D E	58 A B C D E	83 A B C D E
9 A B C D E	34 A B C D E	59 A B C D E	84 A B C D E
10 A B C D E	35 A B C D E	60 A B C D E	85 A B C D E
11 A B C D E	36 A B C D E	61 A B C D E	86 A B C D E
12 A B C D E	37 A B C D E	62 A B C D E	87 A B C D E
13 A B C D E	38 A B C D E	63 A B C D E	88 A B C D E
14 A B C D E	39 A B C D E	64 A B C D E	89 A B C D E
15 A B C D E	40 A B C D E	65 A B C D E	90 A B C D E
16 A B C D E	41 A B C D E	66 A B C D E	91 A B C D E
17 A B C D E	42 A B C D E	67 A B C D E	92 A B C D E
18 A B C D E	43 A B C D E	68 A B C D E	93 A B C D E
19 A B C D E	44 A B C D E	69 A B C D E	94 A B C D E
20 A B C D E	45 A B C D E	70 A B C D E	95 A B C D E
21 A B C D E	46 A B C D E	71 A B C D E	96 A B C D E
22 A B C D E	47 A B C D E	72 A B C D E	97 A B C D E
23 A B C D E	48 A B C D E	73 A B C D E	98 A B C D E
24 A B C D E	49 A B C D E	74 A B C D E	99 A B C D E
25 A B C D E	50 A B C D E	75 A B C D E	100 A B C D E

15

Answers and Explanations for PPST: Mathematics Practice Test 2

PPST: MATHEMATICS PRACTICE TEST 2 ANSWER KEY

1. A
2. E
3. B
4. D
5. D
6. E
7. C
8. A
9. E
10. C
11. B
12. A
13. E
14. B
15. B
16. D
17. E
18. D
19. C
20. A
21. E
22. C
23. C
24. E
25. D
26. A
27. B
28. C
29. B
30. E
31. B
32. A
33. C
34. D
35. A
36. A
37. D
38. D
39. B
40. C

ANSWERS AND EXPLANATIONS FOR PPST: MATHEMATICS PRACTICE TEST 2

1. **A** There are two ways to solve this problem. First, find the percent difference between the red and blue balloons—in this case, 11% (30 – 19). Then find 11% of 300, which is 33. A slower method involves finding the actual number of red balloons, and the actual number of blue balloons, then taking the difference.

2. **E** To find the portion of her earnings that goes to student loans, take that amount ($520) and divide it by the total earnings ($1300). This will give you a fractional amount. To convert it to a percent, multiply by 100.

3. **B** To find the average, sum the items. The total of the nine items is 342 (note the partial answer choice (E) above). Divide 342 by 9 to get the answer 38. Those that selected answer choice (A) likely misread the question—it asks for the average, not the mode.

4. **D** All squares are rectangles, but not all rectangles are squares. We are told that the drawing contains no squares, which means that there are no figures that have four sides of equal length.

5. **D** The fraction asks for the number of dogs over the number of animals. The top part of the fraction is easy—3. Thus, eliminate answer choices (B) and (E). The bottom part of the fraction is the total number of animals—8.

6. **E** 11 hours after 9:45 A.M. is 8:45 P.M. Add 15 minutes to that, and you get 9:00 P.M.

7. **C** Approximate the values to speed up the time it takes to solve this problem. The four values should be estimated as 235, 140, 185, and 200. The sum of these values is 760, or $760,000. (C) is the closest answer.

8. **A** Plot a few points if you want to see how the trends work. If $x = 2$, y is approximately 5. As x increases to 4, y is approximately 10.

9. **E** Multiply 0.6 by 500 to get the value of z, which is 300.

10. **C** There are a total of six possible outcomes when a die is thrown, so eliminate answer choice (A) and (E). Three outcomes are even. Therefore, the probability is 3 out of 6, or $\frac{1}{2}$.

11. **B** To find this answer, plug in values for x and z into the equation.

12. **A** To get a total of 20 crates, it can be bought in six three-pack sets, and two individual sets. The calculation yields $60 for the crates at a special price, and then two individual sets at $4 each, for a total of $68.

13. **E** First, multiply the equation out to get:

$$4x + 6 = 2y - 6$$

Rearrange to get:

$$4x + 12 = 2y$$

Finally, divide by 2 to get:

$$2x + 6 = y$$

14. **B** The easiest unit to start with is likely meters. There are 100 centimeters and 1000 millimeters in a meter, so answer choices (C) and (D) match with (A). 45 meters equals 0.045 kilometers, which does not match (B). Notice that you don't even need to know the meaning of the prefix "hecto" to answer this question correctly, because you're looking for the answer choice that doesn't equal the others.

15. **B** Take each answer choice, add 4 to the number, and determine if it is a multiple of 5. Multiples of 5 end in 0 or 5, so the calculations can be done quickly. Adding 4 to 46 yields 50, which is a multiple of 5.

16. **D** This is a basic subtraction problem. Having completed 31 miles, there are 50 – 31, or 19 miles remaining.

17. **E** If you selected answer choice (D), slow down! The first statement tells us that Kathleen makes $26 for two pies, but states nothing about the amount of time she works, or how long it takes to make each pie. If she works 6 hours, we are not able to determine how much she will earn.

18. **D** $\frac{4}{3}$ is a reciprocal of $\frac{3}{4}$. Multiplying by a number is the same as dividing by the reciprocal of that number.

19. **C** To find the percent decrease, first find the amount of change. The price reduction is $14.00. Be careful not to select answer choice (B), as it is a partial answer choice. The change ($14.00) divided by the original ($70.00) is 20%. Note that 10% of $70.00 is $7, so the $14 difference is 20%.

20. **A** If the total votes is 76, then the number of sandwich votes has to be less than 76, so eliminate answer choice (D) and (E). This is a perfect back-solving question. Start with answer choice (C). If Adam received 42 votes for sandwiches, then he received 76 votes for pizza, which far exceeds the total of 76. If Adam received 21 votes for sandwiches, then he received 55 votes for pizza, and a total of 76. Answer choice (A) works.

21. **E** Answer choices (A), (B), and (C) are rounded to the nearest tenth, so they can be eliminated. When rounding, look at the digit in the thousandths place, which is 9. Because this is greater than 5, round up. (E) rounds up correctly.

22. **C** First, eliminate answer choice (E), because it is larger than the original amount of $120.00. Multiply $120 by 0.15 to get $18.00. However, answer choice (A) is a partial answer. The question asks for the new price of the shoes, which is (C).

23. **C** Start by dividing 412 pictures by 34. This will yield 12 with a remainder. Because there can be no additional pictures left over, a 13th album is needed.

24. **E** The perimeter of a rectangle is twice the length and the width. We are given those two values. The sum is 17, so twice that amount is 34.

25. **D** First, sum up the amount of goods sold by the three employees. The sum is 105,000. Thus, Tom must have sold 45,000 in order for the total to equal 150,000.

26. **A** Rearrange the equation to get:

$$18p - 20 = 16$$
$$18p = 36$$
$$p = 2$$

27. **B** You can eliminate answer choices (C) and (E), as the top fraction of $\frac{7}{10}$ is 70%, which is below the target 71%. Answer choice (B) is between 60% and 75%, so 71% fits within those fractions.

28. **C** The key to this question is knowing that there are 3 feet in a yard. Multiply 485 yards by 3 to get 1455 feet.

29. **B** This is a ratio question. To solve it, set up the following proportion: $\frac{2}{5} = \frac{x}{240}$. Solving gives you $x = 96$.

30. **E** This is a logic question that follows the basic "If A, then B" framework. Given that statement, we know that the one statement which always remains true is "If not B, then not A." If Jed's team did not win, then he did not score a goal.

31. **B** To find a percent increase, use the change formula—difference divided by original. The difference is 50,000, and the original is 250,000. This amount reduces to $\frac{1}{5}$, or 20%.

32. **A** 5% of 20 is 1. 1 additional student would yield a class size of 21.

33. **C** is the correct answer. First, find the total number of shares in the company, which is 300. Lyn owns half of that, or 50%.

34. **D** An average is defined by the total divided by the number of things. The total is 300 and the number of things is 4, which yields an average of 75.

35. **A** There are a total of 52 possible outcomes, and 12 of those are desirable. There are 4 Aces, 4 Kings, and 4 Queens, for a total of 12 favorable cards. 12 out of 52 reduces to 3 out of 13.

36. **A** –14 is a smaller number than –12 (it is farther away from 0 on the number line).

37. **D** Approximate the answer to eliminate answer choices (A), (B), and (C). If you need to do a detailed calculation, multiply 425 by 0.72.

38. **D** The formula for the area of a triangle is $\frac{1}{2}bh$. The formula can be filled in to show: $24 = \frac{1}{2}(b)(6)$.

39. **B** The pattern in the sequence is to add one more value for each following number. So $3 + 1 = 4$, then $4 + 2 = 6$, $6 + 3 = 9$, $9 + 4 = 13$, $13 + 5 = 18$, and finally, $18 + 6 = 24$.

40. **C** The student answered 20% of the 90 questions incorrectly. Multiplying this (.2 times 90) gives a total of 18. Be careful if you selected answer choice (E)—that is the number of questions answered correctly.

PART II

The Praxis II: Subject Assessment Tests

THE PRAXIS II: SUBJECT ASSESSMENT TESTS

If you're reading this chapter, you're probably preparing for a Secondary Education subject-specific test that you need to pass in order to be certified. The Subject Assessment tests are typically taken by testers who have finished or nearly finished their undergraduate educations, and are being asked by a state to demonstrate mastery of a specific subject area.

ETS writes many Praxis II Subject Assessment tests; your state licensing agency can tell you which ones you need to pass to be certified. ETS's website, **www.ets.org,** provides the same information.

How Many Will I Need to Take?

At a maximum, you'll need to take two Praxis II Subject Assessment tests in order to be certified in a specific field: a content test and a pedagogy test. Content tests are multiple-choice tests; pedagogy tests are constructed-response tests, meaning that you'll be asked to write fully-explained answers.

What Do They Measure?

Not surprisingly, content tests measure actual content. There are no "trick questions." General test-taking skills are important to a certain extent, and you'll certainly rely on Process of Elimination as discussed in the introductory chapter, but you'll need to know detailed subject-specific information to answer most questions. If you're taking a test that corresponds to what you studied in college, you probably learned the information you need, but you should spend some time with your old college textbooks brushing up on things that you may have forgotten.

Pedagogy tests ask you how you would teach that content. For instance, you might be asked to come up with classroom examples that show a distinction between two frequently-confused ideas, or design an essay question for a hypothetical final test. For the pedagogy tests, you'll need to rely on your teacher training, but you may also want to study the teacher's edition of a representative textbook to give you ideas.

What Is Covered in This Book?

We've chosen to focus on five content tests in detail, but there is one important thing to know about the Subject Assessment tests in general, regardless of which specific tests you need to take:

All you need to do is pass.

You don't need to ace these tests; you just need to get scores that are at or above the cutoffs set by your state. To understand how this works, let's look at how ETS grades a Subject Assessment test.

How Are the Tests Graded?

Your *raw* score is defined as the number of questions that you answer correctly. For instance, if you answer 36 questions correctly on a 50-question test, your raw score is a 36. If there were 100 questions on the test, your raw score would still be a 36.

Your raw score is then converted to a *scaled* score. The Mathematics: Content Knowledge test, for example, has scaled scores that range from 100 to 200, although raw scores range from only 0 to 50. If your scaled score is above the cutoff established by a particular state for a particular test, you pass; if not, you fail. So, how many questions do you need to answer correctly in order to pass? ETS is notoriously tight-lipped about publishing the conversion tables between raw scores and scaled scores. Nevertheless, our research indicates that on most tests, in most states, answering 75 percent of the questions correctly is sufficient to pass. That's right: You can miss one-quarter of the questions and still get certified. Often, you can miss many more than that. Take a look at the chart on the next page, which is a published conversion table for the Praxis II: Mathematics: Content Knowledge test.

Sample Conversion Table			
Raw Score	**Scaled Score**	**Raw Score**	**Scaled Score**
0	100	26	131
1	100	27	134
2	100	28	136
3	100	29	139
4	100	30	141
5	100	31	144
6	100	32	146
7	100	33	149
8	100	34	151
9	100	35	154
10	100	36	156
11	100	37	159
12	100	38	161
13	100	39	164
14	100	40	167
15	102	41	170
16	105	42	174
17	107	43	178
18	110	44	182
19	113	45	186
20	116	46	190
21	118	47	194
22	121	48	198
23	124	49	200
24	126	50	200
25	129		

Granted, scoring a 200 is a daunting task: You could miss one question at most. But Colorado requires only a 156 to pass (which is the highest standard in the country). A 156 corresponds to 36 correctly answered questions. Arkansas requires only a scaled score of 116 (the lowest), which means that you'd only have to answer 20 of the 50 questions correctly.

Consequently, you have a lot of freedom to decide which questions you want to spend your valuable time on. If you don't know the answer to a certain question, make your best guess (there's no penalty for a wrong answer) and move on. All you're looking for is a passing score.

What's Next?

The rest of this section is dedicated to a more in-depth look at the content knowledge tests in Mathematics, Social Studies, English, Business Education, and Earth and Space Sciences.

16

Mathematics: Content Knowledge

MATHEMATICS: CONTENT KNOWLEDGE

Time: 120 minutes
Format: 50 multiple-choice questions

CONTENT

Content Area	Approximate # of Questions
Arithmetic and Basic Algebra	6–8
Geometry	4–6
Trigonometry	2–4
Analytic Geometry	2–4
Functions and Their Graphs	5–7
Calculus	5–7
Probability and Statistics	3–5
Discrete Mathematics	3–5
Linear Algebra	3–5
Computer Science	2–4
Mathematical Reasoning and Modeling	5–7

WHAT SCALED SCORE DO I NEED TO PASS?

Remember that ETS doesn't determine the cutoff for passing scores; individual states do that. Consequently, the number of questions you need to answer correctly varies dramatically from state to state. Here's the good part: As of this publication, the state with the highest cutoff is Colorado; you'll need a scaled score of 156 to pass. That's only about 36 questions, which means you can miss or skip about 14 of the 50 questions. If you want to teach in Arkansas, you'll need a scaled score of 116; you need only answer about 20 questions correctly.

MANAGE YOUR TIME AND DON'T BE AFRAID TO GUESS

You have a little less than two-and-a-half minutes per question. Many questions will take only a few seconds to answer; some will take much longer. Read each question carefully, and be sure to read all four answer choices. If you know the correct answer, bubble it in and move on. If you don't, use POE (as discussed in the introduction) to eliminate as many incorrect answers as you can, and then take a guess. An incorrect response carries no penalty, so there's no reason not to guess.

NOTATIONS, FORMULAS, AND DEFINITIONS

The first few pages of the test provide you with several pages of notations, formulas, and definitions. Many of these are things you won't need to look up, such as this one from the notation page:

$S \cup T$ union of sets S and T

Some probably won't be much help in any case, such as this one from the definition page:

The set of vectors $v_1, v_2, v_3, \ldots, v_k$ forms a basis for a subspace W of $\mathbf{R}^n$ if $v_1, v_2, v_3, \ldots, v_k$ are linearly independent and their linear span is equal to W.

Still, they're there if you need them.

How to Approach the Questions

As you're deciding which questions to answer and which questions to skip, remember that there are only four answer choices per question, and all you have to do is pick the right one. On the Mathematics: Content Knowledge test, as with all other standardized tests, you will frequently find it easier to eliminate wrong answers than to determine the correct one.

As you read each question, ask yourself the following: *Do I know how to do this?*

If the answer is *yes*, then ask yourself: *Is there an easier way?* Compare the answer choices. Sometimes the format of the answer choices will suggest an approach to the problem. For instance, if the answer choices are in decimal format, you'll probably want to work the problem using decimals. If the choices use fractions, you'll probably want to use fractions, too. Remember to eliminate answers that are obviously wrong, and get to work. If the problem involves many steps, stop at the end of each step and determine whether you can eliminate answers based on the work you've done thus far.

If the answer is *no*, ask yourself: *What can I get rid of?* Look at the answer choices to see if any can be eliminated using common sense, basic mathematical reasoning, or estimation. Then make your best guess and move on.

Let's try an example:

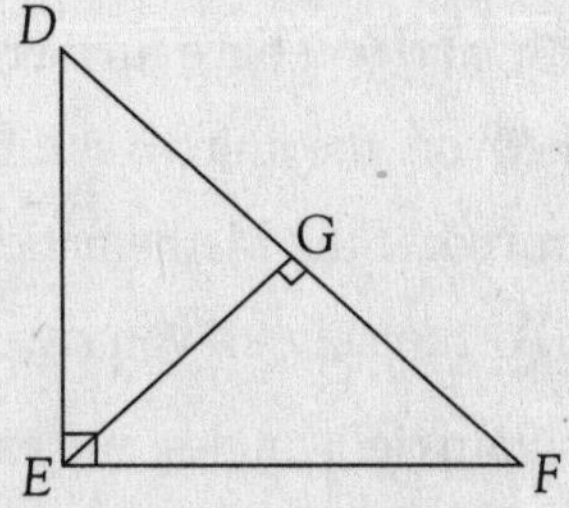

1. In the figure above, DEF is a triangle with a right angle at E. $\overline{EG}$ is perpendicular to $\overline{DF}$. If DG = 3 and GF = 1, then $DE + EF =$

(A) $1 + 2\sqrt{2}$

(B) $2 + 2\sqrt{3}$

(C) $2 + 3\sqrt{2}$

(D) $3 + 3\sqrt{3}$

At first glance, you might assume that the Pythagorean theorem must come into play, because there are three right triangles in the picture. But it may not be obvious how to use it. Ask yourself: *Do I know how to do this?*

Let's assume the answer's *no*. Look at the answer choices. *What can you get rid of?* Remember that $\sqrt{2}$ and $\sqrt{3}$ have numerical values: approximately 1.4 and 1.7, respectively, which means that the answer choices have the following approximate decimal values:

(A) 3.8

(B) 5.4

(C) 6.2

(D) 8.1

That is enough for you to eliminate choice (A), because you're given that the length $\overline{DF}$ is equal to 4. Therefore, the sum of the lengths of the other two sides must be greater than 4. Similarly, you can eliminate choice (D), because it's too big. $\overline{DF}$ is the hypotenuse, so the length of each leg must be less than 4. That means the sum of their lengths must be less than 8.

That leaves you with a 50-50 chance. Can you do better? Compare the remaining choices. One contains the square root of 3, and the other contains the square root of 2. Which is more likely? The square root of 2 tends to show up in problems involving 45-45-90 triangles. You can trust the drawings on the test unless you're explicitly told that they're *not drawn to scale*. Because the drawing doesn't look like half a square, you can eliminate choice (C) and pick choice (B).

Or maybe seeing the square root of three reminded you of a 30-60-90 triangle. If you assume for a moment that each figure is a 30-60-90 triangle, then $\overline{FG}$, which has length 1, is the smaller leg of the smallest triangle, meaning that $\overline{EF}$, the hypotenuse of the smallest triangle, must have length 2, and that $\overline{EG}$, the other leg, must have length $\sqrt{3}$.

$\overline{EG}$, in turn, is the shorter leg of triangle *DEG*, meaning that $\overline{DE}$, the hypotenuse of *DEG*, must have length $2\sqrt{3}$. So $DE + EF = 2 + 2\sqrt{3}$, and you have further confirmation of choice (B).

Granted, the conclusion above relied on the initial assumption that you were dealing with 30-60-90 triangles, which you hadn't proved. If the Mathematics: Content Knowledge test asked you to show your work, you'd be in trouble. Fortunately, all you have to do is pick an answer!

Actually, because the triangles all contain right angles, and each of the two smaller triangles shares another angle with the large triangle, they are necessarily similar to each other. Once you know that, you can set up the proportion $\frac{3}{x} = \frac{x}{1}$, where $x = EG$. Solving that gives you $EG = \sqrt{3}$, proving that all the triangles are 30-60-90 triangles, and the rest of the solution proceeds as above. But don't worry if that didn't occur to you. You can use the answer choices to help you get to the right answer even if you don't know exactly how to do the problem.

Do I Really Need a Graphing Calculator?

Yes. It's required for the test, and there will be about four problems that will be much easier to solve if you have one and you know how to use it. Look at this example:

2. How many solutions does the equation $5x^5 - 14x^4 + 2x^3 + 11x^2 - 7x - 2 = 0$ have?

   (A) Two
   (B) Three
   (C) Four
   (D) Six

Because the function is a 5th degree polynomial, you can get rid of answer choice (D). Then, you could try to factor, but you won't get very far. Without a graphing calculator, you'd just have to guess, unless you wanted to resort to advanced calculus tricks that are beyond the intended scope of the test and that would use up a lot of valuable time. Instead, graph the equation, and you should come up with a graph like on the next page:

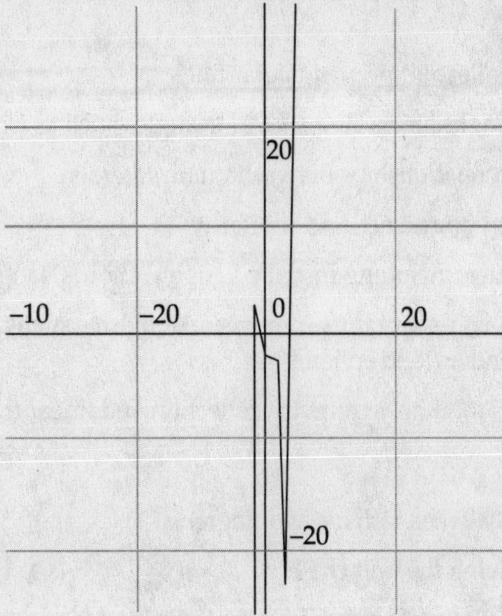

Then, zoom in on the portion of the graph where it crosses the x-axis, and count:

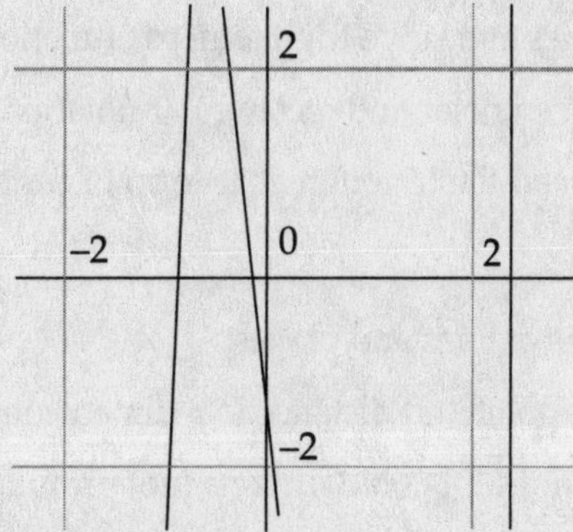

It crosses the x-axis three times, so the answer is (B).

CONTENT AREAS

According to ETS, the following are the things you should know for each content area:

Arithmetic and Basic Algebra

- Definitions of categories of numbers such as rational, real, prime, multiple, etc.
- Properties of operations on these categories such as closure, commutative, associative and distributive
- Concepts such as absolute value, ratio, proportion, percent, average, and weighted average
- How to manipulate algebraic polynomials and fractions
- How to graph linear and nonlinear equations and inequalities
- How to apply Pascal's triangle or combinatorics to solve binomial expansion problems

Geometry

- Properties of parallel and perpendicular lines
- Properties of triangles, including special triangles such as isosceles and equilateral
- Properties of and relationships between quadrilaterals
- Concepts such as congruence and similarity
- Properties of circles, including inscribed angles, chords, tangents, and secants
- Surface area and volume of three-dimensional figures such as right prisms, pyramids, cones, cylinders, and spheres
- Concepts such as rotation, symmetry, reflection and linear translation

Trigonometry

- How to convert between radians and degrees
- Concepts underlying the unit circle
- How to apply the laws of sine and cosine (provided for you)
- How to apply the half-angle, sum, and difference formulas (provided for you)
- How to prove identities and solve trigonometric functions
- How to convert between polar and rectangular notations
- DeMoivre's theorem and the trigonometric form of complex numbers

Analytic Geometry

- How to find equations of lines and planes
- Concepts such as midpoint and distance in 3 dimensions
- Definitions and equations for conic sections (not provided for you)

Functions and Their Graphs

- Different ways of describing a function (e.g., equation, table, chart, description)
- The concepts of domain and range
- The concepts of composite and inverse functions

Calculus

- Definitions and properties of limits
- The concept of continuity
- How to differentiate algebraic, trigonometric, exponential, and logarithmic functions using the sum, product, quotient, and chain rules
- How to use implicit differentiation
- How to solve rate-of-change problems
- The concept of integration with respect to the area under a curve

- How to integrate functions
- How to use integration to calculate the volumes of three-dimensional figures

Probability and Statistics

- How to interpret charts and graphs from a probabilistic and statistical viewpoint
- Concepts of mean, median, mode, range, and standard deviation
- How to solve probability problems by enumeration or counting techniques
- How to model a random variable given a real-world example (such as a loaded die)

Discrete Mathematics

- Understand and use symbolic logic
- How to work with sets
- How to solve problems with permutations and combinations
- Work with numbers expressed in bases other than base ten
- How to solve linear programming problems

Linear Algebra

- How to add, subtract, and multiply matrices and vectors
- Concepts of inverse matrices and linear transformations
- Use matrices to solve linear equations

Computer Science

- Understand functions of computer hardware and software
- Definitions of computer terminology
- Work with computer algorithms

Mathematical Reasoning and Modeling

- Develop and work with mathematical models
- Understand and apply problem-solving strategies
- Estimate answers and identify reasonable results
- Comprehend mathematical concepts such as impossibility and axioms

DRILL

Try these questions.

1. The value of the binomial coefficient $\binom{10}{10}$ is

   (A) 0

   (B) 1

   (C) 10

   (D) Undefined

2. Triangle *ABC* is inscribed within Circle X, which has a diameter of *AB*, and a radius O. Which of the following are true?

   (A) AO = BO = CO

   (B) Angle C must always be a right triangle

   (C) Both (A) and (B)

   (D) Neither (A) nor (B)

3. At what coordinates does the graph of $x = t^2 - t - 6$, $y = 2t$, $-5 < t < 5$, cross the y-axis?

   (A) (–6, 0)

   (B) (0, –4) and (0, 6)

   (C) (0, 6)

   (D) (–2, 3)

4. Let $f(x) = x^2 - 3x$, and $g(x) = 3 + x$. What is a simplified formula for $f(g(x))$?

   (A) $x^2 - 3x + 3$

   (B) $x(x + 3)$

   (C) $2x^2 + 3x$

   (D) $(x + 3)(x + 3)$

5. Using the Mean Value theorem on the function $F(x) = x^4 - 16x^2 + 2;\ -1 \le x \ge 3$, what are the possible values for x, rounded to the nearest thousandth?

   (A) $x = 0.234, 0.657$

   (B) $x = -0.482, 0$

   (C) $x = 0.382, 2.618$

   (D) $x = 1.428, 2.856$

6. A student is organizing 5 notebooks from left to right. Each notebook has a distinct color from the other four: red, green, orange, blue, and yellow. When stacking the notebooks from left to right, how many differently ordered color combinations can be created?

   (A) 14

   (B) 25

   (C) 120

   (D) 3125

7. $i^{12} + i^{14} + i^{20} - i^6 =$

   (A) $-i$

   (B) i

   (C) 1

   (D) 2

8. In an isosceles triangle, the two equal sides measure 24 meters, and they include an angle of 30 degrees. What is the area of the isosceles triangle, rounded to the nearest square meter?

   (A) 48

   (B) 72

   (C) 144

   (D) 288

ANSWERS AND EXPLANATIONS TO DRILL

1. **B** The binomial coefficient can be rewritten as follows:

$$\binom{N}{R} = \frac{N!}{(N-R)!R!}$$

Therefore: $\frac{10!}{0(10!)}$

$$\frac{10!}{1(10!)} = 1$$

Remember that 0! = 1.

2. **C** This is a review of the Inscribed Right Triangle theorem. When a triangle is inscribed in a circle, and one of its sides is the diameter, then the inscribed angle is a right triangle. Statement (A) is true because these are three radii—segments from a point in the triangle to the radius.

3. **B** The equation is an example of a parametric equation. But the question is a basic graphic question, asking you to find points where the function crosses the y-axis. This is something you will likely be able to graph on your calculator. Or, you can solve for the equations when $x = 0$:

$$x = (t + 2)(t - 3)$$
$$0 = (t + 2)(t - 3)$$
$$t = -2, 3$$

When $t = -2$, $x = 0$ and $y = 4$; when $t = 3$, $x = 0$ and $y = 6$. Notice that in both examples, t fits within the limits of the function ($-5 < t < 5$).

4. **B** Solve this composite function problem by taking the value of $g(x)$, and inserting that value as x in the function $f(x)$, as follows:

$$= (3+x)^2 - 3(3+x)$$
$$= 9 + 6x + x^2 - 9 - 3x$$
$$= x^2 + 3x$$
$$= x(x+3)$$

Note that answer choice (A) gives you the answer for the $g(f(x))$. Make sure you work from right to left!

5. **C** To solve for a function using the Mean Value theorem, first calculate the quotient for the limits of x:

$$\frac{f(3) - f(-1)}{3-(-1)} = \frac{-61-(-13)}{4} = -12$$

Next, take the derivative of $f(x)$:

$$F'(x) = 4x^3 - 32x$$

And equate this with the quotient result above:

$$4x^3 - 32x = -12$$

When solving this equation (use your calculator!), you will get two answers, which round to 0.382 and 2.618.

6. **C** The answer to this question is the factorial expression 5! In this sequence and order problem, order does matter. How many different notebooks could be used as the first notebook? 5. How many notebooks could be used as the second notebook? 4. The number is 4 because one notebook will have already been used as the first, and you do not have replacement of notebooks. Therefore, the problem can be solved as $5 \times 4 \times 3 \times 2 \times 1$, or 120.

7. **D** First, translate the functions of *i* into their reduced form, which yields $1 + (-1) + 1 - (-1)$, which equals 2.

8. **C** You will need to use trigonometry to solve this problem. The area of *ABC*

$$= 0.5bc (\sin A)$$
$$= 0.5 (24) (24) \sin 30$$
$$= 288 (.5)$$
$$= 144$$

17

Social Studies: Content Knowledge

SOCIAL STUDIES: CONTENT KNOWLEDGE

Time: 120 minutes
Format: 130 multiple-choice questions

CONTENT

Content Area	Approximate # of Questions
United States History	29
World History	29
Government, Civics, and Political Science	21
Geography	19
Economics	19
Behavioral Sciences	13

PICK YOUR BATTLES

If this sounds like an awful lot of material to cover on one two-hour test, you're right—and there's a fair amount of time pressure; you have less than one minute per question. But even ETS admits that it doesn't expect anyone to be able to ace this test. Concentrate on answering the questions that you know you can answer correctly.

WHAT SCALED SCORE DO I NEED TO PASS?

Your raw score (the number of the 130 questions that you answer correctly) is converted to a scaled score ranging from 100 to 200. ETS doesn't determine the cutoff for passing scores; individual states do that. Consequently, the number of questions you need to answer correctly varies dramatically from state to state. Here's a sampling of states and their passing scaled scores:

State	Passing Score (100–200)
Mississippi	143
Colorado	150
Nevada	152
New Jersey	153
Washington	157
Connecticut	162

You can find a complete listing of each state's requirements on ETS's website: **http://www.ets.org/praxis/prxstate.html**.

MANAGE YOUR TIME AND DON'T BE AFRAID TO GUESS

You have a lot of freedom with respect to the number of questions you will want to spend time answering. Your task is to pick the best of the four answer choices that are in front of you. If you don't like a particular question, use POE (as discussed in the introduction) to narrow down the possibilities. There's no guessing penalty, so there's no harm in taking a shot in the dark, but you'll probably be able to use your own knowledge to eliminate at least one answer choice on any given question.

Try this one:

1. What legal doctrine was established in the Supreme Court's *Plessy v. Ferguson* decision in 1898?

   (A) Right of workers to unionize
   (B) "Separate but equal" laws
   (C) Abolition of slavery
   (D) Sanctity of the flag

Let's assume that you've never heard of *Plessy v. Ferguson*. Note the date mentioned in the question, 1898, and look at the answer choices.

(A) Right of workers to unionize

Maybe. Worker's rights might have been an issue at the time.

(B) "Separate but equal" laws

Maybe. That sounds like something having to do with civil rights and racial issues.

(C) Abolition of slavery

No. Abolition of slavery happened during the Civil War.

(D) Sanctity of the flag

No. The Supreme Court doesn't rule on the "sanctity" of anything.

In this case, we were able to eliminate two incorrect answers by knowing a common fact (that slavery ended during the Civil War) and a basic notion about the role of the Supreme Court (that it makes decisions based on legality rather than theology). This leaves only two answers, so we're now down to a 50-50 chance. (The right answer happens to be (B). *Plessy v. Ferguson* established the doctrine of "separate but equal," meaning that schools and other public institutions were allowed to be racially segregated. This ruling stood until 1954, when the ruling on *Brown v. Board of Education* overturned it.)

CONTENT AREAS

You'll still probably want to do some studying for this test. Some books we recommend for the U.S. and World History areas (as well as some parts of the Geography, Economics, and Government and Civics areas) are the following works by Larry Gonick:

The Cartoon History of the Universe, Vol. I. (Doubleday, 1990)

The Cartoon History of the Universe, Vol. II (Doubleday, 1994)

The Cartoon History of the Universe, Vol. III (Norton, 2002)

The Cartoon History of the United States (Harper Perennial, 1991)

CONTENT AREAS

According to ETS, the following are the things you should know for each content area:

United States History

Native American Peoples

Important political, economic, social, and cultural histories of the following peoples:

- Inuit
- Anasazi
- Northwest Indians
- Plains Indians
- Mound Builders
- Iroquois
- Cherokee
- Seminoles

European Exploration and Colonization

- The major European explorers and the regions they each explored
- The reasons for and approaches to colonization of various countries
- Interactions between explorers and Native Americans and consequences thereof
- Different facets of colonial culture (e.g., society, religion, economy) from different perspectives (e.g., wealthy landowners, small farmers, women, slaves)
- Origins of slavery
- The First Great Awakening

Establishing a New Nation (1776–1791)

- Causes of the American Revolution
- Important people and their roles and contributions (e.g., John Adams, Thomas Jefferson, King George III)
- Important events during the Revolutionary War (e.g., the battle of Yorktown, the Treaty of Paris)
- Ideas expressed in the Declaration of Independence
- The first government of the United States under the Articles of Confederation
- The creation and ratification of the United States Constitution
- Federalism and Anti-Federalism
- The Bill of Rights
- How slavery is addressed in the Constitution

Early Years of the New Nation (1791–1829)

- Early presidential administrations
- The creation and growth of political parties
- The Louisiana Purchase
- The War of 1812
- The Monroe Doctrine

Continued National Development (1829–1850s)

- Slavery's effects on society in the North and South
- "Jacksonian Democracy" (the spoils system, veto of the National Bank, opposition to the Supreme Court)
- Nullification and states' rights
- Westward expansion
- Technological and agricultural innovations and their impact (e.g., cotton gin, steamboat)
- Role of women
- Effects of European immigration
- Treatment of Native Americans (e.g., treaties, Indian Removal Act, "Trail of Tears")
- The Second Great Awakening (e.g., temperance, prison reform)

Civil War Era (1850–1870s)

- Differences between the North and South
- Missouri Compromise and Compromise of 1850
- The abolitionist movement
- The Underground Railroad
- The Women's Movement
- The Fugitive Slave Act
- The Dred Scott decision
- Important people and their roles and contributions (e.g. Abraham Lincoln, Ulysses S. Grant, Jefferson Davis, Robert E. Lee, Frederick Douglass, Harriet Tubman, John Brown)
- Events leading to the Civil War
- Important events during the Civil War (e.g., capture of Fort Sumter, battle of Gettysburg, Lee's surrender, the Gettysburg Address)
- The Emancipation Proclamation
- The 13th, 14th, and 15th Amendments to the Constitution
- Reconstruction
- Jim Crow laws

Emergence of the Modern United States (1877–1900)

- Displacement of Native Americans
- *Plessy v. Ferguson* and segregation
- Federal government's encouragement of business expansion
- Andrew Carnegie, John D. Rockefeller, J. P. Morgan, and their industries
- Sharecropping
- The Industrial Revolution and its impact
- The Labor Movement
- Asian and European immigration
- The Pendleton Act
- The Muckrakers
- Important political and social movements (e.g., Populist movement, Social Darwinism, women's rights, etc.)
- American Imperialism

Progressive Era through the New Deal (1900–1939)

- Direct-ballot
- Mexican immigration
- America's role in WWI
- Isolationism
- The League of Nations
- Important aspects of the 1920s (e.g., the Harlem Renaissance, Prohibition, Women's suffrage, mass-production techniques)
- Causes and Impact of the Great Depression
- Franklin D. Roosevelt and the New Deal

The Second World War and the Postwar Period (1939–1963)

- America's role in WWII
- The attack on Pearl Harbor
- Battles of Midway, Iwo Jima, and Okinawa
- The invasion of Normandy
- Internment of Japanese Americans
- Decision to drop the atomic bombs on Hiroshima and Nagasaki
- The Marshall Plan
- America's role in the Cold War
- The Korean War

- *Brown v. Board of Education*
- G.I. Bill
- Red Scare and McCarthyism
- Cuban missile crisis

Recent Developments (1960s–Present)

- Causes, events, and results of the Vietnam War
- African American Civil Rights movement
- Martin Luther King, Jr.
- Women's movement and the change in family structure
- The "Great Society" and the "War on Poverty"
- Watergate
- Industrial trends (e.g., deregulation, energy crisis, environmental policy)
- The information revolution and its impact

World History

Human Society to Approximately 3500 B.C.E.

- Human societies during the Paleolithic era
- Human societies during the Neolithic era
- Hunter/gatherer societies
- Agricultural revolution
- Specialization of tasks
- Tool making

Development of City Civilization (ca. 3500–1500 B.C.E.)
Important characteristics of the following civilizations:

- Mesopotamia
- Egypt
- Indus River Valley
- Early China
- Olmec society in Mesoamerica

Egypt (ca. 1552–1070 B.C.E.)

- Influence of geography
- Pyramids
- Valley of the Kings
- Important advances in art, writing, and architecture

Greece (ca. 2000–300 B.C.E.)

- Influence of geography
- Concepts of citizenship and democracy
- Athens versus Sparta
- Commerce and the city-state
- Persian Wars
- Peloponnesian Wars
- Alexander the Great
- Important advances in drama, art, sports, architecture, mathematics, and science

Rome (ca. 700–500 B.C.E.)

- Influence of Geography
- Military domination
- Relative size of the empire at various times
- Republic and empire
- Law and citizenship
- Julius Caesar
- Augustus Caesar
- Pax Romana
- Origin and spread of Christianity
- Constantine
- Important advances in architecture, technology, science, law, and engineering
- Causes of the decline and fall of the Roman Empire

India

- Aryan conquest of the Ganges Valley
- Caste system
- Hinduism
- Buddhism

China

- Imperial government and bureaucracy
- Taoism
- Confucianism
- Buddhism
- Important advances and achievements (e.g., printing, compass, paper, gunpowder)
- China's insularity and its effects

Japan

- Influence of geography
- Shinto
- Buddhism
- Emperor, shoguns, and samurai

Disruption and Reversal (ca. 500–1400 C.E.)

- Nomads including Huns and Mongols
- Byzantine Empire
- Origin and spread of Islam
- Difference between Islam and other faiths
- Influence of Muslim learning
- Present-day influences of Islam
- Feudalism and its effects in Europe and Japan
- The Black Death and its effects
- Mayans
- Aztecs
- Incas
- Trading empires and forest kingdoms in sub-Saharan Africa

Emerging Global Interactions (ca. 1400–1750)

- Transition to market economies
- Navigational advancements and their effects
- Chinese voyages
- European voyages of Magellan, Columbus, and de Gama
- Effects of cultural contact
- The Renaissance
- The Protestant Reformation
- Scientific discoveries of Newton, Galileo, and Copernicus
- The Enlightenment's theoretical basis (e.g., works of Locke, Voltaire, and Rousseau)
- The Enlightenment's effects on the American, French, and Latin American Revolutions

Political and Industrial Revolutions, Nationalism (1750–1914)

- Rise of industrial economies, especially in England
- Effects of rapid scientific and technological change
- The factory system
- Liberalism, socialism, Marxism
- Nationalism and imperialism
- Unifications of Germany and Italy
- European colonies in Africa
- The Meiji Restoration of Japan

Conflicts, Ideologies, and Revolutions in the Twentieth Century

- Causes and effects of WWI
- Russian, Mexican, and Chinese Revolutions
- Worldwide economic depression
- Rise of communism
- Rise of fascism
- Important figures (e.g., Lenin, Stalin, Mao Zedong, Adolf Hitler, Franklin D. Roosevelt, Mohandas Gandhi, Kwame Nkrumah, Nelson Mandela)
- Causes and effects of WWII
- The Holocaust
- Origin of the Cold War
- NATO
- Warsaw Pact
- European Economic Community
- Organization of African Unity
- OPEC
- SEATO
- Post–WWII China (e.g., the Cultural Revolution)
- Post–WWII Soviet Union (e.g., uprisings in Hungary and Czechoslovakia, perestroika, and glasnost)
- Decolonization in Africa and Asia
- India and Pakistan
- Rise of a global culture and economy
- Major scientific advances (e.g., atomic power, satellites, computers)

Contemporary Trends

- "New Europe"
- Pacific Rim
- Economic and environmental interdependence
- Judaism

Government, Civics, and Political Science

Basic Political Concepts

- Why government is needed
- Major theorists (e.g., Machiavelli, Hobbes, Locke, Marx, Lenin)
- Major concepts (e.g., citizenship, legitimacy, power, justice, authority, liberty, rights and responsibilities, federalism, and sovereignty
- Orientations (e.g., radical, liberal, conservative, and reactionary)

United States Political System

- The Constitution and Bill of Rights, including procedures for interpretation and amendment
- "Separation of powers" among the three branches of government
- Functions and processes in the federal government
- Relationships among federal, state, and local governments
- Regulatory commissions (e.g., Federal Communications Commission)
- Hierarchy of the federal court system
- Landmark Supreme Court decisions (e.g., *Marbury v. Madison*)
- Judicial activism and judicial restraint

Systems of Government/International Politics
Forms of government such as:

- Classical republic
- Liberal democracy
- Federalism
- Absolute monarchy
- Dictatorship
- Parliamentary system
- Autocracy
- Oligarchy
- Theocracy
- Plutocracy

Geography

The World in Spatial Terms

- Longitude and Latitude
- Geographic features (e.g., continents, oceans, ice caps, mountain ranges)
- Major geographic locations (e.g., seven continents, four oceans)
- General climate patterns for major parts of each continent

Physical Geography of North America

- Physical characteristic and climate patterns of each region
- Main geographic features including mountain ranges, rivers, national parks, etc.

Places and Regions

- Location of major regions, countries, and cities
- Various characteristics of each region

Physical Systems

- Weather patterns, seasons, and climate
- Physical changes (e.g., floods, earthquakes) and their effects

Human Systems

- Causes and effects of settlement patterns
- Population movements
- Difference between developing and industrialized nations

Environment and Society

- Impact of the environment on essentials, transportation, recreation, and economic systems
- Effects of human activity on the environment (e.g., pollution, global warming)
- Renewable and non-renewable natural resources

Economics

Fundamental Concepts

- Scarcity
- Opportunity cost
- Absolute and comparative advantage
- Command, market, and mixed economies
- Circular-flow model

Microeconomics

- Supply and demand
- Equilibrium price
- Perfect competition
- Monopoly
- Distribution of income

Macroeconomics

- Gross National Product
- Gross Domestic Product
- Inflation
- Unemployment
- Consumer Price Index
- Aggregate Supply and Aggregate Demand models
- The Federal Reserve

International Economic Concepts

- Effects of international trade on domestic economy
- Currency fluctuation
- Protectionism

Current Issues and Controversies

- The Balanced-budget amendment
- Protectionism
- Minimum wage
- Government regulation
- Environmental protection
- Fiscal and Monetary policy

Behavioral Sciences

Sociology

- Basic concepts (e.g., networks, norms, groups, status, ethnicity)
- Socialization
- Patterns of social organization (e.g., mores, beliefs, social stratification, social mobility)
- Social institutions (e.g., family, faith, clubs, sports)
- Studies of populations
- Multicultural diversity
- Social problems

Anthropology

- Goals of anthropology and archeology
- Human culture including language, learning of roles, and subcultures
- How cultures change (e.g., adaptation, diffusion, assimilation)

Psychology

- Major theorists (e.g., Freud, Jung, Piaget, Pavlov, Skinner, Erikson)
- Basic concepts (e.g., cognitive development, behavioralism, emotions, motives, values, perception)
- Human development (e.g., physical, cognitive, social, emotional)
- Personality and adjustment (e.g., self-esteem, motivation, assessment)
- Abnormal psychology
- Social psychology

DRILL

Yikes! That's a lot of material! Try these questions.

1. Colonists who were loyal to King George III of England were often known as

   (A) Tories
   (B) Lobsterbacks
   (C) Minutemen
   (D) Patriots

2. Which group's conquering of Russia in the mid 1200s led to a major change in the rural social structure, which lasted several hundred years?

   (A) Huns
   (B) Mongols
   (C) Turks
   (D) Byzantines

3. Which of the following is allowed only in the United States Senate, and not in the House of Representatives?

   (A) The vote of impeachment for the President
   (B) The confirmation of Supreme Court justice nominees
   (C) The right to impose taxes
   (D) The power to regulate interstate commerce

4. Which of the following is NOT an example of spatial diffusion?

   (A) A low-pressure system causing a tornado
   (B) The spread of a wildfire
   (C) The growth of an urban center
   (D) The spread of bubonic plague

5. An increase in United States imports will most likely lead to which of the following events?

   (A) Increased supply of foreign currency on foreign exchange markets
   (B) A stronger United States dollar compared to other currencies
   (C) A decrease in the supply of United States dollars
   (D) A weaker dollar relative to foreign currencies

6. Which sociology theory is most concerned with the contribution the various parts of a society make towards the needs of society?

   (A) Functionalism
   (B) Conflict theory
   (C) Interactionism
   (D) Universal interdependence

7. Which of the following examples is often viewed as a precedent of executive use of United States military force without congressional authority?

   (A) The American invasion of Grenada in 1983
   (B) The United States offensive against Iraq in 1991
   (C) Truman's commitment of United States troops to Korea in the 1950s
   (D) The Bay of Pigs invasion

8. Which United States President completed the Louisiana Purchase?

   (A) Adams
   (B) Washington
   (C) Jefferson
   (D) Madison

ANSWERS AND EXPLANATIONS TO DRILL

1. **A** Tories were supporters of the king, and many fought for the British during the Revolutionary War.
2. **B** Mongol tribes attacked Russia around the 1230s, and ruled over most of Russia for two and a half centuries. Fearful of attacks, many peasants fled to remote areas of the country. The decision of many peasants to become lifetime laborers of the nobility changed the rural social structure within the country.
3. **B** Only the Senate has the ability to confirm the President's Supreme Court nominees. Both the House and Senate register votes of impeachment (though impeachment must be initiated by the House). Answer choices (C) and (D) are fundamental rights granted to Congress.
4. **A** Spatial diffusion is a concept that discusses how a phenomenon moves through geographic space. This concept seeks to explain the movement of cultures, trends, people, and ideas. The spread of wildfires, the growth of an urban center, and the spread of an infectious disease are all examples of spatial diffusion.
5. **D** In general, an increase in U.S. payments (i.e., U.S. imports, investment income outflows, or more U.S. investment abroad) will lead to an increase in the supply of dollars and thus a weaker dollar relative to foreign currencies.
6. **A** Functionalism originally attempted to explain social institutions as collective means to fill individual biological needs; later it came to focus on the ways social institutions fill social needs, especially social solidarity. Famous functionalists include Malinowski, Durkheim, Parsons, and Radcliffe-Brown.
7. **C** Truman's actions have been largely debated for their legality, in relation to the Constitution. Answer choice (B) was also debated, as both relied on UN Security Council resolutions for their declaration of force. However, because the question asks for a precedent, (C) is the correct answer.
8. **C** Acquired from Napoleon in 1803, the Louisiana Purchase marked the beginning of U.S. expansion west of the Mississippi.

18

English Language, Literature, and Composition: Content Knowledge

ENGLISH LANGUAGE, LITERATURE, AND COMPOSITION: CONTENT KNOWLEDGE

Time: 120 minutes
Format: 120 multiple-choice questions

CONTENT

Content Area	Approximate # of Questions
Reading and Understanding Text	66
Language and Linguistics	18
Composition and Rhetoric	36

WHAT SCALED SCORE DO I NEED TO PASS?

Your raw score (the number of the 120 questions that you answer correctly) is converted to a scaled score ranging from 100 to 200. ETS doesn't determine the cutoff for passing scores; individual states do that. Consequently, the number of questions you need to answer correctly varies dramatically from state to state. Here's a sampling of states and their passing scaled scores:

State	Passing score (100–200)
Alaska	158
Mississippi	157
Colorado	162
Nevada	150
New Jersey	155
Washington	158
Connecticut	172

You can find a complete listing of each state's requirements on ETS's website: **http://www.ets.org/praxis/prxstate.html**.

HOW TO PICK THE BEST ANSWER

Fundamentally, there are two types of questions on the test: objective questions that test specific knowledge (e.g., the author of Moby Dick), and subjective questions that are open to interpretation (e.g., the theme of a poem). You should approach these two types of questions differently.

Objective Questions: Let Your Fingers Do the Walking

On any given objective question, you may or may not know the correct answer as you read the question, but if it's on the tip of your tongue, you're likely to know it when you see it. Even if it's not on the tip of your tongue, you can use POE (as discussed in the introduction) to help you make your best guess. (Remember, there's no guessing penalty, so you should answer every question.)

Try this example:

1. Virginia Woolf's *Mrs. Dalloway* and James Joyce's *Ulysses* were both published during which time period?

   (A) 1850–1859
   (B) 1900–1910
   (C) 1920–1930
   (D) 1950–1960

These two titles should be familiar to you, but let's assume that you don't know the exact years for each. Don't waste time trying to rack your brain for more than the first few things that pop into your head—"20th century, I think"—because you won't know how specific you have to be until you've seen the answer choices. In this case, your first thought allows you to cross out only choice (A), but you probably would get rid of choice (D) when you see it, because you might have an inkling that these books were written before World War II, and now that you see it, you might remember that they were both written in the 1920s, and correctly choose answer (C). (And if you're saying to yourself, "But wasn't *Ulysses* published serially in the 1910s?" don't worry about it: it's not an answer choice.) On objective questions, use the answer choices themselves to guide your thinking to the correct answers.

Subjective Questions: Speak for Yourself

By contrast, you should answer subjective questions yourself in your own words before you look at the answer choices. Why? Because the correct answer to a subjective question will be surrounded by answer choices that are included just to confuse you. Cover the answer choices with your hand and try the example below, which features a paragraph from Flaubert's *Madame Bovary*:

Question 2 is based on the following passage.

From early morning, one side of the square was taken up with a row of carts—all tipped up on end, with their shafts in the air, stretching along the house fronts from the church to the hotel. On the other side were canvas booths for the sale of cotton goods, woolen blankets and stockings, horse halters, and rolls of blue ribbon whose ends fluttered in the wind.

2. The imagery used in the passage can best be described as

   (A) pastoral
   (B) religious
   (C) sexual
   (D) satanic

Imagery, of course, is the literary device of using the description of a setting to suggest a deeper or hidden meaning. So what's going on? On the surface, the passage seems to be a description of a country market square, but the imagery tells a different story: descriptions of shafts or other long, cylindrical objects are typically representative of phallic imagery. To balance this, across the square are softer, feminine items that can be construed as vaginal imagery. The scene has strong sexual undertones. Granted, if you were reading this paragraph in the context of the actual novel, you might not have picked up on this. But the question specifically asks about imagery, so you should look for it.

Armed with this revelation, we can quickly pick (C) as the correct answer and move on. If we hadn't stopped to answer this question in our own words, we might have been tempted to pick choice (A), which is a literal description of the scene. We also might have spent valuable time searching for religious or satanic imagery when there was none to be found. For subjective questions, you should answer the questions in your own words first, and then look at the answers to see which choices most closely matches your ideas.

Interpret the Passage, not the Questions and Answer Choices

On the test, you'll be asked to read passages and interpret them with respect to literary devices. One common mistake that test takers often make is to interpret answer choices as though they were part of a literary passage. By design, questions and answer choices are to be taken literally. This knowledge should help reduce uncertainty when you're down to two answer choices.

CONTENT AREAS

According to ETS, the following are the things you should know for each content area:

Reading and Understanding Text

Literal Interpretation

Figurative Interpretation

Theme and Purpose

Literary Devices

- Alliteration
- Allusion
- Analogy
- Characterization
- Cliché
- Dialect/slang
- Diction
- Foreshadowing
- Hyperbole
- Imagery
- Irony
- Metaphor
- Mood

- Personification
- Point of view
- Setting
- Simile
- Style
- Symbolism
- Tone
- Voice

Poetic Forms

- Sonnet
- Haiku
- Epic
- Free verse
- Couplet
- Elegy
- Limerick

Meters and Rhyme Schemes

Fiction Genres

- Novel
- Short story
- Science fiction
- Fable
- Myth
- Legend
- Folk tale
- Fairy tale
- Frame tale
- Mystery
- Historical fiction

Interpretation in a Historical Context
You should be familiar with the following literary schools:

- Harlem Renaissance (Langston Hughes, Zora Neale Hurston)
- British Romantics (Keats, Shelley, Byron)
- Metaphysical Poets (John Donne, Andrew Marvel, George Herbert)
- Transcendentalism (Emerson, Thoreau)

Representative Works of Famous Authors such as:

- Maya Angelou
- Jane Austen
- Ray Bradbury
- Willa Cather
- Stephen Crane
- Emily Dickinson
- Ralph Waldo Emerson
- F. Scott Fitzgerald
- Anne Frank
- Robert Frost
- Zora Neale Hurston
- John Keats
- Harper Lee
- C. S. Lewis
- Herman Melville
- George Orwell
- Edgar Allen Poe
- J. D. Salinger
- William Shakespeare
- Mary Shelley
- Percy Bysshe Shelley
- Amy Tan
- J. R. R. Tolkien
- Mark Twain
- Alice Walker
- Walt Whitman

Instructional Approaches

- Reading appreciation
- Building vocabulary
- Strengthening comprehension

Language and Linguistics

Language Acquisition and Development

- Dialects and other variations in the English language
- Relationships between spelling and spoken language
- Phases of language development
- Strategies for teaching English as a second language

History of the English Language

- Languages related to English
- Etymology
- Common prefixes, suffixes, and roots
- Old English
- Middle English

Grammar

- Parts of speech (e.g., noun, pronoun)
- Syntax (e.g., agreement, tenses)
- Sentence structure (e.g., simple, complex, fragments)

Semantics

- Misplaced modifiers
- Euphemisms
- Jargon

Composition and Rhetoric

Teaching Writing

- Stages of the writing process (e.g., prewriting, drafting)
- Tools for assessing students writing (e.g., peer review, portfolios)
- Research and documentation techniques (e.g., identifying and evaluating sources)
- Bibliographical citations (e.g., MLA, APA)

Rhetorical Features in Writing

- Audience of a passage
- Purpose of a passage
- Organization of a passage
- Relationship of writing to other media
- Types of discourses (e.g., creative, expository, persuasive)
- Distinguishing between fact and opinion

DRILL

Try these questions.

1. "Lindsey Lightning lugged a lot of little lemons" uses what literary device?

   (A) Allegory
   (B) Simile
   (C) Alliteration
   (D) Rhyme

<u>Questions 2–3</u> use the statements below.

I. I'm so hungry I could eat a horse!

II. When the stone was thrown into the lake, a big kerplunk was heard by all.

III. When I saw the way he keeps up his room, I confirmed my suspicions—he was a pig.

IV. Sure, he failed the test, which is a shame, because he studied for all of 10 minutes.

2. Which of the statements above is an example of hyperbole?

   (A) I
   (B) II
   (C) III
   (D) IV

3. The use of the word kerplunk in Statement II is an example of

   (A) alliteration
   (B) onomatopoeia
   (C) oxymoron
   (D) satire

4. A teacher has determined that she will grade her students' essays on two factors—persuasiveness of the arguments, and whether appropriate grammar is used. For each factor, she has determined criteria to give a score between 0–3, and the total score will be determined by averaging these two scores. The teacher's methodology of scoring is an example of what scoring method?

   (A) Analytic scoring rubric
   (B) Holistic scoring rubric
   (C) Answer key
   (D) Conceptual evaluation method

5. At first, the book seemed to be nothing more than a legal thriller—a lawyer in the 1930s defending an accused black man in a sensational crime case. Yet the novel shows the results of prejudice, as well as the healing effects of mutual respect, lessons all learned through the eyes of the lawyer's young daughter.

   The passage above discusses

   (A) Charles Dickens' *Great Expectations*
   (B) John Grisham's *The Firm*
   (C) Harper Lee's *To Kill a Mockingbird*
   (D) John Steinbeck's *The Red Pony*

6. MLA and APA handbooks would most likely agree with which of the following statements regarding proper citations?

   (A) Information found on the Internet does not need to be cited.
   (B) Direct quotations and paraphrases are the only types of information that should be cited.
   (C) Parenthetical acknowledgements are not necessary if there is a complete list of work cited at the end of a research paper.
   (D) It is not necessary to use *Anonymous* or *Anon* when a book has no author's name.

Questions 7–8 use the statements below.

I. The students who did not finish their homework will receive failing grades for today's class.

II. The students, who did not finish their homework, will receive failing grades for today's class.

7. Which of the following best describes the meaning of Statement I ?

(A) Each student will receive a failing grade.
(B) Only students who did not complete their homework will receive a failing grade.
(C) Most students will receive a failing grade.
(D) Some of the students will receive a failing grade.

8. Which of the following best describes the meaning of Statement II ?

(A) Each student will receive a failing grade.
(B) Only students who did not complete their homework will receive a failing grade.
(C) Most students will receive a failing grade.
(D) Some of the students will receive a failing grade.

ANSWERS AND EXPLANATIONS TO DRILL

1. **C** Alliteration is the repetition of the same sounds or of the same kinds of sounds at the beginning of words.
2. **A** A hyperbole is a type of figurative language, which is an exaggeration. Statement III could be considered an exaggeration, but because it is a comparison between two things, it is best described as a metaphor.
3. **B** Onomatopoeia is the use of words whose sounds express or suggest their meaning. The word *kerplunk* expresses the sound of the stone landing in the lake.
4. **A** Often, a rubric is necessary to evaluate the performance of work when qualitative judgments must be used. A scoring rubric attempts to make the evaluation process more objective by outlining expectations at different levels of performance. When the performance expectations can be broken up into distinct items, such as grammar and persuasiveness of an argument, the rubric is said to be an Analytic scoring rubric.
5. **C** The passage describes the key themes and implications in *To Kill a Mockingbird.*
6. **D** While you may not know this specific rule, you should be able to eliminate answer choices (A), (B), and (C). As a general rule, proper citations require you to account for all information that is borrowed—whether it is direct quotations or simply information and ideas. While common knowledge statements are not necessary to cite, any specific information that furthers your ideas must be acknowledged. The first three answer choices all violate this premise.
7. **B** The subject of the sentence is the *students who did not finish their homework.* This is a certain subset of the entire group of students. While (D) seems likely, there is no guarantee from the statement that any student failed to complete his or her homework.
8. **A** We are told that each student failed to complete his or her homework. The phrase is in apposition to the subject *students*, which indicates that all students did not complete their homework.

19

Business Education: Content Knowledge

BUSINESS EDUCATION: CONTENT KNOWLEDGE

Time: 120 minutes
Format: 120 multiple-choice questions

CONTENT

Content Area	Approximate # of Questions
United States Economic Systems	12
Money Management	17
Business and Its Environment	13
Professional Business Education	24
Processing Information	20
Office Procedures and Management, Communications, and Employability Skills	17
Accounting and Marketing	17

WHAT SCALED SCORE DO I NEED TO PASS?

Your raw score (the number of the 120 questions that you answer correctly) is converted to a scaled score ranging from 200 to 800. ETS doesn't determine the cutoff for passing scores; individual states do that. Consequently, the number of questions you need to answer correctly varies from state to state. Here's a sampling of states and their passing scaled scores:

State	Passing Score (200–800)
Arkansas	550
Mississippi	560
Nevada	560
New Jersey	580
Washington	560
Connecticut	620

You can find a complete listing of each state's requirements on ETS's website: **http://www.ets.org/praxis/prxstate.html**.

MANAGE YOUR TIME AND DON'T BE AFRAID TO GUESS

You have exactly one minute per question. Many questions will take only a few seconds to answer; some will take much longer. Read each question carefully, and be sure to read all five answer choices. If you know the correct answer, bubble it in and move on. If you don't, use POE (as discussed in the introduction) to eliminate as many incorrect answers as you can, and then take a guess. An incorrect response carries no penalty, so there's no reason not to guess.

Do I Need a Calculator?

You are allowed the use of a calculator (as long as it doesn't have a QWERTY keyboard). There are a few questions on the test that will require you to do some basic algebra and a calculator might come in handy to help with the small amount of calculation involved. Try this one:

1. A t-shirt factory has fixed costs of $1,600 and variable costs of $2 per unit. How many units must be sold at $10 for the factory to meet the break-even point?

   (A) 16

   (B) 20

   (C) 160

   (D) 200

   (E) 240

The break-even point is the point at which total costs equal total revenue. In this case, the unknown is the number of units, which we'll call x. Total costs are fixed costs (1600) plus variable costs ($2x$), and total revenue is $10x$, so we can write:

$$\begin{aligned} 1{,}600 + 2x &= 10x \\ 1{,}600 &= 8x \\ x &= 200 \end{aligned}$$

The correct answer is (D).

This is as complicated as the math gets on this test. We recommend bringing a calculator with you, just in case, but if you can do this problem without a calculator, you probably won't need one.

CONTENT AREAS

According to ETS, the following are the things you should know for each content area:

United States Economic Systems

Free Enterprise System

- Ways in which businesses can be organized
- Entrepreneurship
- Managing a business
- Business plans

Government and Banking

- Fiscal and monetary policies
- The role of the Federal Reserve
- Gross Domestic Product/Gross National Product
- Banking regulations
- Taxation

Economic Principles

- Supply and demand
- Pricing
- International trade
- Labor versus management
- Cost Benefit Analysis

Money Management

Business Mathematics

- Unit price
- Percent increase/decrease
- Commission
- Simple interest
- Payroll

Consumer Education

- Budgeting
- Consumer rights and responsibilities
- Marketplace decisions

Personal Finance

- Banking
- Investing
- Credit
- Present-value theory
- Risk management

Business and Its Environment

Job Standards

Work Standards

Ethics

Productivity Measurements

Contracts

Principal and Agent

Types of Insurance

Consigned Goods

Negotiable Instruments

Torts

Bankruptcy

Consumer Legislation

Labor Laws

Professional Business Education

Professionalism

- Professional organizations
- Ethics
- Interaction among co-workers

Current Trends and Issues

- Classroom equipment
- Simulations

Methodology and Teaching Strategies

- Competency-based instruction
- Assessments
- Cooperative Education Work-Experience programs
- Special needs students
- Software
- Styles of learning

Student Organizations

- Future Business Leaders of America (FBLA)
- Phi Beta Lambda (PBL)
- DECA—a Marketing Association for Students

Federal Vocational Legislation

Objectives of Business Education

- Occupational preparation
- Lifelong learning
- Responsibilities to business
- Economic literacy

Community and Public Relations

Department Management

- Role of a manager
- Budgeting

Classroom Management

- Attendance records
- Safety hazards
- Lesson plans
- Career goals
- Employment trends

Processing Information

Keyboarding

Production

Word Processing

Proofreading and Editing

Database and Spreadsheet Applications

Graphics

Computer Literacy

Internet Technology

Office Procedures and Management, Communications, and Employability Skills

Office Procedures and Management

- Managerial roles
- Support staff roles
- Records management procedures

Business Communications

- Public speaking
- Speaking aids
- Business letters
- Telephone etiquette
- Office equipment

Employability Skills

- Résumés
- Cover letters
- Job interviews
- Sexual harassment
- Locating jobs

Accounting and Marketing

Account Classification

- Asset
- Liability
- Owner's equity
- Income
- Cost
- Expense

Debit and Credit Theory

Sides of Each Account Classification

Basic Accounting Cycles

Double-entry Accounting Methods

Calculating Depreciation

Calculating Cost of Merchandise Sold

End-of-fiscal-period Statements of Account

Marketing Mix

- The Five Ps

Legislation

- Copyright
- Trademark
- Patent

Sales Techniques

- Telephone marketing
- Personal selling
- Pre-approach

Advertising

- Television
- Radio
- Print
- Direct mail
- Outdoor
- Internet

Merchandise Display

Inventory Control

- Types of inventory-control systems
- Physical inventory
- Perpetual inventory
- Management of stock
- Shoplifting

Inventory Pricing Methods

- Average cost
- Just in Time
- LIFO (Last In, First Out)
- FIFO (First In, First Out)

DRILL

Try these questions.

1. A business structure that is treated as a partnership for tax purposes, but is treated as a corporation for other purposes is best known as

    (A) a limited partnership
    (B) a limited liability
    (C) a sole proprietorship
    (D) a "C" corporation
    (E) an "S" corporation

2. A loan's annual percentage rate (APR) is best defined as

    (A) the interest rate of the loan
    (B) fees paid to the lender for the loan
    (C) fees charged by the lender for processing the loan
    (D) total cost of credit expressed as a yearly rate
    (E) the interest rate plus broker fees that the borrower is required to pay

3. The National Labor Relations Act of 1935 is also known as the

    (A) Taft-Hartley Act
    (B) Wagner Act
    (C) Robinson-Patman Act
    (D) Landrum-Griffin Act
    (E) Norris-La Guardia Act

4. The Office of Vocational and Adult Education (OVAE) is responsible for administering the

    (A) Perkins Act
    (B) No Child Left Behind
    (C) NCLB
    (D) The Report on Education Commission
    (E) The Choices for Parents Plan

5. An increase in the Consumer Price Index may be a leading indicator of

    (A) inflation
    (B) stagflation
    (C) deflation
    (D) credit squeeze
    (E) a contracting money supply

6. A business that chooses to assume its oldest items are to be the first sold follows what inventory accounting practice?

    (A) LIFO
    (B) FIFO
    (C) Depreciation
    (D) Weighted-average costing
    (E) Accounts payable

7. Marketing organizations often use the "3 Cs" to begin a strategic analysis. Which of the following is one of the 3 Cs?

    (A) Capital
    (B) Collateral
    (C) Competition
    (D) Cost
    (E) Customization

8. In a standard process flow, the symbol ♦ is used to indicate a

    (A) connector
    (B) decision point
    (C) user input or action
    (D) conditional branch
    (E) reference

ANSWERS AND EXPLANATIONS TO DRILL

1. **E** A corporation provides limited liability for the investors. A corporation that has made an election to be an "S" corporation is defined by this criteria. Review the different types of business structures, and the differences between them in tax treatment and debt responsibility.
2. **D** APR is the cost of credit expressed as a yearly rate. APR includes the interest rate, points, broker fees, and certain other credit charges that the borrower is required to pay. Answer choices (A), (B), (C), and (D) include items that compose the APR.
3. **B** The Act, signed in 1935, is known as the Wagner Act, so named for Senator Robert F. Wagner, a New York Democrat who sponsored the legislation. It is considered to be the most important piece of labor legislation enacted in the United States in the twentieth century. It was enacted to eliminate employers' disruptions to workers organizing into unions.
4. **A** The Perkins Act was established to support vocational-teaching education programs relating directly to preparing individuals for paid or unpaid employment in current or emerging occupations requiring other than a baccalaureate or advanced degree.
5. **A** Inflation is a general upward price movement of goods and services in an economy. It is usually measured by the Consumer Price Index (CPI) or the Producer Price Index.
6. **B** In a FIFO, or "First In, First Out" system, the oldest inventory is assumed to be the first inventory sold. This is important for valuing the cost of goods sold.
7. **C** (Yes, we know, another C). The 3 Cs of marketing are defined as Company, Competition, and Consumer.
8. **B** A decision point indicates a sequence in the process at which the end user chooses an option, usually a "yes-no" or a "true-false" response.

20

Earth and Space Sciences: Content Knowledge

EARTH AND SPACE SCIENCES: CONTENT KNOWLEDGE

Time: 120 minutes
Format: 100 multiple-choice questions

CONTENT

Content Area	Approximate # of Questions
Basic Scientific Principles of Earth and Space Sciences	8–12
Tectonics and Internal Earth Processes	19–22
Earth Materials and Surface Processes	23–27
History of the Earth and its Life-Forms	13–17
Earth's Atmosphere and Hydrosphere	18–22
Astronomy	8–12

WHAT SCALED SCORE DO I NEED TO PASS?

Your raw score (the number of the 100 questions that you answer correctly) is converted to a scaled score ranging from 100 to 200. ETS doesn't determine the cutoff for passing scores; individual states do that. Consequently, the number of questions you need to answer correctly varies from state to state. Here's a sampling of states and their passing scaled scores:

State	Passing Score (100–200)
Alaska	144
Arkansas	145
New Jersey	134
Missouri	147
Connecticut	157

You can find a complete listing of each state's requirements on ETS's website: **http://www.ets.org/praxis/prxstate.html**.

NO CALCULATOR ALLOWED

You're not allowed to use a calculator on this test. But don't worry, you won't need one. Although some problems may ask you to interpret and manipulate numerical data, you won't be asked to solve anything harder than the question on the next page:

1. Approximately how long will it take light from a star that is 8.78×10^{14} light-years away from the earth to reach the earth? (One light-year = 9.46×10^{12} km)

(A) 1.1 years
(B) 11 years
(C) 55 years
(D) 92.5 years

A light-year is defined as the distance that light travels in a year, so this is just a rate problem. You could set up an equation to solve it like this:

$$x\left(9.46\times10^{12}\right)x = 8.78\times10^{14}$$

$$x = \frac{8.78\times10^{14}}{9.46\times10^{12}}$$

At this point, you could try to do long division, but you're much better off estimating and looking at the answer choices. When estimating values using scientific notation, you should compare the exponents first. Because 14 is two more than 12, we can boil our answer down to:

$$\frac{8.78}{9.46}\times10^{2}$$

Because 8.78 is slightly less than 9.46, we must be looking for a number that's a little less than 100. Choice (D) is the correct answer. Although a calculator would have made this problem easier, it wasn't that hard to do with an understanding of scientific notation.

Manage Your Time and Don't Be Afraid to Guess

You have slightly more than one minute per question. Many questions will take only a few seconds to answer; some will take much longer. Read each question carefully, and be sure to read all five answer choices. If you know the correct answer, bubble it in and move on. If you don't, use good POE to eliminate as many incorrect answers as you can, and then take a guess. An incorrect response carries no penalty, and even ETS says that no one is expected to ace the test.

CONTENT AREAS

According to ETS, the following are the things you should know for each content area:

Basic Scientific Principles of Earth and Space Sciences

The Role of Energy in Earth Systems

- The Sun as an external source
- Internal sources (e.g., radioactive isotopes, gravitational energy)

Heat Transfer in Earth Systems

- Conduction, convection, and radiation
- Greenhouse effect and global warming

Atomic Structures

- States of matter (solid, liquid, gaseous)
- Isotopes

Nuclear Reactions

- Fusion
- Half-life
- Radioactive dating

Basic Biological, Chemical, and Physical Processes

- Evolution
- Biogeochemical cycles
- Chemical reactions
- Gravity
- Waves

Tectonics and Internal Earth Processes

Plate Tectonics

- History of tectonic theory
- Plates and their motions
- Convergent, divergent, and transform boundaries
- Subduction zones
- Trenches
- Rift valleys
- Seafloor spreading
- Hot spots

Processes by which the Crust Is Deformed

- Extension, compression, and shear
- Mountain building
- Folding and faulting of rock layers
- Isostasy

Earthquakes

- Seismic waves
- Internal structure of Earth

Earth's Magnetic Field

- Origin
- Effects
- Shift

Earth Materials and Surface Processes

Characteristics of Minerals

- Composition
- Structure
- Physical characteristics
- Use
- Distribution

Identification of Minerals

- Color
- Streak
- Hardness
- Cleavage
- Specific gravity
- Luster
- Acid test

Changes in Rocks

- The rock cycle
- Mechanical, chemical, and biological weathering
- Soil profiles
- Soil types

Sedimentary Rocks and Processes

- Transportation and deposition of sediments
- Post-depositional processes
- Clastic, biological, and chemical origins of sedimentary rocks
- Identifying sedimentary rocks

Igneous Rocks and Processes

- Types of igneous rocks
- Creation of igneous rocks
- Identification of igneous rocks

Metamorphic Rocks and Processes

- Pressure and heat and their effects on rocks
- Foliated and non-foliated metamorphic rocks

Earth Materials as Resources for Human Civilization

- Fossil fuels
- Minerals
- Building stones

Landscape Evolution

- Erosion
- Mass wasting

Geologic Features as Represented by Maps and Photographs

- Topographic maps
- Geologic maps

Natural Hazards and Human Civilization

- Flood plains
- Volcanos
- Earthquakes

History of the Earth and Its Life Forms

Uniformitarianism

Stratigraphic Correlation

- Superposition
- Original horizontality
- Crosscutting relationships
- Index fossils

Rocks as a Record of Earth's History

- Unconformities
- Types of civilization
- The fossil record
- Paleography
- Paleoclimates

Origin of Earth

- Formation of the earth
- Formation of the atmosphere
- Formation of the hydrosphere

Geologic Time

- Relative age
- Absolute age

Paleontology

- Origin of life
- Development of life
- Use of the fossil record
- Mass extinctions

Earth's Atmosphere and Hydrosphere

Properties of Water

- High specific heat
- Polarity
- Density changes

The Water Cycle

- Energy transfer
- Vapor, phase changes, and precipitation
- Runoff, infiltration, and transpiration

Weather Phenomena and Patterns

- High- and low-pressure regions
- Air masses and fronts
- Absolute and relative humidity
- Cloud formation
- Types of clouds and precipitation
- Hurricanes and tornados
- Weather prediction
- Weather maps

Climate

- Origin
- Distribution
- Variation
- Atmospheric structure and composition
- Atmospheric circulation
- Coriolis effect

- Heat budgets
- Seasonal variations
- El Niño and La Niña
- Climate modification (e.g., desertification)

Civilization and the Atmosphere and Hydrosphere

- Pollution
- Acid rain
- Urban climates

How Water Moves

- Groundwater
- Surface waters
- River systems

Glaciers

- Formation of valley glaciers
- Formation of continental glaciers
- Ice ages

Oceans

- Temperature, salinity, and density
- Chemical cycles, nutrient cycles
- Oceanic circulation patterns and currents
- Upwelling

Oceans and the Solid Earth

- Seafloor topography
- Seafloor sediments
- Waves and tides
- Estuaries
- Erosional and depositional processes, and shore processes
- Sea-level changes

Astronomy

Earth's Rotation and Revolution

- Days, seasons, years
- Time zones and the International Date Line

The Earth, Moon, and Sun

- Moon phases
- Eclipses
- Tides

The Solar System

- The Sun
- The planets and their moons
- Laws of planetary motion
- Retrograde motion
- The asteroid belt
- Meteors, meteoroids, and meteorites
- Comets

Stars

- Temperature
- Color
- Brightness
- The life cycle of stars
- Composition of stars
- Distances in the universe

The Milky Way and Other Galaxies

- Spiral, elliptical, and irregular galaxies
- Types of telescopes
- The Hubble space telescope
- Sensors on space probes
- The International Space Station

Hypotheses Regarding the Origin and Development of the Universe

DRILL

Try these questions.

1. What are the two main metals that make up the outer and inner core of the Earth?

   (A) Nickel and Iron
   (B) Aluminum and Nickel
   (C) Carbon and Iron
   (D) Aluminum and Carbon

2. Which of the following is NOT a type of volcanic cone shape?

   (A) Cinder
   (B) Composite
   (C) Icelandic
   (D) Shield

3. An example of a noncyclic change is the occurrence of

   (A) earthquakes
   (B) ocean tides
   (C) the phases of the Moon
   (D) the seasons of the year

4. Which direct observational evidence provides the strongest evidence that the Earth rotates?

   (A) The seasons repeat in a cycle.
   (B) The apparent shift of nearby stars, as the Earth moves from one side of its orbit to the other.
   (C) The solar diameter varies throughout the year.
   (D) The length of the daylight period varies throughout the year.

5. Which motion causes the Moon to show phases when viewed from Earth?

   (A) The revolution of the Sun around the Moon.
   (B) The rotation of the Sun on its axis.
   (C) The rotation of the Moon on its axis.
   (D) The revolution of the Moon around the Earth.

6. Soil composed of which particle size usually has the smallest capillarity?

   (A) Coarse sand
   (B) Clay
   (C) Silt
   (D) Fine sand

7. Surface winds on Earth are primarily caused by differences in

   (A) air density due to unequal heating of Earth's surface
   (B) ocean wave heights during the tidal cycle
   (C) rotational speeds of Earth's surface at various latitudes
   (D) distances from the Sun during the year

8. Weather-station measurements indicate that the dew point and air temperature are getting farther apart, and that air pressure is rising. Which type of weather is most likely arriving at the station?

   (A) A rainstorm
   (B) A warm front
   (C) Cool, dry air
   (D) Tropical air

ANSWERS AND EXPLANATIONS TO DRILL

1. **A** The core consists mostly of iron, with lesser amounts of nickel and silicon that are combined with a small amount of other elements, most likely sulphur or oxygen.
2. **C** Cinder, composite (also known as a stratovolcano), and shield are all types of volcanic cone shapes. Icelandic is one of six types of volcanic eruptions.
3. **A** A noncyclic change is a change that cannot be predicted, or does not occur on a regular basis.
4. **B** The earth rotates on its axis. This axis extends through the poles. Stars will appear to shift during the night. We know that this is caused by the earth rotating, and not by the stars moving.
5. **D** Each lunar cycle, the moon shows different phases because the earth, moon, and sun are changing. When the moon approaches the opposite side from the earth and sun, its face appears fully lit (i.e., a "full moon").
6. **A** There are nine different textural classes of soils, listed in available water capacity from smallest to greatest: coarse sands; fine sands; loamy sands; sandy loams; fine sandy loam; silt loams; silty clay loams; silty clay; and finally, clay.
7. **A** Wind is caused by air flowing from high pressure to low pressure. Changes in pressure systems are due to different surface temperatures on Earth, where sunlight causes different levels of energy buildup.
8. **C** When the dew point temperature and air temperature are equal, the air is said to be saturated. When there is a large difference between the two temperatures, the air contains very low relative humidity. Therefore (C) is the best answer.

PART III

The PLT: Principles of Learning and Teaching

PRAXIS II: PRINCIPLES OF LEARNING AND TEACHING

There are actually four separate Principles of Learning and Teaching (PLT) tests, each for a specific age range:

- Principles of Learning and Teaching: Early Childhood
- Principles of Learning and Teaching: Grades K–6
- Principles of Learning and Teaching: Grades 5–9
- Principles of Learning and Teaching: Grades 7–12

Because relatively few states require the Early Childhood PLT test, we've chosen to focus on the other three tests.

Each test follows the same format, and tests the same topics, but tailors the content to emphasize each test's specific age range.

WHAT'S ON THE TEST?

The PLT tests measure a range of professional knowledge related to the art and science of teaching. The content covered on the tests is roughly the same as the content you'd see in undergraduate courses in educational psychology and related fields. ETS breaks the content down into four separate areas:

- Students as Learners (about 35% of the content)
- Instruction and Assessment (about 35% of the content)
- Communication Techniques (about 15% of the content)
- Teacher Professionalism (about 15% of the content)

We'll do a thorough review of each of these areas later in this section.

What Does the Test Look Like?

You have two hours to complete a PLT test. The format looks like this:

Part I: 6 short-answer questions based on 2 case histories

Part II: 12 multiple-choice questions

Part III: 6 short-answer questions based on 2 case histories

Part IV: 12 multiple-choice questions

This may seem complicated, but there are really only two types of questions on the PLT tests: multiple-choice and short-answer. You should approach each type of question with a different strategy. Let's take a look at them one at a time.

Multiple-Choice Questions

As you can see above, there are 24 multiple-choices questions on the test, split into two groups of 12. There are only four answer choices per question, and there's no penalty for a wrong answer, so you should answer all of these questions even if you're guessing blindly. A typical multiple-choice question looks like that on the next page:

15. Teacher Melissa Kolbert allows her students to place their desks anywhere in the room while they do seat work. She programmed a computer to play a brief melody 5 minutes before the end of the class period. When the students hear the melody, they know to finish what they are doing and to put all desks back in rows. Why did Melissa do this?

(A) To use technology in the classroom

(B) To achieve a smooth transition

(C) To get students to be seated at the end of class

(D) To reinforce the idea of student-selected seating assignments.

How to Approach Multiple-Choice Questions on the PLT Test

As we discussed in the first chapter, Process of Elimination (POE) is a crucial tool in answering these questions effectively. To help prepare you to eliminate wrong answers on the PLT, you should ask yourself the following questions:

1. What's the scenario?
2. What do I know about that?
3. What would a good teacher do?
4. How would I answer the question?
5. What's the best answer choice?

Let's try this approach on the question we just read:

15. Teacher Melissa Kolbert allows her students to place their desks anywhere in the room while they do seat work. She programmed a computer to play a brief melody 5 minutes before the end of the class period. When the students hear the melody, they know to finish what they are doing and to put all desks back in rows. Why did Melissa do this?

Ask yourself the questions:

1. What's the scenario?
The teacher seems to be making sure that her students have a clear signal and adequate time to get the classroom back in order before the end of class.

2. What do I know about that?
This seems to have something to do with good classroom management. Melissa has her class trained—she doesn't need to yell every day that class is about to end. Giving her students the freedom to sit where they want gives them some control over their learning environment, and they know when they have to give that control back.

3. What would a good teacher do?
A good teacher would do pretty much exactly what Melissa's doing.

4. How would I answer the question?
Answer the question in your own words. Why did Melissa do this? Because she wants a well-managed classroom; because she wants the desks back in their proper places; because she wants to make sure that her students don't just rush off; and because she wants to make sure that the students have enough time to come to a logical stopping point in their work. All of these could be the answer—the right answer should say something like that.

5. What's the best answer choice?
Now, evaluate each answer choice and use good Process of Elimination strategies.

(A) To use technology in the classroom.

(B) To achieve a smooth transition.

(C) To get students to be seated at the end of class.

(D) To reinforce the idea of student-selected seating assignments.

Answer choice (A) has nothing to do with classroom management. Cross it out.

Answer choice (B) is a pretty good encapsulation of all the possible answers we listed above. A smooth transition means that students will have time to stop their work at a logical place, that they'll have to time to put their seats back in their proper places, that they won't just rush off, and that Melissa will have a well-managed classroom. Keep it.

Answer choice (C) is a maybe. That could be Melissa's goal. Keep it.

Answer choice (D) isn't right. Although the scenario is about student-selected seating assignments, programming a computer signal wouldn't reinforce the idea. Cross it out.

Remember now that we're out to find the best answer. Although answer choice (C) might be one goal, (B) does a better job of describing all the things that programming the computer melody accomplishes. The best answer is (B).

Answering the five questions as you're doing each multiple-choice question will help you decide what aspect of the PLT content ETS is trying to test.

Short-Answer Questions

The short-answer questions on the PLT are entirely different. You'll answer these questions in groups of three. Each group is based on a case history—a detailed hypothetical classroom scenario. The scenario is described, sometimes with supporting documentation, such as samples of student work or a transcription of a conversation between a teacher and a student, and then you're asked the questions. Each question typically asks you to identify two ways in which some aspect of the scenario either adheres to or contradicts accepted educational practice, and then to back up your answers using your knowledge of educational theory.

We'll talk about how to approach the case histories later in this chapter. But now, let's take a look at the content you'll need to be familiar with on the PLT.

PLT CONTENT AREAS

As we mentioned earlier, ETS breaks the content on the PLT down into four separate areas:

- Students as Learners (about 35% of the content)
- Instruction and Assessment (about 35% of the content)
- Communication Techniques (about 15% of the content)
- Teacher Professionalism (about 15% of the content)

21

PLT: Students as Learners Test

STUDENTS AS LEARNERS

There are three sub-categories that ETS puts under this umbrella:

- Student development and the learning process
- Students as diverse learners
- Student motivation and the learning environment

STUDENT DEVELOPMENT AND THE LEARNING PROCESS

You'll need to know the basic developmental theories and theorists in cognitive, social, and moral development. Here's a brief overview of the big ones:

COGNITIVE DEVELOPMENT

Piaget's Theory

Jean Piaget was a Swiss psychologist whose theory of cognitive development is often alluded to in Praxis questions. You should be familiar with the basics of this theory and some common examples used to illustrate its principles.

Piaget believed that learning happens as people adapt to their environments. He suggested that cognitive development proceeds as follows: when faced with a situation, you first try to use or apply what you already know, and if that doesn't work, you figure out something else based on what's new or different about that situation. The first idea, using your existing framework or *schema*, he called *assimilation*; the second, developing new frameworks, he called *adaptation*. He believed that we are constantly refining our frameworks.

Based on his observations, Piaget theorized that this ongoing process of assimilation and adaptation leads all children to pass through identical stages of cognitive development, but not necessarily at identical times. He identified four stages:

sensorimotor (approximate age 0–2 years)

preoperational (approximate age 2–7 years)

concrete operational (approximate age 7–11 years)

formal operational (approximate age 11 years old to adulthood)

Let's review them in order:

Sensorimotor Stage

Because most children pass through this stage by the time they reach the age of formal instruction, it is unlikely that you will see questions dealing with it. You should know, however, that things that babies do and the types of games that parents typically play with babies are all relevant to this stage. For instance, one of the characteristics of the sensorimotor stage is understanding *object permanence*—the concept that things continue to exist even though you can't see them. Some educational psychologists and social anthropologists agree that the game of peek-a-boo is practically universally in human cultures specifically because it reinforces the concept of object permanence. Another hallmark of the sensorimotor stage is the early development of *goal-oriented behavior.* For example, a very young child who is able to roll over at will, but not yet able to crawl, may consciously roll over multiple times to reach a bottle or favorite toy.

Preoperational Stage

At this stage, children are developing language skills quickly. They also begin to use symbols to represent objects. Children in this stage will be able to think through simple problems, but only in one direction (i.e., they won't be able to reverse the steps mentally). They also will have difficulty dealing with more than one aspect of a problem at a time. Children in this stage may have difficulty seeing things from another person's point of view. This idea is called *egocentrism.* Although this sounds like a negative quality, it's best understood as the child's assumption that everyone else sees things the same way the child does. For example, a child may assume that everyone likes orange juice simply because she likes orange juice.

Concrete Operational Stage

Children in this stage develop the ability to perform a mental operation and then reverse their thinking back to the starting point, a concept called *reversibility*. They demonstrate the concepts of *transitivity* (they can classify objects according to a specific characteristic, even if the object has many different characteristics) and *seriation* (they can put objects in order according to a given criterion such as height or volume). One important concept is that of *conservation*—the idea that the amount of a substance doesn't change just because it's arranged differently. For example, conservation of mass might be demonstrated by taking a large ball of clay and creating several smaller balls of clay out of it. A child in the concrete operational stage will understand that the total amount of clay hasn't changed; a child in the preoperational stage might think that there is more clay (because there are more balls). Children at this age also understand the concept of class inclusion—they can think about a whole group of objects while also thinking about the subgroups of those objects. For example, while thinking about the whole class, a child could also think about how many girls or boys are in the class. At this stage, children can solve concrete, hands-on problems logically.

Formal Operational Stage

Not all students will reach the formal operational stage. In fact, some theorists estimate that only about 35 percent of the adult population ever achieves this stage. This stage is characterized by the ability to solve abstract problems involving many independent elements. The thought process necessary to frame and solve such problems is called *hypothetical-deductive reasoning.*

Vygotsky's Theories

Lev Vygotsky was a Russian educational psychologist in the early 20th century whose theories you should be familiar with. Here are four of his major ideas that you might see questions about:

- the importance of culture
- the role of private speech
- the zone of proximal development
- scaffolding

Culture

Vygotsky believed that environmental and cultural factors have an enormous influence on what children learn. Piaget argued that children are constantly developing methods of adapting to the world around them; Vygotsky argued that environment and culture dictate what methods the children will find useful, and what their priorities will be.

Private Speech

To Vygotsky, language use is a critical factor in cognitive development. Young children frequently talk to themselves as they play or solve problems. This is called *private speech*. While Piaget would cite private speech as evidence of egocentrism in the preoperational stage, Vygotsky believed that private speech allows children to use language to help break down a problem and solve it—in effect, the children talk themselves through it. He believed that a fundamental stage in development comes when children begin to carry on this speech internally, without speaking the words aloud. Children who routinely use private speech learn complex tasks more effectively.

Zone of Proximal Development

At any given stage, there are problems that a child can solve by herself, and there are other problems that a child couldn't solve even with prodding at each successive step. In between, however, are problems that a child could solve with the guidance of someone who already knows how. That range of problems is what Vygotsky referred to as the *zone of proximal development*. He believed that real learning takes place by solving problems in that zone.

Scaffolding

Scaffolding is another idea fundamental to Vygotsky's notion of social learning. It is about providing children with help from more competent peers and adults. Children are given a lot of support in the early stages of learning and problem solving. Then, as the child is able he/she takes on more responsibility and the supporter diminishes the support. Supportive techniques include clues, reminders, encouragement, breaking the problem into steps, providing examples, or anything that helps a student develop learning independence.

CONSTRUCTIVISM

Piaget's and Vygotsky's theories (among others') led to an educational philosophy called *constructivism,* which essentially says that learning is a constant assimilation of new knowledge and experiences into each student's unique way of viewing the world. Because each student's viewpoint will necessarily be different from everyone else's, a strict constructivist would be in favor of guided hands-on learning rather than traditional lecture-based teaching, because hands-on learning would be more likely to be related to a student's own experience.

Bloom's Taxonomy

- Knowledge
- Comprehension
- Application
- Analysis
- Synthesis
- Evaluation

Students develop thinking skills in roughly the order above. In the early grades, students are limited to facts and other rote knowledge. As they develop, they are capable of processing information at levels of greater and greater complexity. In general, teachers should try to develop higher-order thinking skills (those at the end of the list). Let's take a look at the types of questions that would stimulate these types of thinking. Imagine that a teacher was doing a lesson on the colonization of the United States.

Bloom Taxonomy Level	Description	Question Example
Knowledge	Recalling factual information	What were the names of the New England colonies?
Comprehension	Using factual information to answer a specific question	What crops were common to the New England colonies and the Southern colonies? What were the major religious differences between the New England colonies and the Middle colonies?
Application	Taking an abstract concept together with specific facts to answer a question	In which area of the colonies would a Freethinker have been most likely to find like-minded people?
Analysis	Breaking down a question into concepts and ideas in order to answer a question	What characteristics of the New England colonists made them the most likely to rebel against British rule?
Synthesis	Connecting concepts and ideas to create a new product or idea	What steps could the King have taken to appease the New England colonists that might have prevented the American Revolution?
Evaluation	Making considered judgments by breaking down and reconnecting ideas, concepts, and facts and comparing the judgments to standards	In which area of the colonies did the colonists have the best natural resources from an economic standpoint?

So, in planning a U.S. History unit, a good teacher would build a base of facts and concepts and then develop lessons that would encourage students to ask and answer increasingly complicated sorts of questions based on those facts and concepts.

Cognitive, Affective, and Psychomotor Domains

Bloom's taxonomy deals with skills in the cognitive area, or domain. The other two widely recognized areas are the affective and psychomotor domains.

The affective domain includes class participation, including listening as well as speaking, defending positions, and recognizing the opinions of others.

The psychomotor domain includes abilities related to physical prowess ranging from reflexes through basic motions such as catching and throwing a ball, to skilled motions such as playing tennis, or playing the piano. It also includes the ability to communicate through motion, as in dancing or miming.

SOCIAL DEVELOPMENT

Erikson's Eight Stages of Psychosocial Development

You should be familiar with Erikson's Stages of Psychosocial Development. Erikson, a German-born American psychologist, identified eight stages of personal and social development, each of which takes the form of a resolution of an identity crisis. Here they are in chronological order:

1. Trust vs. Mistrust (birth to 18 months)

If a child is well cared for during this time, he/she will become naturally trusting and optimistic. The goal is for infants to develop basic trust in their families and the world. Again, due to the age range involved, you will probably not see questions dealing with this stage.

2. Autonomy vs. Doubt (18 months to 3 years)

A child learns the mechanical basics of controlling his world—including walking, grasping, and toilet training. The "terrible twos" fall into this stage, with common traits including stubbornness and willful behavior as the child pushes the limits of control and develops autonomy. Children want to become independent and still rely on their support system. Ideally, parents need to be supportive of the child's needs so that the child comes out of this stage proud of his abilities rather than ashamed.

3. Initiative vs. Guilt (3 to 6 years)

After becoming autonomous, children start wanting to do things. They have ideas and plans and carry out activities. Some activities aren't allowed, and it's important for children to feel that their activities are important and valued by adults. If this feeling isn't there, children believe that what they do is wrong, and guilt develops, which restricts growth.

4. Industry vs. Inferiority (6 to 12 years)

In these elementary-school years, children are expected to learn and produce. Parental influence decreases. Teachers and peers become more important. Success creates high self-esteem, while failures lowers self-image. Just the perception of failure can cause children to feel inferior, even if the failure is not real. If children can meet the expectations of themselves, parents, and teachers, they learn to be industrious. If they do not, they risk feeling inferior.

5. Identity vs. Role Confusion (12 to 18 years)

This is when adolescents answer the question, "Who am I?" It's quite common for teenagers to rebel, some very strongly. Erikson believed that the social structure of the United States was a healthy one for teenagers. They are offered the opportunity and leeway to try out different personalities and roles, and decide which ones suit them best. Acceptance by peer groups is of extreme importance.

Because the last three stages, described below, are stages that adults go through, it is unlikely that you will see any questions about them on the exam. They're listed here only for the purpose of completing the list.

6. Intimacy vs. Isolation (Young adulthood)

Being able to form mutually beneficial intimate relationships is the defining characteristic of this stage.

7. Generativity vs. Self-Absorption (Middle adulthood)

Adults need to be productive in helping and guiding future generations, both procreatively and professionally. If adults don't, they risk being self-absorbed.

8. Integrity vs. Despair (Late adulthood)

Finally, adults need to feel complete and comfortable with themselves and the choices they've made in their lives. They need to accept their eventual deaths.

PLAY AS A FORM OF SOCIAL DEVELOPMENT

Play is an important way in which children learn to socialize. Because most children will have reached the final stage of co-operative play by age 7, this is a developmental idea that is most likely to show up on the EC–4 exam. However, it's possible that some wrong answer choices on other exams will make reference to these ideas, so it's a good idea to review these no matter which test type you're preparing for.

Mildred Parten's Stages of Play Development

Mildred Parten, a child psychologist in the 1930s, was one of the first people to study children at play. Here are her stages of play development, which are linked to different levels of social interaction.

1. Solitary Play

Here, children play by themselves. While children may continue to do this throughout their childhoods, in the context of social interaction, this is usually observed in children less than 2 years of age.

2. Onlooker Play

At around 2 years, children will watch others play without doing anything themselves or making any effort to join in. This is closely followed in the same time frame by parallel play.

3. Parallel Play

This is play in which children do the same thing that other children are doing. There is no interaction between the children.

4. Associative Play

Normally, by age 4 or 5, children engage in associative play. Associative play is similar to parallel play, but there is increased interaction. Children will share, take turns, and be interested in what others are doing.

5. Cooperative Play

Finally, usually by age 5 to 7, children will play together in one activity.

MORAL DEVELOPMENT

Lawrence Kohlberg was a developmental psychologist at Harvard University in the late twentieth century who did extensive research in the field of moral education. You should be familiar with Kohlberg's stage theory of moral reasoning. He split moral development into three levels, each of which contains two stages.

Level 1: Preconventional Moral Reasoning (Elementary School)

Rules are created by others.

Stage 1: Punishment and Obedience Orientation

Young children obey rules simply because there are rules, and they understand that they risk punishment by breaking them. Whether an action is good or bad is understood in terms of its immediate consequences.

Stage 2: Instrumental Relativist Orientation

Children internalize the system from Stage 1 and realize that following the rules is generally in their best interests. An action is right or good if it gets you what you want. A simple view of "fair's fair" develops, so that, for example, favors are done with the expectation of something in return.

Level 2: Conventional Moral Reasoning (Junior High—High School)

Kohlberg called this level conventional because most of society remains at this level. Judgment is based on tradition and others' expectations and less on consequences. Individuals adopt rules and sometimes will put others' needs before their own.

Stage 3: Good Boy—Good Girl Orientation

An action is right or good if it helps, pleases, or is approved by others.

Stage 4: "Law and Order" Orientation

An action is right or good if it's expected out of a sense of duty or because it supports the morals or laws of the community or country. This reflects the common sentiment: "It's right because it's the law."

Level three is unlikely to be tested because Kohlberg believed that it's not fully attained until adulthood, if it's ever attained at all. It's included here for completeness.

Level 3: Post-Conventional Moral Reasoning

People determine their own values and ethics.

Stage 5: Social Contract Orientation

An action is right or good if it meets an agreed-upon system of rules and rights (such as the United States Constitution). Unlike stage four, this phase recognizes that rules can be changed for the betterment of society.

Stage 6: Universal Ethical Principle Orientation

Good and right are relative, not absolute, and require abstract thinking in terms of justice, equality, and human dignity. One's conscience determines right from wrong. (In his later years, Kohlberg decided that stages 5 and 6 were actually the same.)

STUDENTS AS DIVERSE LEARNERS

Not all students learn the same way, and students will have strengths and weaknesses in a variety of areas. The major ideas you should be familiar with are multiple intelligences, different learning styles, gender-based and culture-based differences, and exceptional students.

MULTIPLE INTELLIGENCES

What is intelligence? This question may never be fully answered. Nonetheless, you should be familiar with Howard Gardner's work because it might show up on the Praxis. Howard Gardner is a developmental psychologist at Harvard University who, in the mid-1980s, categorized the following eight types of intelligence:

Logical-Mathematical

This type of intelligence relates to the ability to detect patterns, think logically, and make deductions. Scientists and mathematicians tend to be logical-mathematical thinkers.

Linguistic

People who have linguistic intelligence are particularly sensitive not only to words themselves, but also to the relationship between the meanings and sounds of words and the ideas and concepts that words represent. Poets and journalists tend to possess linguistic intelligence.

Musical

Musical intelligence is defined as the ability to recognize and reproduce rhythm, pitch, and timbre—the three fundamental elements of music. Obviously, composers and musicians possess musical intelligence.

Spatial

People with spatial intelligence have the ability to create and manipulate mental images. They also perceive spatial relationships in the world accurately and can use both the mental and actual perceptions to solve problems. Artists and navigators both use well-developed spatial intelligence.

Naturalist

This intelligence relates to being sensitive to natural objects like plants and animals and making fine sensory discriminations. Naturalists, hunters, and botanists excel in this intelligence.

Bodily-Kinesthetic

Bodily-kinesthetic intelligence is the ability to consciously and skillfully control and coordinate your body's movements and manipulate objects. Athletes and dancers need a strong bodily-kinesthetic intelligence.

Interpersonal

Interpersonal intelligence is the ability to understand and respond to the emotions and intentions of others. Psychologists and salespeople make good use of interpersonal intelligence.

Intrapersonal

Intrapersonal intelligence is the ability to understand and respond to your own emotions, intentions, strengths, weaknesses, and intelligences.

Gardner believes that we all possess some degree of these intelligences, and that each of these must be relatively well developed in order for us to function well in society.

Although the intelligences are categorized separately, we rarely use them strictly independently. It is difficult to think of a profession or activity that wouldn't combine some of these intelligences. For instance, a pianist needs not only musical intelligence, but also interpersonal (to be able to relate to an audience) as well as bodily-kinesthetic (to control the actions of her hands on the keyboard).

Different Learning Styles

Not all people learn the same way. Different students will process information differently depending on how it's presented. Many theorists split learning styles into the following three categories:

Visual

Visual learners learn by seeing. They prefer graphs and charts to summarize information, rather than text or a spoken summary. They prefer maps and diagrams to step-by-step directions. They're more likely to remember faces than names when they meet someone. Traditional lecture-based lessons can be good for visual learners as long as the teacher makes good use of visual aids.

Auditory

Auditory learners learn by hearing. They're more likely to remember what was said about a painting they've studied than to be able to describe its appearance. Traditional lecture-based lessons are effective with aural learners.

Kinesthetic

Kinesthetic learners learn by doing. They remember things best if they try them out and see for themselves. They're more likely to remember what they were doing when they met someone than what they talked about. Traditional lecture-based lessons are not good for kinesthetic learners. Lessons that involve laboratory work or hands-on experimentation tend to be effective.

Of course, students do not fall neatly into one of these three categories. According to the ETS, good teachers should take into account these different learning styles and plan lessons accordingly.

Gender-Based and Culture-Based Differences

According to ETS, good teachers should recognize that gender and cultural differences could influence student learning. Teachers should examine their own preconceptions and be careful not to reinforce negative stereotypes.

Here are some key facts concerning gender differences:

- Boys are more likely to have adjustment problems in school than girls are.
- Girls tend to outperform boys in the primary grades.
- Boys tend to outperform girls in the secondary grades.
- Some standardized tests are inherently biased against girls.
- Girls tend to do more poorly in math than boys, probably due to societal influences.

Culture-based differences are too numerous and varied to discuss in detail. Teachers should be aware that societal expectations in a given culture could have an enormous impact upon student learning and behavior. For example, some cultures believe that eye contact from student to teacher is a sign of disrespect, so a teacher would need to be aware that holding such a student to American standards regarding classroom interaction would be inappropriate and possibly traumatic. Similarly, in some cultures less emphasis is placed on a girl's education than a boy's. A teacher faced with a female student from such a culture would need to be especially careful not to offend during parent-teacher conferences.

Exceptional Students

There are some specific requirements for students with specific needs. Because the Praxis is a national exam, individual state requirements won't be tested, but you should be aware of some common terminology:

Individuals with Disabilities Education Act (IDEA)

Passed in its original form in 1975, it now provides special education services to eligible students aged 3 to 21. In 1997, it was reauthorized and modified to allow parents and teachers to be more involved in special education services.

Individual Education Program (IEP)

An IEP outlines the education goals of a child with special needs. It is created by special education staff, school psychologists, the principal, teachers, the parents, other caregivers, and sometimes the student him- or herself. It will also typically include a mechanism and timeline to show that those goals are being achieved. The IEP must be reviewed annually.

"Least Restrictive Environment"

This phrase means that a child with special needs should have the same opportunities as other students to the fullest extent possible. In other words, students with disabilities should be taught with nondisabled students as much as possible. This is regulated by IDEA.

Mainstreaming/Inclusion

In the 1970s, children with special needs began to be placed in classrooms with children without special needs. That process was called *mainstreaming*, and is now called *inclusion*. It can have social and academic advantages, and it promotes a student's self-esteem and greater understanding and compassion from peers. The drawbacks are that it frequently requires extra help in the classroom and adaptation of the curriculum to meet the needs of the student.

Teachers should also know common strategies for adapting their teaching styles to exceptional children. Important areas include those on the following page:

Condition	Recommendation
Hearing impaired	Speak clearly and slowly Face the student when speaking Provide adequate visual instruction Position student in classroom away from other sounds Learn how to assist those with hearing aids
Visually impaired	Read out loud Provide tape-recorded lessons Ensure appropriate lighting Move student near front of classroom
Learning impaired (students who function 2 years below ability level)	Provide adequate structure Provide brief assignments Provide many auditory experiences and hands-on opportunities
Attention deficit/hyperactivity disorder (ADHD)	Reduce distractions Reduce the length of tasks Reward on-task behavior Use progress charts Allow opportunities to be active Make sure student understands rules and the assignment
Gifted students	Provide a variety of challenging learning experiences Do not isolate from rest of students
Lower socioeconomic status (SES)	Be aware of the potential for problems at home that could impact a student's performance Be sensitive to these problems Do not lower expectations Provide extra support and motivation

STUDENT MOTIVATION AND THE LEARNING ENVIRONMENT

Now that we've looked at how children develop and how they learn, let's take a look at how motivation and the classroom environment can have an impact. There are several major theorists you should be familiar with: Edward Lee Thorndike, Ivan Pavlov, Abraham Maslow, B. F. Skinner, and Albert Bandura.

Thorndike's Laws

Edward Lee Thorndike was an early behavioral psychologist whose work led him to three major conclusions:

- Law of effect: An action that produces a positive result is likely to be repeated.
- Law of readiness: Many actions can be performed in sequence to produce a desired effect.
- Law of exercise: Actions that are repeated frequently become stronger.

Pavlov's Conditioned Responses

Ivan Pavlov, a Russian psychologist, proved through experimentation that behavior could be learned according to a system of stimulus and response. His most famous experiment conditioned dogs to salivate at the sound of a bell. He did so by noting that dogs normally salivate at the smell of food, an unconditioned (i.e., innate or reflexive) response to an unconditioned stimulus. The ringing of a bell has no natural meaning for dogs. Such a signal is called a neutral stimulus. He introduced the sound of the bell at feeding time, thereby linking the sound of the bell and the smell of the food in the dogs' minds. Eventually, the dogs salivated at the sound of the bell alone, which was now a conditioned (i.e., learned) response to a conditioned stimulus.

Maslow's Hierarchy of Needs

Abraham Maslow was an educational theorist who believed that children must have certain needs met before they're ready to learn and grow. He organized these needs into a hierarchy, and taught that you couldn't progress to the next level until you'd achieved the previous one. Here's the hierarchy from low to high:

Deficiency Needs

Physiological needs—food, sleep, clothing, etc.

Safety needs—freedom from harm or danger

Belongingness and love needs—acceptance and love from others

Esteem needs—approval and accomplishment

Growth Needs

Cognitive needs—knowledge and understanding

Aesthetic needs—appreciation of beauty and order

Self-actualization needs—fulfillment of one's potential

Maslow called the first four *deficiency* needs. They are the basic requirements for physical and psychosocial well-being. Desire for these declines once you have them, and you don't think about them unless you lack them. He called the other three *growth* needs. They include the need for knowing, appreciating, and understanding. People try to meet these needs only after their basic needs have been met. He believed that meeting these needs created more desire for them. For example, having adequate shelter and food doesn't make you crave more shelter and food. By contrast, learning and understanding sparks the desire to learn and understand more.

Skinner's Operant Conditioning

B. F. Skinner was a psychologist who believed that you could use a system of positive and negative reinforcements to affect voluntary behavior. He called a positive reinforcement a *reinforcing stimulus*, or *reinforcer*, and the behavior that leads to the positive reinforcement an *operant*. The classic lab scenario is that of a rat pressing a bar in a cage in order to receive food. The pressing of the bar is the operant and the food is the reinforcer. If, after a time, the operant no longer leads to positive reinforcement, the behavior will decrease, and eventually stop. That process is called *extinction*.

A *negative reinforcement* is the removal of an unpleasant stimulus after a certain desired behavior occurs. For instance, a parent wishing to reward a teenager for consistently following a 10 P.M. curfew might extend the curfew until 10:30 P.M.

Presentation punishment is what we normally think of as being punished for bad behavior. For instance, a teenager that violated curfew rules might be grounded.

Bandura's Concept of Reinforcement

Albert Bandura, a psychologist, theorized that people learn behavior by watching others, trying the behavior themselves, and deciding whether the behavior was beneficial or detrimental. A positive result means that the behavior is *reinforced*, and therefore likely to be repeated. Bandura believed that peer group modeling and images from the media provided very strong suggestions for new behavior patterns.

EXTRINSIC AND INTRINSIC MOTIVATION

One important idea with respect to classroom management is *extrinsic*, or external, motivation (motivation that comes from outside factors) versus *intrinsic*, or internal, motivation (motivation that comes from within). In general, while external motivation can be used, the long-term goal is that students' motivation for learning be intrinsic.

Creating a Positive Learning Environment

Putting all this together means that children will learn best in an environment where they are encouraged to reach their potential, are inwardly motivated to learn, and are exposed to positive behaviors that allow learning to happen. Sounds easy, right?

Here are important things to keep in mind:

Consistency

Whatever approach you take to classroom management, you must be consistent. Rules that aren't followed consistently cease to have any weight. There should be consistent, regular procedures for daily activities (such as putting chairs on the top of desks at the end of the day).

Structure

Students need structure and direction. Lessons or tasks should have clear, well-articulated goals. Students should always know what they're supposed to be doing at any given point during the day.

Discipline

Discipline techniques that are too harsh and autocratic (such as Lee Canter's Assertive Discipline) run the risk of suppressing students' internal motivation. Discipline techniques that are too laissez-faire run the risk of not providing enough structure. Striking that balance is challenging, but can be made easier by establishing guidelines immediately. Guidelines should be age-appropriate. First-graders can simply be told that they need to raise their hands and wait for a teacher to call on them before they can start speaking. A sixth-grade teacher might use part of the first day of school having the class as a whole decide what types of behavior should be prohibited, and what consequences should arise from prohibited behavior.

Inappropriate behavior should be dealt with immediately, consistently, and in a manner that does not unwittingly provide positive reinforcement. For instance, a verbal reprimand should occur out of earshot from the rest of the class. A troublemaker who craves attention will continue to act out if the teacher gives him/her attention for each inappropriate behavior. For the student, the teacher's attention is positive reinforcement.

Time on Task

It's easy to lose the forest for the trees, but remember that students are there to learn. Structure and discipline serve to make sure there's as much time as possible available for actual learning.

Transitions

Procedures should be in place for getting students from one task to another in an efficient manner. Suggestions include agreed-upon signals such as flipping the lights on and off or clapping your hands.

While you may be preparing for only one specific PLT exam, it won't hurt you to complete the multiple-choice drills for the other age ranges.

DRILL: STUDENTS AS LEARNERS K–6

1. Jean Piaget stated a theory of four stages of cognitive development in young children. Which stage is most associated with a fourth grade student whose thinking becomes organized and logical?

    (A) Sensorimotor
    (B) Preoperational
    (C) Concrete Operational
    (D) Formal Operational

2. Which theorist is most frequently credited for forming the experimental basis for behaviorism?

    (A) Watson
    (B) Pavlov
    (C) Vygotsky
    (D) Bandura

3. Theorist Lawrence Kohlberg would most likely agree with which of the following statements about first grade students?

    (A) Children have no clear morality.
    (B) Children show concern for others and try to live up to expectations.
    (C) Children are able to differentiate between legality and morality.
    (D) Children have a generalized sense of respect for rules and expectations.

4. Students in third grade are given a spelling test. The skills measured in this test are aligned with what stage in Bloom's taxonomy of learning?

    (A) Knowledge
    (B) Comprehension
    (C) Synthesis
    (D) Evaluation

5. Which of the following statements is NOT true about the requirements of an IEP plan?

    (A) It must be in writing.
    (B) Parent consent is required for an IEP plan.
    (C) Special education services or special needs must be included in the plan.
    (D) Objectives, and a timetable to achieve those objectives, can be included in the plan only if requested from the parents.

DRILL: STUDENTS AS LEARNERS 5–9

1. Which of the following examples best demonstrates Vygotsky's theory of the zone of proximal development for a seventh-grade student?

    (A) A student reads a new geometry textbook, and is asked to explain the Pythagorean theorem.

    (B) A student is given a book to read in French, though she has never studied the subject.

    (C) A student is asked to complete a spelling assignment, which reviews words that were assigned last year.

    (D) A student, who can currently solve basic algebra equations, is asked to solve multi-variable algebra equations.

2. "Individuals have the capability to learn from others." This theory was supported by the work of which theorist?

    (A) Albert Bandura

    (B) Jerome Bruner

    (C) John Dewey

    (D) Jean Piaget

3. Which of Jean Piaget's stages of cognitive development is most associated with that of a seventh-grade student who is able to think fully in symbolic terms about concepts?

    (A) Formal Operational

    (B) Concrete Operational

    (C) Preoperational

    (D) Sensorimotor

4. According to Erikson, what is the primary emotional crisis experienced by children in grades 6–9?

    (A) Initiative vs. Guilt

    (B) Industry vs. Inferiority

    (C) Identity vs. Role Confusion

    (D) Intimacy vs. Isolation

5. Ms. Schulman is teaching an eighth-grade class that contains several students for whom English is not a first language. Students in her class have been asked to interview a family member, and then present that information to the class. What can Ms. Schulman do to ensure the ESL students understand the task, and develop their skills effectively?

    (A) Reduce the requirements of the assignment for those students.

    (B) Provide instructions in their natural language.

    (C) Have ESL students work together on the task.

    (D) Use context clues to help students identify the word meaning of the instructions.

DRILL: STUDENTS AS LEARNERS 7–12

1. Mr. Coyne gives a group assignment to his eleventh-grade English Literature class. The grade for each individual will be based on the group's performance on a book report and presentation. By creating a group grade, Mr. Coyne is employing what type of motivation on his students?

   (A) Intrinsic motivation
   (B) Extrinsic motivation
   (C) Prevention
   (D) Extinction

2. Students are given the following assignment in their tenth-grade World History class:

   Describe the challenges that helped to cause the downfall of the Roman Empire? Should America be concerned that we could soon be in a "downfall?" Provide examples between the two cultures to support your beliefs.

   In order to successfully answer the assignment, students will display what type of learning in Bloom's taxonomy?

   (A) Comprehension
   (B) Application
   (C) Knowledge
   (D) Evaluation

3. Which type of diversity might require modification of objectives?

   (A) Academic
   (B) Cultural
   (C) Linguistic
   (D) All of the Above

4. Which of the following is a definition for a schema?

   (A) Providing additional resources for a student, to help them build on the learning he or she already possesses.
   (B) A mental framework by which problems can be perceived and understood.
   (C) Theory that students learn through interaction with the environment.
   (D) The ability to learn by critiquing your past performances.

5. Which of the following would be the LEAST likely reason to explain a girl's sudden drop in math performance?

   (A) Social expectations from her peers.
   (B) Unintentional discrimination by her teacher.
   (C) Difficulty in adjusting to the school regimen.
   (D) Lack of parental involvement.

ANSWERS AND EXPLANATIONS TO DRILL: STUDENTS AS LEARNERS K–6

1. **C** During this period, students' thinking becomes operational, which means that concepts become organized and logical, as long as they are working with or around concrete materials or images.
2. **B** Pavlov, with his conditioning experiments with dogs, is considered the founder of experimental behaviorism. John Watson originated the behaviorist movement in the early 1900s.
3. **A** Kohlberg proposed three levels of moral development, with two stages at each level. For primary grades, he argued that children concentrate on their egocentric needs, and that students do not have a clear sense of morality.
4. **A** In the knowledge stage, students are asked to remember specifics, recalling terms, formulas, and theories.
5. **D** Objectives, short-term goals, and a timetable to achieve both, are a fundamental part of all IEP plans. Parents do not need to request these—they are a standard part of any plan.

ANSWERS AND EXPLANATIONS TO DRILL: STUDENTS AS LEARNERS 5–9

1. **D** When a student can solve problems, with the guidance of someone who has already solved the problems, Vygotsky states that the student is in a Zone of proximal development. The answer choice gives a situation where the student is asked to build upon prior learning, and has a reasonable chance to solve the problem, with some assistance.
2. **A** Bandura studied the area of social modeling, where individuals could learn from others by watching their behavior, and the rewards of punishments for those behaviors.
3. **A** In this stage, students develop and demonstrate concepts without concrete materials or images. Students become able to reason effectively, abstractly, and theoretically.
4. **C** Erikson presented a set of eight psychosocial stages, and an emotional crisis at each stage can lead to a positive or negative result. In this stage, students who establish an identity and sense of self have an easier transition into adulthood.
5. **D** Teaching English as a second language can be accomplished, but with some additional effort is necessary. Many teachers make the mistake of answer choices (A) through (C), which segment the students and erroneously lower the expectations of those students.

ANSWERS AND EXPLANATIONS TO DRILL: STUDENTS AS LEARNERS 7–12

1. **B** Extrinsic motivation is motivation that comes from outside factors. In the example above, there will be peer pressure from other students to perform well on the task, as it will impact their grade as well.
2. **D** In evaluation, students are asked to judge value, and compare works or products to various criteria. While "application" may seem correct, that is not a complete answer. Evaluation does more than application—it presents value judgments on a situation, rather than simply apply a concept to a specific situation.
3. **D** All types may require that teachers modify their objectives to address specific needs of a student.
4. **B** A schema is a mental framework that allows a student to process and absorb new material in relation to previous knowledge.
5. **C** Girls typically wouldn't have trouble adjusting to the routines of a scholastic environment. The other choices could contribute to a sudden drop in mathematics performance.

22

PLT: Instruction and Assessment

INSTRUCTION AND ASSESSMENT

This section makes up another 35 percent of the test content. It deals with the different ways that teachers can teach material and how best to assess student learning.

CREATIVE THINKING VS. CRITICAL THINKING

A good teacher promotes both critical and creative thinking in her students. The difference between the two might best be described by thinking about the following questions:

- How many different ways can you think of to get from New York to San Francisco?
- What's the best way to get from New York to San Francisco?

Answering the first question involves creative thinking. Answering the second involves critical thinking. Let's compare the two:

Creative Thinking

The first question involves *divergent thinking*—there are many possible answers, and no particular answer is necessarily right or wrong. One technique that a good teacher can use to help with questions such as these is *brainstorming*, in which students are encouraged to come up with as many solutions as possible without stopping to evaluate their merits. Imagine posing the question to a group of active sixth graders. At first, you'd probably get some relatively predictable responses that you'd write down as the students came up with them:

- You could fly; you could drive; you could take a train.

Then, you could start to expect some more "outside the box" ideas:

- You could bike; you could run; you could walk; you could take a boat around the tip of South America and come back up the other side.

And some with less critical thought behind them:

- You could hitchhike. How about a hot air balloon? You could drive to Florida and take the space shuttle. You could wrap yourself up and have yourself FedExed. Could you dig a tunnel?

And after a while the responses would taper off, and you'd be left with a large list of possibilities on the board.

You should be familiar with two other important ideas regarding creative thinking:

- *Restructuring* is a term describing the process of thinking about an old problem in a new way. Many educational psychologists believe that time away from the problem is an important element that encourages restructuring—some believe that dreaming is also an important component.
- Also, play encourages creative thinking, and good teachers use well-designed in-class games for this purpose.

Critical Thinking

Let's go back to the results of the brainstorming exercise. There's a large list of possibilities on the board, and you're now ready to ask the second question:

- What's the best way of getting from New York to San Francisco?

This question requires *convergent thinking*—from many possible answers the student is expected to choose and defend the best one. A good teacher will use this opportunity to show how the answer to this question depends on the criteria used. Does "best" mean "cheapest?" If so, then hitchhiking might be a good choice, but you'd have to factor in the cost of food and shelter, because the trip would take longer than it would if you flew. Does "best" mean "quickest?" If so, then flying is probably the best way to go. A good teacher would also seize the opportunity to allow for *transfer*, the application of previously learned skills or facts to new situations. For example, if the class had recently completed a unit on the environment, the teacher could ask, "What if 'best' means 'most environmentally friendly,' but you have to get there within three days?"

Two important aspects of critical thinking are *inductive* and *deductive* reasoning.

Inductive Reasoning

Inductive reasoning occurs when, after viewing several examples, students perceive underlying rules or patterns. For example, students could be given many different parallelograms, and asked what they all have in common. Through measurement and comparison, students might induce that opposite sides of parallelograms are parallel, and that the sum of any two adjacent angles in a parallelogram is 180 degrees.

Deductive Reasoning

Deductive reasoning works in the opposite direction. For example, students might be told that if the sum of any two adjacent angles in a given quadrilateral is 180 degrees, then that quadrilateral is a parallelogram. Then, they'd be given many quadrilaterals, and asked to determine which ones are parallelograms. Both inductive and deductive reasoning are important cognitive skills.

INSTRUCTIONAL STRATEGIES

Different teaching approaches should be taken to stimulate different types of thinking. You should know what options are available to you and which strategies are most likely to accomplish a given educational goal.

Direct Instruction

This is the most common form of teaching, the traditional model in which the teacher stands in front of the room, presents new material, and guides the class toward understanding. You should be familiar with the following concepts:

Hunter's Effective Teaching Model and Mastery Learning

Madeline Hunter, an educational psychologist, expanded on the basic idea of direct instruction and broke the process down into discrete steps:

- Prepare students to learn:

  Review the previous day's material with a question or two.

  Get the students' attention with *an anticipatory set*, a question or problem designed to spark students' curiosity and imagination.

  Outline the lesson's objectives.

- Use input and modeling:

  Teach well.

  Organize your presentation.

  Present the information clearly.

  Connect new ideas to old ideas.

  Use examples and analogies.

  Demonstrate and model new techniques.
- Make sure students understand:

  Ask both individual and group questions.
- Have students apply new techniques immediately:

  Work several short examples—guided practice.

  Monitor student ability—independent practice.

Ausubel's Advance Organizers

David Ausubel's theory expands on some aspects of Hunter's model. *Advance organizers* are the structure (also known as *scaffolding* or *support*) and information that students will need to learn new material effectively. They fall into two categories:

- A comparative organizer relates previously mastered material to the material that's about to be presented. For example, a middle-school lesson about sonnet form might begin with a comparative advance organizer that reminds students of a previous lesson on iambic pentameter or simple ABAB rhyme schemes.
- An expository organizer is a new idea or concept that needs to be understood before a specific lesson can be understood. For example, a high-school literature class already familiar with rhyme schemes might need an expository advance organizer that discussed the purpose of analyzing poetry and showing that rhyme scheme analysis is just one method of doing so.

Spiral Curriculum

Although this is difficult for a single teacher to implement independently, a spiral curriculum revisits topics throughout a student's education, teaching age-appropriate facts and concepts at each stage of the spiral. For instance, a biology curriculum might begin with kindergarteners sorting leaves according to color or shape, whereas a third-grader might learn about the seasonal cycle of leaves, and a sixth grader might learn that leaf shape is an environmental adaptation.

Demonstrations

Visual learners in particular respond well to demonstrations. Showing is more effective than simply telling. New computer technology allows for imaginative and compelling demonstrations. Good teachers take advantage of all tools at their disposal.

Mnemonics

Provide students with memory devices to help them retain factual information. For instance, "Please excuse my dear Aunt Sally" is a common mnemonic for the order of mathematical operations: Parentheses, Exponents, Multiplication, Division, Addition, and Subtraction.

Note-Taking

Students need to be taught how to take notes effectively. One important technique involves giving students a general outline of the major points to be discussed and having them fill in the blanks as the lesson progresses.

Outlining

A clear order of presentation with a well-defined hierarchy of ideas is crucial so that students have an understanding of what the most important parts of a lesson are.

Use of Visual Aids

As with demonstrations, visual aids can make new information stick in students' minds better than it would if it were presented through lecture alone.

Student-Centered Models

In contrast to direct instruction, student-centered models make students, not teachers, the center of attention while new material is being learned. These methods do not lessen the demands on the teacher; in fact, use of student-centered models requires more planning and as much active participation by the teacher as does use of direct instruction. Here are some important student-centered models:

Emergent Curriculum

In this environment, students are given a strong voice in deciding what form the curriculum will take. For instance, students could decide that they were interested in studying leaves. It would then be incumbent upon the teacher to find useful leaf-related activities and experiments that would meet established educational goals. Alternatively, the teacher could present a variety of possible topics, and the students could choose which they wanted to study.

Cooperative Learning

In this model, students are split into mixed-ability groups, assigned very well-defined tasks to accomplish or problems to analyze, and are given individual roles within the group (such as note-taker or illustrator). Students learn from each other and interact in a way that is not possible with direct instruction. One well-known method of organizing cooperative learning in the classroom is called STAD (for Student Teams Achievement Divisions) in which cooperative learning cycles through the following stages:

1. teaching, in which the teacher presents basic material and gives teams a task;
2. team study, in which students work on the project;
3. test, in which students take individual quizzes; and
4. team recognition, in which the best-performing teams are rewarded.

In another model, called the think-pair-share method, students research a topic on their own, discuss their theories and ideas with one other student, and then participate in a classroom discussion.

Discovery Learning

This method is closely aligned with inductive reasoning. Students are given examples and are expected to find patterns and connections with minimal guidance from a teacher during class. Students are encouraged to use *intuitive thinking*, and then make an effort to prove or disprove their intuition given the available information.

Concept Models

Concept models are part of an organizational strategy that helps students to relate new ideas to old ideas. There are three aspects that you should be familiar with:

- Concept development: The concept is promoted by the identification of a prototype, or stereotypical example of the concept. For example, if the concept is polygons, a prototype might be a square or a triangle. From the prototype, students generate the definition, in this case, a closed plane figure with a finite number of straight-line sides.
- Concept attainment: Students learn to identify examples (pentagons, right triangles) and non-examples (circles, open figures) and sub-define the category according to given criteria (a rectangle is a special polygon having four sides and four equal angles).
- Concept mapping or webbing: Students draw a pictorial representation of the concepts or ideas about some topic and the links between them. Teachers can look over these maps and discern areas of misunderstanding. There are several different types of methods that currently go by names like "concept mapping," "mental mapping," or "concept webbing."

Inquiry Method

This method is related to discovery learning. A teacher poses a question, and the students have to gather information, formulate, and test hypotheses in order to answer it. Although this method could conceivably be used in teaching almost any discipline, it's particularly well-suited to teaching science and math. For instance, a teacher could pose the question, "Do all triangles have 180 degrees?" Students could then try to find different ways of proving or disproving the statement (drawing triangles, measuring the angles, and adding them up; comparing the degree measures to a straight line; etc.), and eventually conclude that yes, all triangles have 180 degrees.

Metacognition

Teachers can also encourage students to think about their own learning processes. This is called *metacognition*. For example, a teacher might assign a journal assignment in which students would answer the questions "What did I learn today?" and "How did it relate to things I've learned earlier?"

PLANNING INSTRUCTION

How does a teacher decide what to teach? Ideally, teachers will have long-term and short-term objectives for their students. It's important that these objectives are well-defined, because planning instruction and assessment is easier and more meaningful if goals are clearly specified.

There are two fundamental approaches to defining objectives. Good teachers apply both.

Teaching Objectives

Teaching objectives are defined in general terms. To continue with the geometry example, a cognitive objective might be, "Students will understand the hierarchical relationships among the different types of quadrilaterals." The advantage to a teaching objective is that it's general enough to encompass a wide variety of teaching approaches and techniques. The disadvantage is that it's difficult to measure student understanding of any given concept in all its various forms. Could you write a test that would measure whether students understood all "the hierarchical relationships among the different types of quadrilaterals?"

Learning Objectives

Learning objectives are defined in concrete terms, and can be directly observed. Students are expected to exhibit the desired behavior at the end of the lesson(s). For example, "Students will be able to construct a perfect square of a given length using a compass and straightedge." These goals are easy to assess—you could simply watch a student perform the construction—but their specificity makes it difficult to include large-scale concepts. For instance, imagine how long the list of learning objectives would be to describe the body of knowledge and skills covered in the first semester of a geometry class.

The objective type a teacher will use depends on the plan he/she is creating. A daily lesson plan will require learning objectives; a unit or monthly plan will include teaching objectives. Here's an example:

Type of Lesson	Type of Objective	Example of Objective
Unit Lesson Plan	Teaching objective	Students will understand the hierarchical relationships among the different types of quadrilaterals.
Daily Lesson Plan	Learning objectives	Students will recite the definition of a quadrilateral. Students will be able to demonstrate the hierarchical distinction between squares and rectangles. Students will be able to prove that every rhombus is a parallelogram.

ASSESSMENT STRATEGIES

Types of Assessments

Just as you'd use different teaching strategies to teach different ideas, you should use different assessment strategies to measure student achievement. Here are some terms you should be familiar with:

Norm-Referenced Tests

If you've ever been graded on a curve, then you've experienced a norm-referenced test. That means that your grade depended on how well you did compared to everyone else who took the test.

Criterion-Referenced Tests

Your driver's license test was probably criterion-referenced. Perhaps there were 25 questions, and you needed to answer 20 of them correctly in order to pass. It didn't matter how many people had aced the test and how many people had answered only 10 questions correctly. You needed to prove a certain proficiency in order to pass.

Standardized Tests

If you're reading this book, then we probably have a pretty good idea about what you think of standardized tests. The term *standardized* means that test content, conditions, grading, and reporting are equivalent for everyone who takes the test. We tend to think of them as purely multiple-choice, but that's not true; the Praxis II: PLT is a standardized test, but includes short-answer questions as well.

- Achievement tests—Most standardized tests given are achievement tests, given to measure specific knowledge in a specific area.
- Aptitude tests—These tests purport to measure how well a student is likely to do in the future. The letters SAT used to stand for "Scholastic Aptitude Test," because ETS claimed it measured how well a student was likely to perform in college. (ETS later said it stood for "Scholastic Assessment Test," and now ETS says it doesn't stand for anything at all.)

Remember, of course, that you don't have to give standardized tests to your students. You have a much wider range of options, including the following:

Assessments of Prior Knowledge/Pretesting

It's important to take into account the level of knowledge a student had before beginning a given lesson or semester. Would it be fair to hold a recent immigrant to the same standards as a native English speaker on an oral grammar test? Probably not. Some curricula are designed so that a specific set of knowledge and skills are necessary before instruction in a new area can occur. Such a set of knowledge and skills is called a *prerequisite competency.*

Structured Observations

These are particularly well-suited to situations where cooperative learning is taking place. The teacher can observe the interactions within a group and evaluate student performance accordingly. This is an example of an *informal assessment,* meaning that there is no grading rubric or checklist that a teacher follows. An informal assessment is more subjective and situation-specific than it is during a *formal assessment* such as a standardized test.

Student Responses During a Lesson

This shouldn't necessarily be considered the same as grading on class participation, but a teacher can get a strong sense of student understanding (or lack thereof) based on responses during classroom discussions. This is another example of an informal assessment.

Portfolios

These aren't just used in art classes. Portfolios are often used to give students a place to collect their best work over a longer period of time, such as a unit or even a semester. Teachers can get a sense of the level of student work holistically, without placing undue influence on a specific test. Portfolios allow teachers to assess learning growth over a period of time.

Essays Written to Prompts

While these take longer to grade, and depend upon students possessing sufficient writing skills, essays give insight into student thought in a way that multiple-choice tests cannot.

Journals

Many good teachers use journals not only as tools to promote individual self-expression, but also to gauge understanding.

Self-Evaluation

Sometimes, a good teacher will give students an opportunity to grade their own work. While it's not usually binding, the grade a student chooses to give himself (along with the explanation of why it's deserved) can provide the teacher valuable insight.

CHARACTERISTICS OF ASSESSMENTS

There are some key concepts that you should know with respect to assessment:

Validity

Does the test measure what it's supposed to measure? In addition to ensuring representative content, a well-designed test will correct for factors such as guessing and test anxiety.

Reliability

Barring other factors, would you get the same score on the test if you were to take it today and two weeks from now? If so, the test is said to be reliable.

True Score

The true score is the score you'd get if it measured your knowledge and nothing more. For instance, if you made several lucky guesses you'd get a score higher than your true score; if you didn't sleep at all the night before the test, you'd probably get a score lower than your true score. Sometimes the test itself has variations from administration to administration that could impact your score. A well-designed standardized test minimizes those variations.

Confidence Interval

Test writers acknowledge that not all test-takers will get their true score each time they take the test. To account for that, they suggest that you view any given score within the context of a confidence interval—a range on either side of the score you got. For example, on the GMAT (the business school admissions test), scores range from 200–800, with a confidence interval of 30 points at 66%. Let's say you took the GMAT and got a 510. The confidence interval means that the test writers believe there's a 66% chance that your true score is between a 480 and a 540. (Incidentally, about one-fourth of all GMAT test takers get between a 480 and a 540.)

Mean

The *mean* is the mathematical average of test takers' scores. Add the scores up and divide by the number of test takers.

Median

If you list all the scores in mathematical order, the middle score is called the *median.*

Mode

The *mode* is the score that occurs most frequently.

Standard Deviation

A statistical idea that tells you how wide the variance of scores is with respect to the mean.

Taken together, these last four concepts can lend some insight into what test results looked like as a whole, and how any individual test score compares to the rest of the group. Let's look at two examples:

Here's one group of 20 scores on a test with a maximum score of 100:

Test Scores			
45	59	65	68
69	71	73	73
74	74	79	81
83	84	85	88
92	93	94	100

The average of these scores is 77.5, and the median is 76.5. The mode is 73. In chart form, the distribution of the scores looks like this:

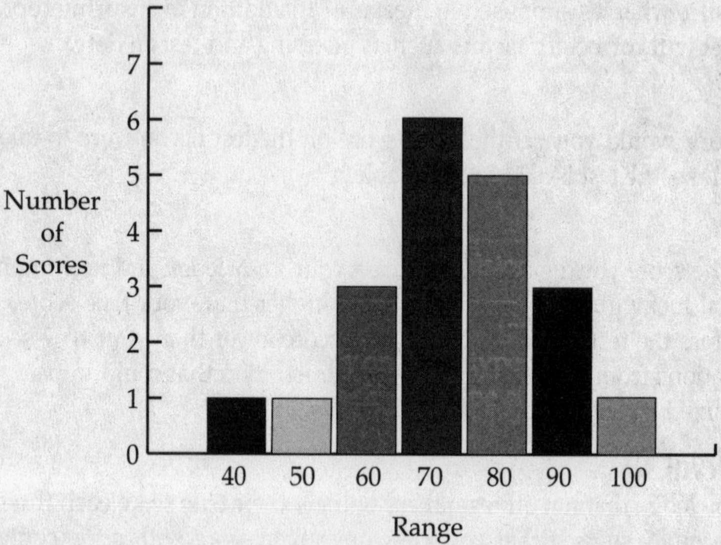

The standard deviation is about 13.2, which means scores are relatively evenly spread out, but tend to cluster around the mean. (The curve resembles a normal distribution, or a typical-looking bell curve).

But what if the scores looked like this?

Test Scores			
52	53	54	56
56	58	59	59
59	59	96	97
98	98	98	99
99	100	100	100

Here, the average is still a 77.5, and the median is only slightly different from the last set: 77.5. In fact, according to those numbers, these results are virtually identical. But the mode is 59, and if you see the results in chart form, the differences are even starker:

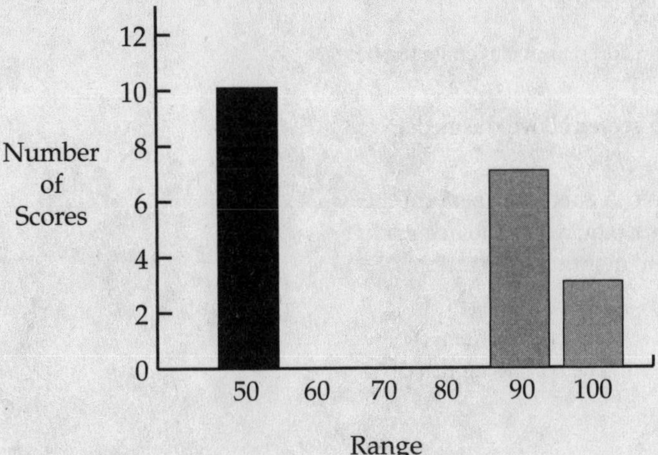

The standard deviation is about 22 points, which means that the scores are not clustered about the mean. But the only way you could tell that without seeing the individual scores (or a graph) would be to know something about the standard deviation.

Finally, there are several different ways that you can put an individual score into a larger context:

Percentile Rank

This tells you what percent of the testing population scored worse than you did. For instance, a score in the 72nd percentile means that you got a better score than 72 percent of the other test takers.

Stanines

The word "stanine" is a contraction of the words "standard nine." Stanines are an artificial scale from 1 to 9 that can be placed on any normal (bell-curved) distribution of scores. The mean is 5, and the standard deviation is 2. For instance, if you had a stanine score of 4, you'd be slightly below average. If you had a stanine score of 8, you'd be well above average. Stanines are meant to be a broad classification of scores, and are often used instead of a more precise measurement to reduce the chance of attributing too much importance to a particular score.

Grade Equivalent Score

This is a score expressed in terms of how an average student performs at a certain grade level. For instance, a grade equivalent score of 10.2 means that your performance on a given test is equivalent to that of an average 10th grader in the second month of the school year.

While you may be preparing for only one specific PLT test, it won't hurt you to complete the multiple-choice drills for the other age ranges.

DRILL: INSTRUCTION AND ASSESSMENT K–6

1. Which of the following is not considered a norm-referenced test?

   (A) An aptitude test
   (B) A standardized test
   (C) A criterion-referenced test
   (D) An achievement test

2. A second-grade student completes a Reading norm-referenced test, and receives a grade equivalent score of 4.2. Which of the following statements must be true?

   (A) The student scored above average for her class.
   (B) The student scored above the median for her class.
   (C) The student can effectively perform the Reading work required of a fourth grader in the second month of instruction.
   (D) The student's score on the test is the average score on the test of a fourth grader in the second month of instruction.

3. Mr. Laky finds that his fourth-grade class loses focus when it switches from subject to subject. Which of the following techniques would help Mr. Laky manage his class more effectively?

   (A) Modeling
   (B) Guided practice
   (C) Transitions
   (D) Assertive discipline

4. Students in Ms. Daniels' kindergarten class are playing a board game. This activity is considered what type of play?

   (A) Active
   (B) Cooperative
   (C) Creative
   (D) Dramatic

5. Which of the following activities does NOT take place in the STAD (Student Teams-Achievement Divisions) method of teaching?

   (A) Team Study
   (B) Individual testing
   (C) Recognition
   (D) Team testing

DRILL: INSTRUCTION AND ASSESSMENT 5–9

1. A definition of prerequisite competencies is

   (A) what a student currently understands

   (B) what a student should know or be able to do before the next level of instruction

   (C) a predetermined order in which instruction is presented

   (D) the ability to assess what a student understands

2. Students complained that Ms. Trinacty's sixth-grade Science test had too many questions that were not discussed in the chapter they were assigned. Students believe the test had which of the following qualities?

   (A) High criterion validity

   (B) Low criterion validity

   (C) Low content validity

   (D) High content validity

3. Ms. Coleman asks her seventh-grade class to determine the next book they will read in English. She presents the class with four choices, and then has each student vote by secret ballot for the book they would like to read. The book with the most votes will be the next assigned book in English. Ms. Coleman is planning instruction using which of the following theories of curriculum?

   (A) Emergent curriculum

   (B) Anti-bias curriculum

   (C) Curriculum webbing

   (D) State curriculum frameworks

4. Students in Ms. Daly's class were having trouble remembering the definition of raconteur, so Ms. Daly told them, "When you think of raconteur, think of 'A raccoon sings on tour,' so you can remember that a raconteur is a storyteller."

   Ms. Daly employed which of the following instructional strategies?

   (A) Demonstration

   (B) Mnemonic

   (C) Outlining

   (D) Allegory

5. After presenting a lecture on the human circulatory system, Mr. Farrell then demonstrated how blood travels towards and away from the heart. Mr. Farrell is in what stage of Madeline Hunter's "Effective Teaching Model?"

   (A) Anticipatory Set

   (B) Input

   (C) Modeling

   (D) Guided Practice

DRILL: INSTRUCTION AND ASSESSMENT 7–12

1. Mr. Thomas evaluated the standardized test scores of two of his students. Billy received a math score of 530, while Cindy received a math score of 540. Mr. Thomas concluded that Cindy is stronger in math than Billy.

   Which of the following statements, if true, would help WEAKEN Mr. Thomas's claim that Cindy is a stronger student?

   (A) Cindy had taken more practices tests than Billy.

   (B) The test has a standard error of measurement of 10%.

   (C) Both scores were below the median performance of the class.

   (D) The test has high content validity with the curriculum.

2. Which of the following tests would best be scored by using a holistic scoring method?

   (A) A multiple choice Calculus test

   (B) A writing sample designed to measure use of grammar

   (C) A student-prompted essay on college admission policies

   (D) An art portfolio used in AP Art

3. Which of the following subjects is typically NOT addressed in a lesson plan?

   (A) Objectives

   (B) Assessment

   (C) Practice

   (D) Punishments

4. "Advance Organizers" are the work of what theorist?

   (A) Madeline Hunter

   (B) David Ausubel

   (C) Abraham Maslow

   (D) John Dewey

5. Ms. Hecox wants her tenth-grade Geometry students to recite the different theorems learned in the class. This task reflects what learning stage?

   (A) Knowledge

   (B) Synthesis

   (C) Evaluation

   (D) Application

ANSWERS AND EXPLANATIONS TO DRILL: INSTRUCTION AND ASSESSMENT K–6

1. **C** Criterion-referenced tests are designed to determine how effectively a student has learned a specific set of material, while norm-referenced tests are designed to compare students in a set of skills.
2. **D** A grade equivalent score gives a score comparable to the average score by a student at a particular level.
3. **C** Mr. Laky likely needs to improve his transitions—the ability to move a class from one task to the next effectively. Poor transitions distract students from the learning process.
4. **B** In a board game, students interact with one another, and learn from watching other children play and interacting with them socially.
5. **D** In the STAD method, there is a lecture, followed by a team study activity, followed by individual testing, and concluded with recognition for the team's collective performance.

ANSWERS AND EXPLANATIONS TO DRILL: INSTRUCTION AND ASSESSMENT K–6

1. **B** While answer choice (A) is close, a prerequisite competency is something the student should know, not necessarily something a student does know.
2. **C** A test that lacks high content validity is unfair, for the test does not related to the subject material covered.
3. **A** Emergent curriculum brings students into the curriculum process.
4. **B** Ms. Daly gave the class a mnemonic, which are tools teachers provide students to help them retain factual information.
5. **C** In the modeling stage, the skills or procedures are being taught or demonstrated. Notice the clue in the question, which indicates that a lecture had already been given. A lecture would qualify as Input, or the presentation of new information.

ANSWERS AND EXPLANATIONS TO DRILL: INSTRUCTION AND ASSESSMENT 7–12

1. **B** Focusing on a single score, and ignoring the scoring range of a student, is one of the most common interpretation errors on standardized tests. With an error of measurement, we can only conclude that Billy and Cindy scored within the same range.
2. **C** In a holistic scoring scale, an overall score is given that focuses on the overall quality of the work. Analytical scoring gives specific scores on individual items, such as grammar.
3. **D** Typically, a teacher does not outline the rewards and punishments associated with a specific lesson plan. Those are a standard part of effective classroom management, which apply to all lessons.
4. **B** David Ausubel built on the work of Hunter to refine the theories of effective learning further. Ausubel's "Advance Organizers" are the structure and information students require to learn new material.
5. **A** Ms. Hecox's communication style is one that asks students to recite facts. Reciting or recalling learned items takes place in the Knowledge learning stage (according to Bloom).

23

PLT: Teacher Professionalism

TEACHER PROFESSIONALISM

Questions dealing with teacher professionalism make up about 15 percent of the test. Because the test can't require knowledge of specific state regulations and requirements, common sense will take you most of the way. Here are the major categories of topics that are tested:

The Reflective Practitioner

ETS believes that all teachers should take advantage of resources available to them in order to become even more effective teachers. Common resources include:

- professional journals and other publications
- professional associations
- professional development activities
- other teachers

ETS also believes that teachers should constantly evaluate themselves and look for ways to improve.

The Larger Community

ETS sees the teacher as a resource and role model for the community in which he or she teaches, and that interaction within the community is an important aspect of the teacher's job.

Home Environment

Many factors outside of school can influence a student's learning. Changes in family situations ranging from the birth of a sibling to parental divorce can markedly affect a child's performance. Similarly, socioeconomic conditions need to be recognized as an influence. While teachers shouldn't lower their expectations of students with unique situations, teachers should be aware of the potential impact of those situations on a child's performance.

Involving Parents

All studies agree that parental involvement is crucial to a child's success in school. Good teachers take steps to encourage this involvement. Pick answer choices that describe parents and teachers as equal partners in a child's education. Also pick choices that display open, two-way communication between parents and teachers. Finally, conferences between parents and the teacher should always begin and end on a positive note.

Legal Responsibilities

Again, the Praxis can't get too specific, but you should be aware of the following:

- Student records are confidential and should be kept private.
- Students should be treated respectfully.
- Teachers are required to report suspicion of child abuse.

Apart from that, use common sense when answering these questions. For instance, an improper relationship between a teacher and a student is always prohibited, so any situation that could be potentially compromising to the teacher or the student should be avoided.

DRILL: TEACHER PROFESSIONALISM K–6

1. Mr. Smith has taught the second grade for 15 years, while Ms. Jackson is teaching second grade for her first year. Which of the following statements is true about the development needs of each teacher?

   (A) Mr. Smith does not have to spend as much time developing his skills as Ms. Jackson.

   (B) If Mr. Smith and Ms. Jackson attend the three teacher development conferences scheduled for the year, they will ensure their personal development needs are met for the year.

   (C) Mr. Smith and Ms. Jackson likely have different development needs, based on their own strengths and familiarity with their curricula.

   (D) If both teachers are reviewed successfully by the principal, there is no need for additional development courses this year.

2. Ms. Pirner is a new third-grade teacher in the Wright District. She has been asked to participate in "Feedback," the school's development program for teachers. Which of the following activities would likely be best for Ms. Pirner, given her experience in the program?

   (A) Discussions of curriculum

   (B) Specific critiques of the teaching methods of other instructors

   (C) Visiting other classrooms, and taking observation notes on the teacher's performance

   (D) As a first year teacher, Ms. Pirner should not participate in any of the activities.

3. Which groups or entities in the United States are legally responsible for education?

   (A) The federal government

   (B) The Department of Education

   (C) Each of the fifty state governments

   (D) The Teachers Association of America

4. Generally, teachers have freedom of speech; however, teachers may not do which of the following?

   (A) Criticize the decisions of the school board.

   (B) Disrupt the school or school curriculum.

   (C) Comment on political affiliation.

   (D) Comment on religious affiliation.

5. Stephanie is a fourth-grade student that is not performing well in class. Recently, her teacher, Ms. Jimenez, noticed that Stephanie wore the same clothes to class for the past three days. Which of the following approaches is best for Ms. Jimenez to take?

   (A) Ask Stephanie in class why she is wearing the same clothes.

   (B) Send a note to Stephanie's parents, asking why Stephanie is wearing the same clothes. Send them a copy of the school dress code.

   (C) Send Stephanie to the school nurse, for a change in clothes.

   (D) Set up a conference with Stephanie's parents, and stress the need for Stephanie to come to class prepared to learn.

DRILL: TEACHER PROFESSIONALISM 5–9

1. A teacher is meeting with Ms. Springer, the mother of a seventh-grade student. Which of the following requests from Ms. Springer should the teacher NOT execute?

   (A) Please show me a folder of my child's work and point out areas needing improvement.

   (B) Please show me a folder of my child's work and point out areas of possible acceleration.

   (C) Please show me my child's report card, so I can see how my child is doing.

   (D) Please show me how my child is doing in comparison to Bobby, Ms. Sullivan's son.

2. Mr. Tankersley is a sixth-grade teacher, who is reviewing the results of his Math midterm. He notices that the boys' average grade is approximately 12 points higher than the girls'. Which of the following actions should Mr. Tankersley take to address this gap most effectively?

   (A) Develop different homework assignments for the boys and the girls.

   (B) Keep the girls for additional time after class, and review the material again.

   (C) Evaluate his own teaching style, and ensure he teaches boys and girls in a similar manner.

   (D) Create a class competition of "Boys vs. Girls" in mathematics, creating extrinsic motivation for the girls.

3. Ms. Smith was extremely impressed with the work of Hank, an eighth-grade ESL student in her class. Hank received the top score in the class for his essay on the environment. In order to show the other students the importance of a structured essay, she passed out Hank's essay to all the other students, and publicly praised a surprised Hank for his hard work.

   What law did Ms. Smith potentially violate in this situation?

   (A) Rights of equal education

   (B) Rights of confidentiality and privacy

   (C) Appropriate treatment of students

   (D) Appropriate treatment of special needs students

4. Tommy, a seventh-grade student, was speaking with his teacher Ms. Purcell after class. When expressing fear of getting a "C" grade in the class, he mentioned, "At least I won't get beat on by my parents like Sven will." Later, Ms. Purcell asked Tommy if he was joking, he shook his head no, and quietly left the room.

   Which of the following is the most appropriate action for Ms. Purcell?

   (A) She should question Sven to see if the allegations are correct, and ask to see any physical evidence.

   (B) She should call Sven's parents and discuss a current "rumor" she has heard.

   (C) She should give the class a lecture on abuse, and ask students who may be abused to stay after class to discuss in private.

   (D) She should report the story to her school's designated representative that handles cases of abuse.

5. Which of the following activities should a teacher invest in to further his or her career?

   (A) Join a professional organization.

   (B) Read research on best practices.

   (C) Personally reflect on past successes and failures of teaching.

   (D) All of the above

DRILL: TEACHER PROFESSIONALISM 7–12

1. Which theorist promoted the use of spiral curriculum?

   (A) Howard Gardner
   (B) Jerome Bruner
   (C) Madeline Hunter
   (D) Jean Piaget

2. Mr. Ascher is a twelfth-grade teacher who frequently interjects his own opinions on politics when he teaches Politics. How could this lessen the learning experience of the students in his class?

   (A) The class is lecture based, thus differing opinions are not distracted.
   (B) The political opinions of Mr. Ascher tend to differ from the most popular views from the parents in that district.
   (C) Mr. Ascher presents his opinions as facts, with no alternative answer.
   (D) Mr. Ascher challenges his students to come up with different opinions.

3. Mr. Moore has heard talk from his ninth-grade class that one of his students, Melissa, may be showing up to school under the influence of marijuana. Which of the following actions is the most effective strategy for Mr. Moore to take?

   (A) Schedule a conference with Melissa's parents, and tell them she is using drugs.
   (B) Schedule a drug test for Melissa with the school nurse.
   (C) Involve Melissa, her parents, and other caregivers in helping identify if Melissa is doing drugs, and if so, how to stop.
   (D) Ignore the situation unless he personally witnesses this action; rumors are quite frequent in the ninth grade.

4. Which of the following situations represents a breach of ethics?

   (A) A science teacher takes a school-owned microscope home so that he can prepare a lab experiment in more comfortable surroundings.
   (B) A teacher has a parent conference in which she accuses a student of cheating. As proof she shows the parents another student's test whose answers were identical.
   (C) A teacher asks another teacher for advice in handling a difficult classroom management situation.
   (D) A teacher asks for student volunteers to help move desks in the classroom.

5. According to a Werner and Smith study, the presence of at least one caring person in a child's life provides healthy support for development and learning. Which of the following statements best describes the role of a teacher when a student does not have the presence of a caring person at home?

   (A) The teacher should be prepared to discipline the student more, as the student will likely not have great classroom behavior.
   (B) A teacher may need to be more than an instructor; the teacher may also need to serve as a confidant and role model for the student.
   (C) Teachers need to fill the gap of parent when students aren't raised properly.
   (D) Teachers should help parents identify their deficiencies in parenting skills.

ANSWERS AND EXPLANATIONS TO DRILL: TEACHER PROFESSIONALISM K–6

1. **C** Learning is a continuous process, even for instructors. Mr. Smith and Ms. Jackson have different needs based on their experience teaching, as well as their own strengths and weaknesses.
2. **A** As a new instructor, Ms. Pirner can likely contribute most effectively by discussing curricula and student work. Over time, researchers find that teachers become more comfortable in providing honest performance assessments of the performance of other instructors.
3. **C** While the right to an education is guaranteed by the Constitution, state governments control education policies and procedures within each state.
4. **B** Teachers may not speak or act in a way that disrupts their responsibilities as a teacher, and their commitment to the school and the established curriculum.
5. **D** It is important that Ms. Jimenez not make any judgments about the behavior she witnesses, or cause any embarrassment to Stephanie. Instead, she must be a part of the shared ownership process (teacher and parents) for Stephanie's learning.

ANSWERS AND EXPLANATIONS TO DRILL: TEACHER PROFESSIONALISM 5–9

1. **D** It is not appropriate to disclose information about the performance of another student. A teacher must be respectful of the privacy of a student's performance.
2. **C** Any step to differentiate boys and girls is inappropriate. However, Mr. Tankersley should reflect on his own teaching behavior. It is possible, like much research has shown, that he may treat boys and girls differently in his lectures on mathematics.
3. **B** In general, Ms. Smith should consult with Hank before distributing his work (along with his name) to the rest of the class.
4. **D** While the other choices may be effective, a teacher has a legal responsibility to report situations related to possible abuse. The proper authorities will then investigate any allegations.
5. **D** A reflective practitioner has many ways to further their development, including the three answer choices listed above.

ANSWERS AND EXPLANATIONS TO DRILL: TEACHER PROFESSIONALISM 7–12

1. **B** The concept of a spiral curriculum, promoted by Jerome Burner, is to constantly review and build on past results, in order to further the learning process.
2. **C** Stating an opinion, especially to older students, is appropriate. However, a teacher must carefully emphasize that the statement is an opinion and not a fact.
3. **C** A helpful strategy for a teacher in these situations is to involve all stakeholders in helping a student. (C) also notes that a step is to identify if Melissa is doing drugs—it should not simply be assumed based on the information Mr. Moore has received.
4. **B** Student records are confidential, and the teacher committed an ethical breach by showing another student's test to the parents.
5. **B** Research shows that students look to their teachers to provide motivation and caring. This is especially true when those needs are not met at home. Answer choices (C) and (D) are too extreme.

24

PLT: Communication Techniques

COMMUNICATION TECHNIQUES

Questions dealing with communication techniques comprise only 15 percent of the test and fall into two major categories:

CULTURE AND GENDER DIFFERENCES

You're not expected to know every potentially offensive gesture in every culture, but you should be aware that ETS considers it incorrect to hold all students to North American cultural standards automatically. Awareness of this fact combined with common sense should guide you to the right answer in multiple-choice questions.

As far as gender differences are concerned, you should know that teachers traditionally hold boys and girls to different standards, and that this is a practice that ETS condemns. For instance, imagine that a teacher is walking around a classroom, monitoring progress on a particularly difficult math problem. Some studies show that the teacher is simply likely to show girls how to get to the right answer, but will encourage boys to think critically to figure out the problem. ETS believes that this is a bad thing to do, so pick answer choices that treat boys and girls equally in terms of academic expectations.

QUESTIONING

Good teachers ask good questions that encourage different kinds of thinking in students. Use Bloom's Taxonomy as a sorting mechanism for different types of questions.

In addition to asking good questions, teachers should also be aware that how questions are asked can have a large impact on student learning. You should be familiar with the following concepts:

Frequency

Frequency simply refers to the number of questions you ask. Socrates notwithstanding, if everything you say is a question, it's difficult for students to learn. On the other hand, nothing is duller than a lecture with no questions. Strike a balance and use questions well to enhance learning.

Equitable Distribution

Call on individual students to ensure that all students are participating. Gear specific questions to specific students, ensuring that a question will be challenging for a given student, but will be something the student has a good chance of answering correctly.

Cueing

Cueing is further prompting by the teacher after the initial question is met with silence or an incorrect or partially correct response. For a rote-memory sort of question such as, "What's the capital of Kansas?" a teacher might cue with a reference to a previously learned mnemonic such as, "Remember: 'Everyone in Kansas wears sandals, so...,'" thereby eliciting the student response of "Topeka!" More complicated questions could require more extensive cueing.

Wait-Time

Wait-time is the amount of time a teacher waits for a response after asking a question. Students need time to process the question, think of the answer, and formulate a response. A wait-time of 3 to 5 seconds is shown to have a strong positive impact on student learning.

Further, a good teacher can use questioning as a mechanism to support classroom management techniques. One common technique is called *group alerting,* in which the teacher asks the whole class the question, waits, and then selects one student to answer. Naming the student before the question is asked increases the likelihood that the other students will stop paying attention.

DRILL: COMMUNICATION TECHNIQUES K–6

1. What is one way in which a second-grade teacher can stimulate student's curiosity about an upcoming subject?

   (A) Cueing

   (B) Group alerting

   (C) Assertive discipline

   (D) Overlapping

2. Which of the following is NOT an ideal method for the organization of a classroom?

   (A) All desks should face the front of the room.

   (B) Desks should be able to be easily rearranged.

   (C) Place a "reading center" in the back corner of one room, away from student desks.

   (D) A teacher should stand where he or she can scan and see the entire class.

3. Canter and Canter recommend that teachers use a technique called assertive discipline. Which of the following statements supports this technique best?

   (A) Students should establish rules, and post those rules in the classroom.

   (B) Teachers should have smoothness and momentum in their transitions.

   (C) Teachers should employ group alerting techniques.

   (D) Teachers should employ a direct approach to problem children.

4. Sheila, a third-grade student, just answered a question about the U.S. government. She correctly indicated that the president was the head of the government. Her teacher, Ms. Grasmick, wants to see if Sheila knows more content about this subject. Which of the following questions would best probe for understanding from Sheila?

   (A) Who is the current president of the United States?

   (B) What is the leader in England called?

   (C) Why did you say president?

   (D) Who is the vice-president?

5. Ms. Calderon wants her fourth grade class to determine how they can help the environment. Which of the following techniques will likely generate participation from her students?

   (A) Brainstorming

   (B) Scaffolding

   (C) Cueing

   (D) Prioritizing

DRILL: COMMUNICATION TECHNIQUES 5–9

1. Mr. Abato, a seventh-grade math teacher, wants to help his students better articulate their ideas and thinking processes on word problems. Which of the following strategies would NOT be effective?

   (A) Have students work in small teams to answer the problems.

   (B) Create an "Ask-3 before me" rule, where students must ask three other students for assistance before asking Mr. Abato.

   (C) Create an "Help from Abato" plan, where you can ask for assistance on any item to Mr. Abato.

   (D) Provide students with all necessary tools (calculators, definitions, etc.) and have the class use them as needed.

2. Which of the following items is NOT a contributing factor to the differences in learning between boys and girls?

   (A) Career aspirations

   (B) Gendered perceptions of a specific subject

   (C) Teacher's expectations

   (D) Socio-economic backgrounds

3. Which of the following is a question designed to encourage students to articulate their opinions?

   (A) What is the boiling point of lead?

   (B) Based on what you read, what is the best way to address the issue of the homeless in San Francisco?

   (C) Who won the football game last night?

   (D) Where would you rather go on vacation—to an island, or to the mountains?

4. Ms. Raeb is concerned about her student Kent, who appears to be very shy. Every time he speaks to Ms. Raeb, he stares down at the ground. What is one possible explanation, that if true, would weaken Ms. Raeb's believe that Kent is shy?

   (A) Kent's siblings are very talkative.

   (B) Kent is from a culture where looking someone in the eye is considered rude.

   (C) Kent is not performing well in school.

   (D) Kent does not like his teachers.

5. Which of the following questions is designed to encourage convergent thinking?

   (A) How may life in the year 2050 differ from today?

   (B) What is the best way to finance the new housing project?

   (C) During what years did Richard III rule?

   (D) Where is the capital of Switzerland located?

DRILL: COMMUNICATION TECHNIQUES 7–12

1. Tim, an African American student, was upset at So Young, a Japanese student, when she smiled through his class presentation about his struggles growing up poor. Tim believed that So Young was mocking him. Which of the following, if true, would help weaken this claim?

   (A) So Young is generally a happy person.

   (B) In So Young's culture, a smile often indicates sadness or embarrassment towards another.

   (C) So Young did not find the presentation thorough.

   (D) Tim is very sensitive to criticism.

2. Ms. Kim noticed that Steven was not paying attention to her lecture. Therefore, she asked Steven to answer the first question in the workbook that corresponds with the lecture. Ms. Kim employed what specific management technique?

   (A) Cueing

   (B) Wait-time

   (C) Group alerting

   (D) Assertive discipline

3. Which of the following characteristics is NOT true about an effective leadership style when managing a class of high-school students?

   (A) Teachers should promote cooperative experiences instead of competitive experiences.

   (B) Teachers should identify and gain the confidence of peer leaders.

   (C) Teachers should spend time establishing rules that describe acceptable classroom behavior.

   (D) Teachers should address student misbehavior immediately, even if that means confrontation, or alienating a student from the class.

4. An increase in wait-time has been shown to have which of the following classroom results?

   (A) Students retain a greater percentage of information taught.

   (B) Fewer students are likely to respond to a question.

   (C) Students who frequently volunteer will not volunteer as often.

   (D) The quantity and quality of student responses increases.

5. Which of the following questions is designed to encourage divergent thinking?

   (A) How may life appear in the year 2050 differ from today?

   (B) Do you support the author's claim?

   (C) In what way did the main character express his frustration?

   (D) Do you prefer strawberries or bananas?

ANSWERS AND EXPLANATIONS TO DRILL: COMMUNICATION TECHNIQUES K–6

1. **A** By asking questions about what students already know about the topic, students can start to think about the next material. An announcement such as "In five minutes we're going to learn how dinosaurs once roamed the earth" can build curiosity, and set boundaries for students. Group alerting is the ability to keep students "alerted" to the task at hand. Assertive discipline promotes effective discipline by establishing rules, regulations, expectations, and procedures in the classroom. Overlapping is the ability to attend to different teaching events simultaneously, and deal with a disruption while continuing the lesson.

2. **C** In general, a room should be arranged so that students do not have to stand in line. Book and supplies should be available in multiple locations.

3. **D** The Canters believe that a passive or hostile communication style with students is not effective, and recommend a direct and assertive approach. (For more info see Chapter 21, "PLT: Students as Learners Test.")

4. **A** Ms. Grasmick's goal is to continue to ask Sheila about the president. One way to do this is to tie Sheila's lesson knowledge with additional knowledge, such as who is the president today. Answer choices (B) and (D) are off topic, while (C) does not test for content.

5. **A** Brainstorming involves a free sharing of ideas, without penalty or punishment. There are no "wrong" answers. After a brainstorming session, students will then clarify ideas, advocate some suggestions, and prioritize into specific results.

ANSWERS AND EXPLANATIONS TO DRILL: COMMUNICATION TECHNIQUES 5–9

1. **C** To develop stronger thinking processes, Mr. Abato should not employ strategies that rely only on asking the teacher for advice.
2. **D** Typically, there is no difference between boys and girls, and their socio-economic status. Answer choices (A) through (C) all help explain how boys and girls learn differently.
3. **D** The answer to this question is purely opinion—there are no answers that are better than others. Answer choice (B) is a decent answer, but is not a pure opinion question—there are likely more rational answers than others. Further, because it is based upon a reading, the question is likely looking for one specific answer.
4. **B** In some cultures, looking away from someone when speaking is normal. This could help explain why Kent looks away when speaking to an authority figure.
5. **B** Convergent thinking questions are those that require students to analyze and integrate given or remembered information, and use that information to present and defend the best answer. Teachers will use convergent thinking questions to demonstrate that the "correct" answer often depends on the criteria used to evaluate the question. Answer choices (C) and (D) do not require analysis of an issue—these are both factual questions that require students to recall the answer (in Bloom's taxonomy, these are "knowledge" questions). Answer choice (A) is an example of creative thinking—there are many possible answers, and no particular answer is necessarily right or wrong.

ANSWERS AND EXPLANATIONS TO DRILL: COMMUNICATION TECHNIQUES 7–12

1. **B** Remember that nonverbal communication techniques can have different meanings across different cultures.
2. **C** In group alerting, the teacher brings uninvolved students back into the lesson by calling their attention to what is happening.
3. **D** The second part of the sentence is NOT an effective technique. Teachers should not draw unnecessary attention to problem students.
4. **D** By waiting an additional few seconds (up to 3) before calling on a student to answer a question, teachers can improve the participation and quality of discussion in their classrooms.
5. **A** Divergent thinking questions are those which represent intellectual operations wherein you are free to generate your ideas independently, or to take a new direction or perspective on a given topic.

25

PLT: Case Histories

HOW TO APPROACH SHORT-ANSWER QUESTIONS ON THE PLT TEST

These are more complex than multiple-choice questions and will require a more detailed strategy. Here are the steps you should follow:

Step 1: Annotate and Predict

Step 2: Read the Questions

Step 3: Brainstorm

Step 4: Write the Answer

Let's break each of these down:

STEP 1: ANNOTATE AND PREDICT

The most important thing to know about the case histories is that every piece of information they give you is there for a reason. So as you're reading the case history for the first time, take notes in the margin. You'll be asked to comment on and improve upon the current situation, so pretend that you are evaluating the scenario. If you notice something that seems odd or unusual, make a note in the margin. If you notice something particularly positive, write that down, too. You'll soon have a good idea of the situation as a whole, and you'll be well on your way to answering the questions before you even see them.

Let's apply this strategy to the following case history:

Case History

Mr. Jackson

Mr. Jackson is a first-year teacher at an elementary school in a working-class suburb of a midsize city. He teaches sixth grade, and has a class of 27 students from a variety of ethnic and socioeconomic backgrounds.

1st year—he doesn't have all the answers. Fairly big, and very diverse class.

One student in Mr. Jackson's class, Tim, is grossly overweight. Tim is an average student, performing at about grade level in all academic areas. The other students in Mr. Jackson's class shun Tim, and he has no real friends in the class. Recently, Mr. Jackson has been hearing students verbally abuse Tim in class. Mr. Jackson's response has been to reprimand the verbally abusive student at the time of the incident, but the incidents seem to be escalating in frequency and severity nonetheless.

The Tim situation is a problem. Mr. Jackson isn't doing the right thing by reprimanding the student in front of the rest of the class—he should either do it alone with the student, or with the student and Tim. Disciplining the verbally abusive student in front of the rest of the class calls attention to the student.

A one-time college athlete, Mr. Jackson has no personal experience with being overweight. He notices that Tim brings unhealthy foods to eat at lunchtime.

Does Mr. Jackson know how to relate to Tim's problem?

Mr. Jackson approached Tim to try to discuss these issues with him. Tim said, "I wish you wouldn't even say anything in class. It just makes it worse at recess." Tim's response to the situation has been to become more withdrawn in class.

Tim's embarrassed.

Parent-teacher conferences are in one week. Mr. Jackson knows that both of Tim's parents are obese themselves. Mr. Jackson sympathizes with Tim, but at some level he is surprised that Tim isn't taking steps to correct the problem on his own. Mr. Jackson understands that the current situation is problematic, and realizes that he must take some further action to ensure a positive learning environment for Tim and the rest of his students.

Sounds like Mr. Jackson needs some sensitivity training to help him understand different reasons for obesity. At least he realizes he doesn't have all the answers.

Even before you see the questions, you can anticipate what they're going to be about. This case history has to do with classroom management, student health and social issues, and dealing with parents.

Step 2: Read the Questions

Question 1

Mr. Jackson is correct to be concerned about Tim's current situation.

- Name TWO ways in which the current situation, if left unchanged, could damage Tim's development. Base your response on the principles of teaching and learning and human development.

Question 2

Mr. Jackson's current method of reprimanding students is not having the effect of stopping the unwanted behavior.

- Suggest TWO alternate strategies that Mr. Jackson might employ to stop the verbal abuse while addressing Tim's concern that punishing other students for teasing him "only makes it worse at recess."
- For each strategy, explain why it would be a preferred strategy to the one Mr. Jackson is using now. Base your response on the principles of learning and teaching and classroom management techniques.

Question 3

Mr. Jackson is concerned about the upcoming teacher conference. He knows that this is a delicate subject, and he wants to be able to have a productive, respectful conversation with Tim's parents.

- Name TWO major issues that Mr. Jackson needs to take into account as he's preparing for the teacher conference.
- Suggest a way of dealing with each issue that will help ensure a positive outcome. Base your response on the principles of teaching and learning and fostering strong school-parent relationships.

Because you've already thought about the situation, none of these questions should come as a complete surprise. Now think about answering them.

Step 3: Brainstorm

Question 1

Mr. Jackson is correct to be concerned about Tim's current situation.

- Name TWO ways in which the current situation, if left unchanged, could damage Tim's development. Base your response on the principles of teaching and learning and human development.

We already knew Tim wasn't happy. If things don't change, what could happen to him? What do we know? He's overweight, and he's being teased to the point where he has no friends in the class. We're asked to find two ways in which his development could be damaged. How about social development and physical development?

Social

- Peer relationships are important.
- Confronting negativism in a constructive manner is an important social skill.

Physical

- Obesity leads to health risks.

Step 4: Write the Answer

These answers can't be long—you have only one page per question. You have to keep two things in mind:

- Be sure to answer the question directly and give supporting reasons for your statements or suggestions. Cite relevant educational theories where appropriate.
- Make your answer easy to read by structuring it well. Graders will be reading lots of these answers—they'll appreciate well-organized thoughts.

A high-scoring sample answer might look like this:

> The current classroom situation is detrimental to Tim's development in two major areas: social and physical.
>
> First, Tim's current social isolation could lead to emotional instability or retardation later in life. Erikson, among other theorists, notes that peer relationships are critical in establishing identity. Having no friends at this age could lead to psychosocial stagnation. In addition, Tim's apparent inability to confront his tormentors suggests that he is incapable of expressing his feelings in a constructive way. This, too, could have negative consequences in terms of interpersonal relationships.
>
> Second, Tim's physical condition needs to be addressed. Childhood obesity rates are rising, as are rates of related medical conditions such as Diabetes. The advantages of balanced nutrition and regular exercise are well-documented. Left unchecked, Tim's obesity could lead to serious negative health consequences in later years.

Most of that probably seems obvious to you (although you may have forgotten about the specifics of Erikson's theories), and much is supported by common sense. All you have to do is answer the question by connecting a few meaningful ideas together into several sentences.

ETS would like the above response for many reasons. First, it quickly answers the question with a sentence that also sets up the structure for what it to follow. The paragraphs are well-organized, with words that link ideas together such as "first" and "in addition." Further, the answers are supported by specific references and examples. Notice that the response wasn't particularly long.

You're not looking to get published, and your answers don't need to be worthy of literary prizes. Answer the question, support your responses, and move on.

Let's try the next one:

Question 2

Mr. Jackson's current method of reprimanding students is not having the effect of stopping the unwanted behavior.

- Suggest TWO alternate strategies that Mr. Jackson might employ to stop the verbal abuse while addressing Tim's concern that punishing other students for teasing him "only makes it worse at recess."
- For each strategy, explain why it would be a preferred strategy to the one Mr. Jackson is using now. Base your response on the principles of teaching and learning and classroom management techniques.

Step 3: Brainstorm

We thought about this when we were reading the text. Mr. Jackson could:

- Take the abusive student aside alone.
- Take the abusive student aside with Tim.
- Address the issue with respect to overall classroom expectations, such as rules of behavior.

If he takes the student aside alone, he runs the risk of alienating the student's relationship with Tim even further. Mr. Jackson should include Tim in the discussion.

Why doesn't Mr. Jackson have a code of behavior in place? That's the type of thing that good teachers establish at the beginning of the year to keep situations like this from happening. It's not too late, as long as he doesn't introduce it in direct response to the situation with Tim.

Now, let's put these ideas into a short answer:

Step 4: Write the Answer

There are two approaches that Mr. Jackson could take that would improve the classroom situation more effectively.

First, rather than simply admonishing the attacker in front of the class, he should take the abuser aside with Tim and not only reprimand the attacker for the teasing, but also give Tim an opportunity to express his feelings to his attacker without having the whole class listening in. The advantages to this method are twofold: first, the attacker doesn't get the attention reinforcement in front of the rest of the class, and second, Tim has an opportunity to work on his peer communication skills. Both of these elements are missing from Mr. Jackson's current approach.

Second, in a general forum not directly linked to any particular attack, Mr. Jackson should take an opportunity to set clear, enforceable standards of behavior for the entire class. These standards should include a ban on abusive speech and a penalty for breaking that rule. That way, if the abuser picks on Tim in the future, Mr. Jackson can punish the abuser without linking the punishment to Tim. In contrast to Mr. Jackson's current method, this makes it less likely that Tim would face repercussions "at recess."

Let's try the same thing again for the last question:

Question 3

Mr. Jackson is concerned about the upcoming teacher conference. He knows that this is a delicate subject, and he wants to be able to have a productive, respectful conversation with Tim's parents.

- Name TWO major issues that Mr. Jackson needs to take into account as he's preparing for the teacher conference.
- Suggest a way of dealing with each issue that will help ensure a positive outcome. Base your response on the principles of teaching and learning and fostering strong school-parent relationships.

Step 3: Brainstorm

This is a much broader question. There could be any number of issues that Mr. Jackson should take into account. But let's use the clues that the case history gave us. First, the parents are overweight themselves. That means they may be particularly sensitive to the topic and feel as though they are being attacked. Second, we know that Mr. Jackson isn't necessarily aware of his own prejudices, and may need some outside information. Surely there must be resources that the district could provide for Mr. Jackson, such as a nurse or health teacher.

Next, let's try writing an answer.

Step 4: Write the Answer

Two issues that Mr. Jackson should take into account are Tim's parents' obesity and his own lack of knowledge about the subject.

First, Mr. Jackson should ask for help in learning about the various causes and effects of obesity. He should speak to an administrator or school nurse to gain a better understanding of how people can become overweight. His own biases need to be addressed so that he can communicate empathetically and effectively with Tim's parents.

Second, Mr. Jackson should open his discussion by mentioning the positive aspects of Tim's performance in class. By starting off with a list of things that Tim is doing well, the parents will be less likely to see a discussion of his obesity as a personal attack.

DRILL: CASE HISTORY APPROACH K–5

Case History

Directions: The case history is followed by three short-answer questions.

Mr. Lewis

Mr. Lewis a fourth-year teacher in a K–6 elementary school. This is Mr. Lewis's second year teaching third grade. This year, his class is comprised of 23 students—12 girls and 11 boys. At the beginning of the third month of school, Mr. Lewis is about to introduce a new activity called "Reading Journal." He did not try this his first year teaching the third grade, but hopes that this activity will help support the goals and Reading curriculum established for third grade students. The first document is a project plan description of the "Reading Journal," while the second document is a conversation with one of Mr. Lewis's students, Cindy.

Document 1

"Reading Journal" Lesson Plan

Goals:

1. Improve reading comprehension abilities.
2. Improve writing skills, and ability to develop critical-thinking skills demonstrated in one's writing.
3. Improve speaking and listening abilities.
4. Improve social skills within the class, creating a more positive classroom environment.

Objectives:

1. Students will use the "Reading Journal" to summarize their readings.
2. Students will discuss their readings, and connect the topics to experiences and people in their own lives.

Assignment:

The "Reading Journal"

Each Friday, we will devote one hour of class time to reading. You may choose any book in the class library, in our school library (ask Ms. Sincoff if the book is approved), or any book from home. If you bring a book from home, please bring it to me for approval.

In addition to the class time each Friday, your homework assignment is to read for about two hours per week outside of class.

Each week, you need to make two entries into your journal.

When you start a journal entry, please indicate the book name, author, page numbers you are writing about, and the date of your entry.

Your journal entry should discuss two things:

1. A summary of the pages you have recently completed.
2. Your thoughts on the material. Do you like the book? What is going to happen next? Do you understand the feelings of the characters? Has this ever happened to you?

Assessment:

Every two weeks, each student will turn in the "Reading Journal" to Mr. Lewis.

I will review the journal for the following criteria:

- quality of book summaries
- number of entries during the week
- number of pages read per week

Document 2

Conversation between Mr. Lewis and a student, Cindy

Mr. Lewis	Cindy, I don't have a record of you turning in your Reading Journal from last week. Did you turn that in? I have seen you reading during our Friday sessions.
Cindy	Yes, sir. I read every night.
Mr. Lewis	What have you been reading?
Cindy	Last week I read a book called "Superfudge." This week I'm reading a book called "The Wind and the Willows."
Mr. Lewis	That is an excellent book. It will probably take you a few weeks to complete.
Cindy	I started reading it this Monday, and so far I've read 200 pages.
Mr. Lewis	Wow, that is just fantastic. Do you enjoy the story so far?
Cindy	It is sometimes confusing. I'm not sure I understand all the parts and what is going on.
Mr. Lewis	Well, I hope that you write about it in your journal. That way, I'll know the types of questions that you have.
Cindy	Okay.
Mr. Lewis	I'm very happy to see that you are reading so much. Yet I'm concerned that this level of work is not reflected in your "Reading Journal."
Cindy	Oh, well you said to turn in two a week. That is what I was doing. But I keep reading because I like to read.
Mr. Lewis	Okay, Cindy. Please turn in your journal from last week so I can give you credit for your efforts.
Cindy	Okay.

Directions: Questions 1 through 3 require you to write short answers. You are not expected to cite specific theories or texts in your answer; however, your responses to the questions will be evaluated with respect to professionally accepted principles and practices in teaching and learning. Be sure to answer all parts of the questions. Write your answers on the answer sheet.

Question 1

Review Document 1, the "Reading Journal" Lesson Plan.

- Identify ONE strength and ONE weakness of the "Reading Journal" Lesson Plan.
- For each strength or weakness, describe how each item is used in planning instruction. Base your response on the principles of effective instructional planning.

Question 2

In Document 2, Cindy's conversation with Mr. Lewis reveals characteristics about herself as a learner.

- Identify ONE characteristic of Cindy as a learner, and suggest ONE strategy Mr. Lewis might use to support her development.
- For the strategy you suggested, describe how it addresses the characteristics of Cindy as a learner. Base your response on principles of varied instructional strategies for different learners and of human development.

Question 3

Review Mr. Lewis' goals at the beginning of Document 1.

- Select TWO goals, and for each goal, identify one strategy Mr. Lewis might use to take the "Reading Journal" plan beyond the stated assignment and assessment plan.
- Explain how each strategy will take the plan beyond its currently stated objectives. Base your response on principles of planning instruction.

DRILL: CASE HISTORY APPROACH 5–9

Case History

Directions: The case history is followed by three short-answer questions.

Ms. Lloyd

Ms. Lloyd teaches a sixth grade Mathematics course to a class of 28 students. There are 14 male students, and 14 female students. Ms. Lloyd is in her third year teaching this course, and in her fifth year of teaching. She is planning for her self-evaluation. In order to prepare a thorough assessment, Ms. Lloyd begins to gather material that may be helpful for the activity. In the documents below, Ms. Lloyd focuses on a specific class, and three of her students. The class takes place during the month of October, which is the second month into the semester. No formal grades have been given at this time.

Document 1

Profiles on three students

Meg is a challenge. She manages to make comments on almost every topic, but they are rarely correct. She seems so eager to participate, but does not have a good grasp on the material. I've noticed that Meg is frequently the last to leave the school day care. Last week, I was working late on some lesson plans, and the afterschool caregiver asked me if I had any additional contact information for Meg since no one had picked her up from school—and it was 7 P.M.! She has also been tardy a number of times—including four times in the last two weeks. I know that Meg lives about 30 minutes from the school, so that could be a factor. But I'd like her to be here on time so we can focus on the more important issues, like building her math skills. With some time and practice, I think she can master the material. She certainly has the right attitude!

Peter is a very quiet student, who is withdrawn from most activities. Yet his performance is just fine. Thus far, he has turned in all the assignments, and would be getting an A– if grades were due this week (they are due in three weeks). Peter seems incredibly shy—he does not like attention from me, nor from other students in the class. He spends most of his breaks or free time playing on his Game Boy, instead of socializing with other students. Previously, I attempted to bring Peter out of his shell, by cold-calling on him in class. He responds extremely timidly, which has drawn some laughter from the rest of the class.

Nicole is an exceptional student who comes from a very proud family. I taught her older brother two years ago; he was the best student in the class. Nicole is like her brother, but she is beyond even where he was two years ago. I'm afraid that I am boring Nicole with the work that we do. She tends to finish each assignment early and get almost all of the questions correct. She raises her hand to answer a question about as often as Meg, except that Nicole knows the answer! I'd like to find ways to keep Nicole entertained and challenged in the class, but with several struggling students, I'm not sure how to do that. I'm afraid that other students may fall further behind.

Document 2

Self-Analysis

Now, that this is my third year of teaching, I'm feeling comfortable with the material, and I can predict the areas that students will struggle on during the year. This year has been somewhat of a challenge, in that the state standards changed, and I know that there is tremendous pressure that this class performs well on the state test, which takes place during the middle of May. As a result, I feel more pressure to keep up the pace—if I don't cover all of the material, the scores of the entire class may suffer. On the other hand, my new pace seems to challenge students more than ever before. I'm not sure if I have a weaker class this year, but more students just "don't get it" than in prior years. The idea of "no one left behind" seems harder than ever.

All of this leaves me with quite a challenge. I'd like to spend more time with students such as Meg, who are struggling with the material. And I don't even have time to think about external issues that are impacting my students—for example, Meg's home life. On the flip side, I'm afraid that students like Nicole are not challenged.

Finally, I'm starting to run low on ideas to keep this course innovative and fun. It was so much easier with the English courses I was teaching. Mathematics is more straightforward. I know that many students don't enjoy this class as much as they enjoy other subjects, such as History and English, which provide greater opportunities for creativity.

Document 3
Notes from Class
Tuesday, October 10

Today, we reviewed some complicated word problems. I had asked that students prepare Questions 1–10 from Page 231 in their 'Workout' workbook. About 13 of the 28 students indicated that they completed all ten questions, so I decided to review each of the questions in class. Nicole was the only student to complete all ten questions correctly—including the final question, which only four students in the class got correct. For each question, I asked two students to come to the board and write their answer on the board. I do this so that I can see how students derive the correct answer, rather than just evaluate if the answer is correct. Meg volunteered to answer Question #4, but unfortunately, she did not get it correct. She was one of the students that did not complete the assignment (in fact, she didn't even get to #4, and I wondered why she volunteered). I asked Peter to answer Question #6, and he gave the correct answer, but did not want to come up to the board. Thomas was very rude to Peter—I didn't hear exactly what he said, but it was not kind. Peter just sulked in his chair after Thomas leaned over and said something. I told Peter he had to come up to the board, and he quickly wrote his explanation on the board, and then quickly walked back to his desk.

Directions: Questions 1 through 3 require you to write short answers. You are not expected to cite specific theories or texts in your answer; however, your responses to the questions will be evaluated with respect to professionally accepted principles and practices in teaching and learning. Be sure to answer all parts of the questions. Write your answers on the answer sheet.

Question 1
Take a look at Document 3 and evaluate Ms. Lloyd's performance for the class on Tuesday, October 10.

- Identify ONE teaching strategy that Ms. Lloyd did well, and ONE teaching strategy Ms. Lloyd could employ to improve her lesson.
- For each strategy identified, explain how it addresses the goals of Ms. Lloyd and the concerns of the class, and how it makes group instruction more effective. Base your response on the principles of effective instructional strategies.

Question 2
Assume that Ms. Lloyd produced a lesson plan before giving the lecture and review on word problems. Assume that no modifications are made for any of her students.

- Suggest TWO modifications, one for Meg and one for Nicole, which Ms. Lloyd could have made that could offer the students a better learning environment.
- For each modification, explain how it will provide for a better learning situation for Nicole and Meg. Base your response on principles of varied instruction for diverse learners.

Question 3
Ms. Lloyd is concerned about her ability to connect with Peter as a student, and wants to learn more about Peter so that she can teach him more effectively.

- Describe TWO aspects of Peter's behavior that Ms. Lloyd, and other school leaders, might discuss in order to understand Peter better as a learner.
- For each aspect, suggest one hypothesis that might be used to understand Peter better as a student. Base your response on the principles of human development and diagnostic assessment.

DRILL: CASE HISTORY APPROACH 7–12

Case History

Directions: The case history is followed by three short-answer questions.

Mr. Erving

Mr. Erving teaches a seventh-grade History class comprised of 26 students. For 12 students, English is the second language; these students represent four different language groups with a wide range of English fluency. Two students are placed in the class on the "least-restrictive environment" provision. Three students have been identified as qualifying for the "gifted and talented" program. One student is repeating the class after having failed it the previous year.

Below is information about Mr. Erving's goals for the year, and specific information about his plans for the week of October 15.

Long-term goals for the class:

1. Students will develop reading and writing skills within the History curriculum.
2. Students will work cooperatively and supportively.
3. Students will develop speaking and listening skills.
4. Students will participate in both formal presentations and informal discussions.

Activities for the week of October 15:

1. Students will begin the class by presenting a history of where they grew up, and of the culture of their native land. Students will work in pairs. Each person will describe where they came from; if they were born in the United States, they will identify the origin of their descendants. They will then present a few facts about that country/region. (1 session)
2. Students will then make a formal presentation on their family background. (1 session)
3. Students will then study the region of their family background in greater detail, using the History text and the Internet. (2 sessions)
4. Students will present "fun facts" about their country of origin. (1 session)

Assessment:

1. Students will be graded on their family background presentation.
2. Students will be graded on their country of origin presentation.

Mr. Erving's impression of three students during the week of October 15

Sarah struggled with the assignment. She is one of the two students in the class under the "least-restrictive curriculum" provision. Sarah seems to have a limited attention span. This was evident during her group work with Cesar, and I could tell that Cesar was frustrated with his partner.

Karen speaks Spanish fluently, and is working hard to improve her English. She performed well during the research portion of the week, but struggled when she was paired with another student. Despite her enthusiasm, it was evident that she did not understand everything that Carrie was telling her during their meeting.

Scott is a gifted student. He spent most of Thursday working on another subject during the class time. When I confronted Scott about this, he indicated that he had completed his research, and was ready to present on Friday. Sure enough, his presentation was one of the best in the class, but I actually believe that Scott could have performed better.

Directions: Questions 1 through 3 require you to write short answers. You are not expected to cite specific theories or texts in your answer; however, your responses to the questions will be evaluated with respect to professionally accepted principles and practices in teaching and learning. Be sure to answer all parts of the questions. Write your answers on the answer sheet.

Question 1
Mr. Erving identifies two items for assessment for this week's lesson plan in History.

- Identify TWO additional formal or informal assessment techniques Mr. Erving could use to provide his students with opportunities to demonstrate their learning.
- For each technique suggested, describe how each item is used to assess student learning. Base your response on the principles of informal and formal assessment.

Question 2
In Mr. Erving's notes, he identified several facts about Karen that reveal characteristics about herself as a learner.

- Identify ONE characteristic of Karen as a learner, and suggest ONE strategy Mr. Erving might use to support her development.
- For the strategy you suggested, describe how it addresses the characteristics of Karen as a learner. Base your response on principles of varied instructional strategies for different learners and of human development.

Question 3
Mr. Erving noted that Scott performed very well on the presentation, but not as well as Scott could have done.

- Identify ONE strategy for keeping a gifted student like Scott motivated in the classroom.
- Explain how this strategy will help Scott and encourage further development. Base your response on principles of effective classroom management and planned instruction.

ANSWERS AND EXPLANATIONS TO DRILL: CASE HISTORY APPROACH K–5

1. **Sample Response that Receives a Score of 2:**

Mr. Lewis' plan has both strengths and weaknesses. One strength is that he has students participate in a writing activity that is connected to a reading activity. By linking the two activities together, Mr. Lewis will help students at this age make connections, and therefore, communicate well. Students will have a better opportunity to learn and demonstrate their learning.

One way that the plan could be improved is that Mr. Lewis can provide examples of what is expected in the "Reading Journal." Under #2, Mr. Lewis asks students for "your thoughts on the material." He then gives three or four sample questions to answer. However, for students in the third grade, this may be too limiting. Students may only answer these specific questions. That is clearly not Mr. Lewis's goal, for his true goal is to get students to reflect on their thoughts and write their personal feelings. Instead of a specific list, Mr. Lewis should encourage students to write what comes to mind. Or, he could add that students can write about anything that comes to mind.

Sample Response that Receives a Score of 1:

The strength of Mr. Lewis' project plan is that it has an assessment section. A necessary part of any project plan is to have an assessment section so that students understand how they will be evaluated. Further, it provides a valuable checkpoint for teachers, so that they can ensure the goals and activities are properly measured with an assessment plan. However, the plan could be improved by listing the average weighting for each of the three categories.

2. **Sample Response that Receives a Score of 2:**

It is clear that Cindy enjoys reading, but does not hold the same passion for writing. The challenge for Mr. Lewis is to make writing more creative and enjoyable for Cindy, based on her enjoyment of reading. While an alternate response mode is likely unnecessary, Mr. Lewis could ask Cindy to mimic her favorite books by asking her to write her own story in the "Reading Journal." She could take one of the characters in the book, and write about what happens to them after the conclusion of the book. This would help to draw direct correlations between her reading and her writing. Cindy has displayed much talent as a reader; the challenge now is to bring those same skills into her writing.

Sample Response that Receives a Score of 1:

Cindy is a very strong reader. The fact that she has read almost two novels in two weeks is a tribute to her time spent reading. In fact, those books are a few hundred pages each! Because Cindy enjoys reading, Mr. Lewis does not need to worry about her reading skills. I'm sure they are just fine, unless she glosses over the material too much. But it is clear that she does not have the same passion, and possibly the same skills for writing. She has not turned in her journal, which means that she likely did not complete the writing assignments, in favor of reading more material in her books.

3. **Sample Response that Receives a Score of 2:**

The third goal of this project plan is to "Improve speaking and listening abilities." Research has shown that strong reading skills do help improve speaking ability. However, Mr. Lewis can take this project further by adding some assignments that directly relate to this goal. For example, he can ask one person each Friday to read from his or her journal. The student would be asked to read the most recent journal entry. Then, other students would be asked if they have read the book, and if so, their thoughts on that particular section. Each week Mr. Lewis would ask one or two other students to read from their journals. This would help students practice their speaking skills. Further, students would need to listen, as they would be asked questions from Mr. Lewis following the presentation. This may also improve the quality of writing, because students know that they may need to present that material to the class.

The second goal mentions the desire to develop critical-thinking skills. However, no part of the current assessment plan addresses this skill. The assessment is based on quantity and the ability to summarize, but there is no measurement on the ability to think critically. Mr. Lewis should add an assessment on critical thinking skills. Further, he should define a rubric to ensure objective grading on this subjective matter. By creating this rubric, he will help link the assessment to the goals, which is a necessary condition for any effective project plan.

Sample Response that Receives a Score of 1:

The third goal of this project plan is to "Improve speaking and listening abilities." Mr. Lewis needs to add more activities to help achieve this goal. First, he can ask students to read their reports aloud. But reading the report aloud, students will listen to the speeches given, and will question the reader, which could help build critical-thinking skills. Another way to achieve this third goal would be to take some of the time devoted for reading on Friday and have Mr. Lewis read a book to the class. He could then quiz students on the book once it is complete. This will test their listening abilities, as the students will not be able to rely on a textbook to demonstrate what they have learned.

ANSWERS AND EXPLANATIONS TO DRILL: CASE HISTORY APPROACH 5–9

1. **Sample Response that Receives a Score of 2:**

Ms. Lloyd needs to be creative and find strategies that will challenge and excite students, even with a topic such as math. Math is often described as not being a very creative topic. One way she did this was to engage the students by having them come up to the board to show their work. This creates more incentive for students to complete their work, as positive peer pressure at this stage can be very helpful from a learning perspective. Ms. Lloyd could make sessions more effective by assigning questions to students based upon their skill level. This will keep students appropriately challenged on material they have learned. One strategy that Ms. Lloyd may need to employ is to give an assessment of student's performance based on the completion of homework assignments. Students may not be conditioned to complete their homework, especially if they learn that there are no adverse consequences to completing the material.

Sample Response that Receives a Score of 1:

Ms. Lloyd did a good job in having an interactive exercise. However, she should improve in the way in which she gives different assignments for different students. Clearly, Nicole needs different things to work. By assigning the same work universally, those at the top of the class will be bored, while those who struggle will not get the attention they need. Ms. Lloyd should plan to maximize her students' scores on the upcoming standardized test. One way to do this is to make sure that advanced students are given the proper material to excel.

2. **Sample Response that Receives a Score of 2:**

Nicole, who is a bright, independent learner, needs the opportunity for enrichment, which will hopefully keep her more engaged and challenged with the class. We know that Nicole often volunteers to give the answer. If she is not called on, she may be frustrated. However, if she is called on too often, other students may feel disengaged or intimidated by not having the correct answer. Thus, the challenge is to keep Nicole focused in a way that will be positive for both her and the entire class. Ms. Lloyd could offer Nicole a more sophisticated Mathematics text, material that focuses specifically on advanced word problems, or to create word problems for the class to complete. Nicole could be asked to complete these activities, and then possibly present this information to the rest of the class. That would challenge Nicole to think about the material in a more complex way, and find ways to communicate more effectively.

For Meg, Ms. Lloyd might have a meeting with her and her parents to discuss her performance in Math—what is going well, and what is challenging. This would also help to involve the parents in the discussion, and potentially to address the external issues such as Meg's attendance, and the fact that her parents often do not pick her up from school on time. As a result of this meeting, Ms. Lloyd should develop specific assignments for Meg. From the passage, we know that Meg likes to volunteer and be involved in the classroom discussion. Thus, Ms. Lloyd could involve Meg, but frame the way in which she asks questions to her differently. For example, Ms. Lloyd could ask Meg to explain the steps of the process to solve a math problem, instead of simply asking the answer. This would keep Meg engaged, and help both Meg and Ms. Lloyd identify possible challenges that Meg has with the material. The specific homework given to Meg should involve doing more work in setting up the problem correctly.

Sample Response that Receives a Score of 1:

Nicole needs to be given more detailed and challenging assignments. Ms. Lloyd should take a look at the Mathematics curriculum tested on the state standardized test, and find out what they teach regarding word problems.

3. **Sample Response that Receives a Score of 2:**

There are several aspects of Peter's behavior that suggest hypotheses about his ability to learn and succeed in a school environment. First, while he does not seem to display any specific behavioral problems, it is important to note how disengaged he is from class and from other students. It is possible that he may have an emotional or behavioral disorder that prevents him from interacting with others. This could cause him to remove himself from what he sees as an unpleasant environment. Further, this is reinforced by the fact that he appeared extremely quiet and passive at times, such as his unpleasant reactions when asked to share information with the class. A second possibility is that Peter is simply not challenged, and therefore removes himself from the classroom environment. We know that Peter tends to do well in his schoolwork. If he feels completely unchallenged, he may have decided it is simply easiest to remove himself from the group.

Sample Response that Receives a Score of 1:

Peter seems very disengaged from the rest of the student body. Peter could be extremely shy, and uncomfortable in social situations. It is possible that he has not developed the necessary social skills to fit in with his peers. Ms. Lloyd should investigate to see if Peter has any history of social disorders or problems interacting with other students. She should speak with his other teachers to see how he interacts in those classes, to make sure it is a general issue, and not one specific to the Mathematics class.

ANSWERS AND EXPLANATIONS TO DRILL: CASE HISTORY APPROACH 7–12

1. **Sample Response that Receives a Score of 2:**

   Mr. Erving currently has two formal assessment measures—the students' performance on each of the two assigned presentations. However, Mr. Erving can take measures to ensure that his overall assessment is more than these two speaking opportunities. In order to be properly aligned with the class long-term goals, Mr. Erving needs to include other measures. First, he could give a team grade for group participation. One of Mr. Erving's goals is to work cooperatively and supportively. To reinforce this, students should receive feedback on their teamwork during the interview sessions. A second formal assessment would be to provide more details about how the presentations will be scored. Identifying a rubric would be helpful for Mr. Erving so that he can be objective during the presentations. For students, they need to understand the types of things that Mr. Erving will want to see in the presentations—will they be judged on length, quality of research, quality of speaking, or organization of material? Knowing this information will help students focus properly.

   Sample Response that Receives a Score of 1:

   The assessment section is currently vague. Sure, the teacher will evaluate the two presentations, but it is not clear how or what criteria will be used to give a score. There is a danger that students will feel that the scoring could be extremely subjective unless Mr. Erving provides more details about the scoring criteria. So by revising these two things (scoring for the first presentation and the scoring for the second), Mr. Erving will have done two additional things to improve the quality of his assessment program for this lesson plan.

2. **Sample Response that Receives a Score of 2:**

   As an ESL student, Karen has several challenges in order to succeed in this History class. Of paramount importance is the need for Karen to improve her English skills. It appears that she has the right attitude, as noted by Mr. Erving. Yet her language skills are taking away from her ability to achieve the classroom goals, such as developing listening skills, and possibly even working cooperatively. Therefore, Mr. Erving should immediately test Karen on her written and oral abilities in both languages. Once Mr. Erving understands Karen's skills, he can then develop a specific plan to get her back up to speed with the rest of the class.

   Sample Response that Receives a Score of 1:

   The quality of Karen as a learner is that she is an ESL student. This means that English is her second language, and that she may not know English as well as the native English speakers. Mr. Erving can take additional steps for all of his ESL students to make sure they understand the activities and assignments for the class. He may need to slow down or present information differently so that students like Karen can feel a part of the group.

3. **Sample Response that Receives a Score of 2:**

Mr. Erving knows that Scott is a gifted student. His challenge is to provide Scott with interesting and challenging material, which may be difficult for Mr. Erving given the diverse set of skills present in his class. Mr. Erving could provide Scott with a much more sophisticated History book than the one given to the remainder of the class. This information would hopefully be more intriguing to Scott, who may be interested in reading this new information during times when he finishes early. Such a move would help engage Scott at a more sophisticated level, while keeping the classroom environment positive for all students. Because many students may model themselves based on Scott's attitude and actions, it is important that top students are given as much attention and special focus as students who are struggling.

Sample Response that Receives a Score of 1:

Scott is a gifted student, and frankly, he is probably the least of Mr. Erving's worries. If Scott finished the assignment a day early, good for him. Mr. Erving cannot be expected to create 26 different plans for his students. Mr. Erving should let Scott know that if he finishes early he should help other students who have not yet completed their assignment. There is a risk that Scott could view this as having to complete additional amounts of work, so Mr. Erving will need to spin it properly. Ideally though, you make Scott an asset to help you manage the class as easily as possible.

26

PLT: K–6 Practice Test

The Praxis Series Professional Assessments for Beginning Teachers

Test Name: Principles of Learning and Teaching

Practice Case Histories and Constructed-Response Questions

Time –120 minutes

12 Short-Answer Questions and 24 Multiple-Choice Questions

Case History 1

Directions: The case history is followed by three short-answer questions.

Ms. Pemble

Ms. Pemble teaches second grade in a K–5 school. This is her fifth year as a teacher, but her first year teaching second grade. Her prior experience was teaching fifth-grade classes. Ms. Pemble was very excited to make the transition to second grade, feeling it would provide a new challenge in her teaching career. She believed that the transition to second grade would be tough, but she has been surprised by just how difficult her first few months have been.

Today, Ms. Pemble invited her colleague Ms. Chaouki to observe her class. Ms. Chaouki has taught second grade for the past seven years at the school. Upon entering, Ms. Chaouki saw a classroom much different than her own. She was delighted to see the room decorated in great detail. She took a seat in the back of the classroom, and sat at Ms. Pemble's desk. The students' desks were arranged in a large rectangle. Students at the front of the class could not easily see their other classmates, while those in the back of the class could see all students. Students on the sides of the classroom could see most other students, and both whiteboards.

Ms. Pemble began today's class by announcing, "Good morning class. Today we're going to cover lots of fun and meaningful lessons. Let's first start with mathematics. Please take out your math workbooks and let's review the addition examples on Page 12." Ms. Chaouki noted that it took some students several minutes to retrieve the correct workbook from their desks, and join in the lesson.

After reviewing a few problems in mathematics, Ms. Pemble instructed the class "to work on your own, completing all problems on page 13." Students quietly worked on these problems, except for Steve, who did not pay attention to the instructions. Instead, Steve made funny faces at his neighbor Tim, who was trying to do the problems, but was distracted by Steve. Ms. Pemble noticed this, and said to the class, "Remember the most important rule in our class—be respectful of your neighbors, and treat them as you wish to be treated." Ms. Chaouki noticed some students recite these words along with Ms. Pemble—it was clear she has said this many times before.

Twenty minutes later, Ms. Pemble said, "Okay class, time is up. Let's put away our mathematics workbooks and take out our reading books." Ms. Pemble watched students followed this task, some much faster than others. Steve was one of the students who took quite some time to complete this task. The noise level began to grow during this time, as some students began to talk with their neighbors. Ms. Pemble stood quietly in front of the room, and did not begin to speak until the classroom was silent. Unfortunately, this took about three minutes.

Ms. Pemble then continued with the day's reading lesson. In her notes, Ms. Chaouki observed:

It is clear Ms. Pemble has great enthusiasm for this job. In watching her class, I now understand why Ms. Pemble has commented that the class was often rowdy—I definitely saw this today. She'll soon get a better understanding on how to manage the classroom more effectively.

GO ON TO THE NEXT PAGE

Directions: Questions 1 through 3 require you to write short answers. You are not expected to cite specific theories or texts in your answer; however, your responses to the questions will be evaluated with respect to professionally accepted principles and practices in teaching and learning. Be sure to answer all parts of the questions. Write your answers on the answer sheet.

Question 1
Ms. Chaouki noticed that Ms. Pemble's room was set up differently than she expected.

- Identify TWO things Ms. Pemble could do to structure her room more effectively.
- For each item above, discuss how these changes would be helpful for Ms. Pemble. Base your response on the principles of establishing an effective climate for classroom management.

Question 2
Ms. Pemble's class often displayed difficulty moving from one event to the next.

- Identify TWO things Ms. Pemble might do that would help the students navigate from one task to the next more effectively.
- For each item above, explain how these will help Ms. Pemble maintain attention in her classroom. Use specific management techniques that a teacher can apply to all classes.

Question 3
Ms. Chaouki observed that Ms. Pemble's class was often "rowdy."

- Identify areas where Ms. Pemble could improve in her ability to influence how her class should act in school. Include specific actions on how she may be able to work more effectively with Steve.

Case History 2

Directions: The case history is followed by three short-answer questions.

Mr. Ascher

Mr. Ascher is a third-year teacher at a K–5 elementary school, and currently teaches the fourth-grade class of 25 students. This class contains 14 boys, and 11 girls; further, the class has several LEP students, as the school is located near the California-Mexico border. Mr. Ascher has prepared a lesson plan for teaching students about the California Gold Rush.

Document 1
Project Plan
California Gold Rush

Objectives: Upon completion of the lesson, students will

1. Understand the events leading up to the California Gold Rush
2. Perform a play about the events
3. Explain the ethnic diversity present in mining towns
4. Discuss concepts of scarcity and diversity

Lesson Plan and Activities:

1. Class Discussion—overview of life in the 1840s. Students will begin Gold Rush Journal—1 session. During this session I will dress up as a miner from the 1940s.
2. Introduction to "gold fever." Students will read Chapter 2, and enter responses in journals—1 session.

GO ON TO THE NEXT PAGE

3. Analyze political cartoons to further discuss "gold fever" and respond to writing prompt—1 session.
4. Record questions from overview chart—1 session.
5. Simulation game—hunting for gold—results to be entered into journals—1 session.
6. Analysis of population charts and recording of inferences in journals—1 session.
7. Compare daguerreotypes of miners and prospective miners. Responses in journal—2 sessions.
8. Students write a letter home from the viewpoint of a miner—1 session.
9. Role-play buying miner's provisions—2 sessions.
10. Finalize what has been learned from overview chart and in Gold Rush journals—1 session.

Focus Questions:

"What are the characteristics of a mining town?"
"How well did the towns incorporate diversity into their society?"

Assessment:

- Performance on the Gold Rush journal
- Level of effort in the play
- Score on the "letter home" writing assignment

Directions: Questions 4 through 6 require you to write short answers. You are not expected to cite specific theories or texts in your answer; however, your responses to the questions will be evaluated with respect to professionally accepted principles and practices in teaching and learning. Be sure to answer all parts of the questions. Write your answers on the answer sheet.

Question 4
Mr. Ascher has produced a detailed lesson plan for the Gold Rush assignment.

- Identify TWO weaknesses in the lesson plan.
- For each item identified, explain how the inclusion of that item will hinder Mr. Ascher's ability to meet his planned objectives effectively.

Question 5
Mr. Ascher's project plan demonstrates many types of effective planning.

- Identify TWO strengths of the plan.
- For each strength, explain how it demonstrates effective planning, based on the principles of planning and instruction.

Question 6
Mr. Ascher has several LEP (Limited English Proficiency) students in the class.

- Identify TWO items that Mr. Ascher has incorporated into his lesson plan that will help LEP students accomplish the objectives, using the principles of learning and teaching.

GO ON TO THE NEXT PAGE

Discrete Multiple-Choice Questions

Directions: Questions 7–18 are not related to the previous case. For each question, select the best answer and mark the corresponding space on your answer sheet.

7. In a third-grade class, teams of three have been assigned to solve a series of multiplication problems. This task is an example of what type of learning?

   (A) Inquiry learning

   (B) Lecture learning

   (C) Demonstrated learning

   (D) Cooperative learning

8. Which of the following is NOT one of the eight types of intelligence identified by Howard Gardner?

   (A) Linguistic

   (B) Musical

   (C) Spatial

   (D) Exploratory

9. Ms. Gemmer's second-grade class is finishing a lesson in mathematics. She then announces, "In five minutes, we will complete work on this subtraction question and begin our discussion of history." This statement is an example of

   (A) cueing

   (B) authoritative leadership

   (C) context clues

   (D) whole language

10. Brady, a first-grade student, announces that his favorite TV Show is "Reference Boy." He becomes upset when another student, Timmy, mentions that he does not like that show. This behavior is an example of what cognitive development theory?

    (A) Piaget's preoperational stage

    (B) Freud's oral stage of personality development

    (C) Eriksen's stage of identify vs. identity

    (D) Thorndike's law of effect

11. Ms. Daniels is a first-grade teacher. Which of the following characteristics of her classroom will likely be the most challenging in establishing effective classroom management?

    (A) All desks are set up so that Ms. Daniels can see the faces of all students in the room.

    (B) Library books, which are used for group reading assignments, are organized in the back left corner of the room.

    (C) Classroom rules are posted on the blackboard at the front of the class.

    (D) Two children with special needs are located at the front of the class.

12. Which of the following statements is a well-formed learning objective?

    (A) I will teach students how to subtract two numbers.

    (B) While in your reading group, pronounce the new vocabulary words on page 12. Help the class pronounce any difficult words.

    (C) Identify where California is located on a map of the United States.

    (D) Bring in a guest speaker to talk about the activities of a fireman.

13. Ms. Larson is writing a spelling test for her second-grade class. This test will likely have which of the following characteristics?

    (A) High content validity

    (B) No error of measurement

    (C) Perfect reliability

    (D) Low criterion validity

GO ON TO THE NEXT PAGE

14. Mr. Elam is in his first year as a fourth-grade teacher. One of his students, Cindy, is struggling in math. Which of the following is likely the most effective step Mr. Elam can take to develop an effective learning plan for Cindy?

    (A) Ask Cindy about her parents, in order to better understand her socio-economic status.
    (B) Assign additional math questions for Cindy—practice makes perfect.
    (C) Discuss Cindy's performance with her third-grade teacher, who still teaches at the school.
    (D) Tell Cindy that girls traditionally don't do well in math, and encourage her to do her best.

15. A teacher is using a phonics approach for her first-grade classroom. Which of the following will the teacher most likely witness in the student's performance?

    (A) Students will know how to associate letters and groups of letters with sounds.
    (B) Students will have a larger vocabulary than those using a whole language approach.
    (C) Students can pronounce words, but will likely not know their meaning.
    (D) Students can only decode words from their context.

16. Which of the following is NOT an effective strategy for teaching a student with ADHD?

    (A) Provide a quiet environment for testing.
    (B) Ensure that each activity is at least one hour long.
    (C) Create a progress plan for the student.
    (D) Use positive reinforcements when activities are completed.

17. In order to determine how well the students in Mr. Brook's third-grade class perform in mathematics compared to other students in the state, he should have his students take what type of test?

    (A) A criterion referenced test
    (B) A low content validity measure
    (C) An authentic assessment
    (D) A norm-referenced test

18. A student in fourth grade is most likely to exhibit which of Erikson's stages of psychosocial development?

    (A) Trust vs. mistrust
    (B) Initiative vs. guilt
    (C) Autonomy vs. doubt
    (D) Industry vs. inferiority

GO ON TO THE NEXT PAGE

Case History 3

Directions: The case history is followed by three short-answer questions.

Ms. Farrell

Ms. Farrell is about to hold a parent-teacher conference to discuss the results of a series of achievement tests. Ms. Farrell is in her twelfth year teaching third grade at Nessland Elementary School, one of several schools in the South District. This year, her class is composed of 23 students—11 boys and 12 girls. Before her conference, Ms. Farrell is reviewing the documents below, in order to prepare her comments about the class's performance.

Document 1

	Reading Grade Equivalent	Math Grade Equivalent	Social Studies Grade Equivalent	Writing Grade Equivalent
Nessland Elementary	3.6	4.5	4.1	3.1
All Schools in South District	3.5	4.0	4.1	3.7

Summary of Results for Third-Grade Classes in South District

	Reading Grade Equivalent	Math Grade Equivalent	Social Studies Grade Equivalent	Writing Grade Equivalent
Nessland Elementary	61%	93%	85%	44%
All Schools in South District	57%	86%	85%	52%

Document 2

Summary of Results for Student Joy Lewis

	Reading Grade Equivalent	Math Grade Equivalent	Social Studies Grade Equivalent	Writing Grade Equivalent
Nessland Elementary	29	34	31%	N/A
All Schools in South District	48%	88%	81%	52%
Grade Equivalent	3.3	4.2	4.0	3.7

Directions: Questions 19 through 21 require you to write short answers. You are not expected to cite specific theories or texts in your answer; however, your responses to the questions will be evaluated with respect to professionally accepted principles and practices in teaching and learning. Be sure to answer all parts of the questions. Write your answers on the answer sheet.

Question 19

Ms. Farrell is pleased with the job she has done for the year, as her class is performing above grade level in all areas but one. She is also pleased to see that her class often performs better than other schools within the district. Yet she feels that more information may be necessary for her to assess her students' progress effectively.

- Identify TWO reports or inputs that Ms. Farrell could use to get a more complete view of the class's performance.
- For each input identified, describe how that assessment information can be used to guide Ms. Farrell's teaching.

GO ON TO THE NEXT PAGE

Question 20

Joy's parents are not familiar with the results of standardized tests, and want some feedback on her performance.

- Interpret Joy's performance on the standardized test.
- Provide TWO recommendations for what Joy should improve on during the last half of third grade.

Question 21

The parents of another student complain that any evaluation from a standardized test is unfair, as their daughter "is not a good test taker" and doesn't perform well under pressure.

- Explain TWO reasons how standardized tests can be a helpful tool in evaluating a students' performance.
- Identify TWO other ways in which student performance can be measured, and how Ms. Farrell can use these to provide a comprehensive assessment of each student.

Case History 4

Directions: The case history is followed by three short-answer questions.

Ms. Gemmer

Ms. Gemmer is a fourth-grade teacher at Abel Elementary School, where she has taught for the past two years. Below is a conversation she recently had with a student in her class:

Tuesday, 10:45 A.M.
Conclusion of Recess

Tiffany (*smiling*)	Ms. Gemmer, the boys are really funny.
Ms. Gemmer	Oh really? What are they up to now?
Tiffany	They just sang a song about Billy.
Ms. Gemmer	About your classmate Billy? What did they sing?
Tiffany	It's pretty funny. It goes, "Billy, Billy, really stinky. You wear clothes from 1950. You take a bath once a year, cause you stink more than dirty underwear!!"
Ms. Gemmer	Which boys are singing this?
Tiffany	Oh, I don't want to get anyone in trouble. It's just funny.
Ms. Gemmer	Please tell me who was singing, so I can deal with them. Otherwise, I may just punish you too.
Tiffany	Scott and Rick.
Ms. Gemmer	Anyone else?
Tiffany	No. But if you tell them I told you, then they'll get mad at me.
Ms. Gemmer	Don't worry about that. Thank you, Tiffany.

Upon returning from class, Billy did not look happy. In fact, it appeared that he had been crying. Ms. Gemmer noticed that while Billy did not in fact smell, that his clothes were somewhat disheveled, and had numerous stains across the shirt. These were not the result of any recess play; in general, Ms. Gemmer knew that Billy wore many "dirty" clothes. As a majority of her class was affluent, she was concerned that Billy's attire was not a function of finances but of someone not properly caring for Billy.

The following conversation took place immediately after recess:

Ms. Gemmer	Before we move on to our Computer assignment, I heard a song I really did not like during recess. Does anyone want to raise their hand and admit that they were singing this song?

GO ON TO THE NEXT PAGE

No hands are raised; many students are laughing at Rick and Scott, who are no longer making eye contact with Ms. Gemmer.

Mark	I know who did it!
Ms. Gemmer	Thank you Mark, but I want the culprits to identify themselves.

No hands are raised.

Ms. Gemmer	Okay. Fine. I'll deal with this during the lunch period, and those of you who did this, but did not admit it now, will now get twice the punishment.

Ms. Gemmer introduced the computer lesson. Part of this lesson involved students working quietly in groups of three. Ms. Gemmer walked around to each group to monitor their progress. As she reached the group Scott was in, she whispered to Scott, "Please see me at lunch regarding the recess incident." Scott was unhappy, and no longer participated in the assignment. She then walked up to Rick and whispered the same thing. Rick immediately began to cry. When she walked pass Billy's group, she asked Billy how we was doing, leading to this exchange:

Ms. Gemmer	Billy, are you doing okay?
Billy	Yes, Ms. Gemmer
Ms. Gemmer	Don't worry, I'll take care of the recess problem.
Billy	I don't want to talk about it.
Ms. Gemmer	Then, I'll talk about it for you.
Billy	I wish you'd just leave this alone.
Ms. Gemmer	I'm sorry, Billy. But I need to teach people what is right and what is wrong. And that song is not nice.

Ms. Gemmer continued teaching until lunch, when she met privately with Rick and Scott.

Directions: Questions 22 through 24 require you to write short answers. You are not expected to cite specific theories or texts in your answer; however, your responses to the questions will be evaluated with respect to professionally accepted principles and practices in teaching and learning. Be sure to answer all parts of the questions. Write your answers on the answer sheet.

Question 22

Ms. Gemmer struggled on how much of this incident she should make public to the entire class versus how much she should deal with it in private.

- Identify one thing Ms. Gemmer did well during this situation.
- Identify two things Ms. Gemmer could do better regarding her handling of this matter. Focus your answers based on your knowledge of managing a positive instructional environment.

Question 23

Ms. Gemmer thinks that Billy's attire may in fact be a sign of problems for Billy.

- Identify TWO things Ms. Gemmer can do to address this issue with Billy and/or his parents.
- Base your response on the principles of teaching and learning and human development.

Question 24

There were two students who gave Ms. Gemmer information about the song—Tiffany and Mark. She treated Tiffany and Mark differently.

- Identify TWO things that Ms. Gemmer could have done differently in her interactions with Tiffany and Mark.
- For each modification you suggested, explain how the modification could have created a better learning environment. Base your response on the principles of effective classroom management.

GO ON TO THE NEXT PAGE

Discrete Multiple-Choice Questions

Directions: Questions 25–36 are not related to the previous case. For each question, select the best answer and mark the corresponding space on your answer sheet.

25. A proper Individualized Education Plan (IEP), includes all of the following EXCEPT

    (A) what should be taught and how

    (B) how much time the student will spend with children who do not have disabilities

    (C) annual goals and short-term objectives for the student

    (D) an agreement signed by parents and teachers that the IEP will not change for the school year

26. Steven, a second grader, completes a standardized reading test. His grade-equivalent score is a 4.3, and his national percentile is 93. Which of the following is true about Steven's national percentile score?

    (A) Steven did as well as 4.3% of the second graders who completed the test.

    (B) Steven scored higher than 93% of students who have completed three months in their fourth year of school.

    (C) Steven scored higher than 93% of second grade students who completed the test.

    (D) The national percentile shows that Steven has not learned concepts taught in the second half of fourth grade.

27. Physical education activities are one way to develop which of the following types of learning?

    (A) Cognitive domain

    (B) Affective domain

    (C) Psychomotor domain

    (D) All of the above

28. According to Skinner's theories on behavioral development, the practice of giving a student a low grade for poor performance on a test is an example of

    (A) positive reinforcement

    (B) negative reinforcement

    (C) extinction

    (D) presentation punishment

29. Ms. Hardy's fourth-grade class is studying the process in which cereal is made. The class is currently answering the following question: "What companies should a cereal manufacturer interact with in order to package the cereal?" This task best models what level in Bloom's Taxonomy of Objectives?

    (A) Knowledge

    (B) Comprehension

    (C) Application

    (D) Evaluation

30. Mr. Bailey started teaching his third-grade class in the following manner: First, he reviewed the prior day's material with two questions designed to reinforce the material. Second, he presented new information for the next lesson. What could Mr. Bailey have done to create a more effective lesson?

    (A) Introduce a statement or question related to the next lesson to get students curious about the future material.

    (B) Call on a quiet student and ask him or her to explain the next lesson.

    (C) Give a pop quiz to the students.

    (D) Have students pre-read the information, and prepare a quiz for other students in the class.

GO ON TO THE NEXT PAGE

31. Several tools are recommended when modifying instruction for students who are learning disabled. Which of the following is NOT a recommended instructional method?

(A) Structured, brief assignments

(B) Manipulative experiences

(C) Cooperative learning

(D) Increasingly longer lessons with less public praise

32. Jamie, a third-grade student, is attempting to learn how to multiply two numbers together. Her teacher recommends that she do 100 problems per day until she is comfortable with the process. Which theory does her teacher employ to help Jamie?

(A) Thorndike's law of exercise

(B) Thorndike's law of effect

(C) Skinner's extinction

(D) Piaget's sensorimotor

33. Which of the following statements about creating an environment for student learning is NOT true?

(A) Objectives should be aligned with the overall goals of the school district.

(B) Objectives should be accepted by appropriate national, regional, or state organizations.

(C) Objectives should be aligned for the achievement desired of students in the class.

(D) Objectives should not be modified for specific student populations; it is important that goals are not compromised.

34. Tanya is a second-grade student who recently completed a standardized test. She received a score of 100 out of 200, which resulted in an equivalent stanine score of 3. Which of the following statements about Tanya's performance must be true?

(A) Tanya scored one grade equivalent above her current grade level.

(B) Tanya scored in the 50th percentile.

(C) The error of measurement on the test is within 20 percent.

(D) Tanya scored below average compared to other students in her class.

35. Students in a sixth-grade class are trying to solve a problem—how to develop a recycling program for their school. They have invited the local commissioner of sanitation and recycling to speak with the class. The students are at which of the following steps in the problem-solving process?

(A) Develop assessment tools to measure the effectiveness of their solutions.

(B) Brainstorm possible solutions to the task.

(C) Gather data and information about the problem.

(D) Develop an implementation plan for the problem.

36. Which of the following instructional strategies is most commonly observed in first-grade classes?

(A) The teacher carefully maps out the day's activities, which include numerous structured lessons.

(B) The teacher focuses on whole group discussions and uses various questioning, explaining, and probing techniques.

(C) The teacher focuses on two or three long lessons per day, which relate to a common integrated theme.

(D) The teacher introduces a topic, and allows students to develop their own plans to address the topic.

STOP

Diagnostic Test Form

Completely darken bubbles with a No. 2 pencil. If you make a mistake, be sure to erase mark completely. Erase all stray marks.

1. YOUR NAME: ______________________________
(Print) Last First M.I.

SIGNATURE: ______________________________ **DATE:** ___/___/___

HOME ADDRESS: ______________________________
(Print) Number and Street

______________________________ **E-MAIL:** ______________________________
City State Zip

PHONE NO.: ____________ **SCHOOL:** ____________ **CLASS OF:** ____________
(Print)

IMPORTANT: Please fill in these boxes exactly as shown on the back cover of your test book.

OpScan *i*NSIGHT™ forms by Pearson NCS EM-255325-1:654321
Printed in U.S.A.

2. TEST FORM

3. TEST CODE

0	0	0	0
1	1	1	1
2	2	2	2
3	3	3	3
4	4	4	4
5	5	5	5
6	6	6	6
7	7	7	7
8	8	8	8
9	9	9	9

4. PHONE NUMBER

0	0	0	0	0	0	0
1	1	1	1	1	1	1
2	2	2	2	2	2	2
3	3	3	3	3	3	3
4	4	4	4	4	4	4
5	5	5	5	5	5	5
6	6	6	6	6	6	6
7	7	7	7	7	7	7
8	8	8	8	8	8	8
9	9	9	9	9	9	9

5. YOUR NAME

First 4 letters of last name				FIRST INIT	MID INIT
A	A	A	A	A	A
B	B	B	B	B	B
C	C	C	C	C	C
D	D	D	D	D	D
E	E	E	E	E	E
F	F	F	F	F	F
G	G	G	G	G	G
H	H	H	H	H	H
I	I	I	I	I	I
J	J	J	J	J	J
K	K	K	K	K	K
L	L	L	L	L	L
M	M	M	M	M	M
N	N	N	N	N	N
O	O	O	O	O	O
P	P	P	P	P	P
Q	Q	Q	Q	Q	Q
R	R	R	R	R	R
S	S	S	S	S	S
T	T	T	T	T	T
U	U	U	U	U	U
V	V	V	V	V	V
W	W	W	W	W	W
X	X	X	X	X	X
Y	Y	Y	Y	Y	Y
Z	Z	Z	Z	Z	Z

6. DATE OF BIRTH

MONTH	DAY		YEAR	
JAN				
FEB				
MAR	0	0	0	0
APR	1	1	1	1
MAY	2	2	2	2
JUN	3	3	3	3
JUL		4	4	4
AUG		5	5	5
SEP		6	6	6
OCT		7	7	7
NOV		8	8	8
DEC		9	9	9

7. SEX

- MALE
- FEMALE

8. OTHER

1 A B C D E
2 A B C D E
3 A B C D E

CASE I

1. Write your response on the appropriate page of the response book.
2. Write your response on the appropriate page of the response book.
3. Write your response on the appropriate page of the response book.

CASE II

4. Write your response on the appropriate page of the response book.
5. Write your response on the appropriate page of the response book.
6. Write your response on the appropriate page of the response book.

7 A B C D
8 A B C D
9 A B C D
10 A B C D
11 A B C D
12 A B C D
13 A B C D
14 A B C D
15 A B C D
16 A B C D
17 A B C D
18 A B C D

CASE III

19. Write your response on the appropriate page of the response book.
20. Write your response on the appropriate page of the response book.
21. Write your response on the appropriate page of the response book.

CASE IV

22. Write your response on the appropriate page of the response book.
23. Write your response on the appropriate page of the response book.
24. Write your response on the appropriate page of the response book.

25 A B C D
26 A B C D
27 A B C D
28 A B C D
29 A B C D
30 A B C D
31 A B C D
32 A B C D
33 A B C D
34 A B C D
35 A B C D
36 A B C D

27

Answers and Explanations for PLT: K–6 Practice Test

ANSWERS AND EXPLANATIONS FOR PLT: K–6 PRACTICE TEST

1. **Sample Response that receives a score of 2:**

   Ms. Pemble should improve the current seating arrangement. The layout of the room is somewhat effective in that she can see the faces of all her students. However, the rectangular approach can prove to be distracting to students, as some are facing other students, and not the front of the room. A more traditional arrangement in rows, all facing front, would help Ms. Pemble navigate her space more effectively.

   A second thing Ms. Pemble should do is to display a list of her expectations for the classroom. While it is impressive that many students knew her "be respectful of your neighbors..." adage, she could reinforce these standards by displaying them on a board. If students violate these rules, Ms. Pemble could ask the student to read the rule aloud to the class, whenever there is an unwarranted disruption.

   Sample Response that receives a score of 1:

   I don't like what Ms. Pemble has done with the seating arrangement. A rectangle makes it difficult to walk around the classroom and closes off open space. Further, her desk should be located in the front of the room, and not the back of the room. This will allow her to make eye contact with her students from their seats. An important challenge of teaching a second-grade class is to establish oneself as an authority figure—this can be best achieved by having a strong presence in front of the class.

   In addition to the seating issue, Ms. Pemble should separate students that are loud, or constantly talk to each other. Separating Steve from Tim may help create a more positive classroom environment, and remove a distraction that could negatively influence other students.

2. **Sample Response that receives a score of 2:**

   Ms. Pemble could be more effective in providing cues to her students about upcoming tasks. Instead of simply announcing the end of the mathematics lesson, Ms. Pemble should provide an alert for students that a transition is coming. By stating, "You have five minutes left to work on this task, and then I will ask you to quickly put away your workbook and take out your reading book," would be helpful. This would help Ms. Pemble reduce the transition time in between tasks. As shown by Kounin, group alerting is an effective technique for effective classroom management.

   Secondly, Ms. Pemble could provide positive reinforcement to those students transitioning between tasks effectively. Ms. Pemble demonstrated techniques when she was not happy with certain behaviors; however, she never demonstrated praise for those who completed their tasks well. When a student quickly retrieves a workbook, she could say, "Thank you [Stacy] for retrieving your mathematics book so quickly." This positive reinforcement will help create learned behaviors within her class.

   Sample Response that receives a score of 1:

   Ms. Pemble's class struggles with effective transitions because she does not tell the students what they are going to do or for how long. When she assigned the math problems, she should indicate the length of the activity, and then could do additional things to reinforce this, such as write the time of the activity on the board. This will help Ms. Pemble create a more focused learning environment. Research shows that when students know what is forthcoming, they make more effective use of their time.

Secondly, Ms. Pemble needs to be more assertive when making transitions. Standing quietly is not an ideal method, because there are no negative consequences to a lengthy transition. Canter and Canter recommend more direct approaches, such as writing the name of the violating student on the board.

3. **Sample Response that receives a score of 2:**

Ms. Pemble's class often turned rowdy when students navigated between two tasks. She should be more active in the transition process, praising students who complete their transitions quickly. Further, Ms. Pemble should play a more active role when students are working individually on mathematics problems. If a student becomes distracted, such as Steve was, she should walk over to Steve and review his work. If Steve finished his problems early, she should challenge him with a bonus problem; if he did not complete his work, she should encourage Steve to complete the problems, possibly explaining how to solve the problem to her. In general, Ms. Pemble needs to identify specifically when Steve is acting out, without causing undue attention to him.

Sample Response that receives a score of 1:

Ms. Pemble should establish a goal whenever she asks the students to do something different. For example, she should establish a one-minute goal for putting away the math book, and retrieving the reading book. Students that complete this task should be rewarded either by a thank you or some reward system. This positive reinforcement would also work for Steve, who needs to know that it is not acceptable to make faces at other students who are still working on problems. More constant eye contact, gestures, or conversations with Steve should help him improve his behavior.

4. **Sample Response that receives a score of 2:**

Mr. Ascher has not specifically identified the necessary set of resources needed to help students reach the objectives. Some of these resources are mentioned in the "Lesson Plan and Activities" section. However, many items, such as the play, do not have a clear identification of the tools necessary to complete that task. Up front identification of resources would help Mr. Ascher make sure he has all materials needed for a successful lesson. Further, once resources are identified, Mr. Ascher can work on transition points, such as distribution or collection of materials. Minimizing these events will create a better environment to learn about the Gold Rush.

Also, Mr. Ascher should provide more specific instructions on how he will accomplish the objective of teaching the concept of scarcity. It is possible that it will be taught in Session 5 as part of the simulation game, but it is not very clear. Linking objectives with specific activities to meet those objectives helps teachers ensure that their work will yield the desired results.

Sample Response that receives a score of 1:

Mr. Ascher could be more specific in how the students will be graded. It is one thing to state "level of effort in the play," but what does that mean? He needs to have a specific idea of what he wants to see from students in this area. By thinking through the desired set of responses, he can create meaningful grades and feedback mechanisms at the conclusion of the class.

Also, he should not give so many activities. There are more than ten sessions required to meet this objective, which may be too long for fourth-graders. Older classes can handle long, focused sessions, but I'm not sure this would work for the fourth grade. Therefore, reduce it to five sessions.

5. **Sample Response that receives a score of 2:**

An often overlooked portion of any project lesson plan is what Hunter calls the anticipatory set—or something that is done to prepare students and focus them on the lesson. In Session 1, Mr. Ascher plans on dressing up like a miner in the 1840s. This should draw immediate student interest. Further, it links to one of the assessment and objective items—that students will perform a play. Students will soon need to be in costumes, so this provides a good preview of what is to come for the class.

A second strength of the plan is the diverse set of activities in the lesson. Students will need to effectively read, write, and perform during this lesson. Learning a subject, and then incorporating that into many different disciplines, helps keep students motivated. Students who are engaged in the learning process tend to be more successful learners.

Sample Response that receives a score of 1:

Mr. Ascher has provided a detailed list of activities in order to accomplish the objectives. This will help Mr. Ascher accomplish his goal, as lesson planning makes the job of a teacher much easier.

Also, he has created an assessment section for his lesson plan. It is important to be able to measure what a class has learned, in order to confirm that the objectives have been met. Assessments help to complete a lesson plan.

6. **Sample Response that receives a score of 2:**

A class that is linguistically diverse must take into account the limits that language places on learning. First, Mr. Ascher has the activity of the simulation game to show how to hunt for gold. If the game is first modeled—that is, showing the skills or procedures being taught—then LEP students should be able to participate in the game just as other students will.

Along the same lines, the role-play of buying miner's provisions will be helpful for all students. Through visual interaction, instead of just language, LEP students can participate and learn about the life of a miner in the 1840s. For example, purchasing supplies can help a student learn about money management, as well as provide some quick mathematics examples. This can be helpful for an LEP student that may struggle if these concepts were only described to him or her.

Sample Response that receives a score of 1:

The first thing that will help the LEP students is the play. Plays are often very interactive, which should get everyone involved. Further, plays often involve studying and memorizing lines, so that will help students learn new words they haven't learned before.

Also, the activities that do not involve writing will be helpful for LEP students. Writing is often considered the hardest part of becoming bilingual. The fact that Mr. Ascher has some non-writing activities should help the students.

7. **D** Cooperative learning involves students working together in groups to learn a concept, or to complete a task.

8. **D** In addition to the first three answer choices, Gardner's list includes logical-mathematical; bodily-kinesthetic; naturalist; interpersonal; and intrapersonal.

9. **A** Cueing defines words or other signals that alert students to a coming transition. Ms. Gemmer's announcement prepares students for the transition from mathematics to history.

10. **A** Piaget's theory has four development stages. The second stage, the preoperational stage, asserts that student's thinking is egocentric, and that some students have difficulty understanding the opinions of others.

11. **B** An effective strategy for classroom management is to have books and supplies available at several locations. Arranging the room so students do not have to stand in line is a key component to classroom management.

12. **C** An objective should describe the actions that students are expected to do once instruction is complete. It should not describe what the teacher will do during the lesson. Answer choices (A) and (D) describe teacher actions, as does the second half of answer choice (B).

13. **A** A test has high content validity if it measures the material covered in a particular lesson or curriculum. Because Ms. Larson is writing a spelling test, it very likely will have high content validity—that is, the test will be based on the recent vocabulary her class has studied. Answer choice (B) is impossible—every test contains some error of measurement. While the spelling test may be reliable, it is a tough argument to say it has perfect reliability. (D) is not valid, as a spelling test is not a predictor for any future type of work.

14. **C** Before Mr. Elam can determine a set of objectives for Cindy, he must determine her prerequisite competencies. The other choices are not aligned with effective techniques to develop Cindy's mathematical skills.

15. **A** This is the standard definition of a phonics approach for reading.

16. **B** Students with ADHD learn most effectively in small, managed tasks. Consistently lengthy activities may prove to be challenging for the student.

17. **D** Norm-referenced tests are designed to compare students or groups.

18. **D** This fourth stage of Erikson's framework is most common for students in elementary school, between ages 6 and 12.

19. **Sample Response that receives a score of 2:**

Document 1 is helpful, in that it shows how Ms. Farrell's class performs overall. However, the figures are summations of individual performance. It would be most helpful to have the individual score reports for each student. This will allow her to identify those who need specific help, or to identify those that are excelling in a subject. Each group requires a specific learning plan, in order to properly develop and challenge the student.

Secondly, Ms. Farrell should seek additional testing information beyond that of one standardized test. From these results, she should create criterion-referenced tests based on her school district curricula. This will help Ms. Farrell specifically identify any concepts or lessons that are difficult for students in her class.

Sample Response that receives a score of 1:

Ms. Farrell should speak with the other teachers in South District about how they teach Writing. Her class did not perform up to the grade-level equivalent, and therefore, she could learn additional techniques from the teachers that were more successful.

An additional piece of information to evaluate is the types of questions that students missed. If many students missed the same questions, then that could provide Ms. Farrell with future lesson plans. She'll need to review those concepts so that students understand them for the future.

20. **Sample Response that receives a score of 2:**

On the whole, Joy performed well on her standardized test. The 'Grade Equivalent' score shows how a student compares to the achievement of all other students at the same grade level. For example, her 4.2 in math indicates that her performance is the average of those in the second month of the fourth grade. Clearly, she is above average with her peer group (3.4 grade equivalent in that category). Across the state, she is performing around the average in Reading and Writing; and above average in Math and Social Studies. Compared to her classmates, she performed above average in Writing, around the average in Math and Social Studies, and somewhat below average in Reading. For the parents, first, I would let them know that Joy is performing well in school, at least as evidenced by this standardized test. Her parents should continue to motivate and encourage her. For specific work, I would recommend to them that they spend extra time with Joy on her Reading. Finally, this class seems to do very well in mathematics, so I would be sure they review mathematics material with Joy, so that she will not fall behind a fast-moving class.

Sample Response that receives a score of 1:

Joy performed above average in Reading and Writing, and above average in Math and Social Studies. This is evidenced by the grade equivalent scores above 4 for the latter two subjects.

I would tell Joy's parents to review Reading with her. She performed under the class average and under her grade equivalent score. Further, I would recommend that her parents help her in Writing, because that appears to be a subject where her class is not strong. If the subject matter is not strong in the classroom, parents may want to supplement at home.

21. **Sample Response that receives a score of 2:**

It is understandable that the parents are concerned about standardized tests, as there is often misconception about them. Standardized tests help provide a comparison between students in a particular group, whether that group is a class, a school district, or a nationwide set of students. Further, standardized tests often have a high degree of reliability; that is, the test will yield similar results to the same person within a short time span. This consistency is very helpful to ensure that a biased test or question is not used to interpret student performance incorrectly.

Yet standardized tests do not evaluate a student's ability to work cooperatively or consistently. In addition to the standardized tests, Ms. Farrell should provide criterion-referenced tests, so the students can display their mastery on certain recently-learned skills. Further, any type of authentic assessment, such as a portfolio review, will help evaluate students and their work in a real-life setting.

Sample Response that receives a score of 1:

Standardized tests are not biased. Otherwise, they wouldn't be around. Teachers often struggle writing purely objective tests. Teacher-made tests don't have the benefit of being reviewed by peers and tested by thousands of students to measure validity. Further, standardized tests help rank people, which can be necessary for identifying candidates for honors courses, etc.

In addition to standardized tests, teachers should use their own day-to-day activities to evaluate a student. Subject-based tests and participation in the classroom are two additional things that can be used to provide a more comprehensive overview of the student.

22. **Sample Response that receives a score of 2:**

Ms. Gemmer only mentioned that there was an incident, and did not mention Billy by name. This saved Billy further embarrassment by having the song at recess discussed again, but this time to the entire class. Further, Ms. Gemmer did not make this incident a public episode for the class when she quietly asked Scott and Rick to meet her after class to discuss the situation. However, this may have been fortunate for Ms. Gemmer, as earlier actions appeared to be designed to having students publicly identify themselves. Even though I disagree with her request for students to raise their hands, I think she made the problem worse by moving on when no one admitted their guilt. This provides a negative reinforcement to students, basically saying that if you don't answer a tough question, Ms. Gemmer will move on to another topic. Therefore, I would recommend that Ms. Gemmer does not bring up these situations to the entire class unless she is determined to resolve them at that time. Secondly, I would recommend that she not threaten Tiffany with punishment. Tiffany provided valuable input to Ms. Gemmer. Her unnecessary comment to Tiffany could potentially create distrust or uneasiness, and she may find it more challenging for Tiffany to open up in the future.

Sample Response that receives a score of 1:

Ms. Gemmer did a horrible job handling this situation. First, she was not friendly to the student that helped her out the most. Second, she didn't punish the kids who made the song. Third, she didn't make the students apologize in front of the entire class to Billy.

I like that she asked Billy if he was okay, which shows that she cares as a teacher. Students who feel appreciated are more likely to do well in school, and likely to develop positive self-esteem, which is critical for students during their elementary school years.

23. **Sample Response that receives a score of 2:**

First, Ms. Gemmer should get more information about Billy's background. She should speak to his teachers from last year, to see if they encountered similar issues with Billy wearing dirty, stained, and torn clothes. If this is a new issue, she can focus on recent changes in Billy's home life. Otherwise, if this behavior has been consistent for a few years, she can use that information when speaking with Billy's parents.

The second thing Ms. Gemmer should do is speak to Billy's parents about his attire. This could be a sensitive topic due to potential financial issues. It is important that Ms. Gemmer describe the problem only in its educational and social context. Specifically, that dirty clothes could cause Billy to become easily distracted or uncomfortable, making it more difficult to pay attention to a lesson. Secondly, these clothes can become a source of teasing, at an age when the need to be accepted by a peer group is quite high. If Billy's parents feel that Ms. Gemmer is describing the issue without any preconceived judgments, they will likely be open to discussing the issue, and taking any suggestions made by Ms. Gemmer.

Sample Response that receives a score of 1:

Ms. Gemmer knows that if Billy is constantly teased, this could have an adverse impact on his development. He could have decreased self-confidence, and ability to relate to his peers. Therefore, she should ask him how he ends up so dirty throughout the day. She should ask if he plays too hard during recess, and ends up dirty. She doesn't want to imply immediately that he comes to school disheveled, even if that is the case.

In addition to asking Billy, she should also ask his parents. Given that the class is generally affluent, Ms. Gemmer may make recommendations such as checking Billy's clothes before leaving for school; or removing any stains prior to doing loads of wash. This will help Billy fit in more with the rest of the class.

24. **Sample Response that receives a score of 2:**

Ms. Gemmer used the threat of punishment to get Tiffany to provide the information she wanted to receive. Tiffany had volunteered information to Ms. Gemmer willingly, but was now threatened to be punished if she did not provide all information. This action could cause Tiffany to believe that there are negative consequences to sharing information with her teacher. This conditioning could lead to distrust, and a closed relationship between teacher and student. Instead, Ms. Gemmer should have encouraged Tiffany to disclose the students' names, informing Tiffany of the good that would come from such an admission. By partnering and encouraging Tiffany, she could help create more trust in the classroom.

Mark wanted to volunteer information, as he attempted to answer the question, but was then told from Ms. Gemmer that his information was not needed. Mark believed he was doing the right thing, only to find out that Ms. Gemmer had different expectations. Ms. Gemmer should have worded her question more carefully, asking for the culprits to identify themselves upfront, rather than ask the ambiguous question of who did it. When students understand what they are being asked, they will be more likely to volunteer information.

Sample Response that receives a score of 1:

Tiffany was not treated fairly. She simply wanted to talk to Ms. Gemmer, and ended up with the risk of getting punished if she did not "tattle" on Rick and Scott. This creates a hostile environment for the classroom, where students cannot share. Instead, they will be taught to hold back information, because giving information can possibly lead to bad consequences. The same is true with Mark. He basically had the right answer, but was then told not to give it. He'll stop volunteering in the future.

25. **D** A key component to an effective IEP is that teachers and parents can change the plan at any time, on an as-needed basis. Parents and teachers should meet if either group feels the needs of the student are changing.

26. **C** Answer choice (B) may be tempting; however, the national percentile provides a comparison to students of the same grade level.

27. **D** While the most obvious type of learning is psychomotor learning (motor skills, etc.), all types of learning can be achieved through physical activities.

28. **D** A negative reinforcement is used to escape an unpleasant situation. For example, students who get an A on the test will not have to do homework for a week. Punishment discourages behavior and we want to discourage students from doing badly on tests. Presentation punishment is to create an undesirable situation as a result of a certain behavior. The student did badly on the test; the student gets a low score.

29. **D** The evaluation stage is defined as "making considered judgments by breaking down and reconnecting ideas."

30. **A** Hunter refers to this as the *anticipatory set*, which is something said or done to prepare students to focus on the next lesson.

31. **D** Notice that answer choices (A) and (D) are contradictory, so one of them must be correct. Learning disabled students should be given structured, brief assignments.

32. **A** Thorndike stated in his *law of exercise* that repeating the response, as in practicing, can strengthen a conditioned response or process.

33. **D** Objectives should be modified to meet the needs of a particular class. The class may be academically diverse, culturally diverse, or linguistically diverse.

34. **D** The word "stanine" is a contraction of the words "standard nine." Stanines are an artificial scale from 1 to 9 that can be placed on any normal (bell-curved) distribution of scores. The mean is 5, and the standard deviation is 2. A stanine score of 3 is below average. Stanines are meant to be a broad classification of scores, and are often used instead of a more precise measurement to reduce the chance of attributing too much importance to a particular score.

35. **C** In the problem-solving process, the students have invited a speaker to offer more information on setting up a program. Therefore, they are in the process of gathering data.

36. **A** Elementary students learn best with more structure, shorter lessons, less explanation, more public praise, and experience with manipulatives and pictures. Answer choices (B), (C), and (D) are more common for middle-school and junior-high school children.

28

PLT: 5–9 Practice Test

The Praxis Series Professional Assessments for Beginning Teachers

Test Name: Principles of Learning and Teaching

Practice Case Histories and Constructed-Response Questions

Time –120 minutes

12 Short-Answer Questions and 24 Multiple-Choice Questions

Case History 1

Directions: The case history is followed by three short-answer questions.

Mr. Dvorak

Mr. Dvorak teaches an eighth-grade class, and it is currently the second month of instruction. Mr. Dvorak is an experienced teacher—he has taught in the district for more than twelve years, but most of his experience is teaching fourth- and fifth-grade classes. Due to a last minute change in staffing, the school principal asked Mr. Dvorak to move from his fourth-grade assignment to the eighth grade. The principal believed that Mr. Dvorak's success in teaching, and veteran experience, would allow him to successfully transition to the eighth grade.

Mr. Dvorak has spent more time planning lessons than he has over the past few years, primarily due to his lack of familiarity with the material and curricula. Known for his innovative teaching methods, he has spent additional time trying to think of creative ways to present the more complex material. He has reviewed his lesson plans with other eighth-grade teachers, and has been complimented many times for the quality and detail of the lesson plans.

While the plans have been well designed, implementing them has been a difficult matter. Frequently, Mr. Dvorak is not able to complete the lesson, and he is concerned about his ability to get the class to participate. Below is a sample of yesterday's discussion:

Mr. Dvorak	Okay, who can tell me about the Pythagorean theorem? Dennis?
Dennis	I didn't do the assignment, Mr. Dvorak.
Mr. Dvorak	That's not good. We'll talk about that later. Who else? Shelly?
Shelly	It's used to find the sides of a triangle.
Mr. Dvorak	What kind of triangle?
Shelly	An isosceles triangle.
Mr. Dvorak	No, that's wrong. Who can give the correct answer?

No one raises their hand for five seconds.

Mr. Dvorak	Anyone?

Tim raises his hand.

Mr. Dvorak	Yes, Tim.
Tim	Can you tell Steve to stop it? He keeps staring at me!

The class laughs.

Mr. Dvorak	Steve, is this true?
Steve	No, sir, I'm just trying to learn about this theorem thing.

The class laughs again.

Mr. Dvorak	I'd like to see you after class. Let's continue...

GO ON TO THE NEXT PAGE

Steve was one of a number of students that were giving Mr. Dvorak trouble. To his surprise, students act differently than he expected. For example, Sven never brings his materials to class. Tina is usually ten minutes late. Many students do not complete homework assignments, and goof off frequently during class time.

This has left Mr. Dvorak frustrated. He has begun to teach in a negative and critical fashion, and it is becomes increasingly difficult for him to hide his anger. He has spoken with some of the veteran eighth-grade teachers, who remind him that the group is at a difficult age, and that some chaos is a normal part of any class. For Mr. Dvorak, who is very accustomed to having complete control in the classroom, this has been a very difficult experience.

Parent conferences have also been a challenge. Several parents have complained that the preliminary grades from Mr. Dvorak are lower than their students usually receive. Further, some parents have complained that the amount of homework given from Mr. Dvorak is greater than the amount given from other teachers.

Directions: Questions 1 through 3 require you to write short answers. You are not expected to cite specific theories or texts in your answer; however, your responses to the questions will be evaluated with respect to professionally accepted principles and practices in teaching and learning. Be sure to answer all parts of the questions. Write your answers on the answer sheet.

Question 1

In his self-analysis, Mr. Dvorak is frustrated at the level of participation by his students in classroom discussion.

- Suggest TWO things that Mr. Dvorak could do to increase the participation in his classroom.
- For each suggestion, explain how its use would make the classroom environment more effective. Base your response on the principles of effective instructional strategies.

Question 2

Mr. Dvorak has had difficulty transitioning from teaching younger students to teaching an eighth-grade class.

- Identify TWO actions Mr. Dvorak can take to ease the transition to teaching an older group of students.
- For each action identified, discuss how the action can help not only Mr. Dvorak, but also the class atmosphere.

Question 3

Several students do not behave appropriately in Mr. Dvorak's class.

- Identify TWO specific actions Mr. Dvorak can take to help promote better behavior in his classroom.
- For each item identified, discuss how Mr. Dvorak's actions will help create a better classroom environment. Base your response on the principles of effective instructional strategies.

Case History 2

Directions: The case history is followed by three short-answer questions.

Ms. Babcock

Ms. Babcock is about to hold a meeting with the school principal to discuss her eighth-grade class's performance on recent achievement tests. These tests were taken during the third month of the school year. Ms. Babcock is in her sixth year teaching eighth grade at Freitas Middle School, one of several schools in the North District. This year, her class is composed of 28 students—7 boys and 21 girls. Before her conference, Ms. Babcock is reviewing the documents below, in order to prepare her comments about the class's performance.

GO ON TO THE NEXT PAGE

Document 1

Summary of Results for Eighth-Grade Classes in the North District

	Reading Grade Equivalent	Math Grade Equivalent	Social Studies Grade Equivalent	Writing Grade Equivalent
Freitas Middle School	8.6	9.5	9.1	8.1
All Schools in North District	8.5	9.0	9.1	8.7
	Reading State Percentile	**Math State Percentile**	**Social Studies Percentile**	**Writing Percentile**
Freitas Middle School	61%	93%	85%	44%
All Schools in North District	57%	86%	85%	52%

Document 2

Summary of Results for Student Darek Lewis

	Reading Grade Equivalent	Math Grade Equivalent	Social Studies Grade Equivalent	Writing Grade Equivalent
Questions Correct (out of 50)	29	34	31	N/A
Percentile	48%	88%	81%	52%
Grade Equivalent	8.3	9.2	9.0	8.7

Document 3

Distribution of Scores for Ms. Babcock's Class

	Reading Grade (%)	Math Grade (%)	Social Studies (%)	Writing Grade (%)
Boys	61%	82%	56%	39%
Girls	61%	95%	86%	47%
Total	61%	93%	85%	44%

GO ON TO THE NEXT PAGE

Directions: Questions 4 through 6 require you to write short answers. You are not expected to cite specific theories or texts in your answer; however, your responses to the questions will be evaluated with respect to professionally accepted principles and practices in teaching and learning. Be sure to answer all parts of the questions. Write your answers on the answer sheet.

Question 4

The school principal asks Ms. Babcock to identify areas that her class can improve on during the second half of the year.

- Identify TWO areas where the class can spend additional time focusing for the remainder of the year. Support your answers with statistics from the documents above.

Question 5

A surprising result of the standardized test was the results of Darek Lewis. Darek is considered by Ms. Babcock to be the best student in the class.

- Identify TWO possible explanations for Darek's performance on the test. For each explanation, identify other ways in which Darek's grasp of the Reading material can be evaluated.

Question 6

Ms. Babcock is preparing to deliver the results of the performance to her class.

- Identify ONE thing that Ms. Babcock should emphasize to the class. Base this information on the principles of effective learning strategies.
- Identify ONE thing that Ms. Babcock should NOT emphasize to her class, again using the principles of effective learning strategies.

GO ON TO THE NEXT PAGE

Discrete Multiple-Choice Questions

Directions: Questions 7–18 are not related to the previous case. For each question, select the best answer and mark the corresponding space on your answer sheet.

7. Matthew is having trouble in his eighth-grade Algebra class. Mr. Peters, a first-year teacher at the school, believes that Matthew's troubles are due to a lack of effort, not due to confusion about the material. Which of the following statements, if true, would weaken Mr. Peters' assessment?

   (A) Matthew has scored below average in six of the seven tests this year.

   (B) Matthew received a score of grade level equivalent of 6.2 in the norm-referenced test last year.

   (C) Matthew has not always turned in his homework on time.

   (D) Matthew has told Mr. Peters that his favorite subject is math.

8. Which of the following statements would behaviorist Skinner argue against?

   (A) Reward systems help lead to desired responses.

   (B) Punishment or extinction is necessary for undesired responses.

   (C) Teachers must teach first things first.

   (D) Students advance at essentially the same rate.

9. Which of the following is NOT a level of cognitive learning according to Bloom's taxonomy?

   (A) Memorization

   (B) Physical

   (C) Understanding

   (D) Application

10. Ms. Benes is concerned that she will not have enough time this semester to teach all of the state required curricula for History. Which of the following actions can Ms. Benes take to maximize her learning time with her class?

    (A) Remove some of the early lessons in the curriculum—students likely already know this review material.

    (B) Assign additional homework to move the class at a faster pace.

    (C) Develop strategies to minimize distributing and collecting materials.

    (D) Ask students to define which sections of the curricula they do not want to study.

11. Mr. Sullivan is requiring that his sixth-grade class prepare oral book reports as a way to evaluate his students' performance in reading. Which of the following best supports Mr. Sullivan's rationale that an oral book report will motivate the students to read?

    (A) It requires that students read the book, or face the embarrassment of a poor oral report.

    (B) Students gain experience with presentation skills.

    (C) Students are less likely to cheat preparing an oral report than preparing a writing sample.

    (D) Students enjoy public speaking more than reading.

12. Steven is a strong visual learner in the seventh grade. Which of the following activities would be most helpful for Steven to learn about immigration patterns in the 1900s?

    (A) Taking frequent breaks while reading a chapter

    (B) Discussing the concepts in a group format in class

    (C) Displaying a diagram that charts movements of certain groups across different continents

    (D) A mathematical representation of immigrants across various segments

GO ON TO THE NEXT PAGE

13. Concept maps are helpful for all of the following activities EXCEPT

    (A) outlining term papers and presentations
    (B) taking notes during a lecture
    (C) brainstorming with a group
    (D) evaluating writing assignments

14. Mr. Windle's plans to teach his seventh-grade class a unit on corporate ethics. His first step was to assign a reading chapter from the Business textbook. Next, he assigned three questions for the class to answer. Before answering the questions, students were able to meet with one other student to discuss the answers. Then, a group discussion would occur, where students will be evaluated based on their participation, and quality of response.

    The cooperative learning strategy employed by Mr. Windle is best known as

    (A) jigsaw
    (B) think-pair-share
    (C) STAD
    (D) demonstration

15. Mr. Martin is teaching his class a unit on nutrition, and wishes to employ a constructivist approach. Which of the following assignments employs this approach?

    (A) Students read an undergraduate level text on nutrition, and its impact on the body.
    (B) Students have a two-part assignment: first, they write a paper on their current nutrition habits. Next, after a lecture about proper nutrition, they add to their paper indicating what they can improve in their own life.
    (C) Students are given a vocabulary list of all important nutrition words. They work within a group of four for one week, before the group is given a spelling test.
    (D) Students are shown two videos on nutrition, and are then asked to give oral reports about what they have learned.

16. One curriculum goal within the sixth-grade mathematics course is to learn strategies of calculator computation. Which of the following objectives for students best reflects that goal?

    (A) Students will use calculators for all mathematical tasks.
    (B) Students will be quizzed daily on basic mathematic formulas.
    (C) Students will understand the order of operations.
    (D) Students will determine whether or not a calculator is needed to solve a problem.

17. Mr. Smith's class is studying American History. They are asked the following three questions:

    - What year did the Revolutionary War begin?
    - Who were the Redcoats?
    - When was George Washington named president?

    These questions reflect which type of learning, according to Bloom's Taxonomy?

    (A) Knowledge
    (B) Application
    (C) Analysis
    (D) Evaluation

18. Which of the following is NOT one of four stages of cognitive development, as proposed by Jean Piaget?

    (A) Proximal
    (B) Sensorimotor
    (C) Concrete Operations
    (D) Preoperational

GO ON TO THE NEXT PAGE

Case History 3

Directions: The case history is followed by three short-answer questions.

Ms. Johnson

Ms. Johnson teaches a seventh-grade English class to 24 students. Fourteen of the students are male, and 10 are female. For nine of the students, English is the second language. These nine students represent three different language groups. The English fluency skill of the nine students varies widely. In addition to these students, Ms. Johnson teaches two more students who have been placed in the class on the "least-restrictive environment" provision. Three other students have been identified as strong performers, and have qualified under the "gifted and talented" program. Finally, one student is repeating the class, after receiving several failing grades the previous year.

Ms. Johnson has determined the following goals for the class.

Goals:

1. Develop skills working cooperatively.
2. Improve reading, writing, and critical thinking skills within the English curriculum.
3. Develop speaking and listening skills, in both group discussions and formal oral reports.
4. Learn to appreciate the diverse works of literature present in our world.

Last week, Ms. Johnson wanted to focus on the third goal. She came up with the following activities:

- Students will meet in pairs to introduce themselves. Then, each student will introduce the other to the class.
- Afterwards, each student will be asked to find something they have in common with another student. Another interview will take place, where they will need to identify another thing the two students share in common.

The exercise did not go as well as Ms. Johnson had hoped. Here are her notes summarizing the exercise:

> *Today was not ideal. The interview exercise seemed like a good idea, but it turned out to be more difficult than I had imagined. Most students simply gravitated to the friends they already knew in the class. As I walked around, I found many pairs discussing random topics, instead of getting to know each other. Some students, like Stephanie, lost focus during the exercise. She couldn't remember anything about her partner, Stephen, when she was asked to present to the group. Other pairs weren't sure what to do. So Young and Kai, neither of whom speaks fluent English, conducted their interviews in Korean, despite my request to carry out the exercise only in English. Other students thought the exercise went too long—it did take up two class periods.*

Today, Ms. Johnson is preparing grades for the first progress report. As she reviews the performance of her students, she talks over the grades with her principal. She notes:

> *I don't feel like I'm really helping anyone. It is such a diverse class. My strong students are probably bored; I spend too much time making sure our IEP students have their needs met; and I'm really frustrated at the poor English skills of some of our students. I just don't know how other teachers let them slip through the cracks, but it's up to me to fix this. At times I feel like I need five separate lesson plans to work effectively with these 24 students. I know that one size never fits all, but right now, one size seems to fit no one!*

GO ON TO THE NEXT PAGE

Directions: Questions 19 through 21 require you to write short answers. You are not expected to cite specific theories or texts in your answer; however, your responses to the questions will be evaluated with respect to professionally accepted principles and practices in teaching and learning. Be sure to answer all parts of the questions. Write your answers on the answer sheet.

Question 19
Ms. Johnson set up four objectives for her class to achieve this year.

- Select TWO of the four objectives, and for each objective, identify one strategy Ms. Johnson might employ to meet her goal, given the current makeup of the class.
- For each of your strategies, explain how the strategy will help Ms. Johnson meet her objectives. Base your response on principles of planning instruction and/or language development and acquisition.

Question 20
Ms. Johnson noted that the "interview" exercise did not go as well as she had hoped.

- Identify TWO things Ms. Johnson could have done to make the exercise more effective.
- For each item identified, explain how that action would have made the exercise more useful to the class. Base your response on the principles of effective instructional planning.

Question 21
Ms. Johnson commented that her students have very diverse needs.

- Identify TWO things Ms. Johnson can do to make sure her efforts reach all students, not just a select few.
- For each strategy, explain how the actions by Ms. Johnson will help to create a stronger learning environment. Base your response on the principles of effective learning.

Case History 4

Directions: The case history is followed by three short-answer questions.

Tammy

Tammy is an eleven-year-old fifth-grade student who lives with her father about an hour from the school district. She attends the school because her permanent address is listed as her mother's address, which is located within the school district. Tammy often arrives at school late. Tammy appears to be often fatigued at school, and on several occasions has fallen asleep at her desk. Despite very strong achievement scores, Tammy is not performing well in school, as her assignments are often incomplete. Ms. Ramos, Tammy's teacher, has asked another teacher to view the class, in hopes that she can provide some additional recommendations on how to improve Tammy's performance. Before Ms. Jimenez views the class, Ms. Ramos sends her this note:

> *Ms. Jimenez, thank you for agreeing to visit my class. I hope that you can help me find some solutions in dealing with Tammy. She has been an excellent student, but her performance has dropped recently, and it is very frustrating. I'm concerned that something may be troubling at home. She looks exhausted when she arrives at school, and is so tired that she simply doesn't concentrate as much as she should. Other students have started to notice, and she is now being teased as "Tired Tammy." I look forward to your comments. Thanks, Ms. Ramos.*

GO ON TO THE NEXT PAGE

Classroom Observation

On the day of Ms. Jimenez's visit, Ms. Ramos begins the class with a discussion of how businesses deal with money. Tammy is not present yet. Ms. Ramos reviews the definitions of income, expenses, and profit, concepts covered during the previous lecture. A few minutes into class, Tammy walks in, and hands Ms. Ramos a tardy slip. A few students giggle at Tammy, who arrives late for the third consecutive class period. Ms. Ramos quiets the class down, and continues to review key definitions.

Next, Ms. Ramos announces that there will be an activity: "Today, we are going to all run a small business by playing a game in your table groups. There are five different roles that you will need to play. Person 1 will be the banker, who holds the money. Person 2 will be the business owner, who pays the bills to the bank. Person 3 will be the accountant, who collects the money from the customer, and tracks the income and the expenses. Person 4 will be the customer, who gives money to the business owner for the product. Person 5 will be the supplier, who will supply the product to the business owner. Use the game pieces and boards that I'm currently distributing to start the game. Please do this for twenty-five minutes, and we will see which group made the most money."

As Ms. Ramos passed around the materials, Tammy's table group starts to discuss the roles that each person will play. There is lots of confusion. "What does Person 2 do again?" asks Tammy. Another student angrily snaps back, "Pay attention, dork." This quiets Tammy, who chooses not to volunteer for a position, but instead waits until the other four students have chosen roles. She is told that she is the banker.

The game progresses, and Ms. Ramos stops by to see how Tammy's group is performing. Cesar drew a card, which said, "Pay business expenses for electricity for $100." When Cesar handed Tammy a $100 bill, she looked confused. Ms. Ramos replied, "Tammy, if you were paying attention, you would know that Cesar just paid an expense. Focus on the game please." Tammy took the money from Cesar, and looked upset as Ms. Ramos walked away. Tammy looked away from the game board, and stared out the window, fighting back tears.

When the activity ended, each group was told by Ms. Ramos to find the amount of profit or loss made by their group. When Carrie, one of Tammy's group members, went to get a calculator, Tammy stopped her and said, "We made a profit of $300. I already added it up." Carrie said thank you, and wrote the figure down. After each group shared their results, each student turned in their summary papers to Ms. Ramos. Ms. Ramos noticed that Tammy had not completely filled out the form. Instead, she had put her head down and rested while the other team members were finishing their roles. Ms. Ramos asked her why she did not complete all aspects of the assignment. Tammy shrugged her shoulders and walked back to her seat.

Post-Observation Notes

Ms. Jimenez writes, "I can understand your confusion about Tammy. There were times when she grasped concepts much faster than other students. At other times, however, she appeared disinterested, and shied away from both participating and in dealing with other students. A few students teased her, which may be reason for concern, but I think there may be something else. She doesn't seem to be your happy-go-lucky fifth-grader, and clearly looks to be a student that is not getting proper amounts of rest."

GO ON TO THE NEXT PAGE

Directions: Questions 22 through 24 require you to write short answers. You are not expected to cite specific theories or texts in your answer; however, your responses to the questions will be evaluated with respect to professionally accepted principles and practices in teaching and learning. Be sure to answer all parts of the questions. Write your answers on the answer sheet.

Question 22
Ms. Ramos believes that Tammy's home environment could be a reason for the challenges Tammy faces at school.

- Identify TWO specific actions Ms. Ramos can take to connect Tammy's home environment with her school performance.
- Explain how each action could benefit Tammy's learning. Base your response on the principles of fostering strong school-parent relationships.

Question 23
It is mentioned that many students were confused before starting the small business game.

- Suggest TWO actions Ms. Ramos could have made in the planning and/or implementation of the group work that would have made the activity more successful.
- For each action, explain how the change could make the activity more successful. Base your response on the principles of planning instruction.

Question 24
Ms. Jimenez suggests that, aside from teasing, there may be other reasons why Tammy's performance has suffered.

- Provide TWO possible explanations for why Tammy's performance has suffered.
- For each explanation, describe one action Ms. Ramos can take to see if those explanations could be correct. Base your response on the principles of human development and motivation.

GO ON TO THE NEXT PAGE

Directions: Questions 25–36 are not related to the previous case. For each question, select the best answer and mark the corresponding space on your answer sheet.

25. Which of the following is NOT an effective strategy in teaching a student with ADHD?

    (A) Seat the student near the teacher's desk, but include them as part of the regular class seating.
    (B) Assign only one task at a time.
    (C) When providing daily announcements to the class, ask the student if he or she remembered to take their medicine.
    (D) Have preestablished consequences for misbehavior.

26. Mr. Smith: Who can tell me the cube root of 64? Cindy?
    Cindy: It is 4.
    Mr. Smith: Correct. Great job. Cindy gains 10 points toward her day of no homework.

    The above exchange is best supported by what theory and theorist?

    (A) Skinner and negative reinforcement
    (B) Maslow and intrinsic motivation
    (C) Bandura and causal relationships
    (D) Vygotsky and hierarchy of needs

27. Mr. Farrell wants his seventh-grade science class to understand how temperatures vary across the United States. What is one technique Mr. Farrell can use as an inductive thinking approach to the problem?

    (A) Ask students to brainstorm about different types of weather.
    (B) Provide students with a chart that shows different temperatures in different regions.
    (C) Give an overview lecture on how temperature is measured.
    (D) Ask students to write out their own theories, then have the class try to disprove them.

28. Ms. Smith likes to conclude her mathematics class with a "lightning round," during which students will shout out the answer to her questions as quickly as possible. This practice is contrary to the benefits associated with what concept?

    (A) Wait-time
    (B) Concept attainment
    (C) Social reasoning
    (D) Memorization and recall

29. Which of the following is NOT part of Madeline Hunter's "seven step lesson plan?"

    (A) Objectives
    (B) Anticipatory Set
    (C) Guided Practice
    (D) Invention

30. Which of the following events is most aligned with the theories of emergent curriculum?

    (A) Students decide what grades they should receive.
    (B) Students help to determine what is taught based upon their interests and desires.
    (C) Parents and teachers align to determine the best course of action for students.
    (D) Teachers will not deviate from state designed curricula.

31. On the sixth-grade Social Studies test at Butterick Middle School, the results were as follows:

    - Mean: 74.5
    - Median: 76.0
    - Mode: 81.0

    Which of the following statements is true?

    (A) Students at Butterick scored below the national average of sixth grade classes.
    (B) More students received a score of 76 than any other score.
    (C) The average score of the class was 81.
    (D) An equal number of students scored above and below 76.

GO ON TO THE NEXT PAGE

32. In a continual effort to improve, Ms. Dooner seeks out different ways to refine her teaching style. Which of the following demonstrates her role as a reflective practitioner?

(A) Brainstorming with other colleagues

(B) Reading professional literature on the latest research

(C) Joining a professional association

(D) All of the above

33. Upon the completion of each test, Ms. Alldredge asks her class to fill out a one-page questionnaire, entitled "Next Time..." The form asks students to think about what they could do next time to learn more effectively. Students receive this form regardless of how they perform on the test. Through this effort, Ms. Alldredge is developing which of the following skills?

(A) Reinforcement

(B) Metacognition

(C) Scanning

(D) Conceptual differentiation

34. Two weeks into the school year, Ms. Brown is worried about a group of eight students, who seem to be falling behind. Of additional concern, she realizes that all eight students are ESL students. In order to address their needs as learners, what could Ms. Brown do to address the situation best?

(A) Begin tutorial sessions with the eight students to review the basic material already covered.

(B) Create a different set of expectations for these students, as they will have more difficulty that students where English is their first language.

(C) She should test all eight students on proficiencies in their first language and English, in order to understand their current performance levels.

(D) Move the students into their own group, to provide more support and allow other students to move at a different pace.

35. In Ms. Nevin's fifth-grade class, the students are given two hours to play in the treasure chest, which contains many common household items. The goal during the play time is to create a representation of an animal out of these items. This type of play is considered

(A) constructive play

(B) parallel play

(C) inductive play

(D) causal play

36. Paul received the results of his eighth-grade computer test. He was told he received a stanine score of 6, and a percentile rank of 61. Which of the following statements are true?

(A) He missed six questions, for a total of 61 percent correct.

(B) He received an average score, scoring above 61 percent of students who completed the test.

(C) His average performance was the equivalent of a sixth-grade student, and he answered 61 percent of the questions correctly.

(D) His performance is the equivalent of an eighth-grade student in the sixth month of instruction.

STOP

Diagnostic Test Form

Completely darken bubbles with a No. 2 pencil. If you make a mistake, be sure to erase mark completely. Erase all stray marks.

OUR NAME: ______________________________ (Print) Last First M.I.

IGNATURE: ______________________________ DATE: ___/___/___

OME ADDRESS: ______________________________ (Print) Number and Street

______________________________ City State Zip E-MAIL: ______________________________

HONE NO.: ______________ (Print) SCHOOL: ______________ CLASS OF: ______________

IMPORTANT: Please fill in these boxes exactly as shown on the back cover of your test book.

OpScan *i*NSIGHT™ forms by Pearson NCS EM-255325-1:654321
Printed in U.S.A.

TEST FORM

3. TEST CODE

0 1 2 3 4 5 6 7 8 9 (four columns)

4. PHONE NUMBER

0 1 2 3 4 5 6 7 8 9 (seven columns)

5. YOUR NAME

First 4 letters of last name				FIRST INIT	MID INIT
A–Z	A–Z	A–Z	A–Z	A–Z	A–Z

DATE OF BIRTH

ONTH	DAY		YEAR	
JAN				
FEB				
MAR	0	0	0	0
APR	1	1	1	1
MAY	2	2	2	2
JUN	3	3	3	3
JUL		4	4	4
AUG		5	5	5
SEP		6	6	6
OCT		7	7	7
NOV		8	8	8
DEC		9	9	9

7. SEX

◯ MALE
◯ FEMALE

8. OTHER

1 (A) (B) (C) (D) (E)
2 (A) (B) (C) (D) (E)
3 (A) (B) (C) (D) (E)

CASE I

1. Write your response on the appropriate page of the response book.
2. Write your response on the appropriate page of the response book.
3. Write your response on the appropriate page of the response book.

CASE II

4. Write your response on the appropriate page of the response book.
5. Write your response on the appropriate page of the response book.
6. Write your response on the appropriate page of the response book.

7 (A) (B) (C) (D)
8 (A) (B) (C) (D)
9 (A) (B) (C) (D)
10 (A) (B) (C) (D)
11 (A) (B) (C) (D)
12 (A) (B) (C) (D)
13 (A) (B) (C) (D)
14 (A) (B) (C) (D)
15 (A) (B) (C) (D)
16 (A) (B) (C) (D)
17 (A) (B) (C) (D)
18 (A) (B) (C) (D)

CASE III

19. Write your response on the appropriate page of the response book.
20. Write your response on the appropriate page of the response book.
21. Write your response on the appropriate page of the response book.

CASE IV

22. Write your response on the appropriate page of the response book.
23. Write your response on the appropriate page of the response book.
24. Write your response on the appropriate page of the response book.

25 (A) (B) (C) (D)
26 (A) (B) (C) (D)
27 (A) (B) (C) (D)
28 (A) (B) (C) (D)
29 (A) (B) (C) (D)
30 (A) (B) (C) (D)
31 (A) (B) (C) (D)
32 (A) (B) (C) (D)
33 (A) (B) (C) (D)
34 (A) (B) (C) (D)
35 (A) (B) (C) (D)
36 (A) (B) (C) (D)

29

Answers and Explanations for PLT: 5–9 Practice Test

ANSWERS AND EXPLANATIONS FOR PLT: 5–9 PRACTICE TEST

1. **Sample Response that receives a score of 2:**

   Mr. Dvorak may want to increase the amount of wait-time before he calls on a student. Studies have shown that increasing wait-time until at least 3 seconds helps to increase the amount of class participation, and increase the quality of response.

   A second strategy to increase participation would be to provide more positive reinforcement. In the case above, Mr. Dvorak was quick to point out when a student made a mistake. For adolescent eighth-graders, his criticism could be interpreted as public humiliation, and may lead others to witness that sharing answers can be dangerous. Skinner's operant conditioning suggests that other students will be hesitant to participate in the face of negative feedback.

   Sample Response that receives a score of 1:

   Mr. Dvorak appears to have lost control of the class in many ways. Students are not fully participating, nor are they following all of the rules set forth in the classroom. In order to increase participation, he first needs to ensure that he has created a positive school environment. This means that students need to feel comfortable sharing answers, and need to know that poor actions will be punished. When students see Sven forget his textbook every day, they may be conditioned to believe that coming to class prepared is not always necessary.

   Mr. Dvorak may also want to be more friendly when he asks students questions. Shelly attempted to answer the question, and got it mostly correct. Yet instead of encouraging her, or congratulating her on the part she did answer correctly, he only pointed out where she made a mistake.

2. **Sample Response that receives a score of 2:**

   Mr. Dvorak should use other teachers as a resource. Mr. Dvorak has been very accomplished in his teaching career, and has demonstrated excellent performance when teaching younger students. While he has consulted with other teachers on matters of curricula, he does not seem to have consulted with them on the social and personal challenges of an eighth-grade class. In working with other teachers, he can get advice on best practices for controlling a classroom, encouraging participation, and understanding the challenges of teaching teenagers. Further, he should consult with last year's seventh-grade teachers to get specific information on his current students.

   A second opportunity for Mr. Dvorak would be to consult professional literature on middle-school students. Mr. Dvorak can incorporate recent articles on teenage classroom behavior and discipline into his current approach to classroom discipline. By employing these techniques, which will likely have him treating his students with more respect, Mr. Dvorak will create a more positive workplace atmosphere.

   Sample Response that receives a score of 1:

   First, Mr. Dvorak must realize that these students are not fourth-graders. They have encountered many experiences, and are at a very difficult age, where puberty and peer pressure can dominate their actions and responses in the classroom. It appears that he may have gone overboard, however, in his expectations of his students. They won't get every question correct, and he may be assigning far more homework than the students can handle. He should scale these back to make the students more at ease.

A second strategy would be to consult with the school board or state-established curricula, to ensure that he is teaching the correct material. Studies have shown that students must have proper pre-knowledge in order to grasp advanced concepts.

3. **Sample Response that receives a score of 2:**

It is important for students to know that the teacher is in charge of the classroom, not the peer leaders. Mr. Dvorak needs to demonstrate that the behavior shown by Steve, Sven, and Tina is not acceptable. Steve's sarcastic answer caused the class to laugh, which indicates that the class seems to be influenced by him. Studies show that peer leaders can interfere with a teacher's effectiveness. It will be important for Mr. Dvorak to work with Steve after class to make sure he understands that such comments are not welcome in the classroom. I recommend he do this outside of class, so as to not draw additional attention to Steve's behavior.

A second strategy to improve the atmosphere in Mr. Dvorak's class is to provide a more positive and uncritical approach to voluntary participation. Studies show that students learn less when teachers are negative and critical, and this is especially true for students at the adolescent stage.

Sample Response that receives a score of 1:

Parents have complained that Mr. Dvorak gives too much homework. If this is true, this can be demotivating for the students, and will likely cause students to give up in the classroom. He should first analyze his goals in teaching the curriculum, and consult with other teachers as to the amount of homework he gives. If he does indeed give too much, he should cut back on the amount. Students will be more likely to complete the work, and therefore classroom discussions should move more effectively.

Further, he needs to create an environment of discipline in the classroom. There needs to be specific penalties for showing up late, forgetting to bring the necessary materials, or for not completing homework. Once other students see discipline, they will be less likely to act out.

4. **Sample Response that receives a score of 2:**

One area where Ms. Babcock's class could improve is in the subject of Writing. The class performed at a percentile rank of 44 percent, which means that 56 percent of equivalent classes performed better than her class. Of the four subjects, this is clearly the weakest area for the class, as it is the only one with a grade school equivalent score closest to their actual year (8.3). A second area where Ms. Babcock should focus is on the difference in scores between boys and girls in the class. In every subject, boys are performing at or below girls. This is especially true in mathematics and social studies, where the percentiles vary greatly. Ms. Babcock should review her teaching methodologies to ensure that her teaching is not biased towards females. Further, with only 7 of the 28 students male, she needs to ensure that her teaching strategies involve all students, not just the majority.

Sample Response that receives a score of 1:

Ms. Babcock's class could improve in Writing, which as the lowest percentile score at 44 percent. After that subject, the class performs at or above grade-level. But if there is another subject to improve, I would recommend she focus on Reading skills, where the percentiles rank second to last out of the four categories.

5. **Sample Response that receives a score of 2:**

Darek performed in the 48th percentile, which is just around average for an eighth-grade student. If Ms. Babcock feels he is normally a stronger student, it may be that Darek performs better with real-world assessment tests. A criterion-referenced test, which is designed to measure a specific set of information, could be used to demonstrate Darek's talents in reading. One other possible explanation is that Darek suffers from a learning disability, and standardized tests are not conducive to him performing his best. One way to validate this would be to see how many questions Darek answered. It is possible that he ran out of time. If this were a likely case, Darek could be evaluated in Reading based on reading passages aloud to Ms. Babcock.

Sample Response that receives a score of 1:

As a boy in the class, Darek may be suffering from a lack of attention. Since boys performed worse than girls in every subject matter, there may be a problem with the way Ms. Babcock works with the boys in her class. One other suggestion is that Darek, as the brightest kid in the class, did not take the test seriously. Darek may simply be bored with activities that are not challenging for him.

6. **Sample Response that receives a score of 2:**

Ms. Babcock should praise the students for their mastery of the material that they have covered throughout the year. She should emphasize that the hard work of the class has been demonstrated through their performance on the test. Further, she can specifically identify extraordinary achievements, such as scoring in the 93rd percentile in mathematics. Students need to receive positive reinforcement for their positive achievements. Students will be conditioned to attempt to repeat the performance if they feel their efforts were worthwhile.

Ms. Babcock should not emphasize that this one test is the sole determinant of success for the classroom. There are many evaluative tools to assess performance, and this is only one of them. If students become fixated on performance of a standardized test, they can often suffer from too much pressure, and actually perform at a level which reflects less than they actually know.

Sample Response that receives a score of 1:

Ms. Babcock should not discuss the disparity between boys and girls on their performance. This is an issue for Ms. Babcock to address as part of her teaching style and strategy. Informing the class that girls performed much better than boys will likely not yield any positive effects. The boys, already in the minority in the class, may begin to feel inferior in Ms. Babcock's classroom, which will only make the challenge to improve their skills more difficult.

7. **B** This score indicates that Matthew is not performing up to a standard consistent with his grade level. His troubles in Algebra may not be due strictly to a lack of effort; prior score results show that he not understand the basic material. Many students have trouble learning because they have not mastered the basic skills necessary for understanding a more complex concept.

8. **D** Many behaviorists, including Skinner, caution that student development, especially in elementary and middle school years, progresses at different rates. Moving students along at the same rate holds some back, and pushes others too quickly.

9. **B** The three levels of cognitive learning are commonly defined as memorization, understanding, and application.

10. **C** Teachers need to maximize their allotted time for learning. Many transitional activities, such as distributing materials, can remove valuable minutes from the day that can be used for learning. Answer choices (A), (B), and (D) would give Ms. Benes more time, but at a cost to the students' education.

11. **A** Most students will read the book to prevent embarrassment. Answer choices (B) and (C) deal with issues outside of motivation. (D) does not provide a reason as to why students would want to read the book.

12. **C** A diagram will be helpful for Steven, who learns best with visual displays. While (D) could be considered, (C) is a more complete answer.

13. **D** A concept map offers a method to represent information visually. Concept maps are not the same as scoring rubrics, which can be helpful in evaluating writing assignments.

14. **B** In a think-pair-share strategy, a concept is introduced; a student gets to review the material with another student; and the material is then discussed with a larger group.

15. **B** The constructivist approach is an approach to teaching and learning based on the premise that learning is the result of mental construction—students learn by fitting new information together with what they already know.

16. **D** Answer choice (A) can be misleading. The goal of the course is to learn strategies for calculator computation. In order to employ any strategies, students must know when it is appropriate to use a calculator. (A) is not a reflection of this goal.

17. **A** Knowledge is the first order of learning in Bloom's taxonomy. The three questions above require remembering, recalling information, and memorizing, which are all traits of knowledge learning.

18. **A** The four stages of Piaget's theory on cognitive development are sensorimotor, preoperational, concrete operations, and formal operations.

19. **Sample Response that receives a score of 2:**

One goal is to develop speaking and listening skills. To develop these skills, Ms. Johnson can include activities such as having students report aloud about the books they've read while other students note what is important about each, and ask questions about the books. Students can then be placed into groups, and choose a book that was important to them. The group would select one or two for presentations to the class. This strategy will develop speaking and listening skills, while possibly generating more interest in books that other students would be interested in reading.

Another goal is to improve reading, writing, and critical thinking skills. Ms. Johnson could have each student maintain a folder of literature entries for several weeks. Then, the student would select two for review and analysis. The student would then rewrite two entries, adding information on why the entries are important to them, and turn them in to Ms. Johnson for evaluation. This adds purpose to the assignment of maintaining a journal.

Sample Response that receives a score of 1:

The second goal listed by Ms. Johnson is to improve reading, writing, and critical thinking skills. One way this can be done is to ask students to find situations of conflict within the books they've read. Students will need to explain why the conflict arose, what the different opinions were from the characters, and what the resolution was. This could be used to start a discussion on the different types of conflict that people go through every day. Ms. Johnson would be helping the class with life lessons in addition to helping them with English. It would also help the class work cooperatively.

20. **Sample Response that receives a score of 2:**

With a number of ESL students in her class, Ms. Johnson may need to give more detailed directions on her expectations for conducting an interview. Before students break off into pairs, she could present a model of an interview and an introduction. One way to do this would be to show a video of a pair of students completing the task. Another way would be to ask a student (either a gifted student, or the one who did the exercise last year) to interview and introduce Ms. Johnson. This would provide a framework and visual understanding so that the ESL students can be successful in the task.

A second recommendation would be to assign students to specific pairs. Part of the goal of the exercise is to meet new students. By determining the pairs in advance, Ms. Johnson can ensure that students have an opportunity to meet new people. The interview will be more effective if you are unfamiliar with a person.

Sample Response that receives a score of 1:

It did not appear that Ms. Johnson put a time limit on how long the interview should take. Students will be more effective if they understand the amount of time allotted to the exercise. Otherwise, some students may finish too early, while others will take so long they may not complete the task in time. More structure is necessary from Ms. Johnson.

Secondly, she has not presented any evaluation criteria. Evaluation criteria will help students understand how their performance will be measured.

21. **Sample Response that receives a score of 2:**

Ms. Johnson is challenged by the fact that she has students at many different skill levels, with many different needs. Her first strategy should be to make sure she understands the exact levels of performance in her students. Ms. Johnson noted how surprised she was in the skills of some of her ESL students. Before she can effectively address their needs as learners, she must first understand their current abilities. She should request an assessment of the students' oral language abilities, in both their first language, and in English. Once she is aware of their specific performance, she can build effective lesson plans to further the development of all students.

A second strategy is to assign students to cooperative learning groups in such a way that the groups combine students of different abilities and backgrounds. This will help all students work together, and succeed in learning the material.

Sample Response that receives a score of 1:

Realistically, Ms. Johnson is in trouble. A class with talents as diverse as hers will likely not be able to survive as one cohesive group. One thing that she should do is group students, so that students don't naturally gravitate to those they are comfortable with. One way to do this is to use a random selection process of group assignment. That way, students can gain trust that Ms. Johnson is not biased, or playing favorites to any one student. By having group work, students of different skills will need to work together to accomplish a goal.

A second strategy would be to seek out the gifted students, and ask them if they want to take on more work. This may keep them challenged by giving them more challenging tasks.

22. Sample Response that receives a score of 2:

First, Ms. Ramos can collect as much information as possible about Tammy to use in a meeting with Tammy's father. Collecting information in advance will help establish a positive relationship with the father, and help identify Tammy's strengths and needs. Observation information could include the number of times Tammy is tardy; the number of times Tammy has arrived at school unkempt; and specific examples of times when Tammy has failed to work to her grade level. This observation information could be augmented by recording Tammy's strengths, and by researching information about how students of Tammy's age deal with parents who are separated or divorced.

Second, Ms. Ramos should organize a parent conference to address her concerns about Tammy. By showing a sincere interest in Tammy's future success, Ms. Ramos can work to establish a positive relationship with Tammy's father.

Sample Response that receives a score of 1:

First, Ms. Ramos needs to call a meeting with Tammy's father, and if possible, her mother. This will help connect the home environment with the school performance. They can discuss Tammy's performance and hopefully identify why her performance has changed, and why she isn't living up to her potential as shown on the standardized tests. Ms. Ramos may also want to bring the observation notes from Ms. Jimenez. In this way, a neutral third party can provide information, so that hopefully the parents and Ms. Ramos can work together to help Tammy improve.

23. Sample Response that receives a score of 2:

Ms. Ramos quickly defined the roles of the five individuals in each group. However, there was nothing present so that students could retain that information. Therefore, Ms. Ramos could display posters that illustrate what students are to do; a poster for each of the five roles would help students remember the different roles, and what each role needs to do.

Secondly, Ms. Ramos allowed the class to become a bit chaotic when she passed out the material. For such a large activity, she could have used volunteers, or even the observation teacher Ms. Jimenez to help pass out material in advance. In this fashion, transition time is reduced, and students would be able to use the visual clues of the game board to understand the rules explained by Ms. Ramos better.

Sample Response that receives a score of 1:

Ms. Ramos should teach or review group work behavior and expectations before the work begins. This would help students to participate appropriately in each activity. Further, she should give warnings on how much time is remaining, so that students know when they are about to finish the activity. This helps them pace themselves appropriately.

24. Sample Response that receives a score of 2:

One possible explanation is that Tammy has ADHD or some other learning disability. Tammy at times has shown the ability to grasp material quickly, but often appears to be withdrawn or removed from most activities. Ms. Ramos could suggest that a nurse or counselor evaluate Tammy in a classroom situation to determine if detailed testing is warranted.

Another possible explanation is that Tammy does not react favorably to any negative feedback. For example, she immediately withdrew when one student called her a "dork." Ms.

Ramos could try to provide frequent positive reinforcement to Tammy. Ms. Ramos would then observe Tammy's behavior to see if her learning improves in an environment where she is frequently praised.

Sample Response that receives a score of 1:

There is likely something wrong in Tammy's home situation. She gets to school late, experiences long drives to and from school, and may not be given the proper attention (notice her often dirty clothes and disheveled look). If something is wrong at home, it's likely hard to focus at school. A second thing that Ms. Ramos could do would be to bring in a professional and have them identify what is wrong with Tammy.

25. **C** While your reminder may be helpful, you want to avoid publicly reinforcing that the student with ADHD is in any way different, or in need of special help. This could lead to ridicule and criticism of the student.

26. **A** Skinner believed that behavior which is reinforced will reoccur, and that negative reinforcement is particularly effective.

27. **B** An inductive approach to learning makes generalizations and theories based on a specific set of information. Once students are provided the data, they can then make theories about temperature changes. (D) and (A) suggest an opposite approach.

28. **A** Recent research on wait-time, the time between a teacher's question and a student's response, indicates that the longer the wait-time, the higher the quality of response and the greater the level of participation. While the practice in Ms. Smith's class is likely entertaining, wait-time research suggests that student's are not given enough time to provide optimal responses.

29. **D** The popular "seven step lesson plan" from Madeline Hunter could have up to nine elements: objectives, standards, anticipatory set, teaching (input, modeling, and check for understanding), guided practice, closure, and independent practice. Not all lesson plans will involve all nine steps.

30. **B** Emergent curriculum describes the kind of curriculum that develops from the interaction of all classroom participants, including the students.

31. **D** The median is defined as the "middle" value in a series of numbers. Therefore, an equal number of students scored above and below 76.

32. **D** On the test, you may be asked questions about how teachers can improve their performance. ETS loves to promote the concept of the teacher as a reflective practitioner.

33. **B** Metacognition is the process of thinking about thinking. By having students reflect on their own learning behaviors, they will be able to determine strategies that enable them to learn more effectively in the future.

34. **C** Before Ms. Brown can devise effective learning strategies, she needs an accurate assessment of her students' current performance and skill set. Answer choices (B) and (D) are absolutely wrong. Lowering expectations is not a long-term effective teaching method.

35. **A** Constructive play is a tool to help stimulate the imagination and creativity of children, and has been found to have a positive impact on the learning and development of children.

36. **B** A *stanine*, or standard nine score, is designed to give students a relative rank of their performance. Generally, scores of 4, 5, or 6 are average. A percentile rank of 61 is used to compare Paul's performance with that of other students. He scored higher than 61 percent of the students that took the test.

30

PLT: 7–12 Practice Test

The Praxis Series Professional Assessments for Beginning Teachers

Test Name: Principles of Learning and Teaching

Practice Case Histories and Constructed-Response Questions

Time – 120 minutes

12 Short-Answer Questions and 24 Multiple-Choice Questions

Case History 1

Directions: The case history is followed by three short-answer questions.

Ms. Pirner

Ms. Pirner teaches an elective Science course to a class of 27 students. There are 13 male students, and 14 female students. The class is composed of 4 sophomores, 15 juniors, and 8 seniors. Ms. Pirner is in her third year teaching this course at the high school. She has a new principal at the school, and is planning for her self-evaluation. In order to prepare a thorough assessment, Ms. Pirner begins to gather material that may be helpful for the activity. In the journal entries below, Ms. Pirner focuses on a specific class, and four of her students. The class takes place early in the semester, before any preliminary grades have been determined.

Journal Entry #1—Student Profiles

Jarrod is an exceptional student who comes from a very proud family. I taught his older brother two years ago, who was the best student in the class. Jarrod is like his brother, but he has additional interests. He does not seem intent on following the family path—medical school. Jarrod has been quiet and focused during most class sessions. He is well respected in the class. Jarrod rarely volunteers information—but whenever I call on him, he always has the correct answer.

Vince is repeating this class. I was surprised to see him enroll in this elective course again, as he received an F last year. Vince and I have a good rapport. During the first week, he offered to help distribute some paperwork for our in-class assignments, stating, "I've seen this stuff before. I should be your teaching assistant!" He did not do well on our quiz last week. When I asked him about his performance, he shrugged his shoulders and said, "Ms. Pirner, some people just can't remember all these details, and I'm one of them. But don't worry about it. Maybe I'll stay here another year."

Ron is a very quiet student, who is withdrawn from most activities. He received a D in Biology last year, and has a GPA of 2.2. Thus far, Ron has completed few of the activities. Ron does not like to receive any attention from me or other members of the class. In a recent activity that required students to pair with others, Ron was left as the odd man out (13 pairs, then Ron). I volunteered to work with Ron, and he snapped at me, "I don't need your pity Ms. Pirner. Just let me complete this on my own!"

Bob is the class clown. He manages to make comments on almost every topic, and while they are often disruptive, I do have to admit that some are quite entertaining. Bob has indicated that this year is important to him, because he doesn't look forward to being a "boring adult" after graduation. Bob has the talent to exceed in this class. Instead, he manages to do slightly above average work. If he really applied himself, he could excel like a few other students in the class.

Journal Entry #2—Self-Analysis

I believe that I have become a fairly competent Science teacher. I attend conferences and read information in an attempt to improve my skill set. This year, I have tried to make my classroom environment more cooperative, by dividing students into different groups for projects and lab work. Yet, I've struggled in making these groups a success. Strong students like Jarrod complain about the groups, claiming that the work is boring and they would learn more if they just do the work themselves, or with a group of their choosing. Some students like Ron seem to dislike anything that brings the class together to perform group work.

GO ON TO THE NEXT PAGE

In discussions, I find that I am trying to manage two different audiences. There is a group that volunteers constantly. At times I feel they are in a competition with each other to see who can answer the most questions. While I appreciate their intent, it seems like more of an attempt to get a strong grade than to really contribute to the classroom. On the other hand, though, I have a core group of students who remain silent. I'm not sure if they are intimidated by the other students, bored, or both. I have tried strategies to increase classroom participation (I attended a workshop on this last year), but I generally fall back into what I'm most comfortable with, which is lecture and the use of a textbook.

Supervisor's Notes on Tuesday's Lesson

Ms. Pirner gave a lecture on Photosynthesis. She encouraged the class to take careful notes, and informed her students that the information on next week's test would be a combination of material found in the reading material, as well as material mentioned only in her lecture. During the lecture, she walked around the class to see if students were taking notes. She spoke generally quickly, but slowed to emphasize key points, such as vocabulary words, and the steps of the photosynthesis process. While many students took notes, I noticed that neither Vince nor Ron took notes.

Directions: Questions 1 through 3 require you to write short answers. You are not expected to cite specific theories or texts in your answer; however, your responses to the questions will be evaluated with respect to professionally accepted principles and practices in teaching and learning. Be sure to answer all parts of the questions. Write your answers on the answer sheet.

Question 1

Ms. Pirner noted that strong performing students, such as Jarrod, say small group work is boring, and not effective for them. Assume that Ms. Pirner wants to continue using cooperative learning groups.

- Identify TWO strategies Ms. Pirner could use to address the concerns of students like Jarrod.
- For each strategy identified, explain how its use could address the concerns of Jarrod, and would make group work more effective. Base your response on the principles of effective instructional strategies.

Question 2

Assume that Ms. Pirner produced a lesson plan before giving the lecture on Photosynthesis. Assume that no modifications are made for any of her students.

- Suggest TWO modifications, one for Vince and one for Jarrod, that Ms. Pirner could have made that could offer the students a better learning environment.
- For each modification, explain how it will provide for a better learning situation for Jarrod and Vince. Base your response on principles of varied instruction for diverse learners.

Question 3

Ms. Pirner feels that she is having difficulty connecting with Ron as a student, and wants to learn more about Ron so he can become a better learner.

- Describe TWO aspects of Ron's behavior that Ms. Pirner, and other school leaders, might discuss in order to understand Ron better as a learner.
- For each aspect, suggest one hypothesis that might be used to understand Ron better as a learner. Base your response on the principles of human development and diagnostic assessment.

GO ON TO THE NEXT PAGE

Case History 2

Directions: The case history is followed by three short-answer questions.

Mr. Gregory

Mr. Gregory is a tenth-grade U.S. History teacher. He teaches to a group of 29 sophomores, 14 boys and 15 girls. This is his sixth year teaching History at Lewisville High School. He is currently planning a lesson on the Civil War, which will be viewed by his supervisor, Mr. Windle, who is the school principal. Attached are Mr. Gregory's notes for his lesson plan, and his reflections after his lecture on Wednesday.

Background Information on Lesson to Be Observed by Supervisor

Goals of Unit on the Civil War:

- Introduce students to the timelines, theories, and important lessons learned from the Civil War.
- Foster students' evaluation skills by identifying similarities between the causes of the Civil War and the causes of today's struggles and wars.
- Develop students' abilities in combining textbook information and lecture information.
- Give students experience in making presentations to the class.
- Link students' textbook reading with information found elsewhere.

Activities:
The pre-assignment for this unit was to read Chapter 13, "Conflict in the United States," and Chapter 14, "The Civil War," by Wednesday, the day of my first lecture on the Civil War. I have asked students to highlight the chapters, and take notes on what they find important in the reading material. I've also asked that students think about what they find most interesting about the Civil War, and to write that down. That topic will be the topic I will ask them to present after our test at the end of the week. Ideally, they will seek out additional information beyond what is in the text.

Assessment:
I will evaluate students based on their performance on Friday's test, as well as their presentation to the class next week. For the presentation, I will evaluate them more on the content of the presentation rather than the delivery. I want to see if students understand how to use outside information effectively to augment the lessons presented directly in class or from our textbook. Further, I will also evaluate them on the quality and quantity of their notes taken while reading the chapter and in their participation in the classroom discussion.

Notes from Thursday
One Day After Wednesday's Lecture

Today students have a free period to study for tomorrow's test. Walking around, I'm somewhat disappointed to see how few students took notes on the chapter, or highlighted the key points of the material. I hope students were paying attention to yesterday's lecture—some information in that lecture will be used on the test, and that information is NOT in the text. I'm not sure that the test tomorrow is the best assessment of student performance on this material. I think I've written it in the best way possible, but I'm never sure about these things.

GO ON TO THE NEXT PAGE

Directions: Questions 4 through 6 require you to write short answers. You are not expected to cite specific theories or texts in your answer; however, your responses to the questions will be evaluated with respect to professionally accepted principles and practices in teaching and learning. Be sure to answer all parts of the questions. Write your answers on the answer sheet.

Question 4

The fourth and fifth goals of Mr. Gregory are to "Give students experience in making presentations to the class" and "Link students' textbook reading with information found elsewhere."

- Recommend TWO activities or strategies Mr. Gregory could use to help students meet one or both of these goals.
- For each activity or strategy suggested, explain how its use will help achieve the goal(s). Base your response on the principles of effective instructional planning and strategies.

Question 5

Mr. Gregory's third goal is to "Develop students' abilities in combining textbook information and lecture information." We know that Mr. Gregory plans to test on information uniquely presented in each medium.

- Suggest TWO additional ways that Mr. Gregory could help to achieve his goal.
- For each strategy suggested, explain how all students would benefit. Base your response on principles of effective instruction.

Question 6

In his reflection, Mr. Gregory wonders if his test is the best way to evaluate his students.

- Identify TWO additional assessment techniques Mr. Gregory could use to provide his students with opportunities to demonstrate their learning.
- For each technique suggested, describe the kinds of information about student learning it could provide. Base your response on the principles of assessment.

GO ON TO THE NEXT PAGE

Discrete Multiple-Choice Questions

Directions: Questions 7–18 are not related to the previous case. For each question, select the best answer and mark the corresponding space on your answer sheet.

7. On a tenth-grade mathematics test, Kathy received a grade-equivalent score of 12.4, and a percentile rank of 91 percent. Which of the following statements is true?

    (A) Kathy missed only 9 percent of the questions on the test.

    (B) Kathy performed as well on the test as the average twelfth-grade student in the fourth month of instruction.

    (C) Kathy can successfully complete 91 percent of the curriculum of a typical twelfth grader in the fourth month of instruction.

    (D) Kathy's ranked 91st of all students that have completed the test nationwide.

8. Archimedes was asked to find a method for determining whether a crown was pure gold, or if it was alloyed with silver. Thinking over how to solve the problem, he stepped into a bath, and realized that a pure gold crown would displace less water than an alloyed crown. "Eureka!" he shouted.

    The learning process of Archimedes is best described as

    (A) accidental learning

    (B) discovery learning

    (C) emergent learning

    (D) cluster learning

9. A teacher would like to get information on how well her class understood her lecture on the Constitution. Which of the following tests would give the best information?

    (A) Criterion-referenced test

    (B) Norm-referenced test

    (C) Portfolio assessment

    (D) Standardized test

10. Lindsey is struggling in her tenth-grade class. Her records show that she has performed above-average in the ninth grade, and her teacher reports that she has a good attitude and desire to succeed. However, Lindsey's performance on most tests is poor.

    Which of the following could Lindsey's teacher do to encourage Lindsey?

    (A) Involve Lindsey's parents, and send them notices whenever Lindsey does poorly on an assignment.

    (B) Match up Lindsey with a student who performs well, and hope that the other student can motivate Lindsey.

    (C) Match up Lindsey with another student who is struggling, so they can work at their own pace.

    (D) Divide Lindsey's work into small pieces, and provide feedback with each part of an assignment.

11. Which of the following statements would Howard Gardner most likely agree with on effective instruction?

    (A) Teachers must find eight different ways to teach each set of material to correspond with the eight different types of intelligence.

    (B) Students must learn different levels of intelligence at different times; they must build on one another.

    (C) Intelligence and morality must be separated, and the two should not work together.

    (D) Educators need to develop new approaches that might better meet the needs of the range of learners in their classrooms.

GO ON TO THE NEXT PAGE

12. Which of the following is an example of a spiral curriculum, as popularized by Jerome Bruner?

(A) Students are given a difficult problem; the tools to address the problem are presented, and then a quiz is given to test comprehension.

(B) Students are given aide from teachers each step of the way, so that they can grasp the material.

(C) Students are given a new lecture; before the work is completed, the basics are reviewed, and then are built upon to further the learning process.

(D) Students move at their own pace, based on successful performance on criterion-referenced tests.

13. Which of the following statements is a well-formed learning objective?

(A) I will teach students how to solve trigonometric functions.

(B) While in your reading group, try to identify the use of foreshadowing. Provide examples to the class on foreshadowing.

(C) Identify the natural resources present in United States that are not present in Asia.

(D) Bring in a guest speaker to talk about the trade deficit.

14. Which of the following is an example of punishment in Skinner's theory of operant conditioning?

(A) Detention

(B) A "no homework day"

(C) Silence in the classroom

(D) A test

15. George is a student in Mr. Martin's tenth-grade class. George has performed well on standardized tests, but his participation and performance on most tasks are poor.

Which of the following practices could Mr. Martin employ to encourage George and assess his needs?

(A) Assign work to George in small steps and review that work immediately.

(B) Have George work with another underachieving student, so that they will encourage each other.

(C) Require George to attend detention, so that he can do his work in a quiet, supervised environment.

(D) Define a set of consequences with George's parents to be administered if George's grades do not improve.

16. Vygotsky's ideas about the "zone of proximal development" are best understood by which of the following learning techniques?

(A) Students should work at their own pace independently, in order to advance in concepts when they are ready.

(B) Students should review basic material of a concept first, and then receive new material with teacher assistance, thus building on previously learned concepts.

(C) A challenging concept is taught and expected to be learned, even if the basic building blocks of that concept were not previously covered.

(D) Seeking help from an instructor is not encouraged, as it may stifle development.

GO ON TO THE NEXT PAGE

17. Students who do not have basic needs met will not be able to achieve the advanced levels of learning, such as the fulfillment of one's potential.

    This statement is best supported by the works of what theorist?

    (A) Abraham Maslow
    (B) Howard Gardner
    (C) John Dewey
    (D) Jerome Bruner

18. Mr. Abato is designing a lesson plan for his twelfth-grade science class. In preparing a lesson on genetics and cell division, he plans to present a short lecture on the basics of genetics, and then show a video explaining how cells divide. What other activity could he employ which would focus on the students that are kinesthetic learners?

    (A) Provide step-by-step instructions on how a cell divides
    (B) Reinforce the lecture with a laboratory session, where students will recreate the cell division process
    (C) Bring in an expert on genetics as a guest-speaker for the class
    (D) Assign a reading assignment in advance of the lecture

GO ON TO THE NEXT PAGE

Case History 3

Directions: The case history is followed by three short-answer questions.

Mr. Watson

Mr. Watson is teaching an elective Economics class to 21 twelfth-grade students, made up of 11 males and 10 females. Students must have completed three years of high school mathematics in order to participate in the class. Some of the brightest students at the high school participate in the class, and Mr. Watson is considered one of the most interesting and dynamic instructors. He is beginning his final month of instruction, five weeks before graduation.

Document 1

Project Plan

Consumer Finance Exercise

May 8

Objectives: Students will:

1. Review and use concepts about consumer finance to problem solve.
2. Demonstrate mathematics skills as they relate to personal finances.
3. Use creativity to finance deals in multiple ways.
4. Use higher-order thinking skills to determine who to approve for credit.

Assignment:

1. Students will work in groups of four; each student will be a member of a credit card consumer finance company.
2. Each group will select ten sample customers from a list I will provide.
3. For each customer, the group will determine whether to approve or deny the applicant based on their credit, and their specific credit request (amount to finance, desired rate).
4. Each customer should also be matched using the "Loss Rate" handout to compare how customers have performed historically.
5. Each team will present their results to the class as a whole, and will make a presentation with their recommendations.
6. Creativity in restructuring deals is encouraged—each team should strive to finance as many customers as possible.
7. All students on the team must participate.

Activities:

1. Discussion on consumer finance principles—2 sessions.
2. Group work—select ten sample customers; determine results—2 sessions.
3. Group work—prepare presentations and Excel worksheets—1 session.
4. Group presentations—3 sessions.
5. Review of work, and quiz on consumer finance—1 session.

Assessment:

1. Group work: individual and group grade
2. Group presentation: individual and group grade
3. Excel spreadsheet: team grade for quality of decisions

GO ON TO THE NEXT PAGE

Document 2

Review after Lesson Plan Complete
May 24

Below are notes taken from Mr. Watson after the conclusion of this lesson plan:

> *I really thought this would be an exciting lesson plan. Students will soon be out in the real world, and I thought they'd enjoy gaining this valuable experience of applying for a credit card. Students need to understand the value of one's credit history, and the role it can plan in consumer finance. But the class was pretty out of control during these sessions—they spent more time discussing prom, graduation, and summer than the FICO scores of their "customers." I think my class may just be lazy right now. I'm not sure I can give assignments like this towards the end of the year—students are just too burnt out, and "senioritis" is at an all time high. The threat of a poor grade just doesn't seem to work anymore, as many are all set about where they will attend college, if they choose to at all. Next year, I'll do this lesson during the first semester.*

Directions: Questions 19 through 21 require you to write short answers. You are not expected to cite specific theories or texts in your answer; however, your responses to the questions will be evaluated with respect to professionally accepted principles and practices in teaching and learning. Be sure to answer all parts of the questions. Write your answers on the answer sheet.

Question 19
Document 1, Mr. Watson's project plan for consumer finance, demonstrates several aspects of effective instructional planning.

- Identify TWO strengths of Mr. Watson's project plan.
- Explain how each strength demonstrates an aspect of effective instructional planning. Base your response on the principles of effective instructional planning.

Question 20
Review Mr. Watson's project plan, described in Document 1.

- Recommend TWO ways in which Mr. Watson could strengthen the assessment section of his project plan in order to provide students with a better opportunity to demonstrate their learning.
- For each recommendation, describe how it would improve Mr. Watson's ability to assess his students' accomplishments on this project. Base your response on the principles of assessment.

Question 21
Review Document 2, where Mr. Watson complains that his students were "lazy."

- Identify TWO behaviors of his class that are typical for students that are Seniors in high school.
- For each behavior, describe how it is typical, and what Mr. Watson can do to create a stronger learning environment. Base your response on the principles of human development and effective learning strategies.

GO ON TO THE NEXT PAGE

Case History 4

Directions: The case history is followed by three short-answer questions.

Kevin

Kevin is a tenth-grade student at Notre Dame High School. Kevin is a very gifted athlete, who plays on the Varsity football, basketball, and baseball teams. Only a sophomore, he is considered the best athlete in the school, and certainly the most popular. The local press has named Kevin "a sure thing" to play professional sports one day, and that day may be as soon as two years away.

Mr. Foster is Kevin's tenth-grade English and homeroom teacher. Mr. Foster is very concerned about Kevin's performance in English, and in other subjects as well. Mr. Foster has gathered the following documentation together, in preparation for a conference with Kevin's parents.

Document 1
Semester 1 Progress Report
November 15

Course	Grade
Geometry	C–
World History	C–
Physical Education	A–
Religion	C–
English	D
Biology	C
Preliminary GPA	**1.97**

Document 2
Results of Kevin's Diagnostic Test
October 15

Results for Kevin			
	Reading Skills	**Mathematics Skills**	**Writing Skills**
# of Questions	50	50	2
# Correct	13	17	N/A
Percentile	37%	23%	42%
Grade Equivalent	9.1	8.3	9.6
Notre Dame High Median	61%	74%	77%

Document 3
Transcript of Meeting Between Mr. Foster and Kevin's Parents, Brian and Jolene

Brian: We're very concerned with this grade of a D. Kevin received a B+ in English last year. How could he drop so quickly?

Mr. Foster: Kevin's grade is based on the number of assignments he has turned in, and the quality of those assignments. Thus far, he has failed to turn in three assignments, and the overall quality of his work has not been up to standards.

Brian: We've spoken with his football coach, who indicated that you grade harder than any other teacher. Kevin can't be penalized because he is in your class. Why isn't there consistent grading?

GO ON TO THE NEXT PAGE

Mr. Foster	I'm sorry you feel that way, but my grading is based upon the work of all students. I have no desire to create a grading scale divergent from others. I simply evaluate the quality of work that students do.
Brian	You need to understand that Kevin needs to get at least a C in this class, in order for him to stay academically eligible. Anything below a 2.0, and Kevin can't play. You seem to know that—everyone else has recognized that Kevin is trying and has given him no worse than a C–. And let's be realistic—keeping Kevin eligible is the most important thing for his future.
Mr. Foster	I understand how much Kevin likes to play sports. By focusing on his work, he can remain eligible to play. I will not use his extracurricular involvement as a factor in my grading.
Brian	Well, maybe Kevin needs a new English teacher.
Mr. Foster	I'm sorry you feel that way. You are welcome to discuss this with the principal.
Jolene	Fine, we will. Everyone seems to help Kevin do his best. You seem determined to punish him for not being as strong as your other students.
Mr. Foster	That's not true, and I'm disappointed you feel that way. This conversation is over.

Directions: Questions 22 through 24 require you to write short answers. You are not expected to cite specific theories or texts in your answer; however, your responses to the questions will be evaluated with respect to professionally accepted principles and practices in teaching and learning. Be sure to answer all parts of the questions. Write your answers on the answer sheet.

Question 22

In Document 3, it is clear that there is tension between Mr. Foster and Kevin's parents.

- Identify TWO things Mr. Foster could do to have a more meaningful conversation with Kevin's parents.
- For each action identified, discuss how each action will help to focus on Kevin's educational welfare and the development of an effective parent-teacher relationship. Base your response on the principles of fostering school-parent relationships to support student learning.

Question 23

Assume Kevin's parents asked Mr. Foster about the results of the standardized test scores, displayed in Document 2.

- Provide TWO unique descriptions of Kevin's performance on the standardized test.
- For each description, provide a comparison of Kevin's performance to his classmates, and to students statewide.

Question 24

Mr. Foster believes that with hard work, Kevin can succeed in his class.

- Identify TWO things Mr. Foster can do to help Kevin in his attempts to improve his performance in class.
- For each item identified, discuss how each strategy can help Kevin improve his performance. Base your responses on the strategies of effective learning.

GO ON TO THE NEXT PAGE

Discrete Multiple-Choice Questions

Directions: Questions 25–36 are not related to the previous case. For each question, select the best answer and mark the corresponding space on your answer sheet.

25. In Ms. Lepson's eleventh-grade computer class, teams of three have been assigned to solve a programming problem. The team will receive one overall grade for their performance on the assignment. This structure is an example of what type of learning?

    (A) Cooperative learning
    (B) Demonstrated learning
    (C) Exploratory learning
    (D) Parallel learning

26. Ms. Chamberlin would like to increase the level of participation by students during class discussions. Which of the following techniques is most likely to improve the level of participation, and the thoughtfulness of students' responses?

    (A) Implement a reward system for answering questions, such as a day with no homework.
    (B) Post a ranking of students, ordered by the number of times they answer a question.
    (C) Ask more leading questions, with clues to the correct answer.
    (D) Increase the wait-time between the conclusion of her questions and calling on a student to give an answer.

27. Which of the following ideas best incorporates the concept of scaffolding?

    (A) Students will role-play important events being studied.
    (B) For a novel currently being studied, new vocabulary can be supported by linking words on a webpage to a separate page with definitions.
    (C) Take students on a field trip to a relevant site, and have them take pictures of items that relate to the subject being studied.
    (D) Assign students to create their own test, based on the subject material currently being studied.

28. Ms. Bryant's eleventh-grade class took the SAT, a standardized test used for admission to many colleges and universities. Her class performance is summarized below:

    - Mean: 1240
    - Median: 1000
    - Mode: 980

    Which of the following statements is true about the performance of Ms. Bryant's class?

    (A) The performance of some individuals was extremely high, raising the overall average.
    (B) An equal number of students scored above and below 980.
    (C) The mean score was below the norm for eleventh-grade students.
    (D) More students scored 1240 than any other score.

29. Today, Noelle attended her twelfth-grade Science class. There was a discussion on genetics. The class attempted two problems as a group. For homework, Noelle will be required to review her notes on the lecture, and to be ready to try three more group problems tomorrow.

    What stage of the lesson plan is Noelle's class currently performing?

    (A) Anticipatory set
    (B) Closure
    (C) Independent Practice
    (D) Guided Practice

GO ON TO THE NEXT PAGE

30. Steven is having problems in his high school classes. The school counselor believes that Steven is having problems at home. His parents have divorced, and there may be abuse within the family. The counselor believes that his home situation must be addressed before his academic issues can be solved.

    What theory and theorist best support the counselor's beliefs?

    (A) Skinner and negative reinforcement
    (B) Maslow's hierarchy of needs
    (C) Bandura's extinction
    (D) Freud's theory of id, ego, and superego

31. Ms. Lloyd has a new student in her class, Cynthia, who was diagnosed with ADHD. Cynthia will be the only student in the class with ADHD. What can Ms. Lloyd do to provide a positive learning environment for Cynthia?

    (A) Introduce Cynthia to the class, and announce that she has ADHD, so that other students can help keep her on track.
    (B) Seat Cynthia in the back of the class, away from the teacher, and most other students.
    (C) Create a consistent class schedule, with predetermined transitions.
    (D) Keep the same set of rules for Cynthia as for all other students.

32. The formal operational stage of Jean Piaget's stages of cognitive development most likely occurs with what age groups?

    (A) Infancy
    (B) Toddler and early childhood
    (C) Elementary and early adolescence
    (D) Adolescence and adulthood

33. Mr. Snow is teaching a tenth-grade class in Literature. The class has completed a novel, and is required to write an essay answering the following questions:

    - What criteria would you use to assess the strength of the main character?
    - Do you agree with the outcome of the novel?
    - What is the most important message from the novel?

    These questions measure what type of learning, according to Bloom's Taxonomy?

    (A) Knowledge
    (B) Comprehension
    (C) Synthesis
    (D) Evaluation

34. Mr. Prior believes that the best way to teach his ninth-grade English class is to employ a constructivist approach? He could do this by using which of the following strategies?

    (A) Students will read material at a level significantly more challenging than the student's reading level today.
    (B) Students will analyze passages to understand the syntax, structure, and vocabulary of each sentence. Then, students should diagram the sentences.
    (C) Students will read a new passage. In writing a summary of the passage, they will be asked to associate the passage with prior readings, and events from their own life.
    (D) Students will read the passage, pair up with another student, then present their summary of the passage to the larger class.

GO ON TO THE NEXT PAGE

35. In Mr. Cockrum's eleventh-grade Business class, the class is currently studying fiscal policy. In order to convey the material, he has broken up the class into groups of six. Then, after a series of lectures, he allows the team to meet for two group sessions to review the material. Next, a test is given, and the cumulative score of all six members is used to determine a grade. Each team member receives the same overall letter grade.

    Mr. Cockrum is using what cooperative learning technique?

    (A) Jigsaw method
    (B) Think-pair-share
    (C) Student Teams-Achievement Divisions (STAD)
    (D) Portfolio

36. Keith, normally a very strong student, is struggling with an assignment in his twelfth-grade History class. The assignment is to analyze the inaugural address of John F. Kennedy, and write a paper discussing the speech's impact. Thus far, the class has been told to read the address contained in their History book. Keith has told his teacher that he is having difficulty understanding the meaning of the speech. What is the most plausible reason Keith is struggling with the assignment?

    (A) Keith is not interested in History.
    (B) Keith does not recognize the reward system in place for completing the assignment.
    (C) Keith may be a strong auditory learner; hearing the speech may help him with the assignment.
    (D) Keith may have difficulty reading.

STOP

Diagnostic Test Form

Completely darken bubbles with a No. 2 pencil. If you make a mistake, be sure to erase mark completely. Erase all stray marks.

1. YOUR NAME: ______________________ (Print) Last First M.I.

SIGNATURE: ______________________ DATE: ___/___/___

HOME ADDRESS: ______________________ (Print) Number and Street

City State Zip E-MAIL: ______________________

PHONE NO.: ____________ (Print) SCHOOL: ____________ CLASS OF: ____________

IMPORTANT: Please fill in these boxes exactly as shown on the back cover of your test book.

OpScan iNSIGHT™ forms by Pearson NCS EM-255325-1:654321
Printed in U.S.A.

2. TEST FORM

3. TEST CODE

4. PHONE NUMBER

5. YOUR NAME

First 4 letters of last name | FIRST INIT | MID INIT

6. DATE OF BIRTH

MONTH	DAY	YEAR
JAN		
FEB		
MAR	0 0	0 0
APR	1 1	1 1
MAY	2 2	2 2
JUN	3 3	3 3
JUL	4	4 4
AUG	5	5 5
SEP	6	6 6
OCT	7	7 7
NOV	8	8 8
DEC	9	9 9

7. SEX

MALE

FEMALE

8. OTHER

1 A B C D E
2 A B C D E
3 A B C D E

CASE I

1. Write your response on the appropriate page of the response book.
2. Write your response on the appropriate page of the response book.
3. Write your response on the appropriate page of the response book.

CASE II

4. Write your response on the appropriate page of the response book.
5. Write your response on the appropriate page of the response book.
6. Write your response on the appropriate page of the response book.

7 A B C D
8 A B C D
9 A B C D
10 A B C D
11 A B C D
12 A B C D
13 A B C D
14 A B C D
15 A B C D
16 A B C D
17 A B C D
18 A B C D

CASE III

19. Write your response on the appropriate page of the response book.
20. Write your response on the appropriate page of the response book.
21. Write your response on the appropriate page of the response book.

CASE IV

22. Write your response on the appropriate page of the response book.
23. Write your response on the appropriate page of the response book.
24. Write your response on the appropriate page of the response book.

25 A B C D
26 A B C D
27 A B C D
28 A B C D
29 A B C D
30 A B C D
31 A B C D
32 A B C D
33 A B C D
34 A B C D
35 A B C D
36 A B C D

31

Answers and Explanations for PLT: 7–12 Practice Test

ANSWERS AND EXPLANATIONS FOR PLT: 7–12 PRACTICE TEST

1. **Sample Response that Receives a Score of 2:**

   Ms. Pirner needs to be creative and find strategies that will challenge and excite all students, even top performing students such as Jarrod. One way she can do that is to make each of the groups interdependent. She can give each student within the group an assigned role, and check to make sure each student fulfills their responsibilities. The roles will likely vary in the skills and abilities required; thus, students like Jarrod should be in the most challenging roles. Another possibility is to use a jigsaw cooperative learning approach. This could segment talented students like Jarrod to a group of his peers, where he is assigned the most challenging material. However, the approach requires that all students are brought together as one group. The challenge for the talented students will be that they need to convey their ideas in a way all students will understand; hopefully, they will also learn from the other students in the class.

   Sample Response that Receives a Score of 1:

   One way to keep students like Jarrod motivated is to ensure that each student has an independent challenge, such as a homework assignment, in addition to the group task. Therefore, students like Jarrod are not penalized by the poor work of other students. Another thing that Ms. Pirner could do is challenge the group to complete the task before the other groups. That way, students like Jarrod will have the proper incentive to participate. The challenge will be to design a task where one student alone cannot complete the task, so other students must learn as well.

2. **Sample Response that Receives a Score of 2:**

   For Jarrod, who is a bright, independent learner, he needs the opportunity to be continuously challenged, which will hopefully keep him more engaged with the class. Ms. Pirner could offer Jarrod a more sophisticated Science text, or material that focuses specifically on photosynthesis. Jarrod could be asked to review this material, then possibly present this information to the rest of the class. That would challenge Jarrod to think about the material in a more complex way, and find ways to communicate more effectively.

   For Vince, Ms. Pirner might have a meeting with Vince to discuss his past year in Science—what went well, and what he struggles with. Ms. Pirner may also want to review the paperwork from last year to identify any patterns of weakness for Vince. This could lead to a set of strategies for Vince for the upcoming year. From the passage, we know that Vince struggles with "remembering details." Thus, Ms. Pirner could task Vince with identifying the important concepts of Science, without focusing on the small details. This could engage Vince, build confidence, and assess his level of understanding.

   Sample Response that Receives a Score of 1:

   Jarrod needs to be given more detailed and challenging assignments. Ms. Pirner should take a look at the Plant Biology curriculum at a local college, and find out what they teach regarding photosynthesis. For Vince, he needs to be given more visual tools to learn the information. A graphic on how Photosynthesis works will motivate Vince and help him become a better learner.

3. **Sample Response that Receives a Score of 2:**

   There are several aspects of Ron's behavior that suggest different hypotheses about his ability to learn. First, while he does not seem to display any specific behavioral problems, it is curious to note how disengaged he is from class. It is possible that he may have some emotional or behavioral disorder that prevents him from focusing on work. This could cause him to remove himself from what he sees as an unpleasant environment. Further, this is reinforced by the fact that he appeared hostile at times, such as his response to Ms. Pirner. It is possible that Ron suffers from "learned helplessness," where he believes that anything he does will not help him.

Sample Response that Receives a Score of 1:

Ron seems very disengaged from the rest of the student body. Ron could be extremely shy and uncomfortable in social situations. It is possible that he has not developed the necessary social skills to fit in with his peers. Ms. Pirner should investigate to see if Ron has family problems at home that have contributed to his inability to get along with others. Further, he does not take notes in class, so it is possible that he could have a learning disorder.

4. **Sample Response that Receives a Score of 2:**

Mr. Gregory could ask students to do research at the library on the Civil War. He could have students work independently, or in small groups to complete this task. Each group would pick a specific topic about the Civil War presented in the textbook, and look to build on that information by doing additional research. The group could then go back to the class and present this additional information. In the final assessment, the students would need to link what they learned from the textbook to what was found in the library.

An additional idea would be to ask students to find information about the Civil War on the Internet. This use of technology to help students access additional information would be useful, as students could then compare what has been learned in addition to the information presented in the text.

Sample Response that Receives a Score of 1:

One thing that Mr. Gregory could do is assign different roles of prominent figures of the Civil War to each student in the class. One student would be President Lincoln, one would be Robert E. Lee, one would be a slave in the South, etc. Each student would then have to do research on how they lived during that time, and would then present that information to the class. In addition to generating experience in public speaking, it would give students a detailed perspective on life during the Civil War.

5. **Sample Response that Receives a Score of 2:**

Mr. Gregory could provide an outline of the text material prior to beginning his lecture. Therefore, students can have a quick reference of the topics that were covered in the text. When Mr. Gregory's lecture begins, students will be able to add notes on the additional material presented from their instructor. This will allow all students to identify what Mr. Gregory believes is important, and will help them tie information from two different sources together.

An additional strategy is to have Mr. Gregory stop at various times during his lecture, and ask students to identify where the information he just mentioned is referenced in the textbook. Students would then need to have their textbooks open, and could add notes to the text with the additional information provided from Mr. Gregory.

Sample Response that Receives a Score of 1:

Mr. Gregory should stop his lecture every time he presents something new, so that students will know for sure that they need to take notes on that part of his lecture. The downside of this is that students could be conditioned not to pay attention to the other parts of his lecture. If you are told every time there is new material, then you may not want to pay attention to the other parts of the lecture. One other thing he could do that may be better would be to give page number references for the material that he discusses, so students can tie the two sources of information together.

6. **Sample Response that Receives a Score of 2:**

   Mr. Gregory seems to have plans for multiple forms of assessment in addition to one test. One item mentioned is the goal of building public speaking skills. He can assign students to a role of a prominent figure in the Civil War, and have students discuss their character and the hardships and joys they faced during the Civil War.

   One additional strategy would be to give students a document which gives a different viewpoint on the Civil War. Students would then be asked to compare and contrast, either formally or informally, the other interpretations of the Civil War with the one found in this document. By doing this, he can determine how well students are able to work and think critically with different sources of information.

   Sample Response that Receives a Score of 1:

   In addition to the formal assessment of a test, Mr. Gregory can give other assessment structures designed to show learning about the Civil War. He could list a few short quotations on the board. These quotations would be taken from the Civil War, and reflect a diverse set of opinions and comments from influential members. Next, he could ask students to explain how much they agree or disagree with each statement. This would challenge students to think about how the material has impacted them, and their views of the battle. This would help students improve their critical thinking skills.

7. **B** A grade-score equivalent shows that a student performs at a level equivalent to the average student of a certain grade. In Kathy's example, she performed as well as the average twelfth-grader in the fourth month of instruction would typically perform on the test.
8. **B** Discovery learning takes place where the learner draws on his own experience and prior knowledge to discover the truths that are to be learned.
9. **A** A criterion-referenced test is designed to test specific information. These tests are often created by teachers to review specific subject material.
10. **D** Immediate feedback is key to both diagnose any learning deficiencies, and to motivate a student properly. Lindsey will learn best when given continuous, positive reinforcement.
11. **D** Gardner's work on multiple intelligences suggests that students have different abilities and strengths, and different ways to learn. While (A) is too extreme (it is neither practical nor effective to try eight different approaches for each topic), the need to develop new approaches is endorsed by Gardner.
12. **C** The concept of a spiral curriculum is to constantly review and build on past results, in order to further the learning process.
13. **C** An objective should describe the actions that students are expected to do once instruction is complete. It should not describe what the teacher would do during the lesson. Answer choices (A) and (D) describe teacher actions, as does the second half of answer choice (B).
14. **A** Detention is often seen as punishment.
15. **A** We know from the information that George is capable of doing the work. Therefore, some strategy for supporting success in class participation and performance is necessary. Assigning work in small steps and providing immediate feedback allows George a greater sense of achievement, and more opportunity for positive feedback. This immediate feedback will also allow George's instructor to identify specific issues or skills that are giving him trouble.

16. **B** The zone of proximal development states that students have an ability to grasp new material that is closely aligned with prior material. In order to learn new concepts, assistance from teachers and other students may be necessary.

17. **A** This question relates to Maslow's theory of the hierarchy of needs. Maslow stated that there was a set hierarchy of needs, and that advanced needs (such as knowledge and understanding, fulfillment of one's potential) could only be possible once deficiency needs (such as shelter, food, love) are met. The statement closely aligns to Maslow's theories.

18. **B** A kinesthetic learner does best when he or she has an opportunity to "learn by doing." A laboratory environment provides the opportunity for students to understand cell division by participating and seeing the results themselves. Students that learn in this fashion learn best by being active participants in the learning process.

19. **Sample Response that Receives a Score of 2:**

Mr. Watson's project plan is strong because it requires each student to participate in the group activities. This ensures that each student will contribute something to the project. Further, this is reinforced in the assessment section with team grades for both the group work and the group presentation. This will help facilitate participation within the groups, and allows each individual to make a contribution. Secondly, Mr. Watson has linked activities to the assessment section in many ways. The group work discussed in activities 2 and 3 are assessed under Assessment 1, and the group presentation activity 4 is assessed under Assessment 2. With the goals, assignments, activities, and assessments closely linked, Mr. Watson is able to deliver an effective instructional plan.

Sample Response that Receives a Score of 1:

This project plan is strong, and demonstrates aspects of effective planning. A very important feature of Mr. Watson's plan is building on prior knowledge. He tells the students that they are going to use their background in mathematics to learn about consumer finance. By reviewing this information first, he provides the necessary backdrop to then move on to a new concept. By building on prior knowledge, students get a much better opportunity for success. This is definitely one strength of Mr. Watson's project plan.

20. **Sample Response that Receives a Score of 2:**

First, while many aspects of the project plan are linked, there are a few gaps that Mr. Watson should address. Students are told that they will have an activity during the final session in which they will take a quiz, but that quiz is not a part of the assessment section. Does the quiz not count? My guess is that it does, and Mr. Watson should add that quiz as part of his overall assessment strategy. Each activity should be linked to the other parts of the project plan, including the assessment section.

Second, Mr. Watson could add some more details about the assessment section. For instance, he could provide the relative weight of each part of the assessment. This might encourage the students to include information that they might have otherwise left out.

Sample Response that Receives a Score of 1:

Mr. Watson needs to make sure that he links the assignments and activities sections with the assessment section. For example, he tells students that they will be evaluated based on the Excel spreadsheet they put together; however, there is no assignment that states that they will be asked to make an Excel spreadsheet. The same aspect is true with the quiz—it appears in the activities session, but is not part of the formal assessment. If he links these things up, he will have a more effective project plan.

21. **Sample Response that Receives a Score of 2:**

Mr. Watson has several challenges teaching a class of seniors during the final weeks of school. A common behavior shown by students nearing the completion of their high school career is a lack of output on classroom assignments. With AP tests and college admissions complete, many students, even top students, do not have the same level of focus and discipline that they had earlier in the year. The desire to graduate, move forward, and begin the next chapter of their lives makes it challenging to focus on the current set of material. Many students indicate that they do not feel it is important, as their time in school is rapidly coming to a conclusion. Therefore, with traditional forms of measurement no longer effective, Mr. Watson needs to find other motivational tools to keep his class focused. Mr. Watson describes them as "lazy," but they are likely lacking motivation. One way to curb this behavior is to appeal to the student's pride—encouraging them to focus for a few more weeks, and to keep pushing towards a good grade because they should be proud of their prior accomplishments, and should work to impress themselves, not simply others.

A second behavior shown by students during this time is anxiety of the future. Students are about to enter a very new and unstructured phase of their lives. As a result, students may be distracted, focusing on the new aspects of their life (moving away from friends, moving to a new city, getting a job, etc.) instead of the current aspects of their life. Mr. Watson should embrace these issues, and build them into his curriculum and lesson planning. Mr. Watson could ask students to discuss what concerns they have about the next phase in their lives, and then build appropriate lessons around them. Mr. Watson employed this approach when he taught the lesson on credit card usage. Customized lessons designed to help students move forward will likely provide a stronger learning environment.

Sample Response that Receives a Score of 1:

This is going to be a tough class for Mr. Watson. First, he is teaching an elective course, which never seems to get the same level of attention as the core curricula classes. Second, at the end of the year, students just want to focus on leaving, and enjoying the summer. He could threaten them with the idea of failing. This would have serious consequences, as it could withhold them from graduation, and force them to take summer school. While it should be used as a last resort, it may provide the wake up call students need in order to get through the final few weeks of the year.

22. **Sample Response that Receives a Score of 2:**

Mr. Foster should be rewarded for not caving to parental pressure in changing Kevin's grade. However, he could employ strategies to make the conversation more meaningful. Mr. Foster should review Kevin's work with his parents to help them identify the areas where he is struggling. This would help to make Kevin's parents an integrated part of the teacher-parent team. Further, it would allow Mr. Foster and Kevin's parents to have an objective discussion about the issues. By reviewing specific work, the conversation will focus on Kevin's learning issues, not outside issues like sports eligibility, or the grading of other teachers.

A second strategy Mr. Foster could employ would be not taking the comments from Kevin's parents personally. While he initially showed good active listening techniques, it appears that Mr. Foster grew frustrated by the end of the conversation, and quickly cut it short. Mr. Foster should recognize that the comments are not directed specifically to him; even if they were, he needs to remain focused on the issues, which are Kevin's learning challenges. By staying objective, Mr. Foster can create good will with the parents.

Sample Response that Receives a Score of 1:

Mr. Foster should bring the principal with him for this conversation to help back him up. It appears that he is being criticized for doing his job as a teacher. Sometimes, it is necessary to ask for administrative support to help a teacher stand strong on an issue, and this appears to be the case. Further, he should bring in other teachers to discuss Kevin's performance. Just because the English score is a D doesn't mean that he is doing well in other courses. This is clearly shown in his preliminary report in Document 1.

23. **Sample Response that Receives a Score of 2:**

Kevin scored in the 37th percentile in the Reading section of the test. This means that he scored better than 37 percent of the students who took the test (and conversely, below 63 percent of students who completed the test). He compares unfavorably to the class median percentile of 61, which shows that students at his class level seem to be performing stronger than an average class. Finally, his grade-score equivalent is 9.1, meaning that his performance is below his expected level (10.2), and that his score is the equivalent to the average score of students in the first month of the ninth grade.

Kevin scored in the 23rd percentile in the Math section of the test. This means that he scored better than 23 percent of the students who took the test (and conversely, below 77 percent of students who completed the test). He compares unfavorably to the class median percentile of 74, which shows that students at his class level seem to be performing stronger than an average class. Finally, his grade-score equivalent is 8.3, meaning that his performance is far below his expected level (10.2), and that his score is the equivalent to the average score of students in the third month of the eighth grade.

Sample Response that Receives a Score of 1:

Kevin scored in the 37th percentile in Reading, and the 23rd percentile in Math, and finally in the 42nd percentile in Writing. So he performs the best in Writing, but he is below the 50th percentile in all areas. This should be reason for concern, as he is below in all categories, and he is below the class median for all subjects as well. It is interesting to note that he got more questions correct in Mathematics than in English, even though he got a lower percentile.

24. **Sample Response that Receives a Score of 2:**

First, Mr. Foster needs to assess the prerequisite competencies that Kevin possesses. It appears that Kevin is struggling to perform well on his assignments. Before Mr. Foster can make a focused plan for Kevin, he needs to understand the baseline skills that Kevin has. This can be done by reviewing Kevin's work from last year, speaking with his teacher, and possibly giving another diagnostic test that will give detailed feedback on different skill sets.

A second strategy for Mr. Foster would be to interview Kevin to discuss what he enjoys about English, and where he struggles. Mr. Foster may learn specific items about how Kevin learns most effectively. As noted above, he often struggles turning in assignments. Mr. Foster needs to determine if this is due to a lack of effort or due to a lack of understanding certain aspects of the assignment. By setting clear expectations that Kevin understands, Mr. Foster will give him the best chance to succeed.

Sample Response that Receives a Score of 1:

Mr. Foster should have Kevin visit a learning specialist, to see if Kevin may be suffering from a learning disability. His poor performance is not limited to just English—it appears that he is struggling in all areas. By identifying any specific disabilities, Mr. Foster can create a more focused learning plan that will meet Kevin's needs. Further, he should test Kevin to see where he performs well and where he struggles. For example, he could review the diagnostic results of the standardized test he recently completed.

25. **A** Cooperative learning involves students working together in groups to learn a concept, or to complete a task.

26. **D** Research on wait-time shows that the longer a teacher waits before calling on a student, the higher the level of participation, and the better the quality of responses. Answer choices (A) and (B) may lead to greater participation, but will not necessarily increase the quality of the response.

27. **B** Scaffolding is coaching or modeling to help students understand material until students develop these new skills and display confidence in their ability to handle the material without support. When the student achieves competence, the support is removed. The student continues to develop the skills or knowledge on his or her own. Answer choice (B) provides an example of scaffolding with new technology tools.

28. **A** You should be able to get to answer choice (A) by eliminating the other three answer choices. (B) and (D) use incorrect definitions for median and mode, respectively. We have no information to support (C). When the mean is higher than the median, it means that the strength of the performance of the students above the median outweighs the performance of those scoring below the median. In the example shown, several students must have scored quite high in order to raise the mean 200+ points above the median.

29. **D** In Madeline Hunter's "seven step lesson plan," the class currently exhibits the stage of guided practice. The class is reviewing problems as a group, before attempting problems on their own. Answer Choice (C) relates to the homework assignment.

30. **B** Maslow believed that certain lower level needs must be met before higher level needs can be fulfilled. If Steven is having issues of safety, shelter, and avoidance of pain, it will be very difficult for him to learn self-confidence, and other traits necessary for strong academic performance.

31. **C** Students with ADHD tend to have difficulty with multiple transitions and frequent distractions. A consistent class schedule will help minimize the distractions. Answer choice (D) may seem correct; however, there should occasionally be different sets of rules, such as the amount of time allocated to complete an test.

32. **D** This is the final of four stages in Piaget's stages of cognitive development. Not all teenagers or adults will reach this stage, but for those that do, it tends to occur during early adulthood.

33. **D** This higher-order of thinking involves making value decisions about issues, as well as the development of opinions, judgments, or decisions.

34. **C** The constructivist approach is an approach to teaching and learning based on the premise that learning is the result of mental construction—students learn by fitting new information together with what they already know.

35. **C** This method, popularized by Slavin in 1995, uses the technique that all individuals will receive the same grade. This encourages team behavior to ensure that all members comprehend the material.

36. **C** We know that Keith is a normally strong student, which makes answer choices (A), (B), and (D) less likely. C provides a plausible explanation. Thus far, Keith has only read the speech. If he were to hear it, and he is a strong auditory learner, he may be able to perform better on the assignment.

Conclusion

EXTRA MATERIALS

At this point, you've read a lot of material, you're an expert on the various forms of the Praxis tests and their content, and you know how to apply strategies to identify correct answers and eliminate wrong ones. If you've done the drills or tests at the back of each chapter, you should have an idea of the areas you still need to review.

If you find you need more content review for the PPST tests, we suggest the following:

- *Grammar Smart*. 2nd Ed. New York: Princeton Review/Random House, 2001.
- *Math Smart*. 2nd Ed. New York: Princeton Review/Random House, 2001.

For extra materials for the Praxis II: Principles of Learning and Teaching test, there are a variety of fine textbooks that cover most areas of educational psychology. We recommend:

- Woolfolk, Anita E. *Educational Psychology*. Boston: Allyn and Bacon, 2004.

Your coursework from your major subject should provide you with adequate study materials for the Praxis II: Subject Assessment tests. ETS also publishes thorough (if expensive) study guides for all other Subject Assessment tests.

WHAT TO DO BEFORE TEST DAY

Establish a Time Routine

If the test is at 9 A.M., and you normally don't get out of bed until 11 A.M., or so, then you'll want to change your habits about a week before the test. Force yourself to adopt the new routine so that your body has enough time to adjust to the new schedule.

Scope Out the Joint

If you can, find the location where you'll be taking the test several days before the actual test administration. You don't want to have to worry about finding a parking space, finding the building, and finding the room, all on the day of the test. Some people find that sitting down inside the room beforehand and imagining taking the test reduces their anxiety on the actual test day.

Take It Easy the Night Before

Obviously, you shouldn't go out partying until 3 A.M. the night before the test. Make sure you get enough sleep to be at your peak. By the same token, don't stay up half the night cramming. Take the night off and rent a movie.

WHAT TO DO ON TEST DAY

Physical Preparation

Watch What You Eat

If you normally eat a light breakfast, don't suddenly decide to have six pancakes, biscuits and gravy, and a ham steak because you read somewhere that a hearty breakfast is important. If you don't normally drink a lot of coffee, the morning of test day is not a good time to start.

Dress in Layers

The testing room will inevitably be too cold or too hot. If you layer up, you'll be able to adjust to a comfortable amount of clothing.

Bring Water and a Light Snack

You'll be there for a couple of hours, at least. Better safe than sorry.

Mental Preparation

It's okay to be nervous before the test. A little nervousness increases adrenaline, which can help you focus your energy and increase your performance. Too much nervousness, however, can be a problem. If you find yourself getting overly stressed during a test, try the following:

- Put your pencil down.
- Lift your head and find the furthest point away from you that you can see. Focus on that point.
- Take two or three deep breaths.
- Tell yourself that no one in the room is better prepared than you are.
- Calmly get back to work.

AFTER THE TEST

When it's over, it's over. ETS will mail your results about three weeks after you take the test, so put it out of your mind until then.

Good luck!

ABOUT THE AUTHORS

Fritz Stewart has been working for The Princeton Review in a variety of capacities since 1988. A former high school teacher, he holds a Master's Degree in Computer Science from Stanford University and a Master's Degree in Orchestral Conducting from the University of Cincinnati College–Conservatory of Music.

Rick Sliter has been a part of The Princeton Review family since 1993, when he started as an SAT, GRE, and GMAT teacher in the San Diego, CA office. Rick has worked as a teacher, a contributor to course materials such as the GMAT, SAT, and SAT Subject Tests, a Director of the Bay Area offices, and an author. This is the fourth book Rick has written—his prior books include *Cracking the CBEST*, the teacher certification test for California and Oregon. Rick holds a Bachelors in Science (Quantitative Economics) from the University of California at San Diego and an MBA from The Anderson School at UCLA. Rick currently enjoys life with his wife and soon to be son in San Diego, where he works for a consumer finance institution.